'Tony Attwood explores in depth the complexity of the mysterious group of clinical pictures known collectively as Asperger's syndrome, part of the wider autistic spectrum. He describes all the puzzling and fascinating aspects of these conditions and brings them vividly to life with illustrations from personal histories. He emphasises the fact that the individuals concerned have special skills as well as disabilities. Most important of all, he makes imaginative but always practical suggestions for helping people with the syndrome, their families and others who are involved. The author has achieved real empathic understanding of children and adults whose basic problem is a biologically based lack of empathy with others. The book is to be highly recommended for those with Asperger's syndrome as well as for families, other carers and professionals in the field.'

– Lorna Wing

'Tony Attwood's *Complete Guide to Asperger's Syndrome* is a boon for all those who are confronted by this intriguing condition in their daily lives. It is full of good sense and the wisdom that comes from years of clinical experience, and full of compassionate advice for a host of problems, vividly illustrated by case material. This is a comprehensively researched and beautifully written state of the art review of what is currently known about Asperger's syndrome. I would recommend this volume as essential reading not only to those who want to learn about Asperger's syndrome, or expand their knowledge, but also to professionals who would like to gain a fuller, wiser and richer picture than can currently be gained from any other source.'

– Uta Frith

'An encyclopedia on Asperger's syndrome written in easy-to-read non-technical language. It will be especially useful for helping individuals with Asperger's, parents and professionals understand the social difficulties. There is a good mix of research information, first person reports and clinical information. The section on sensory over-sensitivity is excellent. Sensory issues prevent many people on the autism/Asperger's spectrum from participating in many social activities because stimuli that do not bother most people are intolerable.'

– Temple Grandin
author of Thinking in Pictures and Animals in Translation

'Ten years ago, I picked up a copy of Tony Attwood's *Asperger's Syndrome: A Guide for Parents and Professionals*. Little did I know it would change me, my family and our lives together. This straightforward, no nonsense book did for me what nothing and no one else in my entire life had ever been able to do. Simply put, it explained the whys behind who I was, and in so doing, it gave me the building blocks that would enable me to become who I am today – a happy and confident, gainfully employed, married mother of three. Now I realize that might not sound like much of a resume, but for someone like me – someone who was not identified as having Asperger's syndrome until they were in their thirties – well, it's stupendous. Until I read Dr. Attwood's book, everything about me was in jeopardy of evaporating into the thin air I had spent my life stumbling through. My marriage, my self-esteem, my identity, my ability to form relationships and keep a job – all those things did I barely have a grasp of, even if all the while others thought I had it made in the shade. Dr. Attwood, or Saint Tony as I call him, gave me the strength to come out to the world and admit I was only pretending to be normal. That strength saved my life, of that I am certain. And now Saint Tony has penned a new book and it is extraordinary. *The Complete Guide to Asperger's Syndrome* is a comprehensive manual filled with useful information, updated research and most importantly, helpful advice and encouragement for those of us who have AS and those who strive to support us.'

– Liane Holliday Willey, EdD
author of Pretending to be Normal: Living With Asperger's Syndrome

'Grounded in research from close to 30 years of direct experience, yet very accessible, Dr Attwood brings understanding of Asperger Syndrome to new heights. Peppered with personal accounts and clear explanations Tony guides the reader with practical solutions to the myriad challenges facing people with Asperger Syndrome, and empowering them in maximizing their considerable strengths for leading fulfilling and productive lives. This book is a "must have" for everyone, including those with Asperger Syndrome.'

— Stephen Shore, AbD
author of Beyond the Wall: Personal Experiences with Autism and Asperger Syndrome

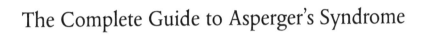
The Complete Guide to Asperger's Syndrome

The Complete Guide to Asperger's Syndrome

Tony Attwood

Jessica Kingsley Publishers
London and Philadelphia

First published in 2006
by Jessica Kingsley Publishers
116 Pentonville Road
London N1 9JB, UK
and
400 Market Street, Suite 400
Philadelphia, PA 19106, USA

www.jkp.com

Library of Congress Cataloging in Publication Data

Attwood, Tony.
  The complete guide to Asperger's syndrome / Tony Attwood. -- 1st hardcover ed.
    p. cm.
  Includes bibliographical references and indexes.
  ISBN-13: 978-1-84310-495-7 (hardcover : alk. paper)
  ISBN-10: 1-84310-495-4 (hardcover : alk. paper) 1. Asperger's syndrome. I. Title.
  [DNLM: 1. Asperger Syndrome. WS 350.6 A886c 2007]
  RC553.A88A88 2007
  616.85'8832--dc22

                    2006020065

British Library Cataloguing in Publication Data
A CIP catalogue record for this book is available from the British Library

ISBN-13: 978 184310 495 7
ISBN-10: 1 84310 495 4

Printed and bound in Great Britain by
Athenaeum Press, Gateshead, Tyne and Wear

In memory of my grandmother
Elsie May Dovey (1903–1987)
and my grandfather
William Howard Dovey (1905–2000)

Acknowledgements

I would like to acknowledge the following people for their encouragement, suggestions and support that has enabled me to acquire the knowledge to complete this book. My wife, Sarah, who also edited each draft chapter to ensure that my sentences make sense and are grammatically correct. This is never an easy task. The many people with Asperger's syndrome and their parents who have described the challenges they face each day and the strategies they have used to succeed. They are my mentors. My friends and colleagues who have commented on the draft chapters and provided valuable advice and encouragement. In particular I would like to acknowledge, in alphabetical order, Kari Dunn, Michelle Garnett, Carol Gray, Isabelle Hénault, Kathy Hoopmann, Janine Manjiviona, Stephen Shore and Liane Willey. Finally, I would also like to thank my clients, friends and family members who have Asperger's syndrome. You bring sunshine into my life.

Extracts from Asperger, H. (1991) [1944] 'Autistic psychopathy in childhood.' In U. Frith (ed) *Autism and Asperger Syndrome*. Cambridge: Cambridge University Press. Reproduced by permission of Springer-Verlag.

Extracts from Asperger, H. (1938) 'Das psychisch abnorme Kind.' *Wiener klinische Wochenschrift 49*, 1–12. ('The mentally abnormal child.' *Viennese Clinical Weekly 49*.) Reproduced by permission of Springer-Verlag. Extracts translated by Brit Wilczek.

Extracts from Jackson, N. (2002) *Standing Down Falling Up: Asperger's Syndrome from the Inside Out*. Bristol: Lucky Duck Publishing. Reproduced by permission of Sage Publications Ltd, Thousand Oaks, London and New Delhi. Copyright © Nita Jackson 2002.

Extracts from Williams, D. (1998) *Nobody Nowhere: The Remarkable Autobiography of an Autistic Girl*. London: Jessica Kingsley Publishers. Reproduced by permission of Jessica Kingsley Publishers. Copyright © Donna Williams 1998.

Extracts from Willey, L.H. (1999) *Pretending to be Normal: Living with Asperger's Syndrome*. London: Jessica Kingsley Publishers. Reproduced by permission of Jessica Kingsley Publishers. Copyright © Liane Holliday Willey 1999.

Gillberg diagnostic criteria in Table 2.1 from Gillberg, I.C. and Gilberg, C. (1989) 'Asperger syndrome – some epidemiological considerations: a research note'. *Journal of Child Psychology and Psychiatry 30*, 631–8. Reproduced by permission of Blackwell Publishing.

DSM-IV (TR) diagnostic criteria in Table 2.2 from American Psychiatric Association (2000) *Diagnostic and Statistical Manual of Mental Disorders*, 4th edition. Washington, DC: American Psychiatric Association. Reproduced by permission.

AAA diagnostic criteria in Chapter 2 from Baron-Cohen, S., Wheelwright, S., Robinson, J. and Woodberry Smith, M. (2005) 'The Adult Asperger Assessment (AAA): A diagnostic method.' *Journal of Autism and Developmental Disorders 35*, 807–819. Reproduced by permission.

Contents

List of figures and tables

Preface

The Complete Guide to Asperger's Syndrome provides a personal perception of children, teenagers and adults with Asperger's syndrome based on my extensive clinical experience and reviewing and contributing to research studies and publications. I am a practising clinician and intend the guide to be of practical value to parents, professionals and people with Asperger's syndrome. I have tried to refrain from indulging in too many technical terms so that the text can be easily read by someone who does not have a postgraduate degree in psychology. For fellow clinicians and academics who seek more information, I have provided the references that can substantiate specific statements and provide further information. I have also included many quotations from the autobiographies of people with Asperger's syndrome. Each chapter starts with a quotation from Hans Asperger and closes with a quotation by a person with Asperger's syndrome. I think that those who have Asperger's syndrome should have the last comment.

The Complete Guide to Asperger's Syndrome was written to provide parents and professionals with the latest information to understand and help a family member or person with Asperger's syndrome, but was also written for the personal benefit of people with Asperger's syndrome. My intention is that reading the guide will enable someone with Asperger's syndrome to understand why he or she is different to other people, and not to feel dejected or rejected. It is also important for others to remember that there is always a logical explanation for the apparently eccentric behaviour of people with Asperger's syndrome. The guide will explain the logic and perspective of the person with Asperger's syndrome.

The year of publication (2006) is the centenary of the birth of Hans Asperger, and the more I explore the world as perceived by people with Asperger's syndrome, the more I acknowledge the accuracy of his detailed descriptions of four children, Fritz, Harro, Ernst and Hellmuth, over 60 years ago. I never met Hans Asperger but have great respect for his understanding and admiration of a distinct group of children who are also my heroes. A few years ago I met his daughter, Maria Asperger-Felder, a child psychiatrist in Switzerland, and I was entranced by her stories about her father, his abilities and personality, but particularly the circumstances in which he worked in Vienna in the late 1930s.

Maria gave me one of her father's papers, published in 1938, when he first described the characteristics that several years later became known as autistic personality disorder, and eventually Asperger's syndrome in 1981. As a paediatrician in Nazi-occupied Austria, he was bravely arguing against the recently introduced law for the 'prevention of offspring suffering from hereditary diseases'. He advocated that education will 'render harmless the dangers which are in a child's genetic disposition'. He wanted to save the children at his clinic from being murdered, and vehemently argued that children who are unusual are not necessarily inferior. He was clearly an opponent of Nazism.

While there is an interesting history regarding the development of our understanding of children and adults with Asperger's syndrome, what are our hopes for the future? In the next decade, we need to reach consensus on the diagnostic criteria, and study the signs of Asperger's syndrome in very young children so that they can benefit from early intervention programs. Governments need to increase the allocation of resources to support children with Asperger's syndrome at school, and help adults with Asperger's syndrome to achieve employment appropriate to their qualifications and abilities. In our modern society we need and benefit from the talents of people with Asperger's syndrome.

I am concerned that government departments rarely have policies and resources specifically for people with Asperger's syndrome. The diagnosis can sometimes actually be used by government agencies to avoid services rather than access services. I hope that greater public awareness of the circumstances and abilities of people with Asperger's syndrome will influence the decisions of politicians, especially as there will soon be a deluge of adults who are seeking a diagnostic assessment. This is the generation that missed the opportunity to be identified and understood.

In the next decade, more professionals will specialize in Asperger's syndrome, and we will see the establishment of local diagnostic and treatment clinics specifically for children and adults with Asperger's syndrome. If the prevalence of Asperger's syndrome is about 1 person in 250, then there will be sufficient referrals for access to expertise to maintain a national network of clinics and specialists.

We clearly need more research on Asperger's syndrome, particularly into aspects of sensory perception. Many people with Asperger's syndrome are desperate to reduce their sensitivity to specific sounds and other sensory experiences. At present, clinicians and therapists have little to offer to reduce auditory, tactile and olfactory sensitivity. We also need to develop and evaluate programs to encourage friendship and relationship skills, the management of emotions and the constructive application of special interests.

I also hope that in the future there will be a more positive and encouraging attitude towards people with Asperger's syndrome, and an increase in their self-esteem. I wrote this guide to disseminate the recent knowledge that has been acquired on Asperger's syndrome, but it was also written to change attitudes. Knowledge changes attitudes, which in turn can change abilities and circumstances.

CHAPTER I

What is Asperger's Syndrome?

Not everything that steps out of line, and thus 'abnormal', must necessarily be 'inferior'.

– Hans Asperger (1938)

The door bell rang, heralding the arrival of another guest for Alicia's birthday party. Her mother opened the door and looked down to see Jack, the last guest to arrive. It was her daughter's ninth birthday and the invitation list had been for ten girls and one boy. Alicia's mother had been surprised at this inclusion, thinking that girls her daughter's age usually consider boys to be smelly and stupid, and not worthy of an invitation to a girl's birthday party. But Alicia had said that Jack was different. His family had recently moved to Birmingham and Jack had been in her class for only a few weeks. Although he tried to join in with the other children, he hadn't made any friends. The other boys teased him and wouldn't let him join in any of their games. Last week he had sat next to Alicia while she was eating her lunch, and as she listened to him, she thought he was a kind and lonely boy who seemed bewildered by the noise and hectic activity of the playground. He looked cute, a younger Harry Potter, and he knew so much about so many things. Her heart went out to him and, despite the perplexed looks of her friends when she said he was invited to her party, she was determined he should come.

And here he was, a solitary figure clutching a birthday card and present which he immediately gave to Alicia's mother. She noticed he had written Alicia's name on the envelope, but the writing was strangely illegible for an eight-year-old. 'You must be Jack,' she said and he simply replied with a blank face, 'Yes'. She smiled at him, and was about to suggest he went into the garden to join Alicia and her friends when he said, 'Alicia's birthday present is one of those special dolls that my mum says every girl wants, and she chose it, but what I really wanted to get her was some batteries. Do you like batteries? I do, I have a hundred and ninety-seven batteries. Batteries are really useful. What batteries do you have in your remote controllers?' Without waiting for a reply, he continued, 'I have a special battery from Russia. My dad's an engineer and he was working on an oil pipeline in Russia and he came home with six triple-A batteries for me with Russian writing on them. They are my favourite. When I go to bed I like to look at my box of batteries and sort them in alphabetical order before I go to sleep. I always hold one of my Russian batteries as I fall asleep. My mum says I should hug my teddy bear but I prefer a battery. How many batteries do you have?'

She replied, 'Well, I don't know, but we must have quite a few…', and felt unsure what to say next. Her daughter was a very gentle, caring and maternal girl and she could understand why she had 'adopted' this strange little boy as one of her friends. Jack continued to provide a monologue on batteries, how they are made and what to do with them when the power is exhausted. Alicia's mother felt exhausted too, listening to a lecture that lasted about ten minutes. Despite her subtle signals of needing to be somewhere else, and eventually saying, 'I must go and get the party food ready,' he continued to talk, following her into the kitchen. She noticed that when he talked, he rarely looked at her and his vocabulary was very unusual for an eight-year-old boy. It was more like listening to an adult than a child, and he spoke very eloquently, although he didn't seem to want to listen.

Eventually she said, 'Jack, you must go into the garden to say hi to Alicia and you must go now.' Her facial expression clearly indicated there was no alternative. He gazed at her face for a few seconds, as if trying to read the expression, and then off he went. She looked out of the kitchen window and watched him run across the grass towards Alicia. As he ran through a group of four girls, she noticed one of them deliberately put out her foot to trip him up. As he fell awkwardly to the ground, the girls all laughed. But Alicia had seen what happened and went over to help him get to his feet.

This fictitious scene is typical of an encounter with a child with Asperger's syndrome. A lack of social understanding, limited ability to have a reciprocal conversation and an intense interest in a particular subject are the core features of this syndrome. Perhaps the simplest way to understand Asperger's syndrome is to think of it as describing someone who perceives and thinks about the world differently to other people.

Although clinicians have only recently described these differences, the unusual profile of abilities that we define as Asperger's syndrome has probably been an important and valuable characteristic of our species throughout evolution. It was not until the late twentieth century that we had a name to describe such individuals. We currently use the diagnostic term Asperger's syndrome, based on the remarkably perceptive descriptions of Dr Hans Asperger, a Viennese paediatrician, who, in 1944, noticed that some of the children referred to his clinic had very similar personality characteristics and behaviour. By the mid-1940s, the psychological study of childhood in Europe and America had become a recognized and growing area of science with significant advances in descriptions, theoretical models and assessment instruments, but Asperger could not find a description and explanation for the small group of similar and unusual children that he found intriguing. He suggested the term *Autistische Psychopathen im Kindesalter*. A modern translation of the original German psychological term 'psychopathy' into current English terminology would be personality disorder – that is, a description of someone's personality rather than a mental illness such as schizophrenia.

Asperger was clearly entranced by children with autistic personality disorder and he wrote a remarkably perceptive description of the children's difficulties and abilities (Asperger 1944). He observed that the children's social maturity and social reasoning were delayed and some aspects of their social abilities were quite unusual at any stage of development. The children had difficulty making friends and they were often teased by other children. There were impairments in verbal and non-verbal communication, especially the conversational aspects of language. The children's use of language was pedantic, and some children had an unusual prosody that affected the tone, pitch and rhythm of speech. The grammar and vocabulary may have been relatively advanced but, at the end of the conversation, one had the impression that there was something unusual about their ability to have the typical conversation that would be expected with children of that age. Asperger also observed and described conspicuous impairments in the communication and control of emotions, and a tendency to intellectualize feelings. Empathy was not as mature as one would expect, considering the children's intellectual abilities. The children also had an egocentric preoccupation with a specific topic or interest that would dominate their thoughts and time. Some of the children had difficulty maintaining attention in class and had specific learning problems. Asperger noted that they often needed more assistance with self-help and organizational skills from their mothers than one would expect. He described conspicuous clumsiness in terms of gait and coordination. He also noted that some children were extremely sensitive to particular sounds, aromas, textures and touch.

Asperger considered that the characteristics could be identified in some children as young as two to three years, although for other children, the characteristics only became conspicuous some years later. He also noticed that some of the parents, especially the fathers of such children, appeared to share some of the personality characteristics of their child. He wrote that the condition was probably due to genetic or neurological, rather than psychological or environmental, factors. In his initial and subsequent publications and a recent analysis of his patient records for children he saw over three decades, it is apparent that he considered autistic personality disorder as part of a natural continuum of abilities that merges into the normal range (Asperger 1944, 1952, 1979; Hippler and Klicpera 2004). He conceptualized the disorder as a life-long and stable personality type, and did not observe the disintegration and fragmentation that occurs in schizophrenia. He also noted that some of the children had specific talents that could lead to successful employment and some could develop life-long relationships.

PATHWAYS TO A DIAGNOSIS

Today, when a child or adult is referred for a diagnostic assessment, they may have travelled along one of several different diagnostic pathways. The child referred for a diagnostic assessment would have had an unusual developmental history and profile of abilities from early childhood, though the average age for a diagnosis of a child with Asperger's syndrome is between 8 and 11 years (Eisenmajer *et al.* 1996; Howlin and Asgharian 1999). I have identified several pathways to that diagnosis, which may commence when the child is an infant, or at other stages of development, or even at specific times in the adult's life history.

Diagnosis of autism in infancy or early childhood

Lorna Wing, who first used the term Asperger's syndrome, considered that there was a need for a new diagnostic category. She had observed that some children who had the clear signs of severe autism in infancy and early childhood could achieve remarkable progress and move along the autism continuum as a result of early diagnosis and intensive and effective early intervention programs (Wing 1981). The previously socially aloof and silent child now wants to play with children and can talk using complex sentences. Where previously there was motivation for isolation, the child is now motivated to be included in social activities. After many hours in intensive programs to encourage communication abilities, the problem is no longer encouraging the child to speak, but encouraging him or her to talk less, listen and be more aware of the social context. As a younger child, there may have been a preoccupation with sensory experiences – the spinning wheel of a toy car or bicycle may have mesmerized the child – but now he or she is fascinated by a specific topic, such as the orbits of the planets. Previous assessments and observations of play would have indicated the possibility of significant intellectual impairment, but now the child is confirmed as having an Intelligence Quotient (IQ) within the normal range.

Peter Szatmari has suggested that those children with autism who develop functional language in early childhood eventually join the developmental trajectory and have a profile of abilities typical of a child with Asperger's syndrome (Szatmari 2000). At one point in a child's early development, autism is the correct diagnosis, but a distinct subgroup of children with autism can show a remarkable improvement in language, play and motivation to socialize with their peers between the ages of four and six years. The developmental trajectory for such children has changed and their profile of abilities in the primary or elementary school years is consistent with the characteristics of Asperger's syndrome (Attwood 1998; Dissanayake 2004; Gillberg 1998; Wing 1981). These children, who may subsequently be diagnosed as having High Functioning Autism or Asperger's syndrome, will benefit from the strategies and services designed for children with Asperger's syndrome rather than autism.

Recognition of Asperger's syndrome in the early school years

During the diagnostic assessment of adults, I usually ask when the person first recognized that he or she was different to other people. Many adults who are diagnosed in their mature years say that the first time they felt different to others was when they started school. They describe being able to understand and relate to family members, including playing socially with brothers and sisters, but when they were expected to play with their peers at school and relate to a teacher, they recognized themselves as being very different from children their age. When I ask these adults to describe those differences, the replies usually refer to not being interested in the social activities of their peers, not wanting to include others in their own activities, and not understanding the social conventions in the playground or classroom.

The diagnostic pathway commences when an experienced teacher observes a child who has no obvious history of characteristics associated with autism, but who is very unusual in terms of his or her ability to understand social situations and conventions. The child is also recognized as immature in the ability to manage emotions and to express empathy. There can be an unusual learning style with remarkable knowledge in an area of interest to the child, but significant learning or attention problems for other academic skills. The teacher may also notice problems with motor coordination such as handwriting, running, and catching a ball. The child may also cover his or her ears in response to sounds that are not perceived as unpleasant by other children.

When in the playground, the child may actively avoid social play with peers or be socially naïve, intrusive or dominating. In class, the teacher recognizes that the child does not seem to notice or understand the non-verbal signals that convey messages such as 'not now' or 'I am starting to feel annoyed.' The child can become notorious for interrupting or not responding to the social context in ways that would be expected of a child of that age and intellectual ability. The teacher may also notice that the child becomes extremely anxious if routines are changed or he or she cannot solve a problem.

The child is obviously not intellectually impaired but appears to lack the social understanding of his or her peers. The teacher knows that the child would benefit from programs to help in his or her understanding of the social conventions of the classroom and school playground. The teacher also needs access to training, in-class support, resources and expertise in Asperger's syndrome to facilitate successful social integration and academic success. The child needs help and the teacher needs help.

My clinical experience suggests that the majority of children with Asperger's syndrome achieve a diagnosis using this pathway. The child's unusual profile of abilities and behaviour are not conspicuous at home but a teacher recognizes qualitative differences in abilities and behaviour in the classroom and playground. At a subsequent meeting of parents and representatives of the school, parents are encouraged to seek a diagnostic assessment both to explain the unusual behaviour and profile of abilities, and for the parents and school to achieve access to appropriate programs and resources.

The previous diagnosis of another developmental disorder

Another diagnostic pathway is that a child's developmental history includes a developmental disorder that can be associated with Asperger's syndrome. The diagnosis of a disorder of attention, language, movement, mood, eating or learning ability can be the start of the formal assessment process that eventually leads to a diagnosis of Asperger's syndrome.

Attention Deficit Hyperactivity Disorder

The general population is reasonably knowledgeable about Attention Deficit Hyperactivity Disorder (ADHD) and the child may be of concern to parents and teacher because of problems with sustained attention, impulsivity and hyperactivity. This diagnosis may account for the child's difficulties in these areas but not explain the child's unusual profile of social, linguistic and cognitive abilities, which are more accurately described by the diagnostic criteria for Asperger's syndrome. The ADHD was accurately diagnosed first but was not the end of the diagnostic trail.

Clinicians have recognized for some time that children with Asperger's syndrome can also have signs of ADHD, which has been confirmed by several research studies and case descriptions (Ehlers and Gillberg 1993; Fein *et al.* 2005; Ghaziuddin, Weider-Mikhail and Ghaziuddin 1998; Klin and Volkmar 1997; Perry 1998; Tani *et al.* 2006). The two diagnoses are not mutually exclusive and a child may benefit from the medical treatment and strategies used for both disorders.

I have observed young children with Asperger's syndrome who have been hyperactive but not necessarily due to having ADHD. The hyperactivity can be a response to a high level of stress and anxiety, particularly in new social situations, making the child unable to sit still and relax. It is important to distinguish between a range of factors that can influence attention span (such as motivation) and hyperactivity before confirming the diagnosis of ADHD.

A language disorder

A young child who has Asperger's syndrome may first be recognized as having a delay in the development of speech and be referred to a speech/language pathologist for assessment and therapy. Formal testing of communication skills may identify both delay in language development and specific characteristics that are not typical of any of the stages in language development. The assessment would indicate language delay and deviance with a pattern of linguistic abilities that resembles Semantic Pragmatic Language Disorder (SPLD). Children with SPLD have relatively good language skills in the areas of syntax, vocabulary and phonology but poor use of language in a social context, i.e. the art of conversation or the pragmatic aspects of language (Rapin 1982). Semantic abilities are affected such that the child tends to make a literal interpretation of what someone says. The diagnosis of SPLD explains the child's language skills but a comprehensive assessment of abilities and behaviour indicates that the broader clinical picture is explained by a diagnosis of Asperger's syndrome.

The diagnostic boundaries between Asperger's syndrome and specific language disorders such as SPLD are not clear cut (Bishop 2000). Receptive language delay in young children is often associated with problems with socialization (Paul, Spangle-Looney and Dahm 1991). A child who has difficulties understanding someone's language and being understood could become anxious and withdrawn in social situations. The reason for the social withdrawal is then due to language impairment rather than the impaired social reasoning that occurs in Asperger's syndrome. During the diagnostic assessment it is important to distinguish between the secondary consequences of a language disorder and Asperger's syndrome. Nevertheless, the child with Asperger's syndrome who also has signs of SPLD will benefit from programs designed for children who have SPLD.

A movement disorder

A young child may be identified by parents and teachers as being clumsy, with problems with coordination and dexterity. The child may have problems with tying shoelaces, learning to ride a bicycle, handwriting and catching a ball, and an unusual or immature gait when running or walking. The child is referred to an occupational therapist or physiotherapist for assessment and therapy. The assessment may confirm a delay in movement skills or a specific movement disorder but the therapist may note other unusual characteristics in the child's developmental history and profile of abilities and be the first professional to suspect that the child has Asperger's syndrome. Although the coordination problems were the start of the diagnostic pathway to Asperger's syndrome, the child will still obviously benefit from programs to improve motor skills.

Some children with Asperger's syndrome can develop involuntary, rapid and sudden body movements (motor tics) and uncontrollable vocalizations (vocal tics) that resemble signs of Tourette's syndrome (Ehlers and Gillberg 1993; Gillberg and Billstedt 2000; Kadesjo and Gillberg 2000; Ringman and Jankovic 2000). A diagnostic assessment for Tourette's syndrome due to the recognition of motor and vocal tics could be a pathway to the further diagnosis of Asperger's syndrome.

A mood disorder

We know that young children with Asperger's syndrome are prone to develop mood disorders (Attwood 2003a), and some children seem to be almost constantly anxious, which might indicate a Generalised Anxiety Disorder (GAD). One of the problems faced by children with Asperger's syndrome who use their intellect rather than intuition to succeed in some social situations is that they may be in an almost constant state of alertness and anxiety, leading to a risk of mental and physical exhaustion.

The child may have developed compensatory mechanisms to avoid anxiety-provoking situations such as school, by refusing to go to school or being mute at school

(Kopp and Gillberg 1997). There may be intense anxiety or a phobic reaction to certain social situations, or to sensory experiences such as a dog barking, or to a change in expectations such as an alteration to the daily school routine. A referral to a clinical psychologist, psychiatrist or mental health service for children with a mood disorder may lead to a diagnosis of Asperger's syndrome when a detailed and comprehensive developmental history is completed (Towbin *et al.* 2005).

Some children with Asperger's syndrome can become clinically depressed as a reaction to their realization of having considerable difficulties with social integration. The depressive reaction can be internalized, leading to self-criticism and even thoughts of suicide; or externalized, resulting in criticism of others and an expression of frustration or anger, especially when the child has difficulty understanding a social situation. Blame is directed at oneself: 'I am stupid'; or others: 'It's your fault.' The signs of a clinical depression or problems with anger management could be the first indicators of a developmental disorder such as Asperger's syndrome.

An eating disorder

Eating disorders can include refusal to eat foods of a specified texture, smell or taste due to a sensory hypersensitivity (Ahearn *et al.* 2001). There can also be unusual food preferences, and routines regarding meals and food presentation (Nieminen-von Wendt 2004). Referral to a paediatrician for problems with food intake, diet or weight can lead to a diagnosis of Asperger's syndrome. Several studies have also suggested an over-representation of low body weight in Asperger's syndrome that may be due to anxiety or sensory sensitivity associated with food (Bolte, Ozkara and Poustka 2002; Hebebrand *et al.* 1997; Sobanski *et al.* 1999).

Serious eating disorders such as anorexia nervosa can be associated with Asperger's syndrome, with approximately 18 to 23 per cent of adolescent girls with anorexia nervosa also having signs of Asperger's syndrome (Gillberg and Billstedt 2000; Gillberg and Rastam 1992; Gillberg *et al.* 1996; Rastam, Gillberg and Wentz 2003; Wentz *et al.* 2005; Wentz Nilsson *et al.* 1999). Thus, concerns about food intake or the diagnosis of an eating disorder could be the starting point for a diagnostic assessment for Asperger's syndrome.

Non-verbal Learning Disability

A young child may be recognized as having an unusual profile of intellectual and academic abilities, and formal testing by a neuropsychologist indicates a significant discrepancy between verbal reasoning abilities (Verbal IQ) and visual-spatial reasoning (Performance IQ). If the discrepancy is a significantly higher Verbal IQ, a subsequent and more detailed assessment of cognitive abilities may indicate a diagnosis of Non-verbal Learning Disability (NLD).

The main characteristics of NLD are deficits in the following: visual-perceptual-organizational abilities; complex psychomotor skills and tactile perception; adapting to novel situations; time perception; mechanical arithmetic; and social perception and social interaction skills. There are relative assets in auditory perception, word recognition, rote verbal learning and spelling. This pattern of abilities suggests right-hemisphere dysfunction and white matter damage to the brain (Rourke and Tsatsanis 2000). The overlap between NLD and Asperger's syndrome is an area of continuing study and discussion among clinicians (Volkmar and Klin 2000). If the child with NLD is subsequently diagnosed as having Asperger's syndrome, information on the child's unusual profile of cognitive skills can be invaluable for a teacher in terms of how to adapt the school curriculum for a distinct learning style.

First recognition of the clinical signs in adolescence

As a child matures into adolescence, the social and academic worlds become more complex and there is an expectation that the child should become more independent and self-reliant. In the early school years, social play tends to be more action than conversation, with friendships being transitory and social games relatively simple with clear rules. In adolescence, friendships are based on more complex interpersonal rather than practical needs, someone to confide in rather than someone to play ball with.

In the early school years, the child has one teacher for the whole year and both teacher and child learn how to read each other's signals and develop a working relationship. There is also more guidance, flexibility and leniency with regard to the school curriculum and expected social and emotional maturity. Life is relatively simple and the child may be less aware of being different to other children, and his or her difficulties may not be conspicuous in the classroom or playground.

During adolescence, a teenager with Asperger's syndrome is likely to have increasingly conspicuous difficulties with planning and organizational skills, and completing assignments on time. This can lead to a deterioration in school grades that comes to the attention of teachers and parents. The teenager's intellectual abilities have not deteriorated, but the methods of assessment used by teachers have changed. Knowledge of history is no longer remembering dates and facts but organizing a coherent essay. The study of English requires abilities with characterization and to 'read between the lines'. A group of students may be expected to submit a science project and the teenager with Asperger's syndrome is not easily assimilated into a working group of students. The deterioration in grades and subsequent stress can lead the adolescent to be referred to the school psychologist who recognizes signs of Asperger's syndrome.

I have noted that the signs of Asperger's syndrome are more conspicuous at times of stress and change, and during the teenage years there are major changes in expectations and circumstances. The child may have coped well during his or her pre-adolescent years, but changes in the nature of friendship, body shape, school routines and support may precipitate a crisis that alerts the relevant diagnostic authorities to the discovery of Asperger's syndrome in a child who was previously coping so well.

Adolescence is also a time of re-appraisal of who one is and wants to be. The influence of parents in an adolescent's life diminishes and the power of and identification with the peer group increases. The teenager is expected to relate to many teachers, each with his or her own personality and teaching style, and to engage in academic assessment that relies on abstract thinking rather than facts. Problems with social inclusion, acceptance and academic success can precipitate a clinical depression, or anger directed to others or the 'system'.

The adolescent may be referred to adolescent psychiatric services for the treatment of depression, an anxiety disorder – which at this age can include Obsessive Compulsive Disorder (Bejerot, Nylander and Lindstrom 2001) – an eating disorder such as anorexia nervosa, problems with anger, or a conduct disorder. I have also seen some children who have various levels of expression of four disorders which can form a cluster, namely Attention Deficit Hyperactivity Disorder, Asperger's syndrome, Tourette's disorder and an Obsessive Compulsive Disorder. Each diagnosis is correct and the child or adult will need treatment for all four disorders.

The suggestion of a conduct or personality disorder

Asperger described a subgroup of children with a tendency to have conduct problems, leading to their being suspended from school – one of the main reasons the children who were subsequently diagnosed as having autistic personality disorder were referred to his clinic in Vienna. Sometimes children with Asperger's syndrome perceive themselves as more adult than child. Indeed, such children may act in the classroom as an assistant to the teacher, correcting and disciplining the other children. In situations of conflict, they are less likely to refer to an adult to act as an adjudicator, and are liable to 'take the law into their own hands'. These children may also learn that acts of aggression can repel other children, ensuring uninterrupted solitude. Conflict and confrontation with adults can be made worse by non-compliance, negativism, and a difficulty in perceiving the differences in social status or hierarchy, resulting in a failure to respect authority or maturity.

The child with Asperger's syndrome is often immature in the art of negotiation and compromise and may not know when to back down and apologize. He or she will not accept a particular school rule if it appears to be illogical, and will pursue a point or argument as a matter of principle. This can lead to a history of significant conflict with teachers and school authorities.

We know that the child with Asperger's syndrome has difficulty with social integration with his or her peers. If that child also has superior intellectual ability, difficulties in social integration may be compounded. Those children who have exceptionally high IQs may compensate by becoming arrogant and egocentric, and have considerable difficulty acknowledging that they have made a mistake. Such children can be hypersensitive to any suggestion of criticism, yet overly critical of others, including teachers, parents or authority figures. The school or parents may turn to professional help with regard to the attitude and conduct of such children, leading to a diagnosis of Asperger's syndrome. Referral to a behaviour management specialist may be the starting point of the pathway to a diagnosis of Asperger's syndrome.

Diagnosis of a relative with autism or Asperger's syndrome

When a child or adult is diagnosed as having autism or Asperger's syndrome, parents and relatives will soon become aware of the different forms of expression of autism, and review their own family history and the characteristics of their relatives for signs of autism spectrum disorder, in particular Asperger's syndrome. Recent research has indicated that 46 per cent of the first-degree relatives of a child with Asperger's syndrome have a similar profile of abilities and behaviour (Volkmar, Klin and Pauls 1998), although usually to a degree that is sub-clinical, i.e. more a description of personality than a syndrome or disorder.

After a child has a diagnosis of Asperger's syndrome confirmed, the clinician may then receive another referral for the diagnostic assessment of a sibling or relative of the child. The diagnosis may be confirmed and clinical experience has indicated that some families have children and adults with Asperger's syndrome within and between generations. This has been confirmed in some of the autobiographies of adults with Asperger's syndrome (Willey 1999). However, the subsequent diagnostic assessment may indicate that the level of expression of the characteristics is too 'mild' for a diagnosis, or the person has a number of 'fragments' of Asperger's syndrome that are insufficient for a diagnosis. Nevertheless, the person may benefit from some of the strategies that are designed for the characteristics or fragments that are present in his or her profile of abilities.

Recognition of the signs of Asperger's syndrome from the media

Watching a television programme or news item that explains Asperger's syndrome, or reading a magazine article or popular autobiography by an adult with Asperger's syndrome, may be the starting point for some people to seek a diagnostic assessment for themselves or a family member, colleague or friend. In Australia, I recently explained the nature of Asperger's syndrome on a national 'live' television programme, and the switchboard of the television company was subsequently inundated with calls from parents who recognized the signs of Asperger's syndrome in their adult son or daughter who, due to their age, had never had access to the diagnostic knowledge that is available for children today. In the next few years there is likely to be a deluge of referrals of adults for a diagnostic assessment for Asperger's syndrome.

Sometimes partners in a relationship may acquire information from the media, and consider that a diagnosis of Asperger's syndrome may explain their husband's (or wife's) unusual hobby and difficulties with empathy and social skills. It is important to remember that many typical women feel that their partner does not understand what they are thinking or feeling, and that many natural characteristics of males could be perceived as signs of Asperger's syndrome. Nevertheless, I have noted an increase in referrals from relationship counsellors who are becoming aware of how to recognize genuine signs of Asperger's syndrome in couples who are seeking relationship counselling (Aston 2003).

Employment problems

Although the person with Asperger's syndrome may achieve academic success, difficulties with social skills may affect his or her performance at a job interview, the social or team aspects of employment, or the understanding of social conventions such as standing too close or looking at someone too long. Getting and keeping a job may be a problem. An assessment by a careers guidance agency, government employment agency or the personnel department of a company may be the first step down the pathway to recognition of Asperger's syndrome. There is probably a high rate of Asperger's syndrome among the chronically unemployed.

Another diagnostic pathway in the area of employment is a change in job expectations. This can be, for example, a promotion to management, requiring interpersonal skills, and conferring responsibilities that demand planning and organizational abilities which can be elusive in some adults with Asperger's syndrome. There can also be issues of not accepting conventional procedures, and difficulties with time management, and recognizing and accepting the organizational hierarchy.

WHY PURSUE A DIAGNOSIS?

The very young child with Asperger's syndrome may not be aware of being different from other children of his or her age. However, adults and other children will become increasingly aware that the child does not behave, think or play like other children. The initial opinion of adults within the extended family and school may be that the child is rude and selfish, while peers may think that the child is just weird. If there is no diagnosis and explanation, others will make moral judgements that will inevitably have a detrimental effect on the child's self-esteem and lead to inappropriate attitudes and consequences.

Gradually the child will recognize that he or she is perceiving and experiencing the world in an unusual way and will become concerned about being different from other children. This is not only in terms of different interests, priorities and social knowledge but also in terms of frequent criticisms by peers and adults. The realization of being different to other children usually occurs when the child with Asperger's syndrome is between six and eight years old.

Claire Sainsbury was about eight years old:

> Here is one of my most vivid memories of school; I am standing in a corner of the playground as usual, as far away as possible from people who might bump into me or shout, gazing into the sky and absorbed in my own thoughts. I am eight or nine years old and have begun to realize that I am different in some nameless but all-pervasive way.
>
> I don't understand the children around me. They frighten and confuse me. They don't want to talk about things that are interesting. I used to think that they were silly, but now I am beginning to understand that I am the one who is all wrong. (Sainsbury 2000, p.8)

The child can then develop compensatory thoughts and attitudes for feeling alienated, socially isolated and not understood.

COMPENSATORY AND ADJUSTMENT STRATEGIES TO BEING DIFFERENT

I have identified four compensatory or adjustment strategies developed by young children with Asperger's syndrome as a response to the realization that they are different from other children. The strategy used will depend on the child's personality, experiences and circumstances. Those children who tend to internalize thoughts and feelings may develop signs of self-blame and depression, or alternatively use imagination and a fantasy life to create another world in which they are more successful. Those children who tend to externalize thoughts and feelings can either become arrogant and blame others for their difficulties, or view others not as the cause but the solution to their problems and develop an ability to imitate other children or characters. Thus some psychological reactions can be constructive while others can lead to significant psychological problems.

A reactive depression

Social ability and friendship skills are highly valued by peers and adults and not being successful in these areas can lead some children with Asperger's syndrome to internalize their thoughts and feelings by being overly apologetic, self-critical and increasingly socially withdrawn. The child, sometimes as young as seven years old, may develop a clinical depression as a result of insight into being different and perceiving him- or herself as socially defective.

Intellectually, the child has the ability to recognize his or her social isolation, but lacks social skills in comparison to intellectual and age peers, and does not know intuitively what to do to achieve social success. Brave attempts by the child to improve social integration with other children may be ridiculed and the child deliberately shunned. Teachers and parents may not be providing the necessary level of guidance and especially encouragement. The child desperately wants to be included and to have friends but does not know what to do. The result can be a crisis of confidence, as described in the following quotation from an unpublished autobiography by my sister-in-law, who has Asperger's syndrome.

> The fact is, no one likes others to know their weaknesses, but with an affliction like mine, it's impossible to always avoid making a fool of yourself or looking indignant/undignified. Because I never knew when the next 'fall' is going to occur, I avoid climbing up on to a 'confidence horse' so to speak.

There can be increased social withdrawal due to a lack of social competence that decreases the opportunities to develop social maturity and ability. The depression can also affect motivation and energy for other previously enjoyable activities in the classroom and at home. There can be changes in sleep patterns and appetite, and a negative attitude that pervades all aspects of life and, in extreme cases, talk of suicide, or impulsive or planned suicide attempts.

Escape into imagination

A more constructive internalization of thoughts and feelings of being socially defective can be to escape into imagination. Children with Asperger's syndrome can develop vivid and complex imaginary worlds, sometimes with make-believe friends.

Thomas has Asperger's syndrome and considerable intellectual ability. In his biography written by his mother, she describes one of the reasons why her son escaped into his imagination:

> During a speech session at school, Thomas was asked by his speech teacher, 'So who do you play with at recess?'
> 'My imagination. What do you think?' he informed her.
> 'Who do you think you should play with at recess?' she enquired.
> 'Anyone that understands me; but that's nobody but you adults and you don't have time for me,' he said bluntly. (Barber 2006, p.103)

In their imaginary worlds with imaginary friends, children with Asperger's syndrome are understood, and successful socially and academically. Another advantage is the responses of the imaginary friends are under the child's control and the friends are instantly available. Imaginary friends can prevent the child from feeling lonely. Liane Holliday Willey explained that:

> When I think of my earliest years, I recall an overwhelming desire to be away from my peers. I much preferred the company of my imaginary friends. Penny and her brother Johnna were my best friends, though no one saw them but me. My mother

tells me I used to insist that we set them a place at the table, include them in our car trips, and treat them like they were real beings. (Willey 1999, p.16)

In a personal communication to me, Liane explained that having imaginary friends 'is not pretend play, so much as the only play that works'.

Having an imaginary friend is typical of the play of many young children and is not necessarily of clinical significance. However, the child with Asperger's syndrome may only have friends who are imaginary, and the intensity and duration of the imaginary interactions can be qualitatively unusual.

Searching for an alternative world can lead some children to develop an interest in another country, culture, period of history or the world of animals, as described in the following passage by my sister-in-law.

> When I was about seven, I probably saw something in a book, which fascinated me and still does. Because it was like nothing I had ever seen before and totally unrelated and far removed from our world and our culture. That was Scandinavia and its people. Because of its foreignness it was totally alien and opposite to any one and any thing known to me. That was my escape, a dream world where nothing would remind me of daily life and all it had to throw at me. The people from this wonderful place look totally unlike any people in the 'real world'. Looking at these faces, I could not be reminded of anyone who might have humiliated, frightened or rebuked me. The bottom line is I was turning my back on real life and its ability to hurt, and escaping. (Unpublished autobiography)

The interest in other cultures and worlds can explain the development of a special interest in geography, astronomy and science fiction, such that the child discovers a place where his or her knowledge and abilities are recognized and valued.

Sometimes the degree of imaginative thought can lead to an interest in fiction, both as a reader and author. Some children, especially girls, with Asperger's syndrome can develop the ability to use imaginary friends, characters and worlds to write quite remarkable fiction. This could lead to success as an author of fiction for children or adults.

The escape into imagination can be a psychologically constructive adaptation, but there are risks of other people misinterpreting the child's intentions or state of mind. Hans Asperger wrote, with regard to one of the four children who became the basis of his thesis on autistic personality disorder, that:

> He was said to be an inveterate 'liar'. He did not lie in order to get out of something that he had done – this was certainly not his problem, as he always told the truth very brazenly – but he told long, fantastic stories, his confabulations becoming ever more strange and incoherent. He liked to tell fantastic stories, in which he always appeared as the hero. He would tell his mother how he was praised by the teacher in front of the class, and other similar tales. (Asperger [1944] 1991, p.51)

Under conditions of extreme stress or loneliness the propensity to escape into an imaginary world and imaginary friends can lead to an internal fantasy becoming a 'reality' for the person with Asperger's syndrome. The person may be considered as developing delusions and being out of touch with reality (Adamo 2004). This could result in a referral for a diagnostic assessment for schizophrenia, as described in the biography of Ben by his mother, Barbara LaSalle (2003).

Denial and arrogance

An alternative to internalizing negative thoughts and feelings is to externalize the cause and solution to feeling different. The child can develop a form of over-compensation for feeling defective in social situations by denying that there is any problem, and by developing a sense of arrogance such that the 'fault' or problem is in other people and that the child is 'above the rules' that he or she finds so difficult to understand. The child or adult goes into what I describe as 'God mode', an omnipotent person who never makes a mistake, cannot be wrong and whose intelligence must be worshipped. Such children can deny that they have any difficulties making friends, or reading social situations or someone's thoughts and intentions. They consider they do not need any programs or to be treated differently from other children. They vehemently do not want to be referred to a psychologist or psychiatrist, and are convinced that they are not mad or stupid.

Nevertheless, the child does know, but will not publicly acknowledge, that he or she has limited social competence, and is desperate to conceal any difficulties in order not to appear stupid. A lack of ability in social play with peers and in interactions with adults can result in the development of behaviours to achieve dominance and control in a social context; these include the use of intimidation, and an arrogant and inflexible attitude. Other children and parents are likely to capitulate to avoid yet another confrontation. The child can become 'intoxicated' by such power and dominance, which may lead to conduct problems.

When such children are confused as to the intentions of others or what to do in a social situation, or have made a conspicuous error, the resulting 'negative' emotion can lead to the misperception that the other person's actions were deliberately malicious. The response is to inflict equal discomfort, sometimes by physical retaliation: 'He hurt my feelings so I will hurt him.' Such children and some adults may ruminate for many years over past slights and injustices and seek resolution and revenge (Tantam 2000a).

The compensatory mechanism of arrogance can also affect other aspects of social interaction. The child may have difficulty admitting being wrong and be notorious for arguing. Hans Asperger advised that:

> There is a great danger of getting involved in endless arguments with these children, be it in order to prove that they are wrong or to bring them towards some insight. This is especially true for parents, who frequently find themselves trapped in endless discussion. (Asperger [1944] 1991, p.48)

There can be a remarkably accurate recall of what was said or done to prove a point, and no concession, or acceptance of a compromise or a different perspective. Parents may consider that this characteristic could lead to a successful career as a defence lawyer in an adversarial court. Certainly the child has had a great deal of practice arguing his or her point.

Unfortunately, the arrogant attitude can further alienate the child from natural friendships, and denial and resistance to accepting programs to improve social understanding can increase the gap between the child's social abilities and that of his or her peers. We can understand why the child would develop these compensatory and adjustment strategies. Unfortunately, the long-term consequences of these compensatory mechanisms can have a significant effect on friendships and prospects for relationships and employment as an adult.

Imitation

An intelligent and constructive compensatory mechanism used by some children is to observe and absorb the persona of those who are socially successful. Such children initially remain on the periphery of social play, watching and noting what to do. They may then re-enact the activities that they have observed in their own solitary play, using dolls, figures or imaginary friends at home. They are rehearsing, practising the script and their role, to achieve fluency and confidence before attempting to be included in real social situations. Some children can be remarkably astute in their observation abilities, copying gestures, tone of voice and mannerisms. They are developing the ability to be a natural actor. For example, in her autobiography, Liane Holliday Willey describes her technique:

> I could take part in the world as an observer. I was an avid observer. I was enthralled with the nuances of people's actions. In fact, I often found it desirable to become the other person. Not that I consciously set out to do that, rather it came as something I simply did. As if I had no choice in the matter. My mother tells me I was very good at capturing the essence and persona of people. (Willey 1999, p.22)

> I was uncanny in my ability to copy accents, vocal inflections, facial expressions, hand movements, gaits, and tiny gestures. It was as if I became the person I was emulating. (Willey 1999, p.23)

Becoming an expert mimic can have other advantages. The child may become popular for imitating the voice and persona of a teacher or character from television. The adolescent with Asperger's syndrome may apply knowledge acquired in drama classes to everyday situations, determining who would be successful in this situation and adopting the persona of that person. The child or adult may remember the words and body postures of someone in a similar situation in real life or in a television programme or film. He or she then re-enacts the scene using 'borrowed' dialogue and body language. There is a veneer of social success but, on closer examination, the apparent social competence is not spontaneous or original but artificial and contrived. However, practice and success may improve the person's acting abilities such that acting becomes a possible career option.

An adult with Asperger's syndrome who is a retired actor wrote to me and explained that, 'As an actor, I find the scripts in theatre far more real than everyday life. The role playing comes naturally to me.' The ability to act a role in daily life is explained by Donna Williams:

> I found it impossible to talk to her in a normal voice. I began to put on a strong American accent, making up a history and identity for myself to go with it. As always, I actually convinced myself that I was this new character and consistently kept this up for six months. (Williams 1998, p.73)

There are several possible disadvantages. The first is observing and imitating popular but notorious models, for example the school 'bad guys'. This group may accept the adolescent with Asperger's syndrome, who wears the group's 'uniform', speaks their language and knows their gestures and moral code; but this in turn may alienate the adolescent from more appropriate models. The group will probably recognize that the person with Asperger's syndrome is a fake, desperate to be accepted, who is probably not aware that he or she is being covertly ridiculed and 'set up'. Another disadvantage is that some psychologists and psychiatrists may consider that the person has signs of multiple personality disorder, and fail to recognize that this is a constructive adaptation to having Asperger's syndrome.

Some children with Asperger's syndrome dislike who they are and would like to be someone other than themselves, someone who would be socially able and have friends. A boy with Asperger's syndrome may notice how popular his sister is with her peers. He may also recognize that girls and women, especially his mother, are naturally socially intuitive; so to acquire social abilities, he starts to imitate girls. This can include dressing like a girl. There are several published case reports and, in my clinical experience, I have seen several males and females with Asperger's syndrome who have issues with gender identity (Gallucci, Hackerman and Schmidt 2005; Kraemer *et al.* 2005). This can also include girls with Asperger's syndrome who have self-loathing and want to become someone else. Sometimes such girls want to be male, especially when they cannot identify with the interests and ambitions of other girls, and the action activities of boys seem more interesting. However, changing gender will not automatically lead to a change in social acceptance and self-acceptance.

When adults with Asperger's syndrome have used imitation and acting to achieve superficial social competence, they can have considerable difficulty convincing people that they have a real problem with social understanding and empathy; they have become too plausible in their role to be believed.

WHAT ARE THE ADVANTAGES AND DISADVANTAGES OF HAVING A DIAGNOSIS?

The advantage to the child of having a diagnosis is not only in preventing or reducing the effects of some compensatory or adjustment strategies, but also to remove worries about other diagnoses, such as being insane. The child can be recognized as having genuine difficulties coping with experiences that others find easy and enjoyable. When an adult has problems with the non-verbal aspects of communication, especially eye contact, there can be an assumption made by the general public that he or she has a mental illness or malicious intent. Once the characteristics of Asperger's syndrome are explained, such assumptions can be corrected.

Children with Asperger's syndrome have no physical characteristics to indicate that they are different, and having intellectual ability may lead others to have high expectations with regard to their social knowledge. Once the diagnosis is confirmed and understood, there can be a significant positive change in other people's expectations, acceptance and support. The child is now understood and more likely to be respected. There should be compliments rather than criticism with regard to social competence, and acknowledgement of the child's confusion and exhaustion from learning two curricula at school: the academic curriculum and the social curriculum.

The advantage of acknowledging and understanding the diagnosis for parents is that, at last, they have an explanation for their son's or daughter's unusual behaviours and abilities, and knowledge that the condition is not caused by faulty parenting. The family may then have access to knowledge on Asperger's syndrome from literature and the Internet, resources from government agencies and support groups, as well as access to programs to improve social inclusion and emotion management that will greatly benefit the whole family. There may also be greater acceptance of the child within the extended family and family friends. The parents can now provide an acceptable explanation to other people regarding the child's unusual behaviour. It is also important that parents explain to the child that having Asperger's syndrome is not an excuse to avoid chores and responsibilities.

Siblings may have known for some time that their brother or sister is unusual and may have been either compassionate, tolerant and concerned about any difficulties, or embarrassed, intolerant and antagonistic. Each sibling will make his or her own accommodations towards the sibling with Asperger's syndrome. Parents can now explain to their children why their brother or sister is unusual, and how the family has had to, and will need to, adjust and work cooperatively and constructively to implement the strategies. Parents and professionals can provide the siblings with age-appropriate explanations about their brother or sister, to give their friends, without jeopardizing their own social networks. Siblings will also need to know how to help their brother or sister at home when friends visit, and be made aware of their role and responsibilities at school and in the neighbourhood.

The advantages for school services, especially teachers, is that the child's unusual behaviour and profile of social, cognitive, linguistic and motor skills are recognized as a legitimate disorder that should provide access to resources to help the teacher. Confirmation of the diagnosis should also have a positive effect on the attitudes of other children in the classroom and other staff who have contact with the child. The teacher can access information from textbooks and resource programs specifically developed for teachers of children with Asperger's syndrome. The teacher can also explain to other children and staff who teach or supervise the child why he or she behaves and thinks in a different way.

The advantages of the diagnosis for the adolescent or adult with Asperger's syndrome can be in terms of support while a student at college or university or in employment. Acknowledgement of the diagnosis can lead to greater self-understanding, self-advocacy and better decision making with regard to careers, friendships and relationships (Shore 2004). An employer is then more likely to understand the profile of abilities and needs of an employee with Asperger's syndrome: for example, the problems that may arise if an employee with visual sensitivity is assigned a work cubicle lit with fluorescent lights.

An adult with a diagnosis of Asperger's syndrome may benefit from joining an adult support group that has local meetings, or an Internet support group or chat room. This can provide a sense of belonging to a distinct and valued culture and enable the person to consult members of the culture for advice. We also know that acceptance of the diagnosis can be an important stage in the development of successful adult relationships with a partner, and invaluable when seeking counselling and therapy from relationship counsellors (Aston 2003).

I have noted that when an adult is diagnosed with Asperger's syndrome there can be a range of emotional reactions. Most adults report that having the diagnosis has been an extremely positive experience (Gresley 2000). There can be intense relief: 'I am not going mad'; euphoria at ending a nomadic wandering from specialist to specialist, at last discovering why they feel and think differently to others; and excitement as to how their lives may now change for the better. A young man with Asperger's syndrome sent me an e-mail which stated, 'I know I have Asperger's, because nothing else comes even close to describing my weirdness as flawlessly and perfectly as Asperger's syndrome does.'

There can also be moments of anger at the delay in being diagnosed and at 'The System' for not recognizing the signs for so many years. There can be feelings of despair regarding how their lives would have been much easier if the diagnosis had been confirmed decades ago. Other emotional reactions can be a sense of grief for all the suffering in trying to be as socially successful as others, and the years of feeling misunderstood, inadequate and rejected.

Nita Jackson provides sound advice for fellow people with Asperger's syndrome:

Because Asperger people can be exceptionally stubborn when they get the chance, denial can pose a big problem. The less they acknowledge their condition, the less they can improve upon their social skills, and consequently the higher the probability of them being friendless and/or victimized. Don't think that acknowledgement solves everything (it doesn't), but at least it brings a certain amount of self-awareness, which can be built upon. Once the person has this acknowledgement, learning the tricks of the trade – or the rules of the game, as some people refer to it – will be feasible, providing they are advised and directed by people who have at least a basic understanding of the syndrome. (N. Jackson 2002, p.28)

There can be a new sense of personal validation and optimism, at last not feeling stupid, defective or insane. As Liane Holliday Willey said exuberantly on learning of her diagnosis, 'That's why I'm different; I'm not a freak or mad' (Attwood and Willey 2000). There can be benefits in terms of self-esteem and moral support in identifying with other adults with Asperger's syndrome by using the Internet and support groups specifically for and organized by adults with Asperger's syndrome. The group meetings can initially be organized by a local parent support group or by disability support staff at a large university or college that has several students registered with Asperger's syndrome (Harpur, Lawlor and Fitzgerald 2004). Some support groups have formed spontaneously in large cities as occurred in Los Angeles when Jerry Newport, a man with Asperger's syndrome, formed and coordinated the support group AGUA (Adult Gathering, United and Autistic). There can be an affinity, empathy and support network with fellow members of the same 'tribe' or clan who share the same experiences, thinking and perception of the world.

When talking to adults with Asperger's syndrome about the diagnosis, I often refer to the self-affirmation pledge of those with Asperger's syndrome written by Liane Holliday Willey.

- I am not defective. I am different.

- I will not sacrifice my self-worth for peer acceptance.

- I am a good and interesting person.

- I will take pride in myself.

- I am capable of getting along with society.

- I will ask for help when I need it.

- I am a person who is worthy of others' respect and acceptance.

- I will find a career interest that is well suited to my abilities and interests.

- I will be patient with those who need time to understand me.

- I am never going to give up on myself.

- I will accept myself for who I am. (Willey 2001, p.164)

I consider the last pledge, 'I will accept myself for who I am,' as a major goal when conducting psychotherapy with an adolescent or adult with Asperger's syndrome.

One reaction, although rare, is for some people to deny that they have Asperger's syndrome, insisting there is nothing wrong with or different about them. Despite acknowledging that the clinical descriptions match their developmental history and profile of abilities, they may question the validity of the syndrome and reject any programs or services. However, this may only be an initial reaction and, given time to reflect, they may eventually accept that their personality and profile of abilities includes the characteristics of Asperger's syndrome, and that this is invaluable information when making major decisions in aspects of life such as employment and relationships.

There could be disadvantages in having a diagnosis in terms of how the person and others perceive the characteristics. If the diagnostic news is broadcast widely, there will inevitably be some children or adults who misuse this disclosure to torment and despise the person with Asperger's syndrome. Care must be taken when using the diagnostic term Asperger's syndrome as some children may consider the condition is infectious (or tease the child that it is), or corrupt the term in a variety of ways – Asparagus syndrome, Sparrow syndrome, Hamburger syndrome or Arseburger syndrome, among others. Children can be quite inventive in stigmatizing differences, but more compassionate people may be able to repair some of the damage to the self-esteem of someone with Asperger's syndrome who has been ridiculed for being different.

One of the concerns of adults with Asperger's syndrome is whether they should include reference to the diagnosis on a job application. If there is considerable competition for a particular vacancy, an applicant having a diagnosis that is unknown to the employer might lead to the application being rejected. A potential solution is for the adult to write a brief, perhaps one-page, description of Asperger's syndrome and the qualities and difficulties that would be relevant to the job. This personalized brochure could also be used to explain Asperger's syndrome to colleagues, juniors and line managers. A shorter version can be reduced to a business card that can be given to anyone who needs to know about the person's diagnosis.

Having a diagnosis of Asperger's syndrome could limit the expectations of others, who may assume that the person will never be able to achieve as well as his or her peers with regard to social, academic and personal success. The diagnosis should facilitate realistic expectations but not dictate the upper limits of ability. I have known adults with Asperger's syndrome whose successful careers have ranged from professor of mathematics to social worker; and those whose ability in the area of relationships ranges from enjoying a fulfilling but celibate life, to having a life-long partner and being a much-loved parent.

As a society, we need to recognize the value of having people with Asperger's syndrome in our multi-cultural and diverse community. In summary, maybe we should consider the comment from an adult with Asperger's syndrome who suggested to me that perhaps Asperger's syndrome is the next stage of human evolution.

KEY POINTS AND STRATEGIES

- Children with Asperger's syndrome have the following characteristics:
  - delayed social maturity and social reasoning
  - immature empathy
  - difficulty making friends and often teased by other children
  - difficulty with the communication and control of emotions
  - unusual language abilities that include advanced vocabulary and syntax but delayed conversation skills, unusual prosody and a tendency to be pedantic
  - a fascination with a topic that is unusual in intensity or focus
  - difficulty maintaining attention in class
  - an unusual profile of learning abilities
  - a need for assistance with some self-help and organizational skills
  - clumsiness in terms of gait and coordination
  - sensitivity to specific sounds, aromas, textures or touch.
- There are several pathways to a diagnosis:
  - Diagnosis of autism in early childhood and progression by the middle school years to High Functioning Autism or Asperger's syndrome.
  - A teacher's recognition of Asperger's syndrome when the child starts primary school.
  - Previous diagnosis of another developmental disorder such as Attention Deficit Hyperactivity Disorder, a language or movement delay or disorder, a mood disorder, eating disorder or Non-verbal Learning Disability.
  - The signs of Asperger's syndrome only becoming conspicuous during adolescence, when the social and academic expectations become more complex.
  - The development of behaviour problems and conflict with parents, teachers and school authorities.
  - The identification of signs of Asperger's syndrome in a relative, where a review of the child's family history identifies other family members who have similar characteristics.
  - Descriptions of Asperger's syndrome in the media and literature may lead someone to seek a diagnosis for him- or herself or a family member.
  - Employment problems, especially achieving and keeping a job appropriate to the person's qualifications and abilities.
- There are four compensatory or adjustment strategies when the child realizes he or she is different to other children:

- o self-blame and depression
- o escape into imagination
- o denial and arrogance
- o imitation of other children and characters.
- The advantages of a diagnosis can be:
  - o Preventing or reducing the effects of some of the compensatory or adjustment strategies.
  - o Removing worries about other diagnoses and being insane.
  - o Being recognized as having genuine difficulties coping with experiences that others find easy and enjoyable.
  - o A positive change in other people's expectations, acceptance and support.
  - o Compliments rather than criticism with regard to social competence.
  - o Acknowledgement of confusion and exhaustion in social situations.
  - o Schools can access resources to help the child and class teacher.
  - o An adult can access specialized support services for employment and further education.
  - o Greater self-understanding, self-advocacy and better decision making with regard to careers, friendships and relationships.
  - o A sense of identification with a valued 'culture'.
  - o The person no longer feels stupid, defective or insane.
- The disadvantages of a diagnosis can be:
  - o Some children or adults could torment and despise the person for having a disorder diagnosed by a psychologist or psychiatrist.
  - o The diagnosis could limit the expectations of others who erroneously assume the person with Asperger's syndrome will never be able to achieve as well as his or her peers with regard to social, academic and personal success.

CHAPTER 2

The Diagnosis

One can spot such children instantly. They are recognizable from small details, for instance, the way they enter the consulting room at their first visit, their behaviour in the first few moments and the first words they utter.

– Hans Asperger ([1944] 1991)

At the same time as Hans Asperger described autistic personality disorder in the 1940s, another Austrian physician, Leo Kanner, then living in Baltimore in the United States, described another part of what we now call the autism spectrum. Leo Kanner, who was apparently unaware of Asperger's studies, described an expression of autism that is characterized as having very severe impairments in language, socialization and cognition: the silent, aloof child with intellectual disability (Kanner 1943). It was this expression of autism, originally considered a form of childhood psychosis, that dominated the subsequent research and therapy literature in the English-speaking countries for the next 40 years. As far as I am aware, Hans Asperger and Leo Kanner never exchanged correspondence regarding the children they were describing, although both used the term autism.

It was not until after Asperger's death in 1980 that we first used the term Asperger's syndrome. Lorna Wing, a renowned British psychiatrist specializing in autism spectrum disorders, became increasingly aware that the descriptions of Leo Kanner that formed the basis of our understanding and diagnosis of autism in America and Britain did not accurately describe some of the children and adults within her considerable clinical and research experience. In her paper, published in 1981, she described 34 cases of children and adults with autism, ranging in age from 5 to 35 years, whose profile of abilities had a greater resemblance to the descriptions of Asperger than Kanner, and did not easily match the diagnostic criteria for autism that were being used by academics and clinicians at the time. Lorna Wing first used the term Asperger's syndrome to provide a new diagnostic category within the autism spectrum (Wing 1981).

Her case examples and conclusions were very convincing, and a group of British and Swedish psychologists and psychiatrists began a closer study of the descriptions of Hans Asperger and the profile of abilities of Asperger's syndrome. Although the original descriptions of Asperger were extremely detailed, he did not provide clear diagnostic criteria. In London, in 1988, a small international conference was held on Asperger's syndrome, with speakers who had begun exploring this newly discovered area of the autism spectrum. One of the results of the discussions and papers was the publication of the first diagnostic criteria in 1989, revised in 1991 (Gillberg 1991; Gillberg and Gillberg 1989). Despite subsequent criteria being published in the two principal diagnostic manuals, and by child psychiatrist Peter Szatmari and colleagues from Canada (Szatmari, Bremner and Nagy 1989b), the criteria of Christopher Gillberg, who is based in Sweden and London, remain those that most closely resemble the original descriptions of Asperger. Thus, these are the criteria of first choice for me and many experienced clinicians. The criteria of Christopher Gillberg are provided in Table 2.1. In clinical practice, a diagnosis of Asperger's syndrome is made if the social impairment criterion is met along with at least four of the five other criteria (Gillberg 2002).

In 1993, the World Health Organization (WHO) published the tenth edition of the *International Classification of Diseases* (ICD-10), and in 1994, the American Psychiatric Association published the fourth edition of the *Diagnostic and Statistical Manual of Mental Disorders* (DSM-IV). For the first time, both diagnostic textbooks included Asperger's syndrome, or to be more precise Asperger's disorder, as one of several Pervasive Developmental Disorders (American Psychiatric Association 1994; World Health Organization 1993). Both criteria are remarkably similar. There was a recognition in both diagnostic manuals that autism, or Pervasive Developmental Disorder, is a heterogeneous disorder and that there appear to be several subtypes, one of which is Asperger's syndrome.

When a new syndrome is confirmed, there is a search of the international clinical literature to determine whether another author has described the same profile of abilities. We now know that it was probably a Russian neurology scientific assistant, Dr Ewa Ssucharewa, who first published a description of children that we would describe today as having Asperger's syndrome (Ssucharewa 1926; Ssucharewa and Wolff 1996). Ssucharewa's description became known as Schizoid Personality Disorder (SPD). Sula Wolff (1995, 1998) has reviewed our knowledge of Schizoid Personality Disorder and suggested that SPD closely resembles the characteristics of Asperger's syndrome. I am relieved that we currently use the term Asperger's syndrome because it is easier for English-speaking people to pronounce (the 'g' is pronounced as in 'get') and spell than Ssucharewa's syndrome.

Hans Asperger died in 1980 and was unable to comment on the interpretation of his seminal study by English-speaking psychologists and psychiatrists. It was only relatively recently, in 1991, that his original paper on autistic personality disorder was finally translated into English by Uta Frith (Asperger [1944] 1991). However, we now have

Table 2.1 **The Gillberg diagnostic criteria
for Asperger's syndrome (Gillberg 1991)**

1. *Social impairment (extreme egocentricity) (at least two of the following):*

   - difficulties interacting with peers
   - indifference to peer contacts
   - difficulties interpreting social cues
   - socially and emotionally inappropriate behaviour.

2. *Narrow interest (at least one of the following):*

   - exclusion of other activities
   - repetitive adherence
   - more rote than meaning.

3. *Compulsive need for introducing routines and interests (at least one of the following):*

   - which affect the individual's every aspect of everyday life
   - which affect others.

4. *Speech and language peculiarities (at least three of the following):*

   - delayed speech development
   - superficially perfect expressive language
   - formal pedantic language
   - odd prosody, peculiar voice characteristics
   - impairment of comprehension including misinterpretations of literal/implied meanings.

5. *Non-verbal communication problems (at least one of the following):*

   - limited use of gestures
   - clumsy/gauche body language
   - limited facial expression
   - inappropriate facial expression
   - peculiar, stiff gaze.

6. *Motor clumsiness:*

   - poor performance in neurodevelopmental test.

over 2000 studies that have been published on Asperger's syndrome, and over 100 books. Since the mid-1990s, clinicians throughout the world have reported an increasing referral rate for a diagnostic assessment of Asperger's syndrome.

QUESTIONNAIRES AND SCALES FOR ASPERGER'S SYNDROME

When a school, therapist, relative, organization or the person him- or herself has identified abilities that could indicate a diagnosis of Asperger's syndrome, the next stage is usually the completion of a questionnaire or rating scale to substantiate a referral to a specialist in Asperger's syndrome. Completing the questionnaire can identify other abilities and behaviour that could be indicative of Asperger's syndrome and confirm whether the person completing the questionnaire is 'on the right track'. We currently have eight screening questionnaires that can be used with children, and six that can be used with adults. There has been a recent review of assessment scales and questionnaires for Asperger's syndrome that concluded that there are problems with validity, reliability, specificity and sensitivity with all the instruments (Howlin 2000). There is, as yet, no questionnaire or scale of first choice. The following are the questionnaires and scales for children, in alphabetical order rather than merit:

- ASAS or Australian Scale for Asperger's Syndrome (Garnett and Attwood 1998)

- ASDI or Asperger Syndrome Diagnostic Interview (Gillberg *et al.* 2001)

- ASDS or Asperger Syndrome Diagnostic Scale (Myles, Bock and Simpson 2001)

- ASSQ or Autism Spectrum Screening Questionnaire (Ehlers, Gillberg and Wing 1999)

- CAST or Childhood Asperger Syndrome Test (Scott *et al.* 2002; Williams *et al.* 2005)

- GADS or Gilliam Asperger Disorder Scale (Gilliam 2002)

- KADI or Krug Asperger's Disorder Index (Krug and Arick 2002).

A recent review of the ASDS, ASSQ, CAST, GADS and KADI suggests that these five published rating scales all had significant psychometric weaknesses, particularly in the use of normative samples, but the KADI showed the strongest psychometric properties while the ASDS had the weakest (Campbell 2005).

The following are questionnaires designed for adults who may have Asperger's syndrome. Most of the current assessment instruments have been developed by Simon Baron-Cohen and Sally Wheelwright and have been published in the appendix of the book *The Essential Difference: Men, Women and the Extreme Male Brain* by Simon Baron-Cohen (2003):

- ASQ or Autism Spectrum Quotient (Baron-Cohen *et al.* 2001b; Woodbury Smith *et al.* 2005)

- EQ or Empathy Quotient (Baron-Cohen and Wheelwright 2004)

- The Reading the Mind in the Eyes Test (Baron-Cohen *et al.* 2001a)

- The Reading the Mind in the Voice Test (Rutherford, Baron-Cohen and Wheelwright 2002)

- FQ or Friendship Questionnaire (Baron-Cohen and Wheelwright 2003)

- ASDASQ or Autism Spectrum Disorders in Adults Screening Questionnaire (Nylander and Gillberg 2001).

Michelle Garnett and I are currently revising the original Australian Scale for Asperger's Syndrome for children and adolescents between the ages of 5 and 18 years. The results of the evaluation of the ASAS-R should be published in 2007.

THE DIAGNOSTIC ASSESSMENT

Screening instruments are usually designed to be over-inclusive so that any potential cases of Asperger's syndrome are identified, but they cannot be a substitute for a thorough diagnostic assessment, which provides an objective validation of the profile of behaviour and abilities identified by the screening instruments. An experienced clinician needs to conduct an assessment of the domains of social reasoning, the communication of emotions, language and cognitive abilities, interests, and movement and coordination skills, as well as examine aspects of sensory perception and self-care skills. Invaluable information can be obtained from reading and highlighting previous reports and assessments that identify characteristics associated with Asperger's syndrome, which can then be examined and confirmed during the diagnostic assessment. The diagnostic assessment will also include a review of the person's medical, developmental and family history (Klin *et al.* 2000). The family history should include questions about any family members who may have a similar profile of abilities, but not necessarily a diagnosis of Asperger's syndrome.

There are two diagnostic tests that have been designed for children with autism: the Autism Diagnostic Interview – Revised or ADI-R (Lord, Rutter and Le Couteur 1994) and the Autism Diagnostic Observation Schedule – Generic or ADOS-G (Lord *et al.* 2000). The ADI-R uses a semi-structured interview with information provided by a parent or caregiver and provides a dimensional measure of the severity of the signs of autism. The ADOS-G is a protocol for the observation of the social and communication abilities associated with autism, with a rating of the quality of behaviours and abilities. However, these diagnostic assessment instruments were primarily designed for the diagnosis of autism, not Asperger's syndrome, and are not sensitive to the more subtle characteristics of Asperger's syndrome (Gillberg 2002; Klin *et al.* 2000).

The diagnostic assessment for Asperger's syndrome requires a protocol (often developed by individual clinicians) that uses a 'script' or sequence of activities and tests that determine whether the pattern of abilities in a particular domain are typical for a child of that age, or adult, or indicative of developmental delay or deviance. The clinician may refer to a checklist: this can include the characteristics of Asperger's syndrome that are included in the diagnostic criteria, and characteristics identified in the research literature or through extensive personal clinical experience as being typical of children or adults with Asperger's syndrome.

Some children and adults are relatively easy to diagnose. A clinician may suspect a positive diagnosis within a matter of minutes, but the full diagnostic assessment will need to be conducted to confirm the initial clinical impression. Some girls and women with Asperger's syndrome, and adults of considerable intellectual ability, can be more difficult to diagnose due to an ability to camouflage their difficulties. The full diagnostic assessment can take an hour or more depending on the number and depth of the assessments of specific abilities. More experienced clinicians can significantly shorten the duration of the diagnostic assessment. Subsequent chapters will include some of the diagnostic assessment procedures that I use to examine specific abilities and behaviour.

The diagnostic assessment should not only examine areas of difficulties, but also areas of ability that may be attributable to the characteristics of Asperger's syndrome. For example, the child may have achieved prizes and certificates for his or her knowledge regarding a special interest, or demonstrated academic skills by winning a mathematics or art competition. The person may draw with photographic realism or invent computer games. Parents can be asked for the endearing personality qualities of their son or daughter, for example being kind, having a strong sense of social justice, and caring for animals.

The Diagnostic Interview for Social and Communication Disorders (DISCO) is a guide for clinicians to enable them to collect, systematically, detailed information on developmental history and current state needed to diagnose autistic spectrum disorders and related developmental disorders in children and adults of all ages (Wing *et al.* 2002). It is available only to those who have been trained in its use.

THE CURRENT DIAGNOSTIC CRITERIA

Clinicians would usually expect to use the DSM-IV criteria of the American Psychiatric Association when conducting a diagnostic assessment for developmental disorders such as Asperger's syndrome. The criteria for Asperger's syndrome or Asperger's disorder in DSM-IV, which were revised for the edition published in 2000, are provided in Table 2.2.

The text in DSM-IV, intended to supplement the criteria, provides only cursory guidelines for the diagnostic process and a superficial description of the disorder. Just reading the DSM-IV criteria as the only source of information from which to make a diagnosis, a clinician would have insufficient knowledge about Asperger's syndrome to

Table 2.2 Diagnostic criteria for Asperger's disorder according to DSM-IV (TR) (American Psychiatric Association 2000)

A. *Qualitative impairment in social interaction, as manifested by at least two of the following:*

1. marked impairment in the use of multiple non-verbal behaviours such as eye-to-eye gaze, facial expression, body postures, and gestures to regulate social interaction

2. failure to develop peer relationships appropriate to developmental level

3. a lack of spontaneous seeking to share enjoyment, interests, or achievements with other people (e.g. by a lack of showing, bringing, or pointing out objects of interest to other people)

4. lack of social or emotional reciprocity.

B. *Restricted repetitive and stereotyped patterns of behaviour, interests, and activities, as manifested by at least one of the following:*

1. encompassing preoccupation with one or more stereotyped and restricted patterns of interest that is abnormal either in intensity or focus

2. apparently inflexible adherence to specific, non-functional routines or rituals

3. stereotyped and repetitive motor mannerisms (e.g. hand or finger flapping or twisting, or complex whole-body movements)

4. persistent preoccupation with parts of objects.

C. *The disturbance causes clinically significant impairment in social, occupational, or other important areas of functioning.*

D. *There is no clinically significant general delay in language (e.g. single words used by age two years, communicative phrases used by age three years).*

E. *There is no clinically significant delay in cognitive development or in the development of age-appropriate self-help skills, adaptive behaviour (other than in social interaction), and curiosity about the environment in childhood.*

F. *Criteria are not met for another specific Pervasive Developmental Disorder or Schizophrenia.*

make a reliable diagnosis. Training, supervision and extensive clinical experience in the nature of Asperger's syndrome are essential before a clinician and client can be confident of the diagnosis.

Problems associated with the current DSM-IV diagnostic criteria

The original inclusion of Asperger's disorder within the DSM-IV was welcomed by clinicians as a wise decision, as was the decision to move the Pervasive Developmental Disorders, including autism and Asperger's syndrome, from Axis II (an axis for long-term, stable disorders with a relatively poor prognosis for improvement) to Axis I (which implies that the signs can improve with early intervention and treatment).

However, there are problems with the diagnostic criteria in DSM-IV, and especially the differential criteria in the manual that distinguish between a diagnosis of autism or Asperger's syndrome.

Language delay

The current criteria in DSM-IV have been criticized by speech/language pathologists with regard to the statement that for children and adults to achieve a diagnosis of Asperger's syndrome, 'There is no clinically significant general delay in language (e.g. single words used by age two years, communicative phrases used by age three years).' In other words, if there have been signs of early language delay, then the diagnosis should not be Asperger's syndrome, but autism, even if all the other criteria, developmental history (apart from language acquisition) and the current profile of abilities are met for Asperger's syndrome. Diane Twachtman-Cullen (1998), a speech/language pathologist with considerable experience of autism spectrum disorders, has criticized this exclusion criterion on the grounds that the term *clinically significant* is neither scientific nor precise and left to the judgement of clinicians without an operational definition. A further criticism is that research on the stages of early language acquisition has established that single words emerge around the child's first birthday, communicative phrases at about 18 months of age and short sentences around two years. In fact, the DSM-IV criteria describe a child who actually has a significant language delay.

Does the development of early language skills actually differentiate between adolescents with autism and an IQ within the normal range (i.e. High Functioning Autism) and Asperger's syndrome? Research has now been conducted on whether delayed language in children with autism can accurately predict later clinical symptoms. Four studies have cast considerable doubt over the use of early language delay as a differential criterion between High Functioning Autism and Asperger's syndrome (Eisenmajer et al. 1998; Howlin 2003; Manjiviona and Prior 1999; Mayes and Calhoun 2001). Any differences in language ability that are apparent in the pre-school years between children with autism and an IQ within the normal range, and those with Asperger's syndrome, have largely disappeared by early adolescence.

Delayed development of language is actually one of the Gillberg and Gillberg diagnostic criteria for Asperger's syndrome (Gillberg 1991; Gillberg and Gillberg 1989). Young children with typical autism who subsequently develop fluent language eventually have a profile of abilities that resembles the profile of children with Asperger's syndrome who did not have early language delay. In my opinion, and that of many clinicians, early language delay is not an exclusion criterion for Asperger's syndrome and may actually be an inclusion criterion, as in the Gillberg criteria. The focus during the diagnostic assessment should be on current language use (the pragmatic aspects of language) rather than the history of language development.

Self-help skills and adaptive behaviour

The DSM-IV criteria refer to children with Asperger's syndrome as having 'no clinically significant delay in cognitive development or in the development of age-appropriate self-help skills, adaptive behaviour (other than in social interaction), and curiosity about the environment in childhood'. Clinical experience and research indicate that parents, especially mothers, of children and adolescents with Asperger's syndrome often have to provide verbal reminders and advice regarding self-help and daily living skills. This can range from help with problems with dexterity affecting activities such as using cutlery, to reminders regarding personal hygiene and dress sense, and encouragement with planning and time-management skills. When parents complete a standardized assessment of self-care skills and adaptive functioning, such abilities in children with Asperger's syndrome are below the level expected for their age and intellectual ability (Smyrnios 2002). Clinicians have also recognized significant problems with adaptive behaviour, especially with regard to anger management, anxiety and depression (Attwood 2003a).

The inclusion of other important or transitory characteristics

The diagnostic criteria of the DSM-IV do not include a description of the unusual characteristics in the pragmatic aspects of language originally described by Asperger and portrayed in the clinical literature, namely the pedantic use of language and unusual prosody. The DSM-IV criteria also fail to make adequate reference to problems with sensory perception and integration, especially auditory sensitivity and hypersensitivity to light intensity, tactile experiences and aromas. These aspects of Asperger's syndrome can have a profound effect on the person's quality of life. The criteria also exclude reference to motor clumsiness, which was described by Asperger and has been substantiated in the research literature (Green et al. 2002).

The diagnostic criteria in the DSM-IV can also be criticized for emphasizing characteristics that can be rare or transitory. The criteria refer to 'stereotyped and repetitive motor mannerisms (e.g. hand or finger flapping or twisting, or complex whole-body movements)', yet clinical experience indicates that many children with Asperger's syndrome never display such characteristics and, for those who do, research indicates that these characteristics have disappeared by the age of nine years (Church, Alisanski and Amanullah 2000).

A hierarchical approach

The DSM-IV guidelines are that if the criteria for autism are confirmed in a diagnostic assessment, then despite the child's cognitive, social, linguistic, motor and sensory abilities and interests being consistent with the descriptions of a child with Asperger's syndrome, a diagnosis of autism should take precedence over a diagnosis of Asperger's syndrome.

The issue of precedence has been examined by several research studies (Dickerson Mayes, Calhoun and Crites 2001; Eisenmajer *et al.* 1996; Ghaziuddin, Tsai and Ghaziuddin 1992; Manjiviona and Prior 1995; Miller and Ozonoff 1997; Szatmari *et al.* 1995). The general conclusion of these studies is that a diagnosis of Asperger's syndrome is almost impossible using current DSM-IV criteria.

Many clinicians, including myself, have rejected the hierarchical rule. The general consensus among clinicians at present is that if the current profile of abilities of the child is consistent with the descriptions of Asperger's syndrome, then the diagnosis of Asperger's syndrome takes precedence over a diagnosis of autism. Thus, contrary to the DSM-IV, if a child meets criteria for both autism and Asperger's syndrome, the child is usually given a diagnosis of Asperger's syndrome by clinicians (Mahoney *et al.* 1998). It is important to recognize that the diagnostic criteria are still a work in progress.

ASPERGER'S SYNDROME OR HIGH FUNCTIONING AUTISM?

DeMyer, Hingtgen and Jackson first used the term High Functioning Autism in 1981, the same year in which the term Asperger's syndrome was first used by Lorna Wing (1981). The term High Functioning Autism (HFA) has been used in the past to describe children who had the classic signs of autism in early childhood but who, as they developed, were shown in formal testing of cognitive skills to have a greater degree of intellectual ability, with greater social and adaptive behaviour skills and communication skills, than is usual with children with autism (DeMyer *et al.* 1981). The child's clinical outcome was much better than expected. However, we currently have no explicit diagnostic guidelines for the diagnosis of HFA.

The cognitive abilities of this group of children have been compared to the cognitive profile of children with Asperger's syndrome, who did not have a history of early cognitive or language delay. The results of the research have not established a distinct and consistent profile for each group. Ehlers *et al.* (1997) found that only a minority of each diagnostic group showed a characteristic cognitive profile. One group of researchers, based at Yale University in the United States, has suggested that the neuropsychological profiles of children with Asperger's syndrome and High Functioning Autism are different (Klin *et al.* 1995). However, other research examining diagnostic differentiation using neuropsychological testing has not identified a distinct profile that discriminates between the two groups (Manjiviona and Prior 1999; Miller and Ozonoff 2000; Ozonoff, South and Miller 2000). A recent study of the past and present behavioural profiles of children with High Functioning Autism and Asperger's syndrome using the Autism Behaviour Checklist concluded that the two groups were indistinguishable in their current behavioural profiles (Dissanayake 2004).

A diagnosis of Asperger's syndrome is usually given if the person has an Intelligence Quotient within the average range. However, children and adults with the clinical features of Asperger's syndrome often have a profile of abilities on a standardized test of intelligence that is remarkably uneven. Some scores may be within the normal range or even superior range, but other scores, within the same profile, may be in the mildly retarded range. Asperger originally included children with some level of intellectual impairment within his description of autistic personality disorder, although mental retardation, according to the DSM-IV, would exclude a diagnosis of Asperger's syndrome. I would view an overall IQ score with some caution and may include those cases with a borderline intellectual impairment when some cognitive skills are within the normal range.

A recent review of the research literature comparing the abilities of children with Asperger's syndrome with those with High Functioning Autism concluded that the number of studies that found a difference in cognitive, social, motor or neuro-psychological tasks probably equal those indicating no difference (Howlin 2000). Clinicians in Europe and Australia are taking a dimensional or spectrum view of autism and Asperger's syndrome rather than a categorical approach (Leekham *et al.* 2000). At present, both terms (Asperger's syndrome and High Functioning Autism) can be used interchangeably in clinical practice. To date, there is no convincing argument or data that unequivocally confirm that High Functioning Autism and Asperger's syndrome are two separate and distinct disorders. As a clinician, I do not think that academics should try to force a dichotomy when the profiles of social and behavioural abilities are so similar and the treatment is the same.

Unfortunately, a dilemma for the clinician is whether a particular diagnosis – autism or Asperger's syndrome – enables the child or adult to have access to the government services and benefits that he or she needs. In some countries, states or provinces, a child may only have support in the classroom, or the parents automatically receive government allowances or medical insurance coverage, if the child has a diagnosis of autism, such services not being available if the child has a diagnosis of Asperger's syndrome. Some clinicians may write reports with a diagnosis of autism or High Functioning Autism rather than the more accurate diagnosis of Asperger's syndrome so that the child has access to resources and the parents do not have to resort to litigation.

HOW PREVALENT IS ASPERGER'S SYNDROME?

The prevalence rates for Asperger's syndrome vary according to the choice of diagnostic criteria. The DSM-IV criteria of the American Psychiatric Association, which are almost identical to the criteria in the *International Classification of Diseases*, or ICD-10, are the most restrictive criteria, and have been the subject of considerable criticism as a result of research studies, and deemed by clinicians as unworkable in clinical practice. The prevalence of Asperger's syndrome using DSM-IV or ICD criteria varies in each study with reported rates of between 0.3 per 10,000 children to 8.4 per 10,000 children (Baird *et al.* 2000; Chakrabarti and Fombonne 2001; Sponheim and Skjeldal 1998; Taylor *et al.*

1999). The expected prevalence rate for Asperger's syndrome, therefore, according to these criteria, would vary between 1 in 33,000 and 1 in 1200 children.

The diagnostic criteria of choice by many clinicians, especially in Europe and Australia, are those of Gillberg and Gillberg (1989) which represent more accurately the original descriptions of Asperger and the profile of abilities of children referred for a diagnostic assessment for Asperger's syndrome. According to the Gillberg criteria, the prevalence rate is between 36 and 48 per 10,000 children, or between 1 in 280 or 210 children (Ehlers and Gillberg 1993; Kadesjo, Gillberg and Hagberg 1999).

There is a difference between the scientific terms of prevalence and incidence. Prevalence figures indicate how many individuals have the condition at a specific point in time, while incidence is the number of new cases occuring in a specified time period, such as one year. Using the Gillberg criteria, it is my clinical opinion that we are currently detecting and diagnosing about 50 per cent of children who have Asperger's syndrome. Those who are not referred for a diagnostic assessment for Asperger's syndrome are able to camouflage their difficulties and avoid detection, or a clinician fails to see Asperger's syndrome and focuses on another diagnosis.

THE DIAGNOSTIC ASSESSMENT OF GIRLS

The majority of children referred for a diagnostic assessment for Asperger's syndrome are boys. Since 1992, I have conducted a regular diagnostic assessment clinic for children and adults with Asperger's syndrome in Brisbane, Australia. A recent analysis of over 1000 diagnostic assessments over 12 years established a ratio of males to females of four to one. From my clinical experience, I have noted that girls with Asperger's syndrome may be more difficult to recognize and diagnose due to coping and camouflaging mechanisms, which can also be used by some boys. One of the coping mechanisms is to learn how to act in a social setting, as described by Liane Holliday Willey in her autobiography, *Pretending to be Normal* (Willey 1999). The clinician perceives someone who appears able to develop a reciprocal conversation and use appropriate affect and gestures during the interaction. However, further investigation and observation at school may determine that the child adopts a social role and script, basing her persona on the characteristics of someone who would be reasonably socially skilled in the situation, and using intellectual abilities rather than intuition to determine what to say or do. An example of a camouflaging strategy is to conceal confusion when playing with peers by politely declining invitations to join in until sure of what to do, so as not to make a conspicuous social error. The strategy is to wait, observe carefully, and only participate when sure what to do by imitating what the children have done previously. If the rules or nature of the game suddenly change, the child is lost.

Girls with Asperger's syndrome can develop the ability to 'disappear' in a large group, being on the periphery of social interaction. One woman with Asperger's syndrome said, when recalling her childhood, that she felt as though she was 'on the outside looking in'. There can be other strategies to avoid active participation in class proceedings, such as being well behaved and polite, thus being left alone by teachers and peers; or tactics to passively avoid cooperation and social inclusion at school and at home, as described in a condition known as Pathological Demand Avoidance (Newsom 1983).

A girl with Asperger's syndrome is less likely to be 'fickle' or 'bitchy' in friendships in comparison to other girls, and is more likely than boys to develop a close friendship with someone who demonstrates a maternal attachment to this socially naïve but 'safe' girl. These characteristics reduce the likelihood of being identified as having one of the main diagnostic criteria for Asperger's syndrome, namely a failure to develop peer relationships. With girls, it is not a failure but a qualitative difference in this ability. The girl's problems with social understanding may only become conspicuous when her friend and mentor moves to another school.

The language and cognitive profile of girls with Asperger's syndrome may be the same as those of boys, but the special interests may not be as idiosyncratic or eccentric as can occur with some boys. Adults may consider there is nothing unusual about a girl who has an interest in horses, but the problem may be the intensity and dominance of the interest in her daily life: the young girl may have moved her mattress into the stable so that she can sleep next to the horse. If her interest is dolls, she may have over 50 Barbie dolls arranged in alphabetical order, but she would rarely include other girls in her doll play.

While in conversation with a boy with Asperger's syndrome, the listener is likely to consider the child a 'little professor' who uses an advanced vocabulary for a child of that age, and is able to provide many interesting (or boring) facts. Girls with Asperger's syndrome can sound like 'little philosophers', with an ability to think deeply about social situations. From an early age, girls with Asperger's syndrome have applied their cognitive skills to analyse social interactions and are more likely than boys with Asperger's syndrome to discuss the inconsistencies in social conventions and their thoughts on social events.

The motor coordination problems of girls may not be so conspicuous in the playground, and they are less likely to have developed the conduct problems that can prompt a referral for a diagnostic assessment for a boy. Thus, where a girl has developed the ability to conceal her signs of Asperger's syndrome in the playground and classroom, and even in the diagnostic assessment, then parents, teachers and clinicians may fail to see any conspicuous characteristics of Asperger's syndrome.

At my clinic I see people with Asperger's syndrome of all ages, and although the sample of adults with Asperger's syndrome is small in comparison to the number of children, I have noticed that the ratio of men to women with Asperger's syndrome is almost two to one. Many of the women who seek a diagnostic assessment have previously not had the self-confidence or a reason to seek a diagnostic assessment. With increasing maturity, they are prepared to seek help, especially when there have been long-term and unresolved problems with emotions, employment and relationships. Another 'pathway' is that of a woman having a child with Asperger's syndrome and recognizing that she had similar characteristics as a child. We need to explore more of what Ruth Baker, a woman with Asperger's syndrome, describes as 'the invisible end of the spectrum' (personal communication).

THE DIAGNOSTIC ASSESSMENT OF ADULTS

The diagnostic assessment of adults will present the clinician with several problems. It may be many years since the adult was a child, and recollections of childhood by the adult and any relatives interviewed during the diagnostic assessment may be affected by the accuracy of long-term memory. An aid to memory and discussion may be the perusal of photographs of the adult as a child. Family photographs are usually taken during a social occasion, and this can provide an opportunity to notice if the child appears to be participating in the social interaction. Conversation during the diagnostic assessment can be about the event in the photograph and the person's competence and confidence in the situation. School reports can be useful in indicating any problems with both peer relationships, and learning abilities and behaviour at school.

We now have questionnaires to identify the ability and personality characteristics of adults with Asperger's syndrome, and the analysis of the responses and scores on these questionnaires can be extremely useful for the clinician. I have found that it can be an advantage to have the person's questionnaire responses validated by a family member such as the person's mother or partner. The adult referred for a diagnostic assessment may provide a response based on personal perception of his or her social abilities, while someone who knows him or her well and does not have Asperger's syndrome may have a different opinion. For example, a man was asked about his friends when he was a child and whether other children would come to his home. He replied that children did come to his house, which would suggest some degree of popularity and friendship. His mother affirmed that other children would visit, but not to play with her son, rather to play with his toys. He preferred to play with his Lego on his own in the bedroom.

It is possible that the adult or adolescent will deliberately mislead the clinician for reasons of maintaining self-esteem or to avoid a diagnosis that may be perceived as a mental illness. For example, Ben described how:

> I was always ashamed of who I was, so I never told the truth about anything that would embarrass me. If you had asked me if I have trouble understanding others, I would have said no, even though the true answer was yes. If you had asked me if I avoided social contact, I would have said no, because I wouldn't want you to think I was weird. If you had asked me if I lacked empathy, I would have been insulted, because everyone knows good people have empathy and bad people don't. I would have denied that I'm afraid of loud noises, that I have a narrow range of interests, and that I get upset by changes in routine. The only questions I would have answered yes to would have been the ones about having unusually long-term

memory for events and facts; reading books for information; and being like a walking encyclopaedia. That's because I liked those things about me. I thought they made me look smart. If I thought it was good, I would have said yes, and if I thought it was bad, I would have said no. (LaSalle 2003, pp.242–3)

During the diagnostic assessment the adult client may provide responses that appear to indicate empathy and ability with social reasoning, but on a more careful examination it may be clear that these responses, given after a fractional delay, were achieved by intellectual analysis rather than intuition. The cognitive processing required gives the impression of a thoughtful rather than spontaneous response.

Some adults with clear signs of Asperger's syndrome may consider that their abilities are quite normal, using the characteristics of a parent as the model of normal interaction skills. If the person had a dominant parent with the characteristics of Asperger's syndrome, this may have influenced the person's perception of normality.

The Adult Asperger Assessment (AAA)

We now have an assessment instrument and diagnostic criteria specifically for adults (Baron-Cohen *et al.* 2005). The Adult Asperger Assessment, or AAA, uses two screening instruments, the Autism Spectrum Quotient (ASQ) and the Empathy Quotient (EQ) and new diagnostic criteria specifically for adults. These criteria include the DSM-IV criteria and several additional criteria. The original research for the AAA was conducted by Simon Baron-Cohen and colleagues at the Cambridge Lifespan Asperger Syndrome Service (CLASS) in the United Kingdom. The clinician asks the client to complete the ASQ and EQ, then validates the answers during the diagnostic assessment and makes his or her own opinion on the diagnosis based on the new diagnostic criteria.

Diagnostic criteria for adults

The diagnostic criteria in the AAA are the same as in the DSM-IV (see page 41), with the addition of ten criteria based on our understanding of the characteristics of Asperger's syndrome in adults rather than children. In section A of the DSM-IV criteria (qualitative impairment in social interaction) there is the additional criterion:

> Difficulties in understanding social situations and other people's thoughts and feelings.

In section B of the DSM-IV criteria (restricted repetitive and stereotyped patterns of behaviour, interests and activities) there is the additional criterion:

> Tendency to think of issues as being black and white (e.g. in politics or morality), rather than considering multiple perspectives in a flexible way.

In the AAA diagnostic criteria there are two sections that are in the DSM-IV criteria for autism but not the DSM-IV criteria for Asperger's syndrome. These two sections are justifiably included in the AAA criteria, being based on the profile of communication and imagination abilities identified in research studies and from clinical experience, as being characteristic of adults with Asperger's syndrome, namely:

Qualitative impairments in verbal or non-verbal communication:

1. Tendency to turn any conversation back to self or own topic of interest.

2. Marked impairment in the ability to initiate or sustain a conversation with others. Cannot see the point of superficial social contact, niceties, or passing time with others, unless there is a clear discussion point/debate or activity.

3. Pedantic style of speaking, or inclusion of too much detail.

4. Inability to recognize when the listener is interested or bored. Even if the person has been told not to talk about their particular obsessive topic for too long, this difficulty may be evident if other topics arise.

5. Frequent tendency to say things without considering the emotional impact on the listener (faux pas).

The diagnostic criteria of the AAA require three or more symptoms of qualitative impairment in verbal or non-verbal communication, and at least one symptom from the following impairments in imagination:

Impairments in imagination:

1. Lack of varied, spontaneous make believe play appropriate to developmental level.

2. Inability to tell, write or generate spontaneous, unscripted or unplagiarised fiction.

3. Either lack of interest in fiction (written, or drama) appropriate to developmental level or interest in fiction is restricted to its possible basis in fact (e.g. science fiction, history, technical aspects of film).

The adult's response to specific questions in the ASQ and EQ provides examples of the symptoms in the five sections of the AAA. Future studies will examine the test sensitivity and specificity of the AAA, but at last we have an assessment instrument and diagnostic criteria that a clinician can use in the diagnostic assessment of adults.

CLOSURE OF THE DIAGNOSTIC ASSESSMENT

At the end of the diagnostic assessment, the clinician provides a summary and review of those characteristics in the person's developmental history, profile of abilities and behaviour consistent with a diagnosis of Asperger's syndrome, and concludes whether the signs are sufficient for a diagnosis. I explain to the client and family the concept of a 100-piece diagnostic jigsaw puzzle. Some pieces of the puzzle (or characteristics of

Asperger's syndrome) are essential, the corner and edge pieces. When more than 80 pieces are connected, the puzzle is solved and the diagnosis confirmed. None of the characteristics are unique to Asperger's syndrome, however, and a typical child or adult may have perhaps 10 to 20 pieces or characteristics. The person referred for a diagnostic assessment may have more pieces than occur in the typical population, but sometimes not enough, or the key or corner pieces, to complete the puzzle or receive a diagnosis of Asperger's syndrome.

The conceptualization of a diagnostic jigsaw puzzle can help explain the diagnostic term Pervasive Developmental Disorder Not Otherwise Specified or PDDNOS. This term describes someone who has many of the fragments or pieces of the diagnostic jigsaw but some pieces are described as atypical or sub-threshold. However, there are sufficient pieces or fragments of Asperger's syndrome to warrant recognition that the person is 'almost there' and needs access to services for the pieces that are there.

Should a diagnosis of Asperger's syndrome be confirmed (the diagnostic puzzle is completed), the summary at the end of the diagnostic assessment needs to acknowledge the positive characteristics of Asperger's syndrome such as being an expert in a particular field, the degree of expression of each of the main characteristics, the overall degree of expression, and which characteristics in the profile of abilities and behaviour are not due to Asperger's syndrome. The clinician may also need to comment on the signs of any secondary or dual disorders such as depression, anxiety or conduct disorder, and whether another disorder is currently the dominant factor affecting the person's quality of life and, as a matter of expediency, should be the priority for treatment.

I make an audio recording for the client or his or her family of the summary stage of the diagnostic assessment, so that participants can listen to the explanation several times to absorb all the information and implications. Other family members and teachers who were not able to attend the diagnostic assessment can listen to the recording to aid their understanding of the rationale for the diagnosis. I have also noted that recording the summary can lessen the likelihood of being misunderstood or misquoted when others are informed of the diagnosis and degree of expression. The next stage is to discuss the known causes of Asperger's syndrome, recommended specific programs, government support services, support groups, relevant publications, the likely prognosis and the monitoring of progress. However, this would be achieved in subsequent appointments once the significance of the diagnosis has been understood and acknowledged.

CONFIDENCE IN THE DIAGNOSIS

My clinical opinion and that of other clinicians is that a diagnosis can be made with some confidence for a child after the age of five years, but cannot be made with sufficient confidence in pre-school children, due to the naturally wide range in abilities in very young children, and the propensity for some children to be developmentally delayed in social, linguistic and cognitive skills. A profile that resembles Asperger's syndrome may 'dissolve' over time; however, the very young child who could be a false positive may still benefit from the programs designed for children with Asperger's syndrome to improve social reasoning and conversation skills. Over time the clinical or diagnostic picture becomes clearer. However, we are developing diagnostic assessment procedures that can be used with pre-school children (Perry 2004). Clinicians can include some of the descriptions of the characteristics of very young children with Asperger's syndrome that are described in subsequent chapters, as part of their assessment procedures for very young children who could be developing the early signs of Asperger's syndrome.

The confidence in the diagnostic assessment of adults can also be affected by the honesty and accuracy in the responses of the client. The person may be able to 'fake it' in terms of denying difficulties with social competence, and using intellect in the artificial circumstances of a clinic room to provide the response of a typical adult, but may in fact have conspicuous difficulties in everyday social interaction. There is a difference between knowledge at an intellectual level and actual practice in real life.

Some adults referred for a diagnostic assessment may have the signs but not the clinically significant impairment in functioning necessary for a diagnosis using the DSM-IV criteria of the American Psychiatric Association. Problems with social understanding may be reduced to a sub-clinical level with the help of a supportive partner who provides the necessary guidance in the codes of conduct and explains or repairs comments or actions that may appear confusing or inappropriate to other people.

Work circumstances may be successful due to sympathetic colleagues and line managers. In such circumstances, the clinician may have to consider whether the person, who appears to be coping reasonably well, perhaps with a high-status profession and having a partner, would benefit from receiving a diagnosis of Asperger's syndrome (Szatmari 2004). At the time of the diagnostic assessment, the person may not need treatment from a psychiatrist or services from government agencies (one of the principal justifications for a diagnosis), although he or she may well benefit from relationship or career counselling. However, should the person experience a divorce or unemployment, the signs may become more conspicuous and then warrant a diagnosis. It is perhaps not the severity of expression that is important, but the circumstances, expectations, and coping and support mechanisms.

The final decision on where you draw the artificial line, namely whether a person has a diagnosis of Asperger's syndrome, is a subjective decision made by the clinician on the basis of the results of the assessment of specific abilities, social interaction, and descriptions and reports from parents, teachers etc. The qualitative impairment in social interaction or social relatedness is central to the diagnosis, but there is no weighting system for the other characteristics to help decide whether, on balance, a borderline case should have the diagnosis. The ultimate decision on whether to confirm a diagnosis is based on the clinician's clinical experience, the current diagnostic criteria and the effect of the unusual profile of abilities on the person's quality of life. Jerry Newport, who has Asperger's syndrome, said to me that the diagnosis occurs when 'human characteristics are at an impractical extreme.'

KEY POINTS AND STRATEGIES

- There are currently eight diagnostic screening questionnaires that can be used with children and six that can be used with adults.

- Girls and women, and children and adults of considerable intellectual ability, can be more difficult to diagnose with Asperger's syndrome due to an ability to camouflage their difficulties.

- The diagnostic assessment should examine not only areas of difficulties, but also areas of ability that may be attributable to the characteristics of Asperger's syndrome.

- There are significant problems with the diagnostic criteria in DSM-IV:
    - The criteria state there should be no clinically significant general delay in language, but the criteria for inclusion actually describe a child who has language delay.
    - Any differences in language ability that are apparent in the pre-school years between children with autism and an IQ within the normal range, and those with Asperger's syndrome, have largely disappeared by early adolescence.
    - The criteria state there should be no clinically significant delay in the development of age-appropriate self-help skills, but clinical experience and research indicate that parents often have to provide verbal reminders and advice regarding self-help and daily living skills.
    - The DSM criteria do not include a description of the unusual language characteristics originally described by Hans Asperger, or make reference to problems with sensory perception, but include characteristics that are rare or transitory.
    - The guidelines state that if the criteria for autism are confirmed, a diagnosis of autism should take precedence over a diagnosis of Asperger's syndrome. Many clinicians have rejected this hierarchical rule.
    - The DSM diagnostic criteria are still a work in progress.

- The diagnostic criteria of Christopher Gillberg most closely resemble the original descriptions of Hans Asperger and are the criteria of first choice by many experienced clinicians.

- There is currently no convincing argument or data that unequivocally confirm that High Functioning Autism and Asperger's syndrome are two separate and distinct disorders.

- Using the Gillberg diagnostic criteria, the prevalence rate for Asperger's syndrome is about 1 in 250 children.

- We are currently detecting and diagnosing only about 50 per cent of children who have Asperger's syndrome.

- A diagnosis can be made with some confidence for a child after the age of five years, but cannot yet be made with sufficient confidence in pre-school children.

- We now have an assessment instrument and diagnostic criteria specifically for adults.

- The confidence in the diagnostic assessment of adults can be affected by the honesty and accuracy in the responses to questions and questionnaires.

- Some adults referred for a diagnostic assessment may have the signs but not the clinically significant impairment in functioning necessary for a diagnosis.

- It is not the severity of expression that is important but the circumstances, expectations and coping and support mechanisms.

CHAPTER 3

Social Understanding and Friendship

The nature of these children is revealed most clearly in their behaviour towards other people. Indeed their behaviour in the social group is the clearest sign of their disorder.

– Hans Asperger ([1944] 1991)

The reader will be interested to know that I have discovered a means of removing almost all of the characteristics that define Asperger's syndrome in any child or adult. This simple procedure does not require expensive and prolonged therapy, surgery or medication, and has already been secretly discovered by those who have Asperger's syndrome. The procedure is actually rather simple. If you are a parent, take your child with Asperger's syndrome to his or her bedroom. Leave the child alone in the bedroom and close the door behind you as you walk out of the room. The signs of Asperger's syndrome in your son or daughter have now disappeared.

SOLITUDE

In solitude, the child does not have a *qualitative impairment in social interaction*. At least two people are needed for there to be a social interaction, and if the child is alone, there will be no evidence of any social impairment. In solitude, there is no one to talk to, so there are no *speech and language peculiarities*; and the child can enjoy time engaged in a special interest for as long as he or she desires, without anyone else judging whether the activity is *abnormal either in intensity or focus.*

In Chapter 6 I will explain how solitude is also one of the most effective emotional restoratives for someone with Asperger's syndrome. Being alone can be a very effective way of calming down and is also enjoyable, especially if engaged in a special interest, one of the greatest pleasures in life for someone with Asperger's syndrome.

Solitude can facilitate learning. The acquisition of knowledge in a classroom requires considerable social and linguistic skills. The difficulties experienced in these areas by children with Asperger's syndrome can impede the understanding of academic concepts. I have observed that some children with Asperger's syndrome acquire academic skills such as basic literacy and numeracy before they attend school, often by looking at books, watching television or playing educational games on a computer. They have successfully taught themselves, in solitude.

When alone, especially in a bedroom, the hypersensitivity for some sensory experiences is reduced as the environment can be relatively quiet, particularly in comparison to a school playground or classroom. The child with Asperger's syndrome may also be sensitive to change and be anxious if things are not where they have been or should be. Furniture and objects in the bedroom will be a known configuration, and family members will have learned not to move anything. The child's bedroom is a refuge that is sacrosanct.

When someone is alone, relaxed and enjoying a special interest, the characteristics of Asperger's syndrome do not *cause clinically significant impairment in social, occupational, or other important areas of functioning*. For the child with Asperger's syndrome, being alone has many advantages; problems only occur when someone enters the room, or when he or she has to leave the bedroom and interact with other people.

I have noted that people with Asperger's syndrome may function reasonably well in one-to-one interactions, using their intellectual capacity to process social cues and non-verbal communication, and using memory of similar social situations to determine what to say and do. The phrase 'two's company, three's a crowd' is very appropriate for someone with Asperger's syndrome. In a group setting, the person's intellectual capacity may not be sufficient to cope with the social interaction of several participants, and the person may take longer to process social information that is normally communicated more quickly in a group than individually. If a one-to-one conversation is a game of tennis, a group interaction is a game of football.

The delay in social processing means the person can become out of synchronization with the conversation and is liable to make a conspicuous social error or have to withdraw. There have been occasions when I have been involved in a reciprocal conversation with an adult with Asperger's syndrome, and noted that when another person or several others join in, the person with Asperger's syndrome becomes quiet and does not participate as actively and fluently as when the conversation was between just the two of us.

When I explained to a teenager with Asperger's syndrome that the degree of stress is proportional to the number of people present, he started to work on a mathematical formula and geometric representation of the number of potential connections between individuals that can occur as more people join a conversation. With two people there is only one link; with three people, three links; with four people, six links; five people, ten links; and so on. This is one of the explanations as to why people with Asperger's syndrome do not like large gatherings of people.

THE ASSESSMENT OF SOCIAL INTERACTION SKILLS

The essential feature of Asperger's syndrome is a qualitative impairment in social interaction, which is acknowledged in all diagnostic criteria. The criteria also refer to a lack of social or emotional reciprocity and failure to develop peer relationships appropriate to developmental level. To date we do not have standardized tests of social interaction and social reasoning for typical children that can be used to produce a 'social quotient' for a child with Asperger's syndrome. The interpretation of aspects of social skills and social understanding such as reciprocity and peer relationships is currently a subjective clinical judgement. The clinician therefore needs to have considerable experience of the social development of typical children to act as a comparison for the child who is referred for a diagnostic assessment for Asperger's syndrome.

To assess social interaction and social reasoning skills, the clinician must socialize with the child, adolescent or adult. With young children, this can be achieved by playing with the child using toys and play equipment in the clinic room. Of clinical significance will be the degree of reciprocity, the child's recognition and 'reading' of social cues expressed by the clinician, and his or her knowledge of how to respond to those cues. The clinician will examine whether the child displays developmentally appropriate social behaviour, and his or her use of eye contact, methods of regulating the interaction, and the degree of spontaneity and flexibility when playing with the clinician. This part of the assessment should be achieved in both structured and unstructured play. For adolescents and adults, the assessment of social interaction skills will be achieved using a conversation that includes a range of topics that explore aspects of friendship, social experiences and social abilities. Some of the topics and conversation questions can be taken from the screening instruments for Asperger's syndrome to provide more information on the person's social maturity and social competence.

An examination of peer relationships or friendships can be achieved by identifying the person's friends, the quality, stability and maturity of the friendships, and his or her thoughts regarding the attributes of friendship. The questions can include:

- Who are your friends?

- Why is _____ your friend?

- What are the things that someone does to be friendly?

- How do you make friends?

- Why do we have friends?

- What makes you a good friend?

I have noted that the child with Asperger's syndrome usually has a concept of friendship that is immature and at least two years behind that of his or her age peers (Attwood 2003a; Botroff *et al.* 1995). The child with Asperger's syndrome typically has fewer friends, playing with other children less often and for a shorter duration in comparison to peers (Bauminger and Kasari 2000; Bauminger and Shulman 2003; Bauminger, Shulman and Agam 2003). This can also occur during adolescence. Liane Holliday Willey explained in her autobiography that at college, 'I was accustomed to defining friendship in very simplistic terms. To me, friends were people I enjoyed passing a few minutes or a few hours with' (Willey 1999, p.43).

Friendships may be unusual in that the child chooses to play with younger children or prefers the company of adults. One child with Asperger's syndrome described to me the friend he regularly met at school during lunch recess. His mother then explained that his 'friend' was the school groundsman, and every lunch recess he helped the grounds-man with his chores. My wife's sister, who is an adult with Asperger's syndrome, wrote to me that, 'As a child, a teenager and a young adult, I seldom got along well with my peers, preferring the company of older adults. Probably because they are likely to be more mellow in temperament and of course quieter.' Stephen Shore, who also has Asperger's syndrome, has explained that adults tend to have more patience to listen to special interests and 'scaffold' a conversation.

A child or adult with Asperger's syndrome can mistake friendliness for friendship and conceptualize friends as though they should be reliable machines. Jamie, a young child with Asperger's syndrome, said of the child he used to play with, 'He can't play with me one day and then other friends another day, he wouldn't be a true friend.' A child with Asperger's syndrome may conceptualize friendship to be about possession, and is intolerant of anyone who breaks his or her personal rules about friendship. Teen-agers and adults with Asperger's syndrome may have problems understanding that friendliness is not necessarily a sign of romantic interest.

The clinician also examines the person's motivation for friendships, ability to make and keep friends and the value and nature of friends in that person's life. Adolescents and adults with Asperger's syndrome can express feelings of loneliness, sometimes being acutely aware and miserable about having so few, if any, friends. As Therese Jolliffe wrote in her personal account of autism, 'contrary to what people may think, it is possible for an autistic person to feel lonely and to love somebody' (Jolliffe, Lansdown and Robinson 1992, p.16).

Young children with Asperger's syndrome can be described by parents and teachers as socially clumsy, such that other children often consider that the child with Asperger's syndrome is not fun to play with, and does not conform with the usual rules of friend-ship, such as sharing, reciprocity and cooperation. As Jerry Newport, a man with Asperger's syndrome, said to me, 'To share, you have to give up control,' and as Holly said to me during her diagnostic assessment, 'My friends don't let me do what I want to do.'

The child with Asperger's syndrome often plays in an unconventional or idiosyncratic way with different priorities and interests to his or her peers, who tend to be bored by monologues or lectures on the child's special interests. In Jean-Paul's reflections on his childhood, he explained, 'I was not very good playing in typical ways or with other children and I rarely got enjoyment from it' (Donnelly and Bovee 2003).

The imaginative play can be qualitatively different to that of other children. In the same reflections on childhood, Jean-Paul described his unusual imaginative play: 'Imagination is something that is different in each person. For me, it was making my lists, creating fictional genealogies of characters, planning imaginary ball games with players on baseball cards, creating different languages, and the list goes on.' Children with Asperger's syndrome can develop imaginative play but usually as a solitary and idiosyncratic activity.

The child with Asperger's syndrome can be on the periphery of the playground, sometimes socially isolated by choice, or actively among the other children and seeking inclusion but being perceived by peers as intrusive and irritating. Such behaviour is often described by teachers as silly, immature, rude and uncooperative (Church *et al.* 2000).

When adolescents are included in the activities and conversations of their peers, there can still be feelings of not being included or popular. This is illustrated by two comments from adults with Asperger's syndrome describing their teenage years: 'I wasn't rejected but did not feel completely included,' and 'I was supported and tolerated but not liked.' A lack of genuine social acceptance by peers will obviously adversely affect the development of self-esteem.

The diagnostic assessment includes an examination of the child's abilities in a range of social situations, such as when playing with friends, parents, siblings or peers, and in new social situations. The signs of Asperger's syndrome are more apparent when the child is playing with peers rather than parents or an adult such as the examining clinician, an important point to remember in a diagnostic assessment. The clinician may supplement the assessment of social interaction skills by observing the child in unstructured play with peers, or obtaining reports on social play from a teacher.

There should be an examination of the child's awareness of the codes of social conduct in a range of situations, particularly the child's recognition of the concept of personal space, and his or her ability to modify greetings, touch and topics of conversation according to the context and cultural expectations. Other valuable information needs to be collected and evaluated with regard to the child's response to peer pressure, the duration and enjoyment of solitary play, the enforcement of social rules, degree of honesty, sense of humour and susceptibility and reaction to teasing and bullying.

To assess social reasoning ability, I show the child a series of pictures of children engaged in various solitary or social activities with associated emotions – for example, a child who has fallen from her bicycle and is crying, a child who appears to be trying to 'steal' a cookie while another child stands guard, and a girl who appears to have lost her parents in the shopping mall. The child is asked to describe what is happening in the pictures. Children with Asperger's syndrome tend to notice and describe objects and physical actions with a relative lack (in comparison to their peers) of reference to the thoughts, feelings and intentions of the participants in the picture. When assessing teenagers and adults, I will ask them to describe events in their personal lives, noting any predominance of descriptions of actions compared to descriptions and interpretations of thoughts, feelings and intentions of themselves and others.

The diagnostic assessment includes an evaluation of the person's social interaction and social reasoning skills from observation, interaction and self-report that can be used to confirm or reject the diagnosis. This evaluation can also be used as the baseline to measure the progress of programs in each of those areas of social understanding that may be delayed or unusual (the 'hallmarks' of Asperger's syndrome). This chapter will now describe strategies to improve social understanding and friendship skills.

THE MOTIVATION TO HAVE FRIENDS

I have observed the social development of children and adults with Asperger's syndrome over several decades and identified five stages in their motivation to have friends.

An interest in the physical world

Very young children with Asperger's syndrome in their pre-school or kindergarten years may not be interested in the activities of their peers or making friends. They are usually more interested in understanding the physical rather than the social world, and may enter the pre-school playground to explore the drainage or plumbing system of the school, or to search for insects and reptiles, or to gaze at the different cloud formations. The social activities of the child's peers are perceived as boring, with incomprehensible social rules. The child is content with solitude, but may be motivated to interact with adults who can answer questions beyond the knowledge of the child's peers, or seek refuge from the noisy and chaotic playground in the quiet sanctuary of the school library to read about topics such as volcanoes, meteorology and transport systems.

Wanting to play with other children

In the early primary or elementary school years, children with Asperger's syndrome notice that other children are having fun socializing and want to be included in the social activities to experience the obvious enjoyment of their peers. However, despite intellectual ability, their level of social maturity is usually at least two years behind that of their peers, and they may have conspicuous difficulties with the degree of reciprocal and cooperative play expected by other children.

At this stage in the motivation to have friends, the child with Asperger's syndrome may long for successful social inclusion and a friend to play with. This is the time when the child can become acutely aware of being different to his or her peers, giving rise to the adjustment and compensation strategies described in Chapter 1, namely depression, escape into imagination, denial and arrogance, or imitation.

The initial optimism about friendship can turn to paranoia, especially if the child fails to make the distinction between accidental and deliberate acts. Children with Asperger's syndrome have difficulty with Theory of Mind tasks – that is, conceptualizing the thoughts, feelings, knowledge and beliefs of others (see Chapter 5). Other children may recognize from the context, and often knowledge of the character of the other person, whether a particular comment or action had benevolent or malicious intent. For example, other children know when someone is teasing with friendly or unfriendly intentions. This knowledge may not be available to the child with Asperger's syndrome.

I have noted that children with Asperger's syndrome are often limited in their ability to make character judgements. Other children will know which children are not good role models and should be avoided; children with Asperger's syndrome can be somewhat naïve in their judgements, and prone to be attracted to and imitate children who may not demonstrate good friendship skills.

Making first friendships

In the middle school years, children with Asperger's syndrome may achieve genuine friendships but have a tendency to be too dominant or to have too rigid a view of friendship. Such children may 'wear out their welcome'. However, some typical children, who are naturally kind, understanding and 'maternal', may find children with Asperger's syndrome appealing, and can be tolerant of their behaviour, becoming genuine friends for several years or more.

Sometimes the friendship is not with a compassionate, typical child, but with a similar, socially isolated child, who shares the same interests, but not necessarily the diagnosis. The friendship tends to be functional and practical, exchanging items and knowledge of mutual interest, and may extend beyond a dyad to a small group of like-minded children with a similar level of social competence and popularity.

Searching for a partner

In late adolescence, teenagers with Asperger's syndrome may seek more than a platonic friendship with like-minded individuals, and express a longing for a boyfriend or girlfriend, and eventually a partner. The partner they seek is someone who understands them and provides emotional support and guidance in the social world – someone to be a 'mother figure' and mentor.

Adolescent peers are usually much more mature and knowledgeable in identifying a potential partner and developing and practising relationships skills. The adolescent boy with Asperger's syndrome may ask forlornly, 'How do I get a girlfriend?' Attempts to develop a relationship beyond platonic friendship can lead to rejection, ridicule and a misinterpretation of intentions. The adolescent with Asperger's syndrome can feel even more socially confused, immature and isolated.

Becoming a partner

Eventually, perhaps when emotionally and socially more mature, the adult with Asperger's syndrome can find a lifetime partner. However, both partners would probably benefit from relationship counselling to identify and encourage the adjustments needed to make an unconventional relationship successful for both. We now have literature on relationship counselling for couples where one partner has Asperger's syndrome. The Resources section towards the end of the book provides a list of recommended books, Internet resources and agencies.

THE IMPORTANCE OF FRIENDSHIP

There must be advantages in having friends. The research evidence suggests that children without friends may be at risk for later difficulties and delay in social and emotional development, low self-esteem and the development of anxiety and depression as an adult (Hay, Payne and Chadwick 2004). Having friends can be a preventative measure for mood disorders.

Another advantage can be an improvement in problem solving (Rubin 2002). If a group of children are engaged cooperatively in a task, they have the benefit of different perspectives and ideas, and greater physical abilities. Another child may literally be in a position to see something of importance, have previous experience of what to do, or can generate an original solution. A group of friends provides greater physical and intellectual strength for problem solving.

Chee is a young man with Asperger's syndrome and he wrote that:

> The worst problem for me in my life is socializing. I cannot make friends and I need friends badly. When you have friends you get more support and you can ask a lot of things from them and they'll help because they're your friends. You also gain a lot of knowledge and experience from your friends. And because I don't have friends it means that I'm cut off from help. Whenever I have a problem I have to handle it on my own. I don't know how to socialize and that means I don't know how to use people to my advantage. To me that is the biggest problem with having Asperger Syndrome. (Molloy and Vasil 2004, p.77)

Being isolated and not having friends also makes the child vulnerable to being teased and bullied. The 'predators' at school target someone who is alone, vulnerable and less likely to be protected by peers. Having more friends can mean having fewer enemies.

Peer acceptance and friendships can benefit the child in terms of providing a second opinion with regard to the motives and intentions of others, preventing a sense of paranoia. Friends can provide an effective emotional monitoring and repair mechanism, especially for emotions such as anxiety, anger and depression. Friends can offer guidance on what is appropriate social behaviour, help develop self-image and self-confidence, and can act as personal counsellors and psychologists. Deborah is an adult with Asperger's syndrome who, in an e-mail to me, stated that in her opinion, 'The best cure for low self esteem…friendship.' This is particularly true during adolescence.

All the qualities of a good friend are the qualities of a good team member, and important attributes for later employment as an adult. I have known of adults with Asperger's syndrome who have impressive academic qualifications, but their lack of teamwork skills has contributed to problems with gaining or maintaining employment or achieving an income appropriate to their impressive qualifications. Having friends and developing friendships skills can determine whether the person acquires the interpersonal abilities for successful employment.

The development of interpersonal skills with friends is also the basis of later success in a relationship with a partner. Concepts of empathy, trust, repairing emotions and sharing responsibilities, developed throughout childhood with friends, are essential in adult relationships.

ENCOURAGING FRIENDSHIPS

In typical children, the acquisition of friendship skills is based on an innate ability that develops throughout childhood in association with progressive changes in cognitive ability, and modified and matured through social experiences. Unfortunately, children with Asperger's syndrome are not able to rely on intuitive abilities in social settings as well as their peers and must rely more on their cognitive abilities and experiences. Children and adults with Asperger's syndrome have difficulty in social situations that have not been rehearsed or prepared for. Thus, it is essential that such children receive tuition and guided practice in the ability to make and keep friends and that their friendship experiences are constructive and encouraging (Attwood 2000). A failure to experience friendship will lead to an inability to grasp the very concept of 'friend' (Lee and Hobson 1998). If you do not have friends, how can you know how to become a friend?

Parents can try to facilitate social play at home with siblings and another child invited to their home on a play date, but will have difficulty providing the range of experiences and degree of supervision and tuition required for a child with Asperger's syndrome. The optimum environment to develop reciprocal play with peers is at school. Education services will need to be aware of the importance of a social curriculum as well as an educational curriculum for a child with Asperger's syndrome. The social curriculum must have an emphasis on friendship skills, and include appropriate staff training and relevant resources. The following suggestions are designed for implementation by teachers and parents for each of the developmental stages of friendship that occur in typical children and can be applied to children with Asperger's syndrome.

The developmental stages in the concept of friendship for typical children

Before the age of three years, typical children will interact and play with members of their family, but their conceptualization of their peers is often one of rivalry for possessions and adult attention rather than friendship. If another child comes to the home, the typical child may hide a favourite toy. However, some basic sharing, helping and comforting can occur after the first year: the first building blocks of friendship. There may be parallel play and curiosity about what is interesting to other children and subsequent copying of what other children are doing, but primarily because it may be interesting, enjoyable and likely to impress a parent. We know that typical children in this age group do have preferred companions and may choose to play alongside a particular child. As children with Asperger's syndrome are usually diagnosed after the age of five years, they have usually progressed beyond the level of friendships associated with very young children when first diagnosed.

Stage one of friendship – three to six years

Typical children from the ages of three to six years have a functional and egocentric conceptualization of friendship. When asked why a particular child is his or her friend, a typical child's reply is usually based on proximity (lives next door, sits at same table) or possessions (the other child has toys that the child admires or wants to use). Toys and play activities are the focus of friendship and the child gradually moves from engaging primarily in parallel play to recognizing that some games and activities cannot happen unless there is an element of sharing and turn-taking. However, cooperative skills are limited, the main characteristics that define a friend being one-way and egocentric (he helps me or she likes me). Conflict is usually associated with the possession and use of equipment and the violation of personal space, but in the last year or two of stage one, conflict can be over the rules of games and who wins. Conflict resolution, from the child's perspective, is often achieved by ultimatums and use of physical force. An adult may not be asked to adjudicate. Children may have some suggestions to comfort or help a distressed friend, but consider emotional repair as the function of a parent or teacher rather than themselves.

If children from three to four years are asked what they did today, they tend to describe what they played with, while over the age of about four years they start to include whom they played with. Social play gradually becomes more than just the construction and completion of the activity. However, friendships are transitory and the child has a personal agenda of what to do and how to do it.

Very young children with Asperger's syndrome have a clear end-product in mind when playing with toys; however, they may fail to communicate this effectively to a playmate, or tolerate or incorporate the other child's suggestions, as this would produce an unanticipated outcome. For example, the child with Asperger's syndrome may have in mind while playing with construction equipment the mental image of the completed structure, and be extremely agitated when another child places a brick where, according to the mental image, there shouldn't be a brick. The typical child, meanwhile, does not understand why his or her act of cooperation is rejected.

The young child with Asperger's syndrome often seeks predictability and control in play activities while typical peers seek spontaneity and collaboration. In her autobiography, Liane Holliday Willey explains about her early childhood:

> Like with my tea parties, the fun came from setting up and arranging things. Maybe this desire to organize things rather than play with things, is the reason I never had a great interest in my peers. They always wanted to use the things I had so carefully arranged. They would want to rearrange and redo. They did not let me control the environment. They did not act the way I thought they should act. Children needed more freedom than I could provide them. (Willey 1999, pp.16–17)

Other children often consider that the child with Asperger's syndrome, who often prefers to play alone, does not welcome them. When other children are included, the child with Asperger's syndrome may be dictatorial, tending not to play by conventional rules and considering the other child as subordinate. Such behaviour is perceived by other children as being bossy and sounding and behaving more like a teacher than a friend. Thus, the child with Asperger's syndrome, who is eventually avoided by other children, inadvertently becomes unpopular. Opportunities are then lost to use and develop friendship skills.

Programs for stage one
An adult acting as a friend

For the young child with Asperger's syndrome, who is probably not interested in playing with peers, but who may be motivated to interact with adults, social play can be taught by an adult who 'plays the part' of an age peer. In much the same way that actors in a theatre play learn how to act, and rehearse their roles, the child can be taught how to engage in reciprocal play. The adult 'friend' in this situation will need to adjust his or her abilities and language to resemble that of the child's peers. The intention is to encourage reciprocal play between equals with neither 'friend' being dominant.

A class teacher has a designated and relatively fixed role, being an adult not a friend. However, an adult who provides support to facilitate integration into the kindergarten or pre-school can sometimes act the role of 'friend'. This adult 'friend' can act as a mentor, or stage director, giving guidance and encouragement to the child in social situations. Games or equipment that are used at school and are popular with other children of the same age may be borrowed or bought to assist in making the interactions more comparable with real social situations with peers.

It is important that adults, especially parents, observe the natural play of the child's peers, noting the games, equipment, rules and language. The strategy is for the parent to play with the child using 'child speak' – the typical utterances of children of that age – and to be equal and reciprocal in terms of ability, interests and cooperation. The adult can demonstrate specific social cues, and momentarily stop and encourage the child to see or listen to the cue, explaining what the cue means and how he or she is expected to respond.

The adult can vocalize his or her thoughts when playing with the child – a commentary of thoughts. This will enable the child with Asperger's syndrome to actually listen to the other person's thoughts rather than be expected to know what the other person is thinking from the context, or by having to interpret facial expressions and body language.

It is important that the adult role-plays examples of being a good friend, and also situations that illustrate unfriendly actions, dominance, teasing and disagreements. Appropriate and inappropriate responses can be enacted by the adult, to provide the child with a range of responses and the ability to determine which response is appropriate and why.

Taking turns and asking for help

In stage one of friendship, a good friend is someone who takes turns and helps. It is important that when the adult is acting as a friend, he or she models and encourages turn-taking. For example, when completing an inset board, the adult and the child should take turns in placing each of the pieces in the puzzle; if looking at a book, the adult first points to one of the pictures and makes a comment or asks a question, and on the next page the child points and asks the adult a question. If the child enjoys being pushed on the swing, the next activity is for the child to push the adult on the swing. The two 'friends' take turns in each activity and in being the leader.

To encourage helping someone, the adult will need to deliberately make a mistake or not be sure what to do in order to solve a problem. The adult then asks the child for help, with the comment that asking for help is the smart and friendly thing to do when you have a problem. The adult will need to ensure that his or her own ability on a task is comparable to that of the child with Asperger's syndrome. Such children may perceive themselves as small adults, and become extremely disappointed or agitated if their level of ability is obviously less than that of their playmate. The adult is also modelling that it is okay to make mistakes.

A dress rehearsal with another child

An adult can easily modify the pace of play and amount of instruction and feedback. After sufficient practice in such a setting, the child can progress to a 'dress rehearsal' with another child. This might be an older sibling, or perhaps a mature child in the class, who can act as a friend to provide further guided practice before the skills are used openly with a peer group.

A video recording of children playing

Children with Asperger's syndrome often enjoy watching the same movie many times. This is a common preferred activity of typical children but the child with Asperger's syndrome may be unusual in terms of the number of times the film or programme is watched. This is not necessarily a self-stimulatory behaviour, as suggested in some of the behaviourist literature on autism, but in my opinion a constructive way of learning without the confusion and effort of having to socialize or talk. Parents can be concerned that watching the same programme so many times is a waste of time; however, the problem may not be what the child with Asperger's syndrome is doing, but what he or she is watching.

I recommend that video recordings be made of the social experiences of the child with Asperger's syndrome – for example, the child and peers playing in the sandpit, 'show and tell' time in class, or playing with cousins at home. The child can then replay, perhaps many times, the 'social documentary' to better understand the social cues, responses, sequence of activities, actions of peers and the child's role as a friend. An adult can use the freeze-frame or pause facility to focus on a specific social cue, identify friendly behaviour and point out what the child with Asperger's syndrome did that was appropriate.

Pretend games

Typical children in stage one of friendship often play make-believe or pretend games based on popular characters and stories from books, television programmes and films. The play of the child with Asperger's syndrome can also be based on characters and events in fiction, but may be qualitatively different in that it is usually a solitary rather than shared activity. It may be an exact re-enactment with little variation or creativity, and may include other children, but only if they follow the directions of the child with Asperger's syndrome and do not change the script. The interaction is not as creative, cooperative or reciprocal as would occur with typical peers. However, the child with Asperger's syndrome can have a remarkable memory and knowledge of popular characters and films, and happily replay scenes for many hours. The child will need to be encouraged to be more flexible in his or her 'imaginative' play, especially when playing with other children. The principle is to learn that something is not wrong if it is different.

Activities to encourage flexible thinking and the ability to engage in pretend play can include games where the objective is to invent as many uses as possible for a given object – that is, to think beyond the most obvious, functional use of that object. For example, how many uses can be thought of for a brick, a paper clip, a section of toy train track, and so on? The section of train track could become the wings of an aeroplane, a sword or a ladder, for example. This will encourage the ability to 'break set' when problem solving and be more comfortable when involved in pretend play with other children.

The adult can act a friend in make-believe games, using the phrase 'let's pretend that…', thus encouraging flexible thinking and creativity. Children with Asperger's syndrome can be very rule-bound and need to learn that, when playing with a friend, it is possible sometimes to change the rules and be inventive, yet still have an enjoyable experience, and that this is not necessarily a cause for anxiety. The child may benefit from a Social Story™ (see page 69) that explains that in friendships, and when solving a practical or intellectual problem, trying another way can lead to an important discovery. Trying to find a quicker way to sail to India led to the European discovery of America.

Once the child with Asperger's syndrome is more comfortable with flexible thinking, the adult and peers can encourage him or her to engage in reciprocal imaginative social play. I have found that when the child discovers the intellectual and social value of being imaginative, the level of creativity can be astounding.

Encouragement for being friendly

When discussing childhood social experiences with young adults with Asperger's syndrome, I have listened to many descriptions of social confusion, and how, very often, the response of adults was criticism of social mistakes but rarely praise for what was appropriate. The child often assumed that at the end of an interaction, a lack of criticism, sarcasm or derisory laughter meant the interaction was successful but had no idea what he or she had done that was socially appropriate. As one young adult said of his childhood, 'The only comments I had were when I did it wrong but no one told me what I was doing right' (personal commuication).

If the child were completing a mathematics activity, the teacher's tick or cross would indicate what was right or wrong. When completing a jigsaw puzzle or construction with building blocks, the child knows he or she has achieved success when all the pieces fit together or the construction is complete and robust. The problem in social situations is that success may not be obvious, and there may be a relative lack of positive feedback. I strongly recommend that when an adult, peer or friend is interacting with a young child with Asperger's syndrome, a conscious effort should be made to point out and comment on what the child did that was appropriate.

For example, if the child was observed playing soccer with other children during the lunch recess, he or she could be informed at the end of the game which actions were friendly and why. Positive feedback could be: 'I noticed that when the ball got lost in the tall grass, you helped to find the ball. Excellent! Helping to find something is a friendly thing to do'; or 'When Joshua fell over and you came up to him and asked if he was okay, that was a caring and friendly thing to do'; or 'When Jessica scored a goal and you went up to her and said "Great goal", that was a nice compliment, and a friendly thing to do.'

The child can have a friendship diary, which records the times during the day or week when he or she demonstrated friendship abilities. The diary can take the form of a 'boasting book' or provide a means of recording friendship 'points' for a particular act of friendship. The diary can record what was done or said and why it was an example of friendship. Memorable acts of friendship could achieve public recognition and an appropriate reward.

Social Stories™

Another strategy to learn the relevant social cues, thoughts, feelings and behavioural script is to write Social Stories™, which were originally developed by Carol Gray in 1991, not from the academic application of a theoretical model of social cognition, but from Carol working directly and collaboratively with children with autism and Asperger's syndrome (Gray 1998). Preparing Social Stories™ also enables other people (adults and peers) to understand the perspective of the child with Asperger's syndrome, and why his or her social behaviour can appear confused, anxious, aggressive or disobedient. Carol Gray (2004b) has recently revised the criteria and guidelines for writing a Social Story™ and the following is a brief summary of the guidelines.

A Social Story™ describes a situation, skill or concept in terms of relevant social cues, perspectives and common responses in a specifically defined style and format. The intention is to share accurate social and emotional information in a reassuring and informative manner that is easily understood by the child (or adult) with Asperger's syndrome. The first Social Story™, and at least 50 per cent of subsequent Social Stories™, should describe, affirm and consolidate existing abilities and knowledge and what the child does well, which avoids the problem of a Social Story™ being associated only with ignorance or failure. Social Stories™ can also be written as a means of recording achievements in using new knowledge and strategies. It is important that Social Stories™ are viewed as a means of recording social knowledge and social success.

One of the essential aspects of writing a Social Story™ is to determine collaboratively how a particular situation is perceived by the child with Asperger's syndrome, abandoning the assumption that the adult knows all the facts, thoughts, emotions and intentions of the child. The structure of the story comprises an *introduction* that clearly identifies the topic, a *body* that adds detail and knowledge and a *conclusion* that summarizes and reinforces the information and any new suggestions.

For younger children, the story is written in the first-person perspective, using the personal pronoun 'I', or the child's name if that is how the child refers to himself or herself, and should provide the child with information that can be personalized and internalized (Gray 2002a). For teenagers and adults, the Social Story™ can be written in the third-person perspective, 'he' or 'she', with a style resembling an age-appropriate magazine article. The term Social Story™ could then be changed to Social Article. For example, one of the expectations of friendship and teamwork abilities for employment as a young adult is the ability to give and receive compliments. A magazine-style article of 16 pages, with cartoon illustrations, was written by Carol Gray to explain to adults with Asperger's syndrome why compliments are expected in friendships, in the relationship with your partner, and with colleagues or customers at work (Gray 1999).

If the person has a special interest, this interest can be incorporated in the text. For example, if the child's special interest is the sinking of the *Titanic*, then scenes from the film or personal recollections in history books or documentaries can be used to illustrate and emphasize some of the key information in the Social Story™ (Gagnon 2001).

Social Stories™ use positive language and a constructive approach. The suggestions are what to do rather than what not to do. The text will include *descriptive sentences* that provide factual information or statements, and *perspective sentences*, which are written to explain a person's perception of the physical and mental world. Perspective sentences, which are one of the reasons for the success of Social Stories™, describe thoughts, emotions, beliefs, opinions, motivation and knowledge. They are specifically included to improve Theory of Mind abilities. Carol Gray recommends including *cooperative sentences* to identify who can be of assistance, and *directive sentences* that suggest a response or choice of responses in a particular situation. *Affirmative sentences* explain a commonly shared value, opinion or rule, the reason why specific codes of conduct have been established and why there is the expectation of conformity. *Control sentences* are written by the child to identify personal strategies to help remember what to do. Carol Gray has developed a Social Story™ formula such that the text describes more than directs. The Social Story™ will also need a title, which should reflect the essential characteristics of the story.

Carol Gray's original work on Social Stories™ has now been examined by many research studies and found to be remarkably effective in improving social understanding and social behaviour in children with autism and Asperger's syndrome (Hagiwara and Myles 1999; Ivey, Heflin and Alberto 2004; Lorimer 2002; Norris and Dattilo 1999; Rogers and Myles 2001; Rowe 1999; Santosi, Powell Smith and Kincaid 2004; Scattone *et al.* 2002; Smith 2001; Swaggart *et al.* 1995; Thiemann and Goldstein 2001).

Social Stories™ can be an extremely effective means of learning the relevant social cues at all stages of friendship, but particularly at stage one. Young children will need guidance to understand the thoughts and feelings of the other person and the role or actions expected in a particular situation. For example, the following is part of an unpublished Social Story™ on gestures of reassurance:

> Sometimes children hug me. They do this to be friendly. Yesterday, I made three spelling mistakes in the class test. When my friend Amy saw my test paper and three mistakes, she thought I would be sad and I was sad. Amy put her arm around me and said, 'It's okay Juanita.' Amy is my friend. She gave me a hug to help me feel better. For some people, having a hug makes them feel better. Having a hug can make Amy feel better. When I have a hug from Amy it is because she knows I am sad and she wants me to feel better. I can say thank you after she has given me a hug.

In the situation described above, the reason for the behaviour of Amy, namely putting her arm around Juanita, may need to be explained to a child with Asperger's syndrome. Such children have difficulty understanding the thoughts, feelings and intentions of others, which can make the behaviour of other people appear illogical and confusing. A gesture of reassurance can repair feelings, not spelling mistakes. Only when the child understands that the action was a gesture of reassurance, intended to repair her feelings of distress, will the behaviour of Amy seem logical and not a cause for confusion and rejection.

After the Social Story™ is written, other people in the child's everyday world will need to know how they can help the child successfully implement the new knowledge and strategies. The child may create a Social Stories™ folder to keep the stories as a reference book at home or school, and have copies of some stories that may be kept in a pocket or a wallet to read again in order to refresh his or her memory just before or during a time when the Social Story™ is relevant.

Other topics for Social Stories™ in stage one of friendship include entry and exit skills (i.e. how to join in and leave an activity), when and how to provide help, and the importance of sharing and accepting play activities suggested by another child. The ability to join a group of children successfully is a particularly difficult skill for children with Asperger's syndrome. The general advice for typical children is to watch, listen, move closer and then ease in (Rubin 2002). Each stage in the entry process may need a Social Story™; for example, the child may need help to recognize and understand the entry signals to ease into a group, such as a welcome look or gesture, the natural pause in conversation or the transition between activities – the 'green-light' signals.

The Social Signals activity

I use a metaphor of a car driver to explain the consequences of not noticing or knowing the social signals. We have developed road signs and driving codes to prevent injuries and damage. A teacher or parent is asked to imagine a driver who does not see or understand the road signs and goes through a red light, exceeds the speed limit or drives too close to another vehicle, any of which can cause an accident.

The child with Asperger's syndrome has difficulty recognizing and knowing how to respond to the social signals that prevent social accidents. When the teacher utters a loud 'Ahem' sound as though clearing his throat, a typical child will know this could be a warning sign similar to the road sign that informs the driver there are traffic lights ahead. The child needs to look at the teachers' face as though looking at traffic lights – if he or she is smiling, a 'green-light' expression, it means you can carry on with whatever you are doing. If the teacher has a frown, but is staring at someone else, this is an 'amber-light' face, meaning be careful, you may have to stop. If he or she is staring at you with an angry expression, a 'red-light' face, it is the clear signal to stop what you are doing or there will be consequences. The child with Asperger's syndrome, however, may interpret the 'Ahem' simply as indicating that the teacher has a dry throat and needs a throat lozenge or a drink.

Children with Asperger's syndrome may not understand the 'no tailgating' signs and encroach on someone's personal space; the 'road closed' sign that indicates 'this will lead nowhere'; or the 'men working' sign that signals 'do not disturb'. In not responding as expected to these social signs, the child with Asperger's syndrome is not being deliberately reckless and provocative, but demonstrating his or her lack of understanding, and will thus be prone to social accidents that damage feelings.

The Social Signals activity uses Social Stories™ to explain the reason for a particular 'rule of the road', and provides clear examples of the signals, and practice in how to respond. The concept of facial expressions as traffic lights can be explored by having a large picture of traffic lights and some pictures of facial expressions. The child with Asperger's syndrome sorts through the pictures and decides which traffic light is associated with each expression. Is this a green-light face, an amber face or a red-light face? The activity includes explaining appropriate comments or questions that the child can use when he or she sees a particular amber or red-light facial expression, such as 'I'm sorry', 'Are you angry with me?', or 'What should I do?'; or when confused as to what the social signal means, questions and comments to prevent further social accidents, such as 'Did I do something wrong?' or 'I am confused.'

Stage two of friendship – six to nine years

At this stage in the development of friendships, typical children start to recognize that they need a friend to play certain games and that their friend must also like those games. Children accept and incorporate the influences, preferences and goals of their friends in their play. Typical children become more aware of the thoughts and feelings of their peers and how their actions and comments can hurt, physically and emotionally. The child is prepared to inhibit some actions and thoughts, to 'think it, not say it', or to tell a 'white lie' in order not to hurt someone's feelings. There is a greater reciprocity and mutual assistance expected in friendships at this stage.

A friendship may develop because both children have similar interests. Aspects of a friend's character rather than possessions are recognized (he's fun to be with, we laugh together). The concept of reciprocity (she comes to my party and I go to hers) and the genuine sharing of resources and being fair in games become increasingly important. When managing conflict the child's view is that the offender must retract the action and a satisfactory resolution is to administer equal discomfort, or 'an eye for an eye'. The concept of responsibility and justice is based on who started the conflict, not what was subsequently done or how it ended. Around the age of eight years the child can develop the concept of a best friend as not only his or her first choice for social play but also as someone who helps in practical terms (he knows how to fix the computer) and in times of emotional stress (she cheers me up when I'm feeling sad). However, not every child has a 'best friend' at this stage.

Programs for stage two

Role-play activities

In stage two of friendship, children develop greater cooperation when playing with their peers and develop more constructive means of dealing with conflict. It is important that the child with Asperger's syndrome learns the theory of, and gains practice in, various aspects of cooperative play using Social Stories™ and role-play activities. These can provide practice in aspects of cooperative play such as giving and receiving compliments, accepting suggestions, working towards a common goal, being aware of personal body space, proximity and touch, coping with and giving criticism, and recognizing signs of boredom, embarrassment and frustration and when and how to interrupt. The role-play and modelling of aspects of social interaction such as giving compliments can be recorded on video to provide practice and constructive feedback (Apple, Billingsley and Schwartz 2005).

In situations of conflict or disagreement, the child with Asperger's syndrome will need encouragement to seek an adult as an adjudicator, rather than act as the person to determine who is at fault and administer the consequences. Social Stories™ and role-play activities can focus on aspects such as the benefits of negotiation and compromise, being fair and the importance of an apology. Issues of control can be a problem. If the child has a tendency to be autocratic or dominant, or to use threats and aggression to achieve his or her goal, other approaches can be explained and encouraged. You are more likely to get what you want by being nice to someone.

A teacher assistant in the classroom and playground

To facilitate successful social inclusion in the classroom and playground, the child will probably need support staff at school. A teacher assistant can observe the child's social behaviour, particularly behaviours indicative of age-appropriate friendship skills, and provide immediate positive feedback and guidance. The teacher assistant has a number of functions including:

- helping the child identify the relevant social cues and responses

- providing individual tuition using specific activities or games, role-play, rehearsal and writing Social Stories™ with the child

- encouraging other children to successfully include the child with Asperger's syndrome in their play

- providing guidance in managing potential conflict between the child with Asperger's syndrome and peers

- providing positive feedback for the child.

The number of hours in the school day that a child with Asperger's syndrome needs a teacher assistant will vary according to the abilities of the child, the social context and abilities of the peer group.

Playing with dolls or figures and reading fiction

In stage two of friendship, I have noted that there can be different coping mechanisms used by girls with Asperger's syndrome in comparison to boys. Girls with Asperger's syndrome are more likely to be interested observers of the social play of other girls and to imitate their play at home using dolls and imaginary friends, or adopt the persona of a socially able girl. These activities can be a valuable opportunity to analyse and rehearse friendship skills.

Girls with Asperger's syndrome can develop a special interest in reading fiction. This also provides an insight into thoughts, emotions and social relationships. A boy with Asperger's syndrome can be encouraged to play with figures, usually masculine action heroes, but to re-enact everyday experiences rather than movies, and to read fiction, perhaps based on a special interest – for example, a book such as *The Railway Children* if the child is interested in trains.

Shared interests

One of the common replies of typical children at this stage in the development of friendship to the question 'What makes a good friend?' is 'We like the same things.' Shared interests are a basis for friendship. I know a child with Asperger's syndrome who had a remarkable interest in and knowledge of insects, especially ants. His peers tolerated his enthusiasm and monologues on ants, but he was not regarded as a potential friend as there was a limit to their enthusiasm for the topic. He was learning friendship skills such as how to have a reciprocal conversation, waiting for the other person to finish what he or she was saying, and how to give and receive compliments and show empathy. When he used these social skills with his class peers, they were achieved by intellectual effort and guidance and perceived by other children as somewhat contrived and artificial. He had few genuine friends.

By chance, another child with Asperger's syndrome lived close by, and also had an interest in ants. Their parents arranged a meeting of the two young entomologists; when they met, the social rapport between the new friends was remarkable. The two boys became regular companions on ant safaris, shared knowledge and resources on insects, made a joint ant study and regularly contacted each other with long and genuinely reciprocal conversations about their latest ant-related discoveries. When observing their interactions, it was clear that there was a natural balance to the conversation, with both children being able to wait patiently, listen attentively, show empathy and give compliments at a level not observed when they were with their typical peers.

Parents and teachers can consider friendship matchmaking, based on the child's special interest. Local parent support groups for families with a child with Asperger's syndrome can provide the names and addresses of families, along with the special interests of the children, in order to arrange a potentially successful friendship. However, I have noted that when the shared interest ends for one partner, the friendship may also end.

The interest can also be used to facilitate friendship with typical peers. My wife's sister has Asperger's syndrome and an outstanding ability in art. She wrote that at school:

> Longing to make friends, when someone complimented a drawing I had done, I started giving people drawings until someone accused me of bragging – a rebuke I never forgot. I was only trying to win friendship. (Personal communication)

If the child with Asperger's syndrome has a particular talent such as drawing, a teacher can arrange for the child to form a working partnership with another child whose abilities are complementary. For example, the artist may become the illustrator for a child whose talent is writing stories. This can demonstrate the value of collaboration and teamwork.

Sense of humour

Another reply to the question 'What makes a good friend?' can be 'Someone with a sense of humour'. Children with Asperger's syndrome tend to make a literal interpretation of what someone says and may not understand when someone is joking; however, there can be a wonderful, though sometimes idiosyncratic, sense of humour (Darlington 2001). The very young child may laugh at the way a word is spoken and repeat the word to himself as a very private joke, but the reason for the humour is not explained or shared. The development of humour can progress to the creation of inventive puns, word associations and word play (Werth, Perkins and Boucher 2001). The next developmental stage of humour can be visual slapstick as occurs in the comedy programmes of *Mr Bean* and subsequently, at an earlier age than expected, an interest in surreal humour such as the comedy style of *Monty Python*.

Among peers, the jokes of children between the ages six and nine years can start to include laughter associated with rude words and actions. Other children will be aware of the nature of the joke, an appropriate context for it, and who would appreciate it. The child with Asperger's syndrome may repeat a rude joke to be popular in circumstances when other children would realize it would not be funny. The joke that causes uproarious laughter among children in the playground is not necessarily the joke to tell your grandmother at the lunch table on Sunday. The child may need a Social Story™ to explain why some jokes are funny for some people and not others.

Hans Asperger wrote that children with Asperger's syndrome lack a sense of humour but this is not consistent with my experience of several thousand children with Asperger's syndrome. Many have a unique or alternative perspective on life that can be the basis of comments that are perceptive and clearly humorous. I agree with Claire

Sainsbury when she writes, 'It is not a sense of humour we lack, but rather the social skills to recognize when others are joking, signal that we ourselves are joking, or appreciate jokes which rely on an understanding of social conventions' (Sainsbury 2000, p.80).

Some adolescents with Asperger's syndrome can be remarkably imaginative in creating original humour and jokes but the topic is often related to the special interest and may not be created to share the laughter with others (Lyons and Fitzgerald 2004; Werth et al. 2001). I know many teenagers with Asperger's syndrome who create abundant jokes, although sometimes I am not sure what I am supposed to be laughing at. However, the laughter of the person with Asperger's syndrome in response to an idiosyncratic joke is very infectious.

Concentric circles

The child with Asperger's syndrome will probably need guidance in the understanding of the different social hierarchies and social conventions for humour, topics of conversation, touch and personal body space, greetings and gestures of affection. I use an activity where a series of concentric circles are drawn on a very large sheet of paper. In the inner circle is written the name of the child and immediate family members. In the surrounding circle are written the names of people well known to the child but not immediate family, such as his or her teacher, aunts and uncles, neighbours and the child's friends. The next circle, closer to the perimeter, can include the names of family friends and acquaintances, distant relatives and children who are known to the child but are not friends. The next circle can include people known but seen only occasionally, such as a doctor or the person who delivers the mail. The outer circle can include people who are initially strangers or seen rarely, such as the distant relative.

Once the circles and occupants of the circles have been agreed, the topic of conversation is an aspect of social behaviour such as different types of greetings. The adult facilitating the activity can work with the child on finding and cutting out pictures of different types of greetings from magazines. The discussion centres around deciding in which circle to place each greeting. A handshake may be an appropriate greeting for the doctor but not the expected greeting for a grandma. The child may really like and admire his or her teachers but giving them a hug and kiss each morning would not be an age-appropriate greeting for a seven-year-old to give a teacher. An alternative affectionate but verbal greeting can be suggested. The concentric circles activity can become more intriguing for older children when considering the greetings of people from different cultures. In northern Europe, the greeting of female friends can be just a smile, but in France, the expectation is a kiss on each cheek. In New Zealand Maori culture, sticking out one's tongue at a respected guest is a traditional form of welcome. However, a parent may have to explain that if the family do not live in New Zealand, sticking out one's tongue is generally not an acceptable greeting.

The concentric circles activity can also be used with programs on friendship to illustrate many of the rules and different aspects of friendship. For example, it is a very clear way of explaining how someone may 'cross the boundaries' and move from being an acquaintance to being a close friend. The great advantage of the concentric circles activity is that it enables the child to visualize a range of complex social conventions and to know what to say and do when socializing with someone within one of the designated circles.

What not to say

Children with Asperger's syndrome are usually brutally honest and speak their mind. Their allegiance is to the truth, not people's feelings. They may have to learn not to tell the truth all the time. While honesty is a virtue, peers at this stage are starting to tell white lies so as not to hurt friends' feelings, or to express solidarity and allegiance to friendship by not informing an adult of the misbehaviour of a friend. Such behaviour may appear immoral and illogical for a child with Asperger's syndrome, who is willing to inform the teacher 'who did it' and that a friend has made a stupid mistake. This is not a recommended way to make or keep friends. The child with Asperger's syndrome may benefit from Social Stories™ to understand why it is appropriate at times to say something that is not the truth, and when to stay quiet.

An anthropologist in the classroom

One way to describe a person with Asperger's syndrome is someone who comes from a different culture and has a different way of perceiving and thinking about the world. Some adults with Asperger's syndrome have suggested that the term Asperger's syndrome should be replaced with 'wrong planet' syndrome. Clare Sainsbury, an Oxford university graduate who has Asperger's syndrome, has written a book entitled *Martian in the Playground* (2000) to help parents and teachers understand Asperger's syndrome. The conceptualization of someone with Asperger's syndrome as being from a different culture or planet can help change the attitudes of adults and peers, but can also be used to substantiate an intervention strategy.

The child with Asperger's syndrome is trying to understand our social customs in much the same way as an anthropologist who has discovered a new tribe will want to study its people and customs. The anthropologist will need someone from that culture to explain the culture, customs and language. A teacher or teaching assistant assigned to the child with Asperger's syndrome can take the role of a guide to explain this new culture or civilization. The process is one of discovery and explanation of the reason for particular customs. A visitor to a new culture will need a guidebook, and writing Social Stories™ is a collaboration between the guide (teacher) and anthropologist (child). Teenagers and adults with Asperger's syndrome would certainly benefit from writing or reading a travel guide to understanding and living with typical people, or, to use a term created by adults with Asperger's syndrome, neurotypicals.

The representative of the culture, or personal guide, can sit with the anthropologist in a corner of the classroom or playground and both watch, comment and make notes on the social interactions of the children, with the guide providing an explanatory commentary. Another activity is the game of 'spot the friendly act', taking turns to identify an act of friendship. The guide comments on why the particular behaviour is considered friendly or not friendly. A people-watching game, with a guide, can provide information on friendship without the child with Asperger's syndrome feeling that he or she is the centre of attention, or the person who inevitably makes mistakes.

After-school social experiences

Children with Asperger's syndrome work twice as hard at school as their peers, as they are learning both the academic and the social curriculum. Unlike other children, they are using cognitive abilities rather than intuition to socialize and make friends. As explained by Stephen, 'It takes all my brain power to be a friend.' At the end of the school day, the child has usually had enough social experiences and desperately needs to relax in solitude. As far as the child with Asperger's syndrome is concerned, friendships end at the school gate. The child can therefore resist parents' suggestions to contact friends from school or play with neighbourhood children. He or she has had enough socializing at school, and parents may need to accept that the child does not have the energy or motivation to socialize any more. If parents arrange social experiences, it is important that the experiences are brief, structured, supervised, successful and voluntary.

Social skills groups

There has been some success reported in the research literature for social skills groups for children, adolescents and young adults with Asperger's syndrome (Andron and Weber 1998; Barnhill *et al.* 2002; Barry *et al.* 2003; Bauminger 2002; Broderick *et al.* 2002; Howlin and Yates 1999; Marriage, Gordon and Brand 1995; Mesibov 1984; Ozonoff and Miller 1995; Soloman, Goodlin-Jones and Anders 2004; Williams 1989). The group members receive information on why certain skills are important, and practise applying those skills using modelling, role-play, reviewing video recordings and receiving constructive feedback from the group leader and fellow participants. The programs have focused on conversation skills, reading and interpreting body language, understanding the perspective of others and friendship skills. A variation on this approach, focusing on the development of emotional intelligence, has been conducted by Andron and Weber (1998), who have coordinated social skills groups using family members, especially siblings, as participants. Their curriculum emphasizes the development of appropriate affect or emotions in social situations.

At present it is extremely difficult to determine whether social skills groups are an effective means of improving the social integration skills of children with Asperger's syndrome. Outcome measures have primarily been qualitative and we do not know if this technique can change specific skills in natural settings. Nevertheless, experience has shown that the groups are perceived as valuable by parents, teachers and participants. In particular, the participants have appreciated the opportunity to meet people similar to themselves who share the same confusion and experiences. This can be the basis of subsequent friendships and self-help groups.

Programs for peers

The other children in the class of the child with Asperger's syndrome will need explanations and guidance in understanding and encouraging the friendship abilities of their classmate. Such children will know that the child with Asperger's syndrome does not play or interact with them in the same way as other children. Without guidance and support from the teacher, the reaction to the child with Asperger's syndrome can be rejection and ridicule rather than acceptance and inclusion in their activities. As much as we have programs to help the child with Asperger's syndrome integrate with his or her peers, the other children need their own programs. They will need to know how to respond to behaviours that appear unfriendly and how to encourage abilities that facilitate friendships. A successful interaction requires a constructive commitment from both parties, and a teacher will need to be a good role model of what to do, and should commend other children who adapt to, welcome and support the child with Asperger's syndrome. The peer group may need their own equivalent of Social Stories™ to improve mutual understanding and to be encouraged to provide guidance for the child with Asperger's syndrome when the teacher is not present or available.

Stage three of friendship – 9 to 13 years

In the third stage in the development of friendships there is a distinct gender split in the choice of friends and companions, and a friend is defined not simply as someone who helps but as someone who is carefully chosen because of special personality attributes. A friend is someone who genuinely cares with complementary attitudes, ideas and values. There is a growing need for companionship and greater selectivity and durability in the friendship alliances. There is a strong desire to be liked by peers and a mutual sharing of experiences and thoughts rather than toys.

With an increase in self-disclosure there is the recognition of the importance of being trustworthy and a tendency to seek advice not only for practical problems but also for interpersonal issues. Friends support each other in terms of repairing each other's emotions. If children are sad, close friends will cheer them up, or if angry, calm them down, to prevent them from getting into trouble.

Friends and the peer group become increasingly important in strengthening or destroying self-esteem and determining what is appropriate social behaviour. Peer-group acceptance and values can override the opinion of parents. The power of the peer group can become greater than the power of adults.

When conflicts occur, friends will now use more effective repair mechanisms. Arguments can be less 'heated', with reduced confrontation and more disengagement, admission of mistakes and recognition that it is not simply a matter of winner and loser. A satisfactory resolution of interpersonal conflict between friends can actually strengthen the relationship. The friend is forgiven and the conflict is put in perspective. These qualities of interpersonal skills that are played out in friendships are the foundation of interpersonal skills for adult relationships.

Programs for stage three
Same-gender friendships

In stage three of friendship, there is usually a clear gender preference in the choice of friends and associates. The activities and interests of boys, who may be playing team games or seasonal sports, may be considered of little interest to boys with Asperger's syndrome. They are also likely to be less able than male peers to understand team games, and clumsy with regard to ball skills, dexterity and coordination. Will Hadcroft explained in his autobiography that:

> I was frightened of the other boys, and this was very apparent to them. Tackling was a nightmare, and I let the ball go without much of a fight, to the fury of my fellow team members. (Hadcroft 2005, p.62)

The boy with Asperger's syndrome knows that he is usually the last person chosen for a team and can be actively shunned and alienated from potential male friends.

When the boy with Asperger's syndrome is alone in the playground, he is likely to be approached by one of two groups: the predatory males who seek someone socially isolated, vulnerable and gullible to tease and torment (see Chapter 4); or girls, who feel sorry for the boy because of his apparent loneliness, and offer inclusion and support in their activities and games. While other boys at this age would usually shun girls, using derogatory and sexist remarks, he can be recruited into the play of girls and actively welcomed. If the boy with Asperger's syndrome is unsure what to do when socializing with girls, his female friends are more likely to be supportive than critical – 'He's a boy so he wouldn't understand, so I'll help him.' There can be the development of genuine 'opposite-gender' friendships.

Having opposite-gender friends at this stage of friendship can have two consequences for boys with Asperger's syndrome; further alienation from boys who consider he is 'fraternizing with the enemy', and absorption within the female culture through imitation, resulting in the development of feminine body language, vocal characteristics and interests. The child may enjoy and benefit from the friendships with girls, but other boys may taunt him as being more like a girl, often using the description 'gay' as an insult. The boy may feel that the only gender to accept and understand him is female – his mother, perhaps his sisters, and his female friends, which could contribute to gender-identity problems.

I have noted that some girls with Asperger's syndrome at this stage of friendship development can reject the companionship of same-gender friends. They may be critical of their peers for enjoying affection and feeling games, and for talking about whom they like or dislike for reasons that seem to be illogical or untrue. The in- and out-group members and rapidly changing friendship cliques are confusing. So too is peer pressure, which can often centre around what is viewed as 'cool' in the way of clothing and accessories. The girl with Asperger's syndrome can have considerable difficulty understanding these new dimensions to friendships, and tends to prioritize logic, truth and comfort over peer pressure. The choice of clothing is likely to be what is comfortable rather than popular or fashionable, and very often this is male clothing, as it is the most comfortable and practical. Hair may be worn very long to create a curtain or wall behind which the girl can 'hide', or very short for convenience, with no desire to appear 'feminine'.

While the activities of other girls can be confusing and illogical to the girl with Asperger's syndrome, the activities of boys can be interesting and based on physical activities rather than emotions. She may be interested in, and then 'adopted' or recruited by, a group of boys. She becomes known as a 'tomboy', with male friends who are more tolerant of someone who has 'come over to their side'; and once again, if she is unsure what to do in a social situation, she is likely to experience support, not ridicule – 'She's a girl, she wouldn't understand. But that's OK, we don't mind.'

The child with Asperger's syndrome needs a balance of same- and opposite-gender friends, and some social engineering could be necessary to ensure acceptance by both gender groups. Teachers will need to monitor group inclusion and exclusion and actively encourage children of the same gender to allow and support the acceptance and integration of the child with Asperger's syndrome.

A mentor or buddy

During stage three of friendship there is a strong desire for companionship rather than functional play, and children with Asperger's syndrome can feel lonely and sad if their attempts at friendship are unsuccessful (Bauminger and Kasari 2000; Carrington and Graham 2001). They will need programs and guidance in friendship, but this may now be achieved by discussion with supportive peers as well as adults. Some typical children who have a natural rapport with children with Asperger's syndrome can be identified and encouraged to be 'buddies' or mentors in the classroom, playground and in social situations. A buddy's advice may be accepted as having greater value than that of parents or teachers, especially if the buddy is socially skilled and popular. A mentor at school, or a sibling, may provide advice and guidance on what is up-to-the-minute from the perspective of the child's peers in terms of what to wear and talk about, so that the child is less conspicuous and less likely to be subjected to ridicule for not being 'cool'.

From the perspective of their peers, children with Asperger's syndrome are 'poor' in terms of the currency of friendship. They may not wear fashionable clothes or be interested in the popular television programmes or merchandise. In return, children with

Asperger's syndrome perceive peers as having limited currency for the Asperger's syndrome culture, namely knowledge. Peta, a girl with Asperger's syndrome who has an encyclopaedic knowledge of the weather, finds other girls her age boring, as they only want to talk about magazines and make-up. She wants to talk about meteorology, which is perceived as equally boring by her peers.

An alternative friendship group

The child with Asperger's syndrome may not easily identify with the new social groups forming during this stage of friendship. The child may be shunned by groups that value sporting abilities due to being clumsy, by academic groups if he or she has a different learning style, and by the groups of socialites because of limited social skills. Unfortunately, there is one group, the disreputable characters, who may accept and include the person with Asperger's syndrome. This group always has an open door, but admission and acceptance is by engaging in inappropriate, anti-social behaviour – not the most appropriate model for children with Asperger's syndrome. A teacher may need to arrange for entry into a more socially acceptable group by encouraging a popular member of that group to act as a mentor or buddy.

Equally, a teacher may consider arranging an alternative group based on the attributes of children with Asperger's syndrome. This group comprises the collectors, scientists or computer experts. Every school will have a few such children who have similar abilities and interests but not the other characteristics needed for a diagnosis. The new group can meet at recess and lunchtime to compare and exchange items of mutual interest (often merchandise based on Japanese animated cartoon characters), undertake a project set by a science teacher, or learn computer-programming techniques from the school information technology teacher. The friendships can be relatively safe from criticism and based on shared interests.

A parent support group may consider publishing a regular newsletter for children and young adolescents with Asperger's syndrome. The contributions can be written by the children and include information on special interests that may be shared by readers and editorial staff, news of group members and examples of their work, reviews of interesting films and books, including books on Asperger's syndrome, and cartoons, editorials, correspondence and advice columns. One teenager considered that his graduation from a social understanding group gave him the qualifications to be a mentor to other adolescents with Asperger's syndrome and provide advice on friendship in the advice column of a school newsletter.

Developing teamwork skills

In early adolescence, children with Asperger's syndrome can become increasingly self-conscious about being different, and resent any suggestion that they might have difficulties making friends or should accept programs. They do not want their social difficulties to be in the 'spotlight' or to be considered a social retard. One option that can enable the pre-adolescent or adolescent to accept programs to improve social and friendship abilities is to change the name of the programs from friendship skills to teamwork skills. All the attributes of a good friend are the same as for a good team member. Class programs on teamwork skills are socially acceptable among peers. Success in sport is valued very highly at this age, especially team sports, and the most successful team does not necessarily comprise the best players, but the most cohesive members. Programs to develop teamwork skills are also relevant to successful employment. Companies often require an applicant to have the ability to be a 'team player', and guidance in teamwork can be accepted by the adolescent with Asperger's syndrome as necessary to achieve his or her career choice. There is then likely to be greater cooperation and motivation.

Drama classes

Another option to help the adolescent who is sensitive to being publicly identified as having few friends and socially naïve is to adapt drama classes. Hans Asperger's nursing sister, Viktorine Zak, at the Vienna Children's Hospital, developed the first programs in the 1940s for children with Asperger's syndrome. She used drama activities to teach the children social skills (Asperger [1944] 1991). When I met Hans Asperger's daughter, Maria, she was able to describe the programs developed by Sister Zak at the children's hospital. Unfortunately, she was killed during an allied bombing raid on Vienna and buried with the child she was clutching and trying to save.

Liane Holliday Willey, in her book *Pretending to be Normal*, describes how she improved her social skills by observation, imitation and acting (Willey 1999). This is an appropriate and effective strategy, especially in stage three of friendship development. The teenager with Asperger's syndrome can learn and practise aspects of adolescent interaction such as suitable conversation topics, the art of being a good listener, expressing affection for someone, and when and how much personal information to disclose. Drama activities can teach appropriate body language, facial expressions and tone of voice, and provide an opportunity for the young person with Asperger's syndrome to act and rehearse responses to specific situations, such as being teased.

Television programmes

Popular television programmes can be used to explain and teach aspects of social behaviour. The *Mr Bean* series in particular can identify the consequences of not being fully aware of someone's thoughts and feelings and of breaking the social codes. The character of Mr Bean and his experiences can be particularly entertaining and informative for children with Asperger's syndrome. The illogical aspects of humans and social conventions can be explored in programmes such as *Third Rock from the Sun*; and science-fiction series such as *Star Trek* provide us with characters (for example, Mr Spock and Data) whose perception, experiences and wisdom are enlightening.

Resources

Towards the end of the book I have provided a list of resources and books that describe and explore aspects of friendship in this age group (and other age groups) for typical children, and are quite informative and entertaining. For example, Judge Judy Sheindlin (2001) has written *You Can't Judge a Book by it's Cover: Cool Rules for School* which includes scenarios associated with friendship that require the child to make social judgements. For example, next to a drawing of a child who has opened his lunch box and looks at his companion with a quizzical expression, there is a description of the situation and a choice of options:

> The salami sandwich that your mother prepared for you is missing from your lunch box. You suspect one of your friends took it because he smells like salami.
> You should:
>
> A.   Ask him if he saw your sandwich
>
> B.   Take his lunch box and search it
>
> C.   Steal his lunch
>
> D.   Tell him your sandwich smells like salami but really is dog food.
>
> (Sheindlin 2001, p.51)

A similar style is used in the book *I Did It, I'm Sorry* by Caralyn Buehner (1998), to explain that there can be more than one correct response to social situations. Unlike the world of science (especially mathematics), there is rarely only one correct solution to a social problem. Children with Asperger's syndrome often seek certainty and the correct and simple solution to a problem. However, the appropriate response or solution in the social world may be based on an evaluation of the merits and consequences of a particular solution for all participants. This requires quite complex reasoning and the ability to make a judgement on the balance of probability and equity, and not certainty. My clinical experience suggests that children with Asperger's syndrome have a limited range of options or solutions for social problems. Some suggestions can be immature, provocative or impulsive, but with encouragement and careful thought, the child can suggest or learn alternative appropriate and more effective solutions.

I also strongly recommend the advice of fellow teenagers with Asperger's syndrome. Luke Jackson, a remarkable and talented young man with Asperger's syndrome, has written a self-help guide for fellow adolescents with Asperger's syndrome (L. Jackson 2002). He provides the following analysis of peer interactions and offers astute advice.

> On the subject of rules, I am sure that all of you AS teenagers have been given some rules on how to behave appropriately. Have you heard of these?
>
> • Don't 'invade people's space' – that means get too close to them.
>
> • Don't stare at someone for whatever reason (however fit they are!).
>
> • Don't make comments about people's bodies, good or bad.

- Don't tell dirty, sexist or racist jokes or make sexual innuendos.

- Don't hug or touch people unless they are part of your family or they have agreed to be your boyfriend or girlfriend and you have both agreed to do it.

If you haven't heard any of those rules, then now you have! Here comes the but…you just watch and listen to a group of teenage boys or girls. First, they will either huddle up together really close or tower over someone in a threatening way. Next they make all sorts of rude comments about the size of people's uh hum…what can I say?! They tell dirty jokes and make sexual innuendos at every opportunity and they will often touch someone or put their arm around them, when they are not a member of their family, their boyfriend or girlfriend.

If these are the rules, then it seems that when boys and girls are in their teenage packs, performing their adolescent rituals, then these rules go out of the window. What a strange world we live in! All in all I would say to stick to the rules and ignore the fact that others seem to be breaking them. (L. Jackson 2002, pp.104–5)

Pre-teens and teenagers with Asperger's syndrome will need advice on puberty and how this will affect their bodies and thinking, but they will also need information and advice on the changing nature of friendship and sexuality. We now have programs and literature developed by Isabelle Hénault to explain puberty and sexuality that have been specifically designed for teenagers with Asperger's syndrome (Hénault 2005).

Stage four of friendship – 13 years to adult

In the previous stage of friendship there may be a small core of close friends but in stage four the number of friends and breadth and depth of friendship increases. There can be different friends for different needs, such as comfort, humour or practical advice. A friend is defined as someone who 'accepts me for who I am' or 'thinks the same way as me about things'. A friend provides a sense of personal identity and is compatible with one's own personality. It is important at this stage that one is able to accept the self before being able to relate to others at an adult level – otherwise friendships may be manipulated as a means of resolving personal issues. There are less concrete and more abstract definitions of friendship, with what may be described as autonomous inter-dependence. The friendships are less possessive and exclusive, and conflict is resolved with self-reflection, compromise and negotiation. During adolescence, friendships are often based on shared interests such as academic achievements, mutual participation in sports and recreational activities and passion for causes such as eradicating world poverty. The person increasingly spends more time with friends than parents, and allegiance can be to friends rather than family.

Young adults with Asperger's syndrome can have a remarkable insight into the difficulties they face in social situations. Scott has Asperger's syndrome and in a college essay wrote:

> Social skills are a foreign language to me. Most of my peer interactions are awkward and unintuitive. I have to guess whether a behaviour is appropriate or not, unlike my friends, who rely on instinct seemingly without effort. These difficulties with navigating life's daily social challenges are the main disadvantage of my neurological disorder, a high-functioning form of autism called Asperger's syndrome that makes it harder for me to lead a normal life. Yet while I get discouraged at times, I do not believe Asperger's syndrome is anything to be ashamed of; it is simply another way of looking at the world. Most people I encounter do not know about Asperger's syndrome and therefore misunderstand my behaviours. My efforts to make friends, for example, have often driven people away. (Personal communication)

Programs for stage four

One of the characteristics of a good friend at stage four is someone 'who accepts me for who I am'. Some adults with Asperger's syndrome have commented to me that no one seemed to accept them for who they were: 'They always wanted me to be different, a copy of themselves.' Eventually the person may find a friend who really does accept him or her – a friend who is not constantly trying to impose change, and who genuinely admires some of the characteristics of Asperger's syndrome.

However, acceptance may come from another source of 'friendship': animals.

Animals as friends

Animals provide unconditional acceptance. The dog is always delighted to see you, despite the day's disappointments and exhaustion. The horse seems to understand you, and wants to be your companion. The cat jumps on your lap, and purrs in your company. I have suggested that cats are autistic dogs, so there may be a natural affinity between cats and people with autism and Asperger's syndrome. Ronald, a mature adult with Asperger's syndrome, wrote to me in an e-mail that 'I only start to be alive and truly natural when alone or with my cats'. Thus, pets, and animals in general, can be effective and successful substitutes for human friends, and a menagerie becomes a substitute 'family'. Animals identify with, and feel relaxed in the company of, a non-predator (the person with Asperger's syndrome), and pets can be a source of comfort and reassurance. A special interest in and natural understanding of animals can become the basis of a successful career (Grandin 1995). And I have found that children and adults with Asperger's syndrome are sometimes more able to perceive and have compassion for the perspective of animals than humans.

Internet friends

The Internet has become the modern equivalent of the dance hall in terms of an opportunity for young people to meet. The great advantage of this form of communication to the person with Asperger's syndrome is that he or she often has a greater eloquence in disclosing and expressing thoughts and feelings through typing rather than face-to-face conversation. In social gatherings the person is expected to be able to listen to and process the other person's speech, often against a background of other conversations, to reply immediately, and simultaneously analyse non-verbal cues such as gestures, facial expression and tone of voice. When using the computer, the person can concentrate on social exchange without being overwhelmed by so many sensory experiences and social signals.

As in any social situation, the person with Asperger's syndrome may be vulnerable to others taking advantage of his or her social naïvety and desire to have a friend. The person with Asperger's syndrome needs to be taught caution and not to provide personal information until he or she has discussed the Internet friendship with someone who can be trusted. However, genuine and long-lasting friendships can develop over the Internet based on shared experiences, interests and mutual support. The Internet provides an opportunity to meet like-minded individuals who accept the person because of his or her knowledge rather than his or her social persona and appearance. Internet 'friends' can share experiences, thoughts and knowledge using chat lines, web pages and message boards dedicated to people with Asperger's syndrome.

Support groups

An interesting recent development is the formation of support groups for adults with Asperger's syndrome, with regular meetings to discuss topics that range from employment issues to personal relationships, and social occasions for the participants, such as excursions to the train museum, or the cinema to see the latest science-fiction film. Friendships can develop between like-minded individuals who share similar experiences and circumstances. There is a variety of ways that support groups can begin. For example, a group can initially be formed by parents of young adults with Asperger's syndrome; or by individuals with Asperger's syndrome who originally met each other in group counselling or therapy sessions and wanted to maintain contact. Older adults with Asperger's syndrome who want to help others who share the same diagnosis and difficulties may form support groups. Groups can be started by final-year college students wanting to help newly enrolled students with Asperger's syndrome; or by someone who used to belong to and benefit from being a member of a support group, who moves to another town and wants to start a support group locally.

In Los Angeles, Jerry Newport founded AGUA, a support group for adults with Asperger's syndrome, and it was at one of the support group meetings that he met Mary, a woman with Asperger's syndrome. The relationship gradually became less platonic and more romantic and eventually Jerry and Mary married each other. Their romance and relationship are portrayed in the film *Mozart and the Whale*.

Information on relationships

Teenagers with Asperger's syndrome may be keen to understand and experience the social and relationship world of their peers, including sexual experiences, but there can be some concerns regarding the source of information on relationships. If the teenager with Asperger's syndrome has few friends with whom she or he can discuss personal topics, such as romantic or sexual feelings for someone, the source of information on relationships may be television programmes ('soap operas' and situation comedies in particular) or pornography. The television dramas and situation comedies often portray intense and dramatic emotions and relationships. The teenager with Asperger's syndrome may remember and apply the actions and script in an inappropriate context. For example, Tim watched a popular situation comedy in which the line 'I want to have sex with you' resulted in considerable laughter from the audience. Tim did not consider the context, only the request, and could not understand why his peers did not laugh when he said the same line to a girl in class. Reading or watching pornography, the teenager with Asperger's syndrome may presume intimate acts occur very quickly in a relationship and will be less aware of any concerns regarding consent.

The source of information on relationships can be same-age peers who may recognize that the person with Asperger's syndrome is naïve, gullible and vulnerable. Peer advisors with cruel intent can provide information and make suggestions that cause the person with Asperger's syndrome to be ridiculed, or encourage others to assume malevolent intentions. The person with Asperger's syndrome can easily be 'set up' and suffer the consequences of deliberately misleading suggestions. It is important that the teenager with Asperger's syndrome has access to accurate information on relationships, especially the early stages in a relationship that goes beyond friendship, and to have someone he or she trusts to provide guidance.

I have known previously socially isolated teenage girls with Asperger's syndrome who, after the physical changes that occur at puberty, have become flattered by the attention of boys. Due to their naïvety, they have not realized that the interest was sexual, and not simply to enjoy their conversation and company. When the teenage girl lacks female friends to provide advice on dating and intimacy there can be concern with regard to promiscuity and sexual experiences. Teenage girls with Asperger's syndrome are often not 'street wise' or able to identify sexual predators, and may become vulnerable to sexual exploitation when desperate to be popular with peers.

Social anxiety

Adolescents, especially girls, with Asperger's syndrome can be increasingly aware of being socially naïve and making a social mistake. The worry about social incompetence and conspicuous errors can lead to the development of a social phobia and increased social withdrawal. Carrie said to me that 'I live in a constant state of performance anxiety over day-to-day social encounters.'

The anxiety can be especially acute at the end of the day, and before falling asleep, when the teenager reviews the social experiences of the day. He or she may now be very aware of what other people may think and this can be a significant cause of anxiety ('I probably made a fool of myself') or depression ('I always make mistakes and always will').

It is essential that teenagers and young adults with Asperger's syndrome receive positive feedback on social competence from parents and peers, and guidance and preparation for what to do and say in social situations. The intention is to change a negative self-perception to a positive or optimistic self-perception, to focus on achievements, not errors. Strategies to change attitudes and self-perception will be explained in the Cognitive Behaviour Therapy section of Chapter 6 and in Chapter 14 on psychotherapy.

Maintaining the friendship

When a friendship does occur, one of the difficulties for people with Asperger's syndrome is knowing how to maintain it. At this stage, the issues are those of knowing how often to make contact, appropriate topics of conversation, what might be suitable gifts, empathic comments and gestures, as well as how to be generous or tolerant with regard to disagreements. There can be a tendency to be 'black or white', such that when a friend makes a transgression the friendship is ended rather than reconciliation sought. A useful strategy is to encourage the person to seek advice from other friends or family members before making a precipitous decision.

Providing a reason for the characteristics of Asperger's syndrome

If a young child is diagnosed with Asperger's syndrome, early intervention designed to improve social abilities in primary or elementary school and continued up to the end of high school can achieve remarkable success. Although so far we do not have any longitudinal research data to substantiate the progress in social understanding and peer relationships, clinical experience can testify to the benefits of social understanding programs for individual children. When someone first acquires the diagnosis in his or her adolescent or adult years, the person has missed the opportunity to benefit from early intervention and, as an adult, is less likely to have access to programs and resources.

An option for such adults is not to seek elusive programs that may take decades to achieve success, but simply to acquire a means of explaining why an attribute of Asperger's syndrome is confusing to friends, colleagues or acquaintances. For example, the person with Asperger's syndrome may not look at the other person as much as would be expected in a conversation, and especially when answering a question. Rather than undertake a program to know when to look at someone and read facial expressions, I recommend explaining the avoidance of eye contact: for example, 'I need to look away to help me concentrate on answering your question. I am not being rude, dishonest or disrespectful.' When talking about a special interest that is likely to be perceived as boring, the person with Asperger's syndrome may say, before starting the monologue, 'Sometimes I talk too much about my interests. If I am boring you, please ask me to stop. I will not think you are being rude.' The person creates a spoken Social Story™ for typical people to explain what appears to be eccentric or rude behaviour.

When given a succinct and accurate explanation, the typical person can be less confused by and more tolerant of the characteristics of Asperger's syndrome. The person with Asperger's syndrome may need some guidance in thinking of an explanation. However, I have noted that the parent or partner of an adult with Asperger's syndrome may have been providing such explanations to other people for many years.

Moving to another culture

I frequently give presentations on Asperger's syndrome in many countries throughout the world. When in countries with a very different culture to my own, I am amazed at the number of people from English-speaking countries who have Asperger's syndrome in the audience. When I was last in Japan, I met Richard, a charming man from England, who has lived in the Far East for several years. Richard explained that if he makes a social error in Japan, his behaviour is acknowledged as being due to cultural differences, not a deliberate attempt to offend or confuse. The Japanese are remarkably tolerant of his social clumsiness, especially as he is very keen to speak Japanese and clearly admires the culture. Stephen Shore explained to me in an e-mail that 'some people (me included) with Asperger's syndrome enjoy visiting and even living in foreign countries for extended periods of time. Their differences and "social blindness" are then attributed to being in a foreign country rather than a mistaken assumption of wilful behaviour.'

The person with Asperger's syndrome may also make friends with visitors to his or her culture. Visitors sometimes share the same challenges integrating into a new culture as the 'native' with Asperger's syndrome.

Friendships with colleagues

Due to a developmental delay in the conceptualization of friendship, when the person with Asperger's syndrome reaches stage four of friendship development, he or she may have left high school and be seeking friends through work, college and recreational pursuits. Attempts to change a relationship from colleague or workmate to friend can present some challenges to the young adult with Asperger's syndrome. A mentor at work who understands his or her unusual personality and friendship skills can provide guidance and act as a confidant and advocate.

The mentor can also help determine the degree of genuine interest in friendship from the colleague. Sometimes people with Asperger's syndrome assume that a friendly act, smile or gesture has greater implications than was intended, and this may lead to the development of an intense interest or infatuation with a person who appears kind and friendly.

The duration of socializing

We each have a limited capacity for the duration of social contact. I use the metaphor of filling a 'social bucket'. Some typical individuals have a large social bucket that can take some time to fill, while the person with Asperger's syndrome has a small bucket, or cup, that reaches capacity relatively quickly. Conventional social occasions can last too long for someone with Asperger's syndrome, especially as social success is achieved by intellectual effort rather than natural intuition. Socializing is exhausting.

The person with Asperger's syndrome is more comfortable if social interactions are brief and purposeful, and when complete, he or she is able to end the interaction or participation. It is important that others are not offended by an abrupt ending to a conversation or social gathering, as offence was not intended. The person must leave due to exhaustion and is not being inconsiderate.

Another characteristic that can affect the duration of social contact is the difficulty people with Asperger's syndrome have in finding someone that they want to talk to and spend time with. As Darren said to me, 'It's not that I'm anti-social, it's that I don't meet many people that I like.'

THE PROGNOSIS FOR THE DEVELOPMENT OF SOCIAL UNDERSTANDING

Hans Asperger considered that:

> Normal children acquire the necessary social habits without being consciously aware of them, they learn instinctively. It is these instinctive relations that are disturbed in autistic children. Social adaptation has to proceed via the intellect. (Asperger [1944] 1991, p.58)

There may be two ways to acquire a skill – intuition or instruction. Children and adults with Asperger's syndrome will need tuition in specific social skills. I recommend that the learning process include an explanation of the rationale for the specific social rule. The child with Asperger's syndrome will not change his or her behaviour unless the reason is logical. The teaching style is that of making a mutual discovery in the social world. The person with Asperger's syndrome is almost an anthropologist, conducting research on a newly discovered culture; and the 'teacher' or representative of the culture will need to discover and appreciate the perspective, different way of thinking and culture of the person with Asperger's syndrome. It is important not to make a value judgement that one culture is superior to the other.

Those with Asperger's syndrome can perceive typical people as social zealots who assume that everyone can and should socialize without effort, and that anyone who does not prioritize and excel at socializing must be defective, ridiculed and corrected. There needs to be a compromise between the two cultures. Those in the typical culture communicate in 'social telegrams' assuming the other person can fill in the gaps.

Such assumptions should not be made when engaged in a social interaction with someone with Asperger's syndrome. Also, typical people may complain that the person with Asperger's syndrome is not good at explaining why he or she did something that appeared to contravene the social codes; but, equally, typical people are not good at explaining the exceptions to the codes and reasons for their social behaviour.

When considering the prognosis for social interaction skills, Hans Asperger (1938) wrote that:

> These children can take note of 'rules of etiquette' given to them in a down-to-earth kind of way, which then they can fulfil – like they would a sum. The more 'objective' such a law is – maybe in a form of schedule, which includes all possible variations of daily routines, and which must be stuck to by both parties in the most pedantic kind of way – the better it will be. So it is not through a habit, which unconsciously and instinctively grows by itself, but through conscious, intellectual training, in years of difficult and conflict-ridden work, that one will achieve the best possible assimilation to the community, which will be more and more successful with growing intellectual maturity. (Asperger 1938, p.10)

Gradually the person with Asperger's syndrome can build a mental library of social experiences and social rules. The process is similar to learning a foreign language with all the problems of exceptions to the rule for pronunciation and grammar. Some adults with Asperger's syndrome consider that social conversations appear to use a completely different language, for which they have no translation and which no one has explained to them.

I use the metaphor of a social jigsaw puzzle of 5000 pieces. Typical people have the picture on the box of the completed puzzle, the innate ability to know how to relate or connect to fellow humans. The social puzzle is completed in childhood relatively easily. The picture on the box, or intuition, can generally be relied on to solve a social problem. The child with Asperger's syndrome does not have the picture, and tries to identify the connections and pattern from experience and, one would hope, some guidance. Eventually, some pieces of the social puzzle fit together in small groups of disconnected 'islands', and after three or four decades, a pattern is recognized and the completion of the puzzle accelerates. Some people with Asperger's syndrome are eventually able to socialize reasonably well, with typical people unaware of the mental energy, support, understanding and education that is required to achieve such success. Perhaps the final words in this chapter should be from Liane Holliday Willey who, in her autobiography *Pretending to be Normal*, wrote:

> Looking far over my shoulder, I can call to mind people who must have been interested in friendship. I can see a boy I knew as if it was yesterday. I can remember his face and the expressions he made as we talked. Today if he looked at me like he did then, I believe I would have seen the kindness and gentleness that was his. I never did much with this boy when I had the chance. I missed his offer of friendship. I would not miss that offer if it were made today. His face would make sense to me today. (Willey 1999, pp.61–2)

KEY POINTS AND STRATEGIES

Stage 1

- An adult can act as a friend to the child.
- Teach the child to take turns and ask for help.
- Organize a dress rehearsal with another child.
- Encourage the child to watch a video recording of children playing.
- Play pretend games with the child.
- Give encouragement to the child for being friendly.
- Write Social Stories™ to help the child understand specific social situations.
- Use 'social signals' activity to teach the social signs to prevent social accidents.

Stage 2

- Use role-play activities to provide practice in aspects of cooperative play.
- Provide a teacher assistant in the classroom and playground to offer guidance and feedback for the child and his or her friends.
- Encourage boys and girls to play with figures or dolls and read fiction.
- Seek shared interests with like-minded children.
- Help the child to develop a sense of humour.
- Use concentric circles to help the child to learn social conventions for greetings, topics of conversation, touch and personal body space and gestures of affection.
- Teach the child what not to say.
- Be the guide to the child as 'anthropologist' in the classroom to explain social customs.
- Ensure that after-school social experiences are brief, structured, supervised, successful and voluntary.
- Enrol the child in social skills groups.
- Provide programs for peers on how to play with and be a friend of someone with Asperger's syndrome.

Stage 3

- Encourage same-gender and opposite-gender friendships.
- Encourage a peer to become a mentor or buddy to the child.
- Help the child to find and join an alternative group of friends who have similar interests and values.
- Introduce programs to develop teamwork skills as a way to teach friendship skills.
- Encourage the child to attend drama classes.
- Use television programmes, especially situation comedies and science fiction, to illustrate aspects of social behaviour.
- Use books and resources to teach friendship skills.

Stage 4

- Encourage the person to view animals as potential friends.
- Encourage the person to use the Internet as a source of friendship.
- Suggest the value of support groups for young adults with Asperger's syndrome.
- Provide information on relationships.
- Explore different strategies to reduce performance anxiety in social situations.
- Provide guidance on how to maintain a friendship.
- Teach the person how to explain the characteristics of Asperger's syndrome to someone.
- Explore the advantages of moving to another culture.
- Provide guidance on friendships with work colleagues.
- Encourage the person to limit the duration of socializing if necessary.

CHAPTER 4

Teasing and Bullying

Autistic children are often tormented and rejected by their class-mates simply because they are different and stand out from the crowd. Thus, in the playground or on the way to school one can often see an autistic child at the centre of a jeering horde of little urchins. The child himself may be hitting out in blind fury or crying helplessly. In either case he is defenceless.

– Hans Asperger ([1944] 1991)

The programs and activities described in Chapter 3 were designed to increase the social knowledge and integration of children and adolescents with Asperger's syndrome. Parents and teachers hope that the integration will be enjoyable and successful, but while some children will be welcoming, 'maternal' and kind to the child with Asperger's syndrome, some will be 'predatory' and consider the child with Asperger's syndrome as an easy target for teasing and bullying.

TYPES OF TEASING

From my clinical experience, the comments most frequently used as an act of verbal teasing or abuse when the target is a child with Asperger's syndrome are 'stupid' (or 'retard'), 'psycho' and 'gay'. These comments, intended to be derogatory, can be observed in the interactions of typical children but can have more significance for children with Asperger's syndrome. Such children value intellectual ability as one of their strengths, which can be a constructive form of compensation for low social self-esteem if they are not successful in social situations. To be called 'stupid' is a signifi-cant personal insult and likely to create considerable distress. The insult of 'psycho' can also be perceived as a personally meaningful insult, especially if the child has to see psy-chologists and psychiatrists and take medication. The child may start to question his or her sanity and worry about the potential for future mental disturbance. Unfortunately, in schools today, the description 'gay' is perceived as a powerful insult. Children with Asperger's syndrome may make a literal interpretation of the comments of other children, and assume that the description could be genuine and that they may indeed be homosexual. Thus, a few comments designed to confuse, tease or infuriate can have life-long implications for the child with Asperger's syndrome.

Sometimes the play of other children includes teasing and physical discomfort though the intention is friendly. Children, especially boys, will engage in 'puppy fighting', and tease with the intention of sharing the humour. Typical children as young as three years can distinguish between real and pretend or play fighting, when the intention is not malicious (Rubin 2002). When both parties laugh and enjoy the experience it is not bullying, but the child with Asperger's syndrome will have difficulty determining the intention – was it a friendly act or not? Other children may soon become reluctant to interact with a child who is too quick to assume malicious intent.

WHAT IS BULLYING?

If one asks friends, colleagues and children to define bullying, the responses are considerably varied. One person's example of bullying can be another person's idea of entertainment. It is important for a school to agree on a definition to ensure consistency in policies and strategies. Clearly, bullying includes a power imbalance, intent to harm (physically or emotionally) and a distressed target. Gray (2004a) reviewed the literature on bullying in childhood, and used her extensive knowledge of children with Asperger's syndrome to define bullying as 'repeated negative actions with negative intent towards a targeted individual over time, with an imbalance in the power (physically, verbally, socially and/or emotionally) within the interaction' (p.8).

There are some places and circumstances at school where bullying is more common, such as hallways, on school transport, during sports and in situations when the incident is less likely to be detected by an adult. Bullying can also occur close to the child's home by children of neighbours, family friends and older siblings. Bullying usually occurs with a peer audience or bystanders and can take a wide variety of forms. The most common are verbal or physical confrontation and intimidation, injury and destruction of personal property, and derogatory gestures or comments. If adults committed such actions, they would be liable to receive criminal convictions for assault, be reprimanded by their employers for harassment, or dismissed.

There are other types of bullying that are perhaps more subtle but devastating in their effects. Someone might openly steal a possession such as a hat and torment the child as he or she tries to retrieve it; or engage in malicious gossip, spreading rumours; or make comments that cause humiliation; or use obscene gestures. Another form of bullying that frequently occurs with children with Asperger's syndrome is peer shunning or social exclusion, such as not being included in a group at meal times, not having questions answered, deliberately being chosen last in a game or team, or not being invited to a social event. While parents and teachers are encouraging the child with Asperger's syndrome to interact with his or her peers, some typical children do not welcome the child's request to join the conversation or activity. Improved social skills are of little practical value if peers deliberately and maliciously reject the child with Asperger's syndrome.

There are types of bullying experienced by children but committed by adults, such as a relative or family friend enjoying teasing or playing practical jokes. However, this may also include examples of educational bullying by a teacher. The definition of a bullying act is confirmed when a teacher uses his or her position of authority to ridicule and humiliate a child, respond with sarcasm, be overly critical or punitive, or use facial expressions that discredit or reflect non-acceptance (such as a glance that indicates to the class 'I think he's stupid'). Such actions can create a model of behaviour and demonstrate approval for similar acts between class peers and the child who is the target of the adult's acts of bullying.

Some forms of bullying are relatively rare for typical children but in my clinical experience appear to be more common when the target of a bullying action is a child with Asperger's syndrome. Because such children are often socially naïve, trusting, and eager to be part of a group, they are able to be 'set up' by other children. For example, another child may make a socially inappropriate or bizarre suggestion, and the child with Asperger's syndrome, who has limited social understanding and is not 'street wise' (and therefore does not recognize the social meaning, context, cues and consequences), can be persuaded to follow this through. Another child or adult, unaware of what went before, assumes that the child with Asperger's syndrome was fully aware of the significance and implications of what he or she said or did. The consequent rebuke or punishment of the child with Asperger's syndrome becomes a cause for amusement by those who made the suggestion or gave false information.

In Will Hadcroft's autobiography he explained that:

> Being quite shy and timid often proved to be traumatic. The bullies would home in on these traits and take advantage of them. I was very easy to wind up because I believed everything I was told. Often when children innocently asked me questions I would be unable to discern whether they were being sincere or were in fact setting me up. (Hadcroft 2005, p.38)

Another act of bullying is to torment the child with Asperger's syndrome (ensuring that a teacher does not detect the provocation) and enjoy the benefits of the child's reaction. Children with Asperger's syndrome can be impulsive in their response to such goading without thinking of the consequences to themselves. Other young children in the same situation would delay their response so as not to be 'caught', or would recognize how to respond without getting into trouble. When the child with Asperger's syndrome retaliates with anger to this provocation, perhaps causing damage or injury, the covert 'operative' appears to be the innocent victim, and receives compensation from the supervising adult.

Covert bullying, because of the havoc that often ensues, can also be used to avoid a class activity or examination. When I was examining the circumstances regarding several disruptive classroom incidents involving a child with Asperger's syndrome, I was told by the child's classmates that they encouraged his emotional outbursts. Since the teacher would then be preoccupied with taking the child to the school principal for punishment, they could successfully avoid having to do a class test or exam.

The social naïvety of children with Asperger's syndrome can lead to an unusual form of bullying, described by Gray (2004a) as backhanded bullying. The other child initially appears friendly but subsequent actions are certainly not friendly. An example is provided by Luke Jackson, a teenager with Asperger's syndrome who has written a self-help guidebook for adolescents with Asperger's syndrome (L. Jackson 2002). He described how another child approached him with apparently friendly gestures and conversation while his accomplice crouched down on his hands and knees directly behind Luke. The 'friend' in front of him then pushed Luke so he fell backwards over the accomplice, was unable to prevent his fall and hit his head on concrete, resulting in his being concussed.

Nita Jackson's autobiography provides another example of backhanded bullying.

> They would approach me – the short, timid fat girl – at break time, saying how guilty they felt for taunting me and asking me to accept a seemingly unopened packet of crisps, can of fizzy drink or bag of chips as a token of apology. They would stand around while I reached into the bag of crisps (which I suddenly noticed were already open but thought nothing more of it) or chips, shoved a huge handful into my mouth and chomped…and chomped until I suddenly noticed a tingling sensation inside my mouth. The tingling sensation grew and before I knew it my whole mouth was burning – the kids had sprinkled the crisps or chips with hellishly spicy curry powder.
>
> But it was the cans of drink that were the worst. The bullies would put ants, worms, maggots or even wasps in the drinks. Fortunately, I never got stung by the wasps, but I did swallow a few ants, maggots and worms. (N. Jackson 2002, p.26)

HOW COMMON IS BULLYING FOR CHILDREN WITH ASPERGER'S SYNDROME?

A recent study of the prevalence and frequency of bullying in a sample of more than 400 children with Asperger's syndrome, whose ages were between 4 and 17 years, found the reported rate of bullying to be at least four times higher than for their peers (Little 2002). More than 90 per cent of mothers of children with Asperger's syndrome who completed the survey reported that their children had been the target of some form of bullying within the previous year. The pattern of bullying was different from that in the general population, with a higher-than-expected level of shunning and, in the teenage years, one in ten adolescents with Asperger's syndrome was a victim of peer gang attack. Another form of bullying reported in the survey that occurred at a greater level than experienced by peers was non-sexual genital assaults on boys. Unfortunately, this prevalence study by Little may be a conservative estimate of bullying experiences, as targets can be reluctant to report acts of bullying to their parents (Hay *et al.* 2004).

WHY ARE CHILDREN WITH ASPERGER'S SYNDROME MORE LIKELY TO BE A TARGET?

A study of the bullying of typical children suggests that there are passive and proactive bullying targets (Voors 2000). Passive targets are usually physically weaker children, who are anxious in a social setting, have low self-esteem and lack confidence. They are shy, loners and, while having academic abilities, may not be successful in sports nor have an extensive network of friends. They also tend to be passive in terms of their response to being a target, more likely to relinquish possessions and less likely to retaliate with anger or be supported by peers. This could be a description of the 'passive' personality and abilities of some children with Asperger's syndrome.

Proactive bullying targets also have difficulties with friendship skills. Peers and adults perceive the social skills and social maturity of these children as being intrusive, irritating and provocative. They may not know how to read a social situation or have a constructive role in the interaction. For example, the child may not know how to join or play with a group of children, and relies on inappropriate behaviour such as wrestling, being 'attention seeking', or dominating, and fails to respond to the signals to stop. The response of other children can be that 'he deserved it' or 'it was the only way to stop her'. The profile of a typical child who is a proactive target is also applicable to some young children with Asperger's syndrome, who want to participate but do not know how.

Another reason that children with Asperger's syndrome are more likely to be the target of bullying acts is that they often actively seek and need quiet solitude in the playground. They may be able to cope reasonably well with the social demands of the classroom, but when class is over they are mentally and emotionally exhausted. Their restorative for mental and emotional energy is solitude, in contrast to other typical young children whose emotional restoratives in the playground are being noisy, active and sociable. Unfortunately, one of the prime characteristics of a target for bullying is being alone. When children with Asperger's syndrome re-energize by isolating themselves from their peers, they are placing themselves in circumstances that are more likely to make them potential targets of teasing and bullying.

My clinical experience suggests that children with Asperger's syndrome can have difficulties with aspects of characterization: that is, the capacity to identify the personality descriptions of their peers (see Chapter 14, p.321). Consequently, children with Asperger's syndrome have problems distinguishing the 'good guys' from the 'bad guys'. Other children will instinctively know which children to avoid and whether or not someone is to be trusted. Without this 'radar' and identification system, children with Asperger's syndrome are often unable to avoid those children who are notorious for teasing and bullying.

One of the reasons some adolescent boys or girls with Asperger's syndrome may become a target is that they may not adopt the conventional signs of masculinity or femininity in terms of clothing, hair style, mannerisms and interests expected of their gender. As Clare Sainsbury describes, 'We are largely immune to gender stereotyping and do not limit ourselves on the basis of what is deemed proper for girls or boys – but it can also be yet another cause for bullying and isolation' (Sainsbury 2000, p.82).

THE SIGNS OF BEING BULLIED

Children with Asperger's syndrome are less likely than their peers to report being a target for bullying or teasing as they have impaired Theory of Mind abilities; that is, they have difficulty determining the thoughts and intentions of others in comparison to their peers (Attwood 2004d; Baron-Cohen 1995). Children with Asperger's syndrome may not intuitively know that the acts of other children are examples of bullying. They sometimes consider that such behaviour is typical play and something that they have come to accept as yet another example of the confusing behaviour of their peers.

Other children will know the advantages of telling someone their practical, social and emotional problems. Children with Asperger's syndrome tend to solve academic and social problems on their own; asking for guidance and help from another person may not be considered as a solution to the problem of being a target of bullying. Adults may become aware of the child being a target for bullying and teasing from evidence other than the child disclosing what has happened. Stephen Shore explained to me that 'It never occurred to me to tell my parents of my difficulties with bullying in elementary school. They found out from a lunch monitor.'

There may be physical evidence in terms of lost or damaged possessions or torn clothing, and visible evidence of injury in terms of abrasions, cuts and bruising. There can be some psychological evidence in terms of an increase in anxiety, which in turn may affect the gastro-intestinal system, such that the child suffers genuine stomach pains, constipation or diarrhoea. There may be evidence of other potentially stress-related conditions such as sleep disturbance and a reluctance to go to school, with an avoidance of certain areas.

I have noted that the frequent bullying of children with Asperger's syndrome, sometimes as young as six years, has led to their being referred for the treatment of clinical depression. Sometimes, when repeated requests by the child with Asperger's syndrome for the bullying to stop have failed, as have ignoring the bullying or reporting it to an adult, the degree of depression experienced by the child is such that he or she feels there is no other option but suicide. This is perceived as the only way to stop the emotional pain that bullying is causing in the child's daily life.

Another extreme outcome is for the child to respond with violence in an attempt to deter the bullying. This can include an unexpectedly ferocious physical response, or the use of weapons that could lead to a fatal injury. The child with Asperger's syndrome may be suspended from school for violent retaliation, or face criminal charges for assault; but a close examination of the circumstances that led to the assault indicate that the escalating frequency and nature of the bullying had become intolerable for the child. He or she felt driven to this violent response due to the failure of all other conventional and recommended strategies to stop the bullying.

I have identified other signs of being a target of bullying. There can be a change in the special interests, from relatively benign topics, such as vehicles and insects, to an interest in weapons, the martial arts and violent films, especially films with a theme of retribution. The child's drawings may also express violence, retaliation and retribution.

In her autobiography, Nita Jackson describes the effects of bullying on her imagination and self-esteem:

> Despite being a loser in every sense, I maintained a belief that somehow I'd get my revenge. I devised elaborate plots, detailing how I'd do this. I drew pictures, I wrote stories. In my fantasy life I was victorious, courageous, strong and popular. I intended to achieve this by the time I reached my teens.
>
> But the courage never arrived, and my planned revenge never happened. Thirteen came miserably, and went, with me still a loner and a pathetic weakling, easily suppressed by the bullies and subservient to their demands – mute and grovelling like some unworthy slave to his master's feet. I felt like less of a person and more of a corpulent object to be abused. I had the personality of a slug on valium, never uttering a word to my peers except 'sorry'. I actually didn't feel worthy to be liked. (N. Jackson 2002, p.24)

Children with Asperger's syndrome may also mimic the acts of the children who are bullying them, when they are playing with younger siblings at home. However, the child may not be aware that such behaviour is unacceptable and may simply be imitating the behaviour experienced when interacting with peers, or repeating the acts of bullying to try to understand why someone would choose to behave that way.

THE EFFECTS OF BULLYING ON CHILDREN WITH ASPERGER'S SYNDROME

Research has confirmed that typical children who are the target of bullying are at greater risk for low self-esteem, increased levels of anxiety and depression, lower academic achievement, and increased social isolation (Hodges, Malone and Perry 1997; Ladd and Ladd 1998; Olweus 1992; Slee 1995). The psychological consequences of bullying in the typical population can last for more than ten years (Olweus 1992). Children with Asperger's syndrome are more prone to these consequences because of their already low self-esteem, predisposition to anxiety (see Chapter 6) and difficulty understanding why someone would behave that way, questioning why they were the target and what else they could have done to stop it. Clinical experience suggests that the psychological consequences of being the target of frequent bullying and teasing are likely to last many years and be a major contributor to clinical depression, anxiety disorder and problems with anger management.

I have discussed incidents of bullying during childhood with adults with Asperger's syndrome, and noted that they have considerable difficulty understanding why they were the target so often, or the motivation of the children who tormented them. Their main way of trying to understand why they were singled out is to repeatedly replay the events in their thoughts. The person is re-living but not resolving past injustices. This can be a daily experience, even though the incidents occurred decades earlier. As the event is repeated in their thoughts, so are the emotions experienced again. Adults with Asperger's syndrome may require psychotherapy to overcome the deep and entrenched traumas caused by being the target of persistent bullying, which often began in early childhood. They cannot easily forgive and forget, or have closure, until they understand why.

STRATEGIES TO REDUCE THE FREQUENCY AND EFFECTS OF BULLYING

Unfortunately, acts of bullying occur in all schools and this behaviour is not exclusive to childhood. Bullying occurs in the workplace. Over hundreds of years there have been various strategies that have been accepted as conventional wisdom to reduce the frequency and the effects of bullying, but we have only recently had research to determine the proven effectiveness of these strategies (Smith, Pepler and Rigby 2004). The following strategies are based on recent evaluation studies that have significantly reduced the frequency of bullying.

A team approach

It is essential to have a team approach to reduce the frequency of bullying. The team includes the target of the bullying, school administration, teachers, parents, a child psychologist, other children, and the child who engages in acts of bullying (Gray 2004a; Heinrichs 2003; Olweus 1993). It is important that schools develop and implement a code of conduct that specifically defines bullying and ways to stop it. The definition should be broad and not restricted to acts of intimidation and injury. There will need to be staff education, and consensus and consistency in determining what are bullying actions and what are appropriate consequences.

Staff training

The first stage in a program to reduce bullying in a school and for an individual child is a staff in-service training program. Staff will need to be trained in how to supervise situations where bullying is more likely to occur, how to respond to acts of bullying, and how to provide appropriate consequences and resolution.

Equitable justice

The concept of justice is extremely important. Before considering the degree of responsibility, it will be necessary to conduct a calm and objective assessment of all the facts – to be an impartial detective. The degree of injury or damage should not be viewed as the *only* measure of the degree of responsibility and consequences. The child with Asperger's syndrome may have been the target of many acts of bullying over a considerable length of time and has eventually responded with an act of physical aggression, which may be dramatic but is sometimes the only means the child knows of stopping such acts.

If the educational setting has consequences for acts of physical aggression, then the child with Asperger's syndrome must experience those consequences. However, it is my opinion that those who tormented the child and caused the act of aggression should receive the same punishment. This would be consistent with the concept of equitable justice, the notion of having a moral responsibility for the acts of others, and the criminal justice system for adults. If children with Asperger's syndrome do not perceive justice to have been done, they may take the law into their own hands to seek retribution, using the conflict resolution strategy of 'an eye for an eye', with the intent of inflicting equal discomfort. Children with Asperger's syndrome are more likely to seek retribution by physical than by verbal retaliation.

The Scales of Justice activity

I developed the 'Scales of Justice' activity to help a child who tends to make immature, egocentric or incorrect attributions of the degree of responsibility in situations of conflict, which can include teasing and bullying, between the child and others. Typical children with a developmental level of under nine years tend to attribute the degree of responsibility for an action in terms of who started it, which can appear to justify almost any retaliation, and fail to make an accurate judgement of the severity of their own response and the degree of consequences for themselves and others in making that response. At this stage of cognitive development, conflict resolution can be 'an eye for an eye' with the infliction of at least equal, if not more, discomfort. When an adult administers 'justice', the response of the child can be that it is not fair, according to his or her perception of responsibility, conflict resolution and retribution.

The 'Scales of Justice' is an interactive, educational strategy using visual reasoning to help the child understand the degree of importance – the 'weight' – given to particular acts and why, 'on balance', the 'weight' of evidence is used to determine the degree of responsibility and consequences. In English, we may use the comment 'six of one and half a dozen of the other' when attributing responsibility for conflict, and this was the comment on which I based this activity.

The first stage is to determine who was involved in a particular incident. Each participant has his or her name on a separate piece of paper, and all the named pieces of paper are placed on a table in front of the child. If there are only two participants in the sequence of events, then it is possible to dispense with the names on pieces of paper and actually use a set of scales. The adult has at least 20 wooden or plastic blocks in a container. The number of blocks measures the degree of importance that we attribute to a particular act. A relatively minor infringement of the codes of behaviour may be 'judged' as worth one or two blocks while actions that are major transgressions of the code that perhaps could or did result in serious harm or damage would be represented by many more blocks.

The child is asked to describe the sequence of events, from his or her perspective. As the story progresses, when a participant in the sequence of events makes a decision to do or say something that breaks the codes of conduct, the child is asked to determine what he or she thinks the words or actions (or lack of actions) are 'worth' in terms of the number of blocks. The child may need some guidance with regard to why the number of blocks that he or she attributes to the act may need to be adjusted. This can include information on the effect of the act on a person's feelings, the degree of potential physical injury and cost of repairing damaged items. When the number of blocks is determined, that number of blocks is placed on the name of the person who did the act. This procedure continues during the recall of the events. Each participant will acquire a number of blocks and, at the end of the description of events, the number of blocks for each participant is calculated by the child.

This procedure is designed to enable the child to see the relative importance of what he or she and others did that justified the consequences for all those involved. Perhaps one of the most effective ways of describing the procedure is to provide a summary of how the Scales of Justice activity was used when debriefing a child with Asperger's syndrome who had a strong feeling of injustice for being suspended from school.

There were three participants in the incident: Eric, a child with Asperger's syndrome, who was 11 years old but whose level of conflict resolution and empathy was as least two years behind his chronological age; another child, Steven; and a teacher who was a temporary replacement for the usual class teacher.

Steven started the conflict by calling Eric a 'w***er' (an obscene expression in Australia). I asked Eric how many blocks that comment was worth and he replied, and we agreed on, a weight of two blocks for Steven. I asked Eric what he did next and he replied that he ignored him. My judgement was that that was the wise thing to do, so no blocks for Eric. I asked him if the teacher (who had overheard the comment about Eric) reprimanded Steven and Eric replied 'No' so we agreed that the teacher's lack of intervention was worthy of one block. Then Steven called Eric a 'f***ing w***er' and we agreed that that was worth four blocks. I asked Eric what the teacher did and he replied that the teacher did not hear Steven's comment, so no blocks for the teacher; but I asked Eric if he told the teacher what Steven had said and he replied 'No' so I suggested that Eric should have one block for not reporting the next level of provocation. I then asked Eric what he did when he heard the description of himself and he replied that he said the same words to Steven, so he had four blocks placed on his name.

I asked what happened next. Eric described how Steven came up to his desk and scribbled over Eric's work that he had been doing in class. We agreed that this act was worth two blocks. At this stage, Steven's piece of paper had eight blocks, Eric's paper five and the teacher's one. After the scribbling on his work (which was not seen by the teacher), I asked Eric if he reported the incident, and he replied 'No,' so he had another block. I asked what he did next and he described how he hit Steven in the face with his fist as retribution and to make him stop tormenting him.

'Was there lots of blood?'

'Yes.'

'Where on his face did you hit him?'

'His nose.'

I then explained the degree of potential injury from hitting someone in the face, how painful it would be and the school rules on violence. We agreed that his response was valued at 12 blocks. He could see that although Steven started it, and committed more provocative acts than Eric, by hitting Steven in the face, Eric eventually had 18 blocks, Steven eight, and the teacher one. This was used to explain and to encourage him to accept why he was suspended from school and Steven was not suspended.

A map of the child's world

Carol Gray (2004a) recommends creating a map of the child's world and identifying places where the child is vulnerable to or safe from acts of bullying. Some areas will need more supervision, and more safe havens can be created. One of the problems with a prevention program that relies primarily on staff surveillance is that acts of bullying are usually covert, with only around 15 per cent of such actions observed by a teacher in the classroom and only 5 per cent in the playground (Pepler and Craig 1999). However, other children often witness acts of bullying and they will need to be key participants in the program.

Positive peer pressure

The code of conduct on bullying in schools should include input from peers. There should be regular class discussions to review the code, specific incidents and strategies. The children themselves may need their own training program on bullying. The program can include information on the long-term consequences for both those children who commit acts of bullying and for their targets. Those children known to bully others need to be reminded of the short-term consequences in terms of the agreed code of conduct and punishments, as well as of the long-term consequences on their ability to form friendships and achieve successful employment. They should also be alerted to their risk of developing mood disorders and the greater possibility of committing criminal offences. The 'silent' majority of children, who are not involved in bullying as either perpetrator or target, need to be encouraged to rescue both the child who is the target of, and the child who engages in, bullying.

Bystanders, who generally find it disturbing to witness acts of bullying, will need new strategies and encouragement to respond constructively to such acts. Their previous responses may have included relief that they are not the target; being immobilized by fear of being a target themselves if they intervene; having a diffused sense of responsibility by being in the majority group; not being sure what to do; being advised not to get involved; and adherence to a code of silence, with peer pressure not to report what is happening. Unfortunately, some bystanders can perceive the event as being humorous or deserved by the target, which provides overt encouragement for the child committing the bullying act. They can be taught to state clearly that what is happening is wrong, that it must stop, and that if it does not stop it will be reported. This may mean stepping between the perpetrator and the target. There are some children within the silent majority who have a high social status, a strong sense of social justice and natural assertiveness. These children can be personally encouraged, and can be highly successful in intervening, to stop bullying. Their high social status may also encourage other children to express their disapproval. Peer pressure can reduce bullying.

I suggest that part of the children's code on bullying should include commendations for a positive intervention by a bystander, but that other children who were present but did not try to intervene should experience some consequences for their inaction, which has indirectly enabled the bullying to occur. There needs to be group responsibility for acts of omission rather than commission: in other words, consequences for what they did *not* do.

A guardian

The teacher can encourage a 'buddy' or guardian system, with the guardian recruited from the group of high social status children with a social conscience. His or her role is to monitor the circumstances of the child with Asperger's syndrome, to report any incident confidentially, to encourage the target to report the incident, and to state publicly that the situation is not funny and that the teasing or bullying must stop.

Another valuable characteristic of the guardian is to repair the emotional and self-esteem damage inflicted on the child or adolescent with Asperger's syndrome. An adult may be sympathetic and provide reassurance but the restorative value of a supportive comment from a popular peer can be a very effective antidote.

Sometimes the child with Asperger's syndrome is unaware that the actions of another child are acts of teasing and bullying. The monitor or guardian should be a socially aware child who is easily able to distinguish between friendly and non-friendly acts, and respond accordingly. The guardian can also rescue the child with Asperger's syndrome in situations that adults find difficult to monitor.

Liane Holliday Willey describes in her autobiography an example of the benefits of her guardian, Craig.

> I am amazed my peers put up with me and my peculiarities. Truth be known, they may not have, had it not been for a very good friend of mine named Craig. This friend was very bright and very funny and very well-liked. With him by my side, I was given an instant elevated status among our group and beyond. He had been my friend almost forever and over the years he had become almost like a guardian to me. In subtle and overt ways, he would show his support for me by saving me a seat at lunch, walking me to class, or picking me up to take me to a party. Craig jumped in to my rescue even before I knew I needed to be rescued. (Willey 1999, p.40)

Every school will have a potential Craig, a role that is sometimes taken in the playground by the sibling of a child with Asperger's syndrome. If genuine friends or relatives provide such support, their guardianship should be recognized, commended and encouraged. During a high-school speech, Bill Gates said, 'Be nice to nerds. Chances are you'll end up working for one.'

Strategies for the target

There are strategies that can be used by the child who is the target of a bullying act, such as trying to avoid potentially vulnerable situations. A child with Asperger's syndrome may try to find a socially isolated sanctuary but this can be one of the most vulnerable situations. Luke Jackson, a teenager who has Asperger's syndrome, offers some advice:

> One day things just got too much to bear. I had tried to hide in the changing rooms away from my tormentors – I wish I had written my book then as I would have realized that hiding away is the worst thing to do. These two lads (low-lifes) found me and began toying with me in much the same way as a cat plays with a mouse. (L. Jackson 2002, p.137)

> Don't go to a quiet corner somewhere at school breaks. Try to be somewhere safe such as the library. I know it sounds strange but when you think you are hiding you are most likely to be found and bullied. AS kids are not good at working out how other people think. The best thing to do is stay with your friend if you have one, or at least a place where there are lots of people around. (L. Jackson 2002, p.151)

Safety is in numbers. The best place to 'hide' is in a group of children, or at least near them. It is important that children with Asperger's syndrome are welcomed into, or nearby, a group of children when predators are approaching a potential target. That welcome will need to be part of the class code on bullying. Other options can be the provision of activities in a supervised classroom during break times, such as a chess club; or an opportunity for like-minded individuals to meet as a group in the playground.

There are conventional recommendations regarding what to do when being the target that can actually make the situation worse. The advice to ignore the words and actions of the bully *does not work*. Ignoring acts of bullying as a means of preventing such behaviour is a myth. The bully will escalate his or her actions until the child responds. Donna Williams wrote to me regarding the bullying she experienced as a child, explaining how her lack of or delay in response, especially to pain, led other children to think 'it doesn't matter…she can't feel it'.

The child must respond in some way, but what should he or she say or do? The general advice is for such children to try to stay calm, maintain their self-esteem, and respond in an assertive and constructive way. Staying calm and maintaining self-esteem is difficult for children with Asperger's syndrome, but self-talk strategies can be used to maintain self-control. Children who are a target need to know and remember that they are not at fault, they do not deserve the comments or actions, and the people who need to change their behaviour are those who are committing the bullying acts.

Gray (2004a) recommends the creation of one simple spoken response that is true and used consistently. Examples are, 'I don't deserve this, stop it'; and 'I don't like that, stop it.' It is advisable to avoid telling a lie (for example, to say 'I don't care'). This would in any case be difficult for children with Asperger's syndrome, who are known for their reluctance to lie. Another response to avoid is replying with a sense of humour. Children with Asperger's syndrome would have considerable difficulty creating humour in such a situation. If the target child is unsure whether the actions of the other person are friendly or not, a reply could be, 'Are you teasing me to be friendly or not friendly?' The child will need to state his or her feelings clearly: 'What you are doing/saying is making me feel… [confused, angry, etc.].' It is important that the child states that the bullying will be reported. The child can then try to leave the situation, moving towards an adult or a safe group of children. If the bullying occurs in class, then the teacher can allow the child who is the target to move to another part of the classroom, perhaps without having to ask permission first.

The child with Asperger's syndrome will especially need guidance when he or she transfers to middle school or high school where the predatory students are at their peak in terms of teasing and bullying. Nita Jackson, in her autobiography, has very wise words of advice:

> Having Asperger's syndrome does not make me less human, less emotional, but simply more vulnerable. So I conclude that other Asperger teenagers like myself should always be forewarned of the problems they can and will encounter with mainstreamers. Parents – talk to your kids; and kids – listen to your parents! I didn't…and see what happened to me. (N. Jackson 2002, p.83)

Strategies for specialist staff

There are strategies that can be implemented by a psychologist, school counsellor or learning support teacher. The first stage is to explore with the child why someone would engage in a bullying act. The thoughts and motivations of others are not obvious for children with Asperger's syndrome, owing to inherent difficulties with Theory of Mind abilities. The child can be very confused as to why someone would be so unkind, why he or she became the target, and what he or she is supposed to think and do. I recommend two strategies developed by Carol Gray (1998), namely Comic Strip Conversations, which can be used to discover and explain the thoughts and feelings of each participant in the incident, and Social Stories™, to determine what to do if similar circumstances occur again.

Comic Strip Conversations

Comic Strip Conversations involve drawing an event or sequence of events in story-board form, with stick figures to represent each person involved, and speech and thought bubbles to represent each participant's words and thoughts. The child and teacher use an assortment of fibre-tipped coloured pens, with each colour representing an emotion. As he or she fills in the speech or thought bubbles, the child's choice of colour indicates his or her perception of the emotion conveyed or intended. This can clarify the child's interpretation of events and the rationale for his or her response. This activity can also help the child to identify and rectify any misperception, and to determine how alternative responses will affect each participant's thoughts and feelings. When new responses have been identified, the child will benefit by being able to rehearse those responses using role-playing activities, and by being encouraged to report back when a particular strategy has proved effective. The child with Asperger's syndrome can enjoy creating a 'boasting book' of the new successful responses, especially if the successful management of the event achieves a commendation and a suitable reward.

Resources

The child can read age-appropriate fiction in which the central character experiences bullying and responds in ways intended to serve as a model for the young reader. I recommend careful selection of any reading material relevant to bullying, as some of the strategies in the text may not be consistent with conventional wisdom on preventing bullying, or are not appropriate for children with Asperger's syndrome.

There are many programs on the prevention of bullying in schools for typical children, and some of the activities in these programs can be used with children with Asperger's syndrome (Rigby 1996). However, there are school-based programs on bullying that are specifically designed by specialists in Asperger's syndrome (Attwood

2004c; Gray 2004a; Heinrichs 2003). Parents of children with Asperger's syndrome will be requesting that schools implement these new programs.

What can parents do?

Parents are essential to the team approach to reducing bullying, and they will need to be aware of the policies and relevant programs at their child's school, and be active participants in encouraging specific responses. Parents also have a role in encouraging the child to have the confidence and ability to disclose his or her experiences as a target and to talk to a friend, teacher, parent or counsellor.

A parent may consider enrolling the child in a martial arts course to increase skills in self-protection as a deterrent to acts of bullying. However, I would recommend the martial arts course focus on how to remain calm and escape particular holds and actions, rather than to injure the other child. Parents may also need to know that research on typical children has indicated that simply changing school has little effect on reducing the likelihood that a child will be a target of bullying (Olweus 1993). However, parents may transfer the child to a different school that has a renowned intervention program to reduce the incidence and effects of teasing and bullying.

I am often amazed at the stoicism and optimism of some children with Asperger's syndrome when they are the target for chronic bullying. Perhaps the final words of this chapter on teasing and bullying should be from a child with Asperger's syndrome. Kate said to her mother, 'Mum, I can't tell when people are teasing me or being nice, but someday someone will really want to be my friend, and I want to be available.'

KEY POINTS AND STRATEGIES

- Children and adults with Asperger's syndrome are often the target of teasing and bullying.
- The effects on the child's self-esteem and mental state can be extremely detrimental.
- Strategies to reduce the frequency and effects of bullying:
  - Use a team approach, and include the target, school administration, teachers, parents, a child psychologist, other children and the child who engages in bullying.
  - Provide staff training in how to react to and reduce acts of teasing and bullying.
  - Ensure that justice is equitable based on motivation, knowledge and facts.
  - Use the Scales of Justice activity to determine and explain the degree of responsibility and consequences.

- Create a map of the child's world to identify safe havens.
- Use positive peer pressure to prevent acts of teasing and bullying.
- Select a guardian who is 'street wise' and has high social status among peers to protect the child and repair self-esteem.
- Teach the target that he or she can find safety in numbers, and 'hide' in a group of children.
- Acknowledge that ignoring acts of bullying rarely, if ever, reduces the likelihood of being the target of bullying.
- Teach the child who is a target to have an assertive and honest response.
- Seek the help of specialist staff, such as clinical psychologists, who can use activities such as Comic Strip Conversations to discover the thoughts, feelings and interpretation of intentions of the person with Asperger's syndrome and any other participants, and explain why he or she was a target and what to do in similar situations in the future.
- Use books, resources and programs to provide information and strategies to reduce teasing and bullying.
- Encourage parents to consider enrolling the child in a course for self-protection from physical acts of bullying.
- Be aware that changing school may have little effect on reducing the likelihood that a child will be a target of teasing and bullying.

CHAPTER 5

Theory of Mind

How odd is his voice, how odd his manner of speaking and his way of moving. It is no surprise, therefore, that this boy also lacks understanding of other people's expressions and cannot react to them appropriately.

— Hans Asperger ([1944] 1991)

The psychological term Theory of Mind (ToM) means the ability to recognize and understand thoughts, beliefs, desires and intentions of other people in order to make sense of their behaviour and predict what they are going to do next. It has also been described as 'mind reading' or 'mind blindness' (Baron-Cohen 1995) or, colloquially, a difficulty in 'putting oneself in another person's shoes'. A synonymous term is empathy (Gillberg 2002). The child or adult with Asperger's syndrome does not recognize or understand the cues that indicate the thoughts or feelings of the other person at a level expected for someone of that age.

The diagnostic assessment should include an examination of the child or adult's maturity in ToM skills and we have a range of tests that can be used with children, adolescents and adults (Attwood 2004d). There are stories with comprehension questions that can be used, at different age levels, to assess the ability to determine what someone in the story would be thinking or feeling. The 'Strange Stories' have been developed by Francesca Happé for children from 4 to 12 years (Happé 1994) and the 'Stories from Everyday Life' by Nils Kaland and colleagues for adolescents (Kaland *et al.* 2002). Simon Baron-Cohen and Sally Wheelwright have developed ToM tasks for adults (Baron-Cohen 2003), in which the clinician records whether the child or adult provides an answer that demonstrates ToM abilities, but also the time taken to achieve the answer in comparison to the person's peer group and whether the correct reply appears to have been achieved by intellectual analysis, rote learning and memory rather than being immediate and intuitive.

Typical children, especially after the age of five years, are remarkably astute at perceiving and understanding social cues that indicate thoughts and feelings. It is as though their mind prioritizes social cues above other information in their environment, and they have a mental theory as to what the social cues mean and how to respond. This ability dominates the perception of typical people to such a degree that we become anthropomorphic and project human social behaviour on animals and even objects.

An intriguing study by Ami Klin (2000) used the Social Attribution Task (SAT) that was originally developed by Heider and Simmel (1944). They made a cartoon animation film with a cast of 'characters' that are geometric shapes, which move in synchrony against one another, or as a result of the action of the other shapes. The film lasts only 50 seconds but has six sequential segments presented one at a time. After each segment, the observer is asked 'What happened there?' to provide a narrative to the silent film. The observer is also asked questions such as 'What kind of a person is the big triangle or the small circle?' The authors of the task found that college students used anthropomorphic words to describe the actions (chasing, entrapping and playing) and feelings (frightened, elated or frustrated) of the 'characters'.

When the SAT was used with adolescents with Asperger's syndrome it was found that there were significant differences between such subjects and their peers. Their narratives were shorter with less elaborate social plots. Many of their comments were not pertinent to the video and they identified only one quarter of the social elements identified by the control subjects. They used fewer ToM terms and less social sophistication. They also produced fewer and more simplistic personality attributions. The narratives of the control subjects, who easily attributed social meaning to the ambiguous scene, included descriptions of bravery or elation, complex personalities and social attributions that provided a coherent Social Story™. In contrast, the narrators with Asperger's syndrome used different terms to explain the movements of the shapes. Their attributions tended to focus on the physical aspects, describing such movements as bouncing or oscillating because of a magnetic field. The person with Asperger's syndrome perceives the physical world more than the social world.

A subsequent study using animated geometric shapes found, as expected, that adults with Asperger's syndrome gave fewer descriptions of the actions in terms of mental states but was able to identify which areas of the brain were involved (Castelli *et al.* 2002). In typical adults, the attribution of mental states is mediated by the prefrontal cortex, the superior temporal sulcus and temporal poles, but participants in the study who had Asperger's syndrome showed less activation of these regions of the brain. There is a neurological explanation for impaired or delayed ToM abilities.

It has been suggested that impaired ToM also affects self-consciousness and introspection (Frith and Happé 1999). I was talking to Corey, a teenager with Asperger's syndrome, about the ability to 'mind read'. He said, 'I'm not good at working out what other people are thinking. I'm not sure what I'm thinking now.' Thus there may be a pervasive difficulty in thinking about thoughts and feelings, whether they are the thoughts and feelings of another person or oneself.

It is important to recognize that the person with Asperger's syndrome has immature or impaired ToM abilities or empathy, not an absence of empathy. To imply an absence of empathy would be a terrible insult to people with Asperger's syndrome, with the implication that the person does not recognize or care about the feelings of others. The person does care, very deeply, but may not be able to recognize the more subtle signals of emotional states or 'read' complex mental states.

EFFECTS OF IMPAIRED THEORY OF MIND ABILITIES ON DAILY LIFE

Although we can appreciate that the person with Asperger's syndrome has difficulty knowing what another person may be thinking or feeling, it is much harder to imagine what it must be like on a day-to-day basis, as typical people 'mind read' relatively easily and intuitively. We can 'read' a face, and translate the meaning of body language and the prosody of speech. We also recognize the contextual cues that indicate the prevailing or expected thoughts of others. The following are some of the areas of daily life in children and adults with Asperger's syndrome that are affected by impaired or delayed ToM skills.

Difficulty reading the social/emotional messages in someone's eyes

How do we know what a person may be thinking or feeling? One way is our ability to read a face, in particular the region around the eyes. We have known for some time that children and adults with an autism spectrum disorder, including Asperger's syndrome, appear to engage in less eye contact than anticipated, tending to look at a person's face less often, and therefore missing changes of expression.

Chris was a teenager with Asperger's syndrome who had a special interest in astronomy. Prior to attending a diagnostic assessment, his parents had asked him not to talk to me about the interest as his enthusiasm and tendency to bore people made him appear eccentric. However, I knew of his remarkable knowledge of astronomy and started to ask Chris about some recent photographs of the surface of Mars that had been shown on television news programmes. Chris was aware that while I was keen to continue the conversation on astronomy, as was Chris, his parents, who were present and watching him, would not approve of the topic of conversation. He was confused and withdrew by closing his eyes, but continued to talk about astronomy. I then explained to Chris the difficulty I had in continuing a conversation with someone whose eyes were closed. Chris replied, 'Why would I want to look at you when I know where you are?'

Looking at people is not just to locate where they are and to see if they have moved. We look at a face to read the expression to determine what someone may be thinking or feeling. When children and adults with Asperger's syndrome do look at a face, where exactly do they look? Most typical people focus on the eyes to help determine the other person's thoughts and feelings. The eyes are considered as 'windows to the soul'. Eye-tracking technology can be used to measure visual fixation, and recent research has indicated that adults with Asperger's syndrome tend to look less at the eyes and more at the mouth, body and objects than do control subjects (Klin *et al.* 2002a, 2002b). These ingenious studies determined where someone was looking as they watched a filmed interaction between actors. In one scene, where the control subjects fixated on the look of surprise and horror in the actor's wide-open eyes, the subjects with Asperger's syndrome or High Functioning Autism were focusing on the actor's mouth. The research showed that control subjects visually fixated on the eye region twice as often as the group of subjects with Asperger's syndrome or High Functioning Autism. By looking at someone's mouth, the person may help process linguistic communication, but will miss the information that can be conveyed by the eye region of the face.

Other research has shown that when the person with Asperger's syndrome does look at someone's eyes, he or she is less able to read the meaning in the eyes than control subjects (Baron-Cohen and Jolliffe 1997; Baron-Cohen *et al.* 2001a). A quotation from a person with Asperger's syndrome confirms the difficulty in reading the messages conveyed by the eye region of the face: 'People give each other messages with their eyes, but I do not know what they are saying' (Wing 1992, p.131). People who have Asperger's syndrome have two problems in using information from the eyes to determine what someone is thinking and feeling. First, they tend not to look at the eyes as the dominant source of information regarding social/emotional communication and, second, they are not very good at reading the eyes that they do look at.

Making a literal interpretation

One of the consequences of impaired or delayed ToM skills is a tendency to make a literal interpretation of what someone says. I have noted the literal response of children with Asperger's syndrome to requests such as 'Hop on the scales,' the emotional reaction to comments such as 'Let's toast the bride,' and confusion regarding English metaphors such as 'It's about time that you pulled your socks up.' Another example of making a literal interpretation was that of a child with Asperger's syndrome who had completed his homework essay, and his mother was bewildered as to why at the end of the essay he had drawn pictures. He explained that the teacher had told him that at the end of the essay he must draw his own conclusions.

We have known for some time that children and adults with Asperger's syndrome have difficulty recognizing the relevant social cues and reading the thoughts or emotions in another person's face, but we have new evidence that they also have difficulty understanding the significance of the person's tone of voice, or prosody (Kleinman, Marciano and Ault 2001; Rutherford, Baron-Cohen and Wheelwright 2002), which normally would enable the listener to go beyond a literal interpretation. We are able to understand the incongruence between facial expression, tone of voice and context, and realize when someone is teasing or being sarcastic. Children or adults with Asperger's syndrome can be confused by sarcasm, and prone to teasing by others, as they are remarkably gullible and assume that people say exactly what they mean.

Being considered disrespectful and rude

The child with Asperger's syndrome may not notice or read an adult's or another child's subtle cues that they are becoming annoyed with his or her egocentric or dominating behaviour or conversation. The child appears to break the social rules and does not respond to the warning signs. If the adult or other child does not know that this behaviour is due to impaired or delayed ToM skills, the interpretation of the behaviour is to make a moral judgement: that the child with Asperger's syndrome is being deliberately disrespectful and rude. However, the child does not necessarily have any malicious intent, is usually unaware of causing offence and can be bewildered as to why the other person is angry.

People with Asperger's syndrome have a remarkable enthusiasm for their special interests. However, they may not recognize that other people do not share the same level of enthusiasm. Because people with Asperger's syndrome tend to look less at the other person when they are talking, they may not see or recognize the subtle signs of boredom or be able to judge whether the topic is relevant to the context or priorities of the other person.

When a mother asks her child, 'What did you do at school today?', typical children will know what their mother already knows and what she would like to know, or would find interesting, that happened at school. Children with impaired ToM abilities may not know how to answer that question. Does she want to know everything, from the moment the child entered the classroom to the moment he or she left? What would be important for her? How much does she know already? The child with Asperger's syndrome may have difficulty identifying the key events from a mother's perspective, and will either refuse to answer the question as it is too difficult, or provide a commentary of the whole day, with every detail. The monologue then becomes very tedious.

Stephen Shore sent me the following comment. 'When I am asked what I would like to eat or drink when at another person's home as a guest, it is impossible for me to answer. My response is to ask 'What is available?' Once the options are laid out for me it is easy to make a choice. Otherwise the question just feels too big.'

Equally, those topics or activities that are of interest to others may be perceived as boring by the person with Asperger's syndrome. For example, at school young children usually sit still during 'show and tell' and take a genuine interest in the experiences of the child who is standing before the group. The child with Asperger's syndrome may not be able to empathize with the storyteller or be interested in his or her experiences. He or she can become bored and be criticized for not paying attention. The tendency therefore to talk at length without recognizing another person's boredom, or to be inattentive to others' interests, may be due to impaired ToM rather than a lack of respect or a desire to misbehave.

Honesty and deception

I have noted that young children with Asperger's syndrome are often remarkably honest. Asked by a parent if they have committed an act that they know is not allowed, they are likely to admit readily that they did it. Other children will recognize that there are some occasions when the adult would not have enough knowledge (i.e. he or she did not actually see who did it), and the child can use deception to avoid the consequences.

Another characteristic associated with Asperger's syndrome is that the person does not know when he or she would be expected to tell a 'white lie', making a comment to someone that is true but likely to cause offence. For example, the child with Asperger's syndrome may notice that a woman in the line at the supermarket checkout is obese, and remark, in his or her usual tone of voice and volume, that the lady is fat and needs to go on a diet. The child's opinion is that she should be grateful for the observation and advice; the likelihood that his or her mother will be embarrassed or the woman offended at such a rude comment is not part of the child's thinking process. Other children would normally inhibit such a response, based on the understanding of the other person's thoughts and feelings. Children and adults with Asperger's syndrome appear to have a greater allegiance to honesty and the truth than to the thoughts and feelings of others.

Another such example may occur at school. For instance, while the teacher is distracted, a child may commit a disobedient act. When the teacher recognizes something has happened but does not know who did it, he may ask that the culprit confess. The other children often know who it was but they will usually not say, as their allegiance is to the social code of, as the Australians would say, 'not dobbing in your mates'. However, for the child with Asperger's syndrome, the allegiance is to the truth, not the social group. The teacher asked a question and he or she quickly provides the answer, but is then confused by the annoyance of the other children, especially if they did not do the act. As far as the child is concerned, he or she has given the logical, correct answer to the teacher's question.

The ability to understand the value of deception and recognize when it might be expected occurs later in the development of the child with Asperger's syndrome, sometimes as late as the early teens. This can cause confusion to parents and teachers, as the previously honest (perhaps to a fault) child recognizes that one can deceive people and avoid anticipated consequences. However, the type of deception can be immature and the deceit easily identified by an adult.

Where lying is becoming an issue for the family and friends of the person with Asperger's syndrome, explanations will be sought. First, due to impaired or delayed ToM abilities, the person with Asperger's syndrome may not realize that the other person is likely to be more offended by the lie than by any apparent misdemeanour. Second, he or she may consider that a lie can be a way of avoiding consequences, or a quick solution to a social problem. What the person might not acknowledge is that lying can also be a way of maintaining self-esteem should he or she have an arrogant self-image, whereby the making of mistakes is unthinkable.

Adults with Asperger's syndrome can be renowned for being honest, having a strong sense of social justice and keeping to the rules. They strongly believe in moral and ethical principles. These are admirable qualities in life but can cause considerable problems when the person's employer does not share the same ideals. I suspect that many 'whistle-blowers' have Asperger's syndrome. I have certainly met several who have applied a company's or government department's code of conduct to their work and reported wrongdoing and corruption. They have subsequently been astounded that the organizational culture, line managers and colleagues have been less than supportive; this can lead to disillusionment and depression.

A sense of paranoia

One of the consequences of impaired or delayed ToM skills for the person with Asperger's syndrome is a difficulty in distinguishing between deliberate or accidental actions of another person. I observed a child with Asperger's syndrome who was sitting on the classroom floor with the other children in the class, listening to the teacher read a story. The adjacent boy started to tease him by poking his fingers in his back while the teacher was not looking. The child with Asperger's syndrome became increasingly annoyed and eventually hit the boy to make him stop. The teacher was looking at the children at this point but, being unaware of the preceding events, reprimanded the child with Asperger's syndrome for being aggressive. Other children would have explained that they were provoked, and would recognize that if the teacher knew the circumstances, the consequences would be less severe and more equitable. Yet he remained silent. The teacher continued with her story and a few moments later another child returned to the classroom from the toilet. As he carefully moved past the child with Asperger's syndrome, he accidentally touched him; the child with Asperger's syndrome was not aware that in this situation the action was accidental, so he hit him in the same way as he had the child who had been tormenting him. Fortunately, in this case, the teacher was aware of the child's difficulty in distinguishing accidental and deliberate acts, and was able to calm the situation with an explanation.

I would add that the apparent paranoia in children and adults with Asperger's syndrome might also be due to very real social experiences, where they encounter a greater degree of deliberate and provocative teasing than their peers. Once another child has been hostile, any subsequent interaction with that child is confusing; the child with Asperger's syndrome can make the assumption that the interaction was intentionally hostile, while typical children would be better able to interpret the other child's intentions by the context and social cues.

Problem solving

At a very young age, typical children realise that someone else may have a solution to a practical problem and that others might be interested and able to help. This insight into the thoughts and abilities of other people is not automatic for children with Asperger's syndrome. When presented with a problem, seeking guidance from someone who probably knows what to do is usually not a first or even a second thought. The child may be sitting or standing next to someone who could obviously help but appears 'blinkered' and determined to solve the problem by him- or herself.

Managing conflict

As children develop, they become more mature and skilled in the art of persuasion, compromise and management of conflict. They are increasingly able to understand the perspective of other people and how to influence their thoughts and emotions using constructive strategies. Managing conflict successfully requires considerable ToM skills, therefore one would expect difficulties in conflict resolution for children and adults with Asperger's syndrome. Observations and experience of conflict situations suggest that children with Asperger's syndrome are relatively immature, lack variety in negotiating tools and tend to be confrontational. They may resort to 'primitive' conflict management strategies, such as emotional blackmail or an inflexible adherence to their own point of view. They may fail to understand that they would be more likely to achieve what they want by being nice to the other person. When an argument or altercation is over, the person with Asperger's syndrome may also show less remorse, or appreciation of repair mechanisms for other people's feelings, such as an apology.

An adult often needs to provide guidance for the child with Asperger's syndrome in conflict resolution at all stages of childhood, but during adolescence the child is expected to be able to compromise, identify and acknowledge the point of view of the other person, negotiate and forgive and forget conflicts. These attributes can be elusive for the child with Asperger's syndrome, who can be considered as displaying signs similar to Oppositional and Defiant Disorder. The relevant conflict resolution characteristics associated with Asperger's syndrome at this stage are:

- a difficulty conceptualizing the other person's perspective and priorities
- limited skills in persuasion
- a tendency to be confrontational and rigid
- reluctance to change a decision and admit making a mistake
- an aversion to being interrupted
- a compulsion for completion
- a tendency to punish rather than praise

- a tendency to avoid demands
- a lack of knowledge of alternative strategies.

Thus children with Asperger's syndrome can appear to oppose the decisions of others, defy their priorities and deny their reason. They may have a history of pursuing their decision until the other person capitulates, and not recognize the signals that it would be wise not to continue the argument. Other children can recognize their friend's perspective, priorities and reasoning, and at least for the sake of their friendship be accommodating of the request and decision of their friend. They expect reciprocity in this aspect of friendship. Children with Asperger's syndrome and their friends may need guidance in when and how to make a request, to listen to and absorb the point of view and priorities of the other person, to negotiate some areas of agreement and compromise and to seek and accept the decision of an adjudicator. Above all, they need to learn not to let emotion, especially anger, inflame the situation. Role-play games can be used to illustrate inappropriate and appropriate conflict resolution strategies.

Introspection and self-consciousness

Uta Frith and Francesca Happé (1999) have suggested that due to differences in the acquisition and nature of ToM abilities in the cognitive development of children with Asperger's syndrome, they may develop a different form of self-consciousness. The child may acquire ToM abilities using intelligence and experience rather than intuition, which can eventually lead to an alternative form of self-consciousness as the child reflects on his or her own mental state and the mental states of others. Frith and Happé (1999) have described this highly reflective and explicit self-consciousness as similar to that of philosophers.

I have read the autobiographies of adults with Asperger's syndrome and would agree that there is a quasi-philosophical quality. When a different way of thinking and perceiving the world is combined with advanced intellectual abilities we achieve new advances in philosophy. It is interesting to note that the philosopher Ludwig Wittgenstein had many of the characteristics of an intellectually 'gifted' person with Asperger's syndrome (Gillberg 2002).

Understanding embarrassment

A study that examined the understanding of embarrassment in children with High Functioning Autism or Asperger's syndrome, as would perhaps be expected, found a link between ToM skills and the understanding of embarrassment; but a detailed examination of the children's responses found that there were some interesting characteristics (Hillier and Allinson 2002). The children with Asperger's syndrome tended to rate some situations as embarrassing whereas typical children did not, and they had some difficulty justifying why someone would be embarrassed. At an intellectual level, they had an understanding of the concept of embarrassment but were less able to use the concept in novel situations. In practical terms, I have noted that some children with Asperger's syndrome can appear to have little embarrassment or 'stage fright' when making a presentation or acting in front of others. Observation of social situations that would be expected to include the body language of embarrassment suggests that people with Asperger's syndrome make fewer gestures of embarrassment (such as a hand over the mouth, or a red face) than their peers (Attwood, Frith and Hermelin 1988).

Simon Baron-Cohen and colleagues developed a faux pas detection test using a series of stories, and examined whether children with Asperger's syndrome recognized a faux pas (Baron-Cohen *et al.* 1999a). A faux pas is defined as 'an indiscreet remark or action', and the study confirmed the experience of many parents that, in comparison to typical peers, the children with Asperger's syndrome were less skilled at detecting faux pas and more likely to commit faux pas in their everyday behaviour.

Children at around eight years can inhibit their comments or criticism on the basis of their prediction of the emotional reaction of the other person; that is, they keep their thoughts to themselves so as not to embarrass or annoy their friend. The person with Asperger's syndrome can be very astute at identifying mistakes and can be very keen to point out another person's mistakes. The comments can be interpreted as deliberately critical and hostile, but the motivation of the person with Asperger's syndrome may have been to encourage perfection and to enlighten the other person about the error. I have observed teenagers with Asperger's syndrome criticize the teacher in front of the whole class. The teacher's mistake can be trivial, such as an incorrect spelling of a word, but for the young person with Asperger's syndrome the desire to correct the mistake takes precedence over the feelings of the teacher.

Anxiety

Being unsure of what someone may be thinking or feeling can be a contributory factor to general feelings of uncertainty and anxiety. Marc Fleisher is a talented mathematician with Asperger's syndrome and, like most people with Asperger's syndrome, is a very kind person who does not want to cause someone to be confused or distressed. In his autobiography he wrote:

> Because of my lack of confidence, I am terribly afraid of upsetting others without realising it or meaning to, by saying or doing the wrong thing. I wish I could read minds, then I would know what they wished for and I could do the right thing. Socialising is harder than any maths equation for me. What works for one person doesn't for another. People do not always say what they mean, or stick to what they say. (Fleisher 2003, p.110)

The speed and quality of social reasoning

Typical people are very quick and efficient in using ToM abilities when engaged in social situations. Research has shown that while some children and adults with Asperger's syndrome can demonstrate quite advanced ToM skills, they can take longer with the cognitive processing of the relevant cues and responses than one would expect, and require more encouragement and prompts. Their answers to questions that rely on ToM abilities can be less spontaneous and intuitive and more literal, idiosyncratic and irrelevant (Bauminger and Kasari 1999; Kaland *et al.* 2002).

An adolescent with Asperger's syndrome, who has a special interest in computers, said to me that he considered that when typical people are in a social situation their brain is like a computer that has a 'Windows' to the social world operating system, while the brain of someone with Asperger's syndrome is trying to use DOS (a metaphor that will only make sense if the reader is conversant with computer terminology).

One of the consequences of using conscious mental calculation rather than intuition is the effect on the timing of responses. In a conversation or social interaction, the person with Asperger's syndrome can be slow in processing aspects that require ToM skills. The time delay for intellectual processing leads to a lack of synchrony to which both parties try to adjust. This delayed reaction time can cause the other person to perceive the person with Asperger's syndrome as unusually formal or pedantic, or even to consider that he or she is intellectually retarded. Other children often torment children with Asperger's syndrome, calling them stupid, which adds insult to injury and can lead to low self-esteem or anger.

I have also noted that ToM abilities in children and adults with Asperger's syndrome can be influenced by the complexity of the situation, the speed of the interaction and the degree of stress. In large social gatherings the amount of social information can be overwhelming for someone with Asperger's syndrome. The person may have reasonable ToM abilities but have difficulty determining which signals are relevant and which are redundant, especially when inundated with social cues.

The time taken to process social information is similar to the time it takes for someone who is learning a second language to process the speech of someone fluent in that language. If the native speaker of the language talks too quickly, the other person can only understand a few fragments of what has been said. I have learned to adjust my interaction with a person with Asperger's syndrome to be within the person's processing capacity for social reasoning.

When relaxed, the person with Asperger's syndrome can more easily process mental states, but when stressed, as with any skill, performance declines. This can have an effect on the formal testing of ToM abilities and may explain some of the differences between formal knowledge in an artificial testing situation, and real life, which is more complex, with transitory social cues and greater stress.

Exhaustion

We know that the acquisition of ToM skills can be delayed in those with Asperger's syndrome, and that over time they can eventually achieve advanced ToM abilities. However, we also need to recognize the degree of mental effort required by people with Asperger's syndrome to process social information. Using cognitive mechanisms to compensate for impaired ToM skills leads to mental exhaustion. Limited social success, low self-esteem and exhaustion can contribute to the development of a clinical depression. One of my clients has an excellent phrase to describe her exhaustion from socializing. She says, 'I'm all peopled out.'

STRATEGIES TO IMPROVE THEORY OF MIND ABILITIES
Social Stories™

We now have several strategies to improve ToM abilities, in particular Social Stories™ (see page 69). The perspective sentences in a Social Story™ provide the valuable information to develop ToM abilities. They describe each person's knowledge, thoughts, beliefs and feelings that are relevant to the situation. One of the essential elements of preparing and writing a Social Story™ is the acquisition of information on the perspective of all participants, especially the child with Asperger's syndrome. A Social Story™ dictionary can improve knowledge and vocabulary with regard to mental state terms, with pictorial explanations of vocabulary such as know, guess, expect and opinion.

Social Stories™ can also be developed to become exercises on specific ToM skills; for example, the child completes the following sentences:

I often talk about trains. I often think about _____.

I often talk about bus schedules. I often think about _____.

Matt often talks about dinosaurs. I guess Matt often thinks about _____.

Matt may like it if I ask him about _____.

Social Stories™ are a strategy that would be expected to improve ToM abilities, but to date there have been no published studies that have examined whether and how Social Stories™ improve such abilities using the standard ToM tests. However, I recognize that teachers, parents and practitioners need strategies such as Social Stories™ now, and cannot wait until the research studies determine whether they improve maturity in ToM abilities.

THEORY OF MIND TRAINING PROGRAMS

Several studies have examined whether ToM abilities can be improved using training programs specifically designed to improve social cognition. The programs have used social skills training with a group format (Ozonoff and Miller 1995), simple computer programs (Swettenham *et al.* 1996) and a teaching manual and workbook (Hadwin *et al.* 1996). Pre- and post-treatment assessment using the standard measures of ToM abilities has confirmed that the programs improve the ability to pass ToM tasks. However, these studies have not found a generalization effect to tasks not included in the training program.

Two studies used an interesting approach to teach ToM abilities in pre-school children with Asperger's syndrome, by using a 'picture in the head' strategy (McGregor, Whiten and Blackburn 1998; Swettenham *et al.* 1996). The training procedure included placing a photograph into a slot in a doll's head to explain the concept that another person can see or know something different to that seen or known by oneself.

Comic Strip Conversations

Comic Strip Conversations (see page 109) were originally developed by Carol Gray and use simple drawings such as 'stick figures', thought and speech bubbles, and text in different colours to illustrate the sequence of actions, emotions and thoughts in a specific social situation (Gray 1994). Children are familiar with thought bubbles from reading comics and cartoons. We know that children as young as three to four years understand that thought bubbles represent what someone is thinking (Wellman, Hollander and Schult 1996). Recent studies examining whether thought bubbles can be used to acquire ToM abilities in children with autism found some success with this method (Kerr and Durkin 2004; Rajendran and Mitchelle 2000; Wellman *et al.* 2002).

With Comic Strip Conversations, a single 'cartoon' or comic strip is a 'conversation' between the child and adult, with the drawings used to determine what someone is thinking, feeling, said or did, or could do. Colour can be used to identify the emotional 'tone' or motivation, and a colour chart can be used to associate a specific colour or depth of colour with a specific emotion. For example, the child may decide to use a red crayon to indicate that the words spoken by the other child were perceived as being said in an angry tone of voice. This provides an opportunity to learn the child's perception of the event and to correct any misinterpretations. One of the advantages of this approach is that the child and adult have a conversation, but are not looking at each other; their joint focus is on the evolving drawing in front of them.

The general approach is one of joint discovery, of the thoughts and feelings being portrayed, rather than an attempt to determine who is at fault. Comic Strip Conversations provide a clear, visual explanation of what someone is thinking and feeling. They can be used to explain misinterpretation of intentions (of both parties), figures of speech such as sarcasm, and to illustrate alternative outcomes by changing actions, speech and thoughts. It is interesting that when we express our new understanding, we say 'Yes, I see what you mean,' rather than 'I hear what you mean.'

I make regular use of Comic Strip Conversations in my clinical treatment of mood disorders (see Chapter 6). Children with Asperger's syndrome often communicate their thoughts and feelings more eloquently using drawings rather than speech. Although children with Asperger's syndrome have difficulty identifying what someone else may be thinking or feeling, clinical experience suggests they have even greater difficulty estimating the degree of expression of a particular emotion. Their perception can be very 'black and white', without understanding the shades of grey. I add a component to Comic Strip Conversations: the use of a numerical scale to measure the degree of expression (for example, how sad someone is feeling), using a scale from one to ten. This strategy is particularly useful for children who have a limited vocabulary for the subtle and precise description of emotional intensity.

A guide for teachers

Teaching Children with Autism to Mind-Read: A Practical Guide by Howlin, Baron-Cohen and Hadwin (1999) provides resource materials, assessment and teaching procedures, and outlines the principles underlying theory and practice. The understanding of mental states is divided into three separate components:

- understanding informational states

- understanding emotion

- understanding pretence.

The section on informational states provides a range of activities to teach visual perspective taking, the principle that seeing leads to knowing, and how to predict actions on the basis of another person's knowledge. The section on teaching emotions examines several levels of emotional understanding, namely recognizing facial expression from photographs and schematic drawings through to identifying both situation-based emotions, and desire- and belief-based emotions.

The material requires the child to have a language age of at least five years and knowledge of the concept that other people have desires and thoughts. In some activities the child is required to make a choice as to how the person will feel according to the situation. One example depicts a car stalled between closed railway crossing barriers, with a train approaching. The text describes the scene. *Jamie is in the car. The barrier comes down. The train is coming. How will Jamie feel when the train is coming?* The child has a prompt of happy/sad/angry/afraid. Although the answer appears to be obvious, I have observed that, if the young child with Asperger's syndrome has a special interest in trains, he might consider the situation solely from his perspective, and would be happy to be so close to a train. If this was the child's response, one can discuss that while Jamie might be happy, his father, who is driving the car, probably feels afraid. This can help explain how two people would perceive the same situation in very different ways.

The resource material uses simple drawings with clear cues and no irrelevant detail. The child is also provided with a logical and progressive structure with sufficient time to think about his or her response. With practice, as provided by the wide range of examples, the child becomes more fluent and able to interpret mental states. The authors of the guide have conducted a quantitative analysis of the program and found that improvements in ToM abilities were maintained long after intervention ceased.

Computer programs

A remarkable DVD is an electronic encyclopaedia of emotions, entitled *Mind Reading: The Interactive Guide to Emotions*. Simon Baron-Cohen and colleagues at the University of Cambridge identified 412 human emotions (excluding synonyms). They examined the age at which children understand the meaning of each emotion, and developed a taxonomy that assigned all the distinct emotions into one of 24 different groups. A multimedia company then developed interactive software that was designed for children and adults to learn what someone may be thinking or feeling.

On the DVD, actors (including Daniel Radcliffe, the actor who plays Harry Potter) demonstrate facial expressions, body language and speech qualities associated with a specific emotion. The DVD also includes audio recordings that illustrate aspects of prosody, and stories that illustrate the circumstances and contexts for each emotion. There is an emotions library, a learning centre and a games zone. Further information on the DVD is provided in the Resources section towards the end of the book.

I recommend the interactive DVD program as particularly suitable for children and adults with Asperger's syndrome. Such individuals can have considerable difficulty learning cognitive skills in the 'live' social theatre of the classroom, where they have to divide their attention between the activities in front of them and the social, emotional and linguistic communication of the teacher and the other children. With a computer, the feedback is instantaneous; they do not have to wait for a response from the teacher and they can repeat a scene to identify and analyse the relevant cues many times without annoying or boring others. They are also not going to receive public criticism for mistakes and are more likely to relax when engaged in a solitary activity. The program is designed to minimize any irrelevant detail, highlight the relevant cues and to enable the 'student' to progress at his or her own pace. It may be somewhat ironic that those with Asperger's syndrome may be better able to learn about someone's thoughts and feelings by using a computer program than observing real-life situations. Every day people make intuitive guesses regarding what someone may be thinking or feeling. Most of the time we are right but the system is not faultless. We are not perfect mind readers. Social interactions would be so much easier if typical people said *exactly* what they mean with no assumptions or ambiguity. As Liane Holliday Willey wrote to me in an e-mail, 'You wouldn't need a Theory of Mind if everyone spoke their mind.'

KEY POINTS AND STRATEGIES

- Effects of impaired Theory of Mind abilities in daily life:
  - difficulties reading the messages in someone's eyes
  - a tendency to make a literal interpretation of what someone says
  - a tendency to be considered disrespectful and rude
  - remarkable honesty
  - a sense of paranoia
  - an inability to see that another person may have the knowledge and a desire to be of help
  - delay in the development of the art of persuasion, compromise and conflict resolution
  - a different form of introspection and self-consciousness
  - problems knowing when something may cause embarrassment
  - anxiety
  - a longer time to process social information, due to using intelligence rather than intuition
  - physical and emotional exhaustion.
- Strategies to improve Theory of Mind abilities:
  - Social Stories™
  - Theory of Mind teaching programs
  - Comic Strip Conversations
  - computer programs.

CHAPTER 6

The Understanding and Expression of Emotions

The children cannot be understood simply in terms of the concept 'poverty of emotion' used in a quantitative sense. Rather what characterises these children is a qualitative difference, a disharmony in emotion and disposition.

— Hans Asperger ([1944] 1991)

Extensive clinical experience and autobiographies confirm that while the person with Asperger's syndrome can have considerable intellectual ability, especially in the area of knowing facts, there is invariably confusion and immaturity with regard to feelings. The diagnostic assessment for Asperger's syndrome will need to include an evaluation of the person's ability to understand and express emotions, not only to confirm the diagnosis, but also to screen for the possibility of an additional mood disorder, especially anxiety or depression.

A qualitative difference in the understanding and expression of emotions that was originally described by Hans Asperger is acknowledged in the diagnostic criteria. The DSM-IV criteria for Asperger's syndrome refer to 'lack of social or emotional reciprocity' (p.84) and the diagnostic criteria in ICD-10 refer to 'a failure to develop peer relationships that involve a mutual sharing of interests, activities and emotions'. The lack of socio-emotional reciprocity is expressed as 'an impaired or deviant response to other people's emotions; and/or lack of modulation of behaviour according to the social context; and/or a weak integration of social, emotional and communicative behaviours'. The criteria of Christopher Gillberg refer to 'socially and emotionally inappropriate behaviour and limited or inappropriate facial expression' (Gillberg and Gillberg 1989, p.632). The diagnostic criteria of Peter Szatmari and colleagues refer to 'difficulty sensing feelings of others, detached from feelings of others, limited facial expression, unable to read emotion from facial expressions of child, and unable to give message with eyes [sic]' (Szatmari *et al.* 1989b, p.710). In other words, these criteria state that the person with Asperger's syndrome has a clinically significant difficulty with the understanding, expression and regulation of emotions.

The explanatory text included in the DSM-IV description of Asperger's syndrome refers to an association between Asperger's syndrome and the development of an additional or secondary mood disorder, especially depression or an anxiety disorder. Current research indicates that around 65 per cent of adolescents with Asperger's syndrome have an affective or mood disorder. Perhaps the most common is an anxiety disorder (Ghaziuddin *et al.* 1998; Gillot, Furniss and Walter 2001; Green *et al.* 2000; Kim *et al.* 2000; Konstantareas 2005; Russell and Sofronoff 2004; Tantam 2000b; Tonge *et al.* 1999). However, the prevalence of depression is also high (Clarke *et al.* 1999; Gillot *et al.* 2001; Green *et al.* 2000; Kim *et al.* 2000; Konstantareas 2005). Research has indicated a greater risk of developing bipolar disorder (DeLong and Dwyer 1988; Frazier *et al.* 2002) and there is evidence to suggest an association with delusional disorders (Kurita 1999), paranoia (Blackshaw *et al.* 2001) and conduct disorders (Green *et al.* 2000; Tantam 2000b). For teenagers with Asperger's syndrome, an additional mood disorder is the rule rather than the exception.

Research has been conducted on the family histories of children with autism and Asperger's syndrome and has identified a higher than expected incidence of mood disorders in family members (Bolton *et al.* 1998; DeLong 1994; Ghaziuddin and Greden 1998; Lainhart and Folstein 1994; Micali, Chakrabarti and Fombonne 2004; Piven and Palmer 1999). The research studies acknowledged the ironic comment that 'madness is hereditary: you get it from your children' and examined the parents' mood states before the child with Asperger's syndrome was born. We do not know why there is an association between a parent (mother or father) having a mood disorder and having a child with Asperger's syndrome. Research studies will eventually explain the association.

If a parent has a mood disorder, a child with Asperger's syndrome could have a genetic predisposition to strong emotions. This may be one of the factors that explain problems with the intensity and management of emotions that are characteristics of Asperger's syndrome. However, there are other factors. When one considers the inevitable difficulties people with Asperger's syndrome have with regard to social reasoning, empathy, conversation skills, a different learning style and heightened sensory perception, they are clearly prone to considerable stress, anxiety, frustration and emotional exhaustion. They are also prone to being rejected by peers and frequently being teased and bullied, which can lead to low self-esteem and feeling depressed. During adolescence, there can be an increasing awareness of a lack of social success, and greater insight into being different to other people – another factor in the development of a reactive depression. Thus, there may be genetic and environmental factors that explain the higher incidence of mood disorders.

The theoretical models of autism developed within cognitive psychology, and research in neuropsychology and neuro-imaging also provides some explanation as to why children and adults with Asperger's syndrome are prone to secondary mood disorders. The extensive research on Theory of Mind skills (see Chapter 5) confirms that people with Asperger's syndrome have considerable difficulty identifying and conceptualizing the thoughts and feelings of other people and themselves. The interpersonal and inner world of emotions appears to be uncharted territory for people with Asperger's syndrome. This will affect the person's ability to monitor and manage emotions, within themselves and others.

Research on executive function and Asperger's syndrome suggests characteristics of being disinhibited and impulsive, with a relative lack of insight that affects general functioning (Eisenmajer *et al.* 1996; Nyden *et al.* 1999; Ozonoff *et al.* 2000; Pennington and Ozonoff 1996). Impaired executive function can also affect the cognitive control of emotions. Clinical experience indicates there is a tendency to react to emotional cues without thinking. A fast and impulsive retaliation can cause the child with Asperger's syndrome to be considered to have a conduct disorder or a problem with anger management.

Research using neuro-imaging technology with people who have autism and Asperger's syndrome has also identified structural and functional abnormalities of the amygdala, a part of the brain associated with the recognition and regulation of emotions (Adolphs, Sears and Piven 2001; Baron-Cohen *et al.* 1999b; Critchley *et al.* 2000; Fine, Lumsden and Blair 2001). The amygdala is known to regulate a range of emotions including anger, anxiety and sadness. Thus we also have neuro-anatomical evidence that suggests there will be problems with the perception and regulation of emotions.

Research studies have also suggested that people with Asperger's syndrome may have signs of *prosopagnosia*, which is rather difficult to pronounce and means face blindness (Barton *et al.* 2004; Duchaine *et al.* 2003; Kracke 1994; Nieminen-von Wendt 2004; Njiokiktjien *et al.* 2001; Pietz, Ebinger and Rating 2003). The person with Asperger's syndrome has difficulty reading facial expressions. Typical people have special areas of the brain that process facial information, but this seems not to be the case for people with Asperger's syndrome, who process faces as if they were objects and appear to focus only on the individual components of the face. This can contribute to the misinterpretation of someone's emotional expression. For example, a furrowed brow can be one of the facial signs of being angry. However, a furrowed brow can also indicate feelings of confusion. Typical children would consider and integrate all the facial signs and context to determine which emotion is being conveyed.

We now have a psychological term, *alexithymia*, to describe another characteristic associated with Asperger's syndrome, namely someone who has an impaired ability to identify and describe feeling states. Clinical experience and research have confirmed that alexithymia can be recognized in the profile of abilities of people with Asperger's syndrome (Berthoz and Hill 2005; Hill, Berthoz and Frith 2004; Nieminen-von Wendt

2004; Rastam *et al.* 1997; Tani *et al.* 2004). Children and adults with Asperger's syndrome often have a limited vocabulary of words to describe feeling states, especially the more subtle or complex emotions.

THE ASSESSMENT OF THE COMPREHENSION AND EXPRESSION OF EMOTIONS

The first stage in the assessment of the communication of emotions is to establish the child's or adult's maturity of emotional expression, range of vocabulary to express and describe feelings, and ability to regulate or control emotions and stress (Berthoz and Hill 2005; Groden *et al.* 2001; Laurent and Rubin 2004). I have noted that the emotional maturity of children with Asperger's syndrome is usually at least three years behind that of their peers, and we now have some research evidence to confirm this observation (Rieffe, Terwogt and Stockman 2000). The child may express anger and affection at a level expected of a much younger child. There can be a limited vocabulary to describe emotions and a lack of subtlety and variety in emotional expression. When other children would be sad, confused, embarrassed, anxious or jealous, the child may have only one response, and that is to feel angry. The degree of expression of negative emotions such as anger, anxiety and sadness can be extreme, and described by parents as an on/off switch set at maximum volume.

The ability to identify emotions in facial expressions can be assessed by showing the child or adult photographs of faces and asking the person to say what emotion is being expressed, noting any errors or confusion and the time taken to provide the answer. The answer may be correct, but achieved by time-consuming intellectual analysis of the features and reference to previous experiences of a similar facial expression. Typical children or adults can find these activities relatively easy and achievable with little intellectual effort. A child with Asperger's syndrome can usually identify the extremes of basic emotions, such as intense sadness, anger or happiness, but the understanding of more subtle expressions such as confusion, jealousy or disbelief may be elusive.

During the diagnostic assessment I usually ask the person to make the facial expression for a designated emotion. Typical pre-school children can easily make a happy, sad, angry or scared face on request. In contrast, I have noted that some children, and even some adults, with Asperger's syndrome have considerable difficulty with this task. The person may achieve the facial expression by physically manipulating his or her face, providing only one element, such as the mouth shape associated with being sad, or producing a grimace that does not appear to resemble the facial expression of any human emotion. The person may also explain that it is difficult to express the emotion as he or she is not experiencing that feeling at that moment.

The ability to understand, express and regulate emotions can be assessed by asking parents specific questions, for example:

- Does the child have any unusual emotional mannerisms, such as flapping his or her hands when excited or gently rocking when trying to concentrate or relax?

- Does the child understand the need in some situations for an expression of gratitude, an apology or an expression of remorse?

- Does the child have difficulty reading the signs of someone being bored, annoyed or embarrassed?

- Does the child lack subtlety or maturity in his or her expression of anger, affection, anxiety and sadness?

- Does the child have rapid mood changes?

- How does the child express and respond to affection?

Conversations with parents can examine whether the child suppresses feelings of confusion and frustration at school but releases such feelings at home. I describe some children with Asperger's syndrome as being a 'Dr Jekyll and Mr Hyde' – an angel at school but a devil at home. This has been described in the literature as masquerading (Carrington and Graham 2001). Unfortunately, a parent may be personally criticized for not being able to manage his or her child with Asperger's syndrome at home. A teacher reports that the child has exemplary behaviour in class so the behaviour must be due to a defect in how the parents manage the child's emotions. It is important that school authorities recognize that children with Asperger's syndrome can sometimes consciously suppress their feelings at school and wait until they are home to release their anguish on younger siblings and a loving parent. Such children are more confused, frustrated and stressed at school than their body language communicates, and the constrained emotions are eventually expressed and released at home. The cause of the problem is the child not communicating extreme stress at school, and not a parent who does not know how to control his or her child.

The diagnostic assessment should also include an examination of any examples of inappropriate or unconventional emotional reactions when distressed, such as giggling (Berthier 1995), or a delayed emotional response. The child may worry about something, not communicate his or her feelings to parents and eventually, perhaps hours or days later, release the build up of emotions in a 'volcanic' emotional explosion. Such children keep their thoughts to themselves and replay an event in their thoughts to try to understand what happened. Each mental action replay causes the release of the associated emotions and eventually the child can cope no longer. The frustration, fear or confusion has reached an intensity that is expressed by very agitated behaviour. When parents discover what the child has been ruminating about, they often ask the child why he or she did not tell them so that they could help. However, such children are unable to effectively articulate and explain their feelings to alert a parent to their distress, and do not seem to know how a parent could help them understand or solve the problem.

Some children and adolescents with Asperger's syndrome can feel responsible for another person's agitation or distress and apologize or appease when they did not cause the other person's feelings. Wendy Lawson explained:

> Until recently I always believed that if someone close to me was 'angry' then it must be because of me. Now I am beginning to realise that people can be unhappy or even angry, for many different reasons. In fact it may have nothing to do with me at all! (Lawson 2001, pp.118–19)

The child may have a history of being overly attached to a parent, or detached; or having an intense emotional reaction to changes in routines or expectations, or when experiencing frustration and failure. The child may rapidly switch from one emotion to another. I ask parents if the child's emotions over a short period of time are sometimes like a pinball in a pinball machine, bouncing between and lighting up intense emotions. Wendy Lawson wrote about her emotions and explained that:

> Life tends to be either 'happy' or 'not happy', 'angry' or 'not angry'. All the 'in between' emotions on the continuum get missed. I jump from calm to panic in one major step. (Lawson 2001, p.119)

I have noted that many parents say that the child or adult may be most happy when alone (McGee, Feldman and Chernin 1991), or when engaged in his or her special interest (Attwood 2003b). The person with Asperger's syndrome may not associate happiness with people or not know what to do when someone is happy. Sometimes happiness is expressed in an immature or unusual way, such as literally jumping for joy or flapping hands excitedly.

Observation of the child by a clinician can reveal aspects that are qualitatively different from typical children. Hans Asperger noted that the child's face might lack subtle emotional expressions and be unusually 'wooden' or mask-like, sometimes having an unnatural expression, or appear unusually serious (Hippler and Klicpera 2004). An adult with Asperger's syndrome said to me, 'I've just got one facial look,' and another said, 'People tell me to smile, even though I feel great inside.'

During the diagnostic assessment of children with Asperger's syndrome, I tell several stories and ask the child specific questions to determine the degree of maturity in Theory of Mind abilities (see Chapter 5). The stories include descriptions of someone's feelings, including feelings of excitement and disappointment. I carefully observe the facial expressions and body language of the child who is listening to the story, to see if the child's expressions mirror the emotion being described. I have found that typical children will show facial expressions that indicate they are sympathizing with the central character, but children with Asperger's syndrome often have a look of attention but not emotion. I have also noted that adults with Asperger's syndrome may not sympathize with characters in a film, and have a 'poker face' when other people in the cinema are clearly expressing emotions sympathetic to the actors.

When discussing emotions, adults with Asperger's syndrome may intellectualize feelings, despise emotionality in others and describe difficulties understanding specific emotions such as love. There is often a conspicuous emotional immaturity; the professor of mathematics may have the emotional maturity of a teenager. Despite their being notorious for becoming irritable over relatively trivial matters, I have noted that some adults with Asperger's syndrome are renowned for remaining calm in a crisis when some typical adults would panic. This ability has been very useful for adults with Asperger's syndrome who have been medical staff in Accident and Emergency departments of hospitals, or soldiers on active duty.

The person with Asperger's syndrome may have an unusual or immature concept of emotions in terms of understanding that someone can have two feelings at the same time, for example being delighted to have a promotion at work but also anxious about the new responsibilities. Sean Barron explained that:

> I was in my early twenties before I learned a simple rule of social interactions that opened the door to greater understanding of others: that people can and usually do feel more than one emotion at the same time. It was inconceivable to me, for instance, that someone could be happy in general, yet furious with a specific incident, etc. – that two contradictory emotions could be operating at once in the same person. (Grandin and Barron 2005, p.255)

The assessment includes an examination of the ability to identify and express emotions but also the ability to repair emotions. For children, I use a story to assess a child's ability to understand how to repair someone's feelings. The child is asked to imagine coming home from school, walking into the kitchen, and seeing his or her mother at the kitchen sink. She has her back to the child, who greets her, and she turns round. As she turns round, the child notices she is crying and appears to be very sad. The child is reassured that her sadness is not due to anything the child has done. I then ask, 'If she was crying and very sad, what would you do?'

The initial response of both typical children and those with Asperger's syndrome is to ask her what's wrong. I commend the response and then say, 'But what could you say or do that would make her feel better?' Typical children quickly suggest words or gestures of affection to cheer her up. Children with Asperger's syndrome tend to prefer a practical action to make her feel better, such as getting her some tissues for the tears, making her a cup of tea, doing their homework, talking to her about their special interest (which is what would cheer up the child) or leaving her alone so that she will get over it more quickly.

Sometimes children with Asperger's syndrome will suggest a hug but, when asked why that would help, may reply that they don't know why, but it is what you are supposed to do. The child with Asperger's syndrome does care and genuinely wants her to feel better, but emotional repair is achieved by a practical action, solitude or imitating the observed response of others. The conspicuous absence or quality of words and gestures of affection is clinically significant, not only in terms of a diagnosis but also in identifying the emotional repair mechanisms that are effective for the child. The clinician examines the quality and quantity of emotional repair suggestions as part of the diagnostic assessment, but the information can be valuable in determining which emotional repair strategies are likely to be effective if the child needs treatment for a mood disorder.

As much as there can be problems with the understanding, expression, regulation and repair of emotions, there can also be problems regarding the confidence to respond appropriately. I had just diagnosed Asperger's syndrome in a young boy during a diagnostic assessment at the family home. The son went to the neighbour's house so that we could discuss the diagnosis, remedial strategies and likely prognosis. As I confirmed the diagnosis, the child's mother, who had suspected for several years that her son had Asperger's syndrome, released her feelings in a torrent of tears. The tears were of relief, not despair. I intuitively knew that she needed comforting. As she was sitting next to her husband, I anticipated that her husband would comfort her. However, he showed no emotion or attempt to console her. A little later, after some discussion of the family and relationship history, and while her husband was out of the room, she asked me if there were signs of Asperger's syndrome in her husband. There were in fact many signs in his descriptions of his childhood and current profile of abilities. When he returned to the room, I asked him if he could tell me what he was thinking when his wife was crying a short while ago. He said, 'I knew she was upset, but I didn't want to do the wrong thing.'

In summary, the person with Asperger's syndrome may have difficulty understanding the cues that indicate feelings; as one child said, as his mother was crying, 'Why is it raining in your eyes?' There can be difficulty knowing how to respond to the cues. A child saw his young sister fall from a swing. As she approached him and his mother, in tears, he asked his mother, 'What face do I make?' Those who do develop the ability to read the signals may not have the confidence to respond in case they make a mistake and there can be a limited range of emotional repair mechanisms.

Rating scales for emotions

There are several self-rating scales used by clinicians to measure the degree of depression, anxiety or anger that have been designed for typical children and adults but can also be administered to children and adults with Asperger's syndrome. However, there are specific modifications that can be used for someone with Asperger's syndrome. He or she may be more able to quantify an emotional response accurately using a numerical representation of the gradation in experience and expression of emotions rather than a precise and subtle vocabulary of words. I use the concept of an emotion 'thermometer', bar graph or a 'volume' scale. These analogue measures are used to establish a baseline assessment as well as being incorporated in the emotion education component of the treatment of a mood disorder.

The assessment of the understanding and expression of emotions should include the construction of a list of behavioural indicators of mood changes. The indicators can include changes in the characteristics associated with Asperger's syndrome: for example, an increase in time spent engaged in solitude or in the special interest; rigidity or incoherence in thought processes due to anxiety or depression; or behaviour intended to impose control in the person's daily life and over others. This is in addition to conventional indicators such as panic attacks, comments indicating low self-worth, and episodes of anger.

The person and his or her family can also complete a daily mood diary to determine whether there is any cyclical nature to, or specific triggers for, mood changes. For example, if the child has an anxiety disorder, parents can consider the child's level of anxiety during the day and rate the level of anxiety on a scale from zero to 20. A score near zero would indicate a relatively relaxed day, ten a typical level of anxiety and a score near 20 would indicate the child was extremely anxious that day. Over time a pattern can emerge. This can be related to a menstrual or lunar cycle, a particular time of year or a clear cycle or wave pattern that may or may not be related to environmental factors. Medical investigations can then determine whether the person has an unusual fluctuation in hormones or a cycle of mood swings that suggests a diagnosis of bipolar disorder.

ANXIETY DISORDERS

We all feel a little anxious sometimes, but many children and adults with Asperger's syndrome appear to be prone to being anxious for much of their day, or to be extremely anxious about a specific event. The late Marc Segar had Asperger's syndrome and in his essay 'The Battles of the Autistic Thinker' (Segar undated) wrote that one thing autistic people are often good at is worrying. I have talked to adults with Asperger's syndrome who have needed treatment for chronic anxiety, and many have said that they cannot think of a time in their lives when they did not feel anxious, even in very early childhood. I am not sure if this is a constitutional feature for some people with Asperger's syndrome or a result of being overly stressed from trying to socialize and cope with the unpredictability and sensory experiences of daily life.

The specific event that can elicit feelings of anxiety can be anticipated change such as a replacement class teacher for the day, unexpected changes in routines, public criticism or praise, or a sensory experience. Very sensitive sensory perception, especially for sounds, can cause the person with Asperger's syndrome to worry about when the next painful sensory experience will occur. My sister-in-law has Asperger's syndrome, and the sound of a dog barking is an excruciating experience for her. At times, this has caused her to be almost agoraphobic, fearing leaving her home as a journey to the local shops could include hearing a dog bark. The sensory sensitivity will create a feeling of anxiety, but unfortunately feeling anxious also heightens sensory perception, and the combination of sensory sensitivity and anxiety thus has a profound effect on the person's quality of life.

Being anxious will affect the person's thinking and lead to the development of strategies to reduce the level of anxiety. When we are relaxed, our bodies are flexible but when anxious we tense our muscles and become rigid. The same occurs for thinking and problem solving. When a person with Asperger's syndrome is anxious, his or her thinking tends to become more rigid. One of the signs of anxiety for such individuals is 'tunnel vision' or a 'one-track mind' in thinking. Marc Segar said that 'The problem with worrying is that it will often distract you from what you need to be concentrating on if you are to solve the problem' (Segar undated).

A means of avoiding anxiety-provoking situations is to develop the type of personality that is unfortunately perceived as controlling or oppositional. The child can use tantrums, emotional blackmail, rigid defiance and non-compliance to ensure he or she avoids circumstances that could increase anxiety. Another way of avoiding situations associated with anxiety is to retreat into solitude or the special interest. The greatest anxiety is usually associated with social situations, and being alone ensures the person does not make any social errors or suffer humiliation or torment by others. The special interest can be so engrossing and enjoyable that no anxious thought intrudes into the person's thinking. Clinicians also need to be aware that one way of reducing anxiety is self-medication, such as using alcohol or cannabis.

When the level of anxiety is extreme and long-standing, there can be a breakdown of the sense of reality such that the person develops mood-congruent delusions. The obsession can become a delusion, especially when resistance to obsessive or intrusive thoughts is abandoned and insight disappears. The thinking appears disorganized and psychotic, and clearly the person displaying such characteristics should be referred to a psychiatrist who specialises in the treatment of mood disorders in someone with Asperger's syndrome.

Having suffered long-term anxiety, the person will become extremely sensitive to any situation that could increase anxiety. There can be a tendency to 'press the panic button' too quickly. This will also affect the quality of life of those who support the person with Asperger's syndrome who has a chronic anxiety disorder. Family life is affected in terms of avoiding potentially anxiety-provoking situations, with the person with Asperger's syndrome and family members feeling they are 'walking through an anxiety minefield'.

For some people with Asperger's syndrome, there can be worries about events and experiences that are very unlikely to happen. Marc Fleisher has written a book on survival strategies for people with Asperger's syndrome. He describes his own anxiety and that:

> One critical observation is the fact that as much as 99 per cent of the things that worried me never happened. Autistic people can waste an incredible amount of energy getting every part of their body tensed up in a state of anxiety while

dwelling on something that they will probably never have to face. (Fleisher 2006, p.32)

The most common types of anxiety disorders for children and adults with Asperger's syndrome are Obsessive Compulsive Disorder (OCD), Post Traumatic Stress Disorder (PTSD), school refusal, selective mutism and social anxiety disorder (Ghaziuddin 2005b).

Obsessive Compulsive Disorder

About 25 per cent of adults with Asperger's syndrome also have the clear clinical signs of Obsessive Compulsive Disorder (Russell *et al.* 2005). In OCD the person has intrusive thoughts that he or she does not want to think about: the thoughts are described as *egodystonic*, i.e. distressing and unpleasant. In typical people the intrusive thoughts are often about cleanliness, aggression, religion and sex. Clinical experience and research studies indicate that the obsessive thoughts of children and adults with Asperger's syndrome are much more likely to be about cleanliness, bullying, teasing, making a mistake and being criticized than the other categories of intrusive thoughts (McDougle *et al.* 1995). The vulnerable times to develop OCD in the general population and for those with Asperger's syndrome are between 10 and 12 years and the early adult years (Ghaziuddin 2005b). Treatment for OCD is a combination of psychotherapy such as Cognitive Behaviour Therapy (CBT – see page 151), and medication.

Sometimes parents describe the person's special interest as an 'obsession' which suggests a diagnosis of OCD, but there is a distinct qualitative difference between an interest and a clinical obsession. The person with Asperger's syndrome clearly enjoys the interest: it is not egodystonic and therefore not necessarily indicative of OCD (Attwood 2003b; Baron-Cohen 1990).

Compulsions are a sequence of actions and rituals, usually with a repetitive quality, to reduce the level of anxiety. This can include actions such as washing hands to prevent contamination by germs, or checking several times that all the electricity switches in a house are in the off position. The typical behaviour of children with Asperger's syndrome includes repetitive or compulsive actions. This can include ensuring that objects are in a line or symmetrical, hoarding and counting items or having a ritual that must be completed before the child can fall asleep. While these are known characteristics of Asperger's syndrome, the additional diagnosis of OCD is made when the intensity or degree of expression has gone beyond that expected of someone with Asperger's syndrome, and reached clinical significance. However, what is clinically significant is the subjective decision of the psychologist or psychiatrist.

Post Traumatic Stress Disorder

Post Traumatic Stress Disorder (PTSD) can be the consequence of experiencing a traumatic event or series of events. The clinical signs of PTSD include attempts to avoid the incident or memories of the incident, and signs of anxiety, depression, anger and even hallucinations associated with the precipitating event or events. In the general population, PTSD is associated with war experiences and sexual, physical and emotional abuse. I know that severe and repeated bullying can precipitate the clinical signs of PTSD in children with Asperger's syndrome (see Chapter 4) and a fear of physical injury through bullying is often reported by children with Asperger's syndrome who are anxious (Russell and Sofronoff 2004).

The person can have intrusive memories of the traumatic event that are very difficult to 'block'. An adolescent with Asperger's syndrome explained to me that the intrusive thoughts (about being the target of very malicious bullying) appear almost to argue with him. He explained that his inner voice 'does not let me calm down easily. It keeps on going on about what happened and going on how wrong the other person was to me.' The original event was obviously traumatic but intrusive thoughts and mental re-enactments will cause the person repeatedly to experience the same feelings of fear and distress.

The treatment is medication and psychotherapy. I use Comic Strip Conversations (i.e. drawings of stick figures and thought, feeling and speech bubbles) to explore the child's or adult's traumatic experiences and to provide explanations of why the event may have occurred, the person's perception of the event, and the thoughts and motives of various participants, including the person with Asperger's syndrome. The cognitive restructuring component of CBT is then used to change thoughts and reactions, and achieve resolution or closure (see page 158).

School refusal

Typical children can refuse to go to school for many reasons, including being anxious, wanting to avoid specific lessons and to be with friends outside the school grounds. School refusal for children with Asperger's syndrome is usually due to anxiety. With young children this can be separation anxiety and not wanting to leave the company of their mother. The child needs the presence of a parent to provide reassurance and guidance. The classroom can be a very daunting environment which creates considerable anxiety. This can result in genuine physiological signs associated with anxiety such as nausea, headaches and bowel problems.

Later in childhood, the contrast between the lifestyle and circumstances at home and those at school can lead to school refusal. A lack of academic and social success, fear of being teased, and a sense of being overwhelmed by the experiences in the classroom and playground can lead to a phobic reaction to school. Treatment programs will need first to determine which aspects of school provoke anxiety and then to encourage success in school work and social integration.

Selective mutism

Girls are more commonly affected by selective mutism than boys, and the cause of the avoidance of speech is usually anxiety. When anyone is anxious, the reaction can be one of fight, flight or freeze. Thus anxiety may make the person agitated and restless (fight), try to escape or avoid the situation (flight), or freeze in terms of being unable to participate or talk. Children with Asperger's syndrome who develop selective mutism in their early years can talk fluently when relaxed, for example at home, but when in school, their level of anxiety is so severe that they are unable (not unwilling) to speak. Treatment programs should focus on which aspects of the context provoke anxiety, and developing strategies to encourage relaxation and confidence.

Social anxiety disorder

Social phobia, or social anxiety disorder, would be expected to be relatively common for those with Asperger's syndrome, especially in the teenage and adult years when they are more acutely aware of their confusion in social situations, of making social mistakes, and possibly suffering ridicule. A typical person who develops social phobia is very concerned as to what others will think of him or her, with a fear of being embarrassed. I have noted that young people with Asperger's syndrome who develop signs of social phobia are more avoidant of self-criticism than the criticism of others, and have a pathological fear of making a social mistake. Treatment includes medication and CBT, but someone with Asperger's syndrome who has social phobia will also need guidance in improving social skills, and encouragement to be less self-critical and to cope with social mistakes.

DEPRESSION

Our psychological and biological models of mood disorders suggest a continuum between long-standing anxiety and depression. When anxious, the person thinks 'What if X happens?' But in depression, the person assumes the worst outcome is unavoidable. It is interesting that anxiety and depressive disorders both respond positively to the same medications and CBT.

There are a number of characteristics of depression: physical and mental exhaustion; feeling sad or empty; and having little interest in previously pleasurable experiences. There can be social withdrawal, a change in appetite with either weight gain or loss, and a change in sleep pattern with little, or excessive, sleep. The person talks about feeling worthless and guilty, is unable to concentrate, and may have thoughts about death.

People with Asperger's syndrome appear vulnerable to feeling depressed, with about one in three children and adults having a clinical depression (Ghaziuddin *et al.* 1998; Kim *et al.* 2000; Tantam 1988a; Wing 1981). The reasons for people with Asperger's syndrome to be depressed are many and include the long-term consequences on self-esteem of feeling unaccepted and misunderstood, the mental exhaustion from trying to succeed socially, feelings of loneliness, being tormented, teased, bullied and ridiculed by peers, and a cognitive style that is pessimistic, focusing on what could go wrong. I have listened to adolescents with Asperger's syndrome who are clinically depressed and often heard the comment, 'I feel I don't belong.' The depression can lead to a severe withdrawal from social contact and thoughts that, without social success, there is no point in life.

People with Asperger's syndrome are often perfectionists, tend to be exceptionally good at noticing mistakes, and have a conspicuous fear of failure. There can be a relative lack of optimism, with a tendency to expect failure and not to be able to control events (Barnhill and Smith Myles 2001). As the adolescent with Asperger's syndrome achieves greater intellectual maturity, this can be associated with an increased insight into being different and self-perception of being irreparably defective and socially stupid.

Some of the characteristics of Asperger's syndrome can prolong the duration and increase the intensity of depression. The person with Asperger's syndrome may not disclose his or her inner feelings, preferring to retreat into solitude, avoiding conversation (especially when the conversation is about feelings and experiences), and trying to resolve the depression by subjective thought. Typical people are better at, and more confident about, disclosing feelings and knowing that another person may provide a more objective opinion and act as an emotional restorative. Family and friends of a typical person may be able to temporarily halt, and to a certain extent alleviate, the mood by words and gestures of reassurance and affection. They may be able to distract the person who is depressed by initiating enjoyable experiences, or using humour. These emotional rescue strategies are sometimes less effective for people with Asperger's syndrome, who try to solve personal and practical issues by themselves and for whom affection and compassion may not be as effective an emotional restorative.

The signs of depression can be the same as would be expected of typical children and adults, but clinicians who specialize in Asperger's syndrome have noted another feature that can be indicative of depression. The special interest of the person with Asperger's syndrome is often associated with pleasure and the acquisition of knowledge about the physical rather than the social world (see Chapter 7). However, when the person becomes depressed the interest can become morbid, and the person preoccupied with aspects of death.

Sometimes the reason for the change in the focus of the interest to the macabre can be mystifying, but is the child's attempt to communicate confusion, sadness and uncertainty about what to do. In her book on autism and Asperger's syndrome, Pat Howlin described Joshua, whose father was a news cameraman on war assignment. His father was missing for several days and the family was extremely worried. Joshua began asking his mother incessant questions about the weapons used by each side, and how many people were being killed. During this time of anxiety for the family, Joshua did not express worry or seek comfort from family members. On his father's return, he wanted to know how many dead bodies he had photographed. When Joshua was asked about his apparent lack of concern or compassion, he said that he was aware that his mother and sister were upset but he was unable to reassure them since he did not know what had happened to his father, and he did not want to tell a lie – he did not know what to say. His morbid interest and questions were actually 'a cry for help', and his attempt to try to communicate and understand his own feelings (Howlin 2004). Parents and clinicians may need to look beyond the focus of the interest and recognize a mood disorder (anxiety or depression) that is being expressed in an unconventional way, but a way that may be expected in someone who has difficulty understanding and expressing emotions.

Clinical experience confirms that some adolescents and adults with Asperger's syndrome who are clinically depressed can consider suicide as a means of ending the emotional pain and despair. The person carefully plans a means of suicide over days or weeks. However, children and some adolescents with Asperger's syndrome can experience what I describe as a 'suicide attack', a spur-of-the-moment decision to make a dramatic end to life. Liliana, an adult with Asperger's syndrome, conceptualized her intense depression as a 'soul migraine'. We recognize the occurrence of a panic attack in typical people, which can occur very quickly and be unanticipated; the person has a sudden and overwhelming feeling of anxiety. In a depression attack, the person with Asperger's syndrome has a sudden and overwhelming feeling of depression and there can be an impulsive and dramatic attempt at suicide. The child can suddenly run in front of a moving vehicle or go to a bridge to jump from a height to end his or her life. Those who have been with the person may not have identified any conspicuous preceding depressive thoughts, but a minor irritation, such as being teased or making a mistake, can trigger an intense emotional reaction, a depression attack. The person can be restrained and prevented from injury, and remarkably, a short while later, usually returns to his or her typical emotional state, which is not indicative of a severe clinical depression.

When a person is depressed, there is also the risk of self-injury. Nita Jackson explained in her autobiography that:

> Another thing about depression is that anything can cause a tear: a tune, chord sequence, a picture, an object out of place, a speck of dust on a picture frame…and then all I can think about is how to escape the pain in my head, of which the only route is through the physical. Self-abuse can take many forms. It's not all about razors and knives. (N. Jackson 2002, p.63)

> It is not always true that Asperger people are self-centred and uncaring. A number of my Asperger friends say they keep their self-mutilation secret because they don't want to upset their families. (N. Jackson 2002, p.63)

Treatment for a conventional clinical depression in someone with Asperger's syndrome should be a combination of medication, CBT and programs to encourage social success, self-esteem and a more optimistic outlook. This is discussed in a subsequent section of this chapter.

ANGER

We do not know how common anger management problems are with children and adults with Asperger's syndrome, but we do know that when problems with the expression of anger occur, the person with Asperger's syndrome and family members are very keen to reduce the frequency, intensity and consequences of anger. The rapidity and intensity of anger, often in response to a relatively trivial event, can be extreme. Using the metaphor of a volume control for the emotional intensity of expression, with a gradation from one to ten, a typical child will gradually increase his or her expression of anger through all volume levels. The child or adult with Asperger's syndrome may only have two settings, between one and two, and nine and ten. Events that may precipitate a three to eight reaction in a typical child can precipitate a nine or ten level of expression in someone with Asperger's syndrome. Thus, for some people with Asperger's syndrome, there appears to be a faulty emotion regulation or control mechanism for expressing anger.

When feeling angry, the person with Asperger's syndrome does not appear to be able to pause and think of alternative strategies to resolve the situation, considering his or her intellectual capacity and age. There is often an instantaneous physical response without careful thought. When the anger is intense, the person with Asperger's syndrome may be in a 'blind rage' and unable to see the signals indicating that it would be appropriate to stop.

Feelings of anger can also be the response in situations where we would expect other emotions. I have noted that sadness may be expressed as anger. When conducting a CBT program on emotion management for a group of teenagers with Asperger's syndrome, I asked the group members how each of them expressed feeling sad. Some of the responses were typical of their peers, for example 'be alone', 'go for a walk' and 'sometimes cry'. However, several members of the group said 'try and smash glass', 'play violent computer games' and 'hit my pillow'. Observation of these behaviours in a typical teenager would indicate feelings of anger, not sadness. The confusing combination of anger and depression occurred when Luke said, 'When I'm angry I say I want to kill myself.'

One of the teenagers with Asperger's syndrome in the group informed me that when he feels sad, he 'gets angry with someone who is trying to cheer me up'. Words and gestures of affection are not an emotional restorative for him, and can result in an angry and aggressive response. A teenage girl in the group said, 'Crying doesn't work for me, so I get angry instead and throw sticks.' For her, too, tears are not an emotional release. However, a physical and destructive action does repair the sad feeling. Unfortunately, others would interpret such behaviour as indicative of feeling angry and aggressive.

When typical children and adults have a 'negative' emotion or thought such as feeling sad, anxious, confused or embarrassed, they have an extensive vocabulary of emotional expression that can be subtle, precise and easily understood by others. Those with Asperger's syndrome have a limited vocabulary of emotional expression that lacks subtlety and precision and can easily be misinterpreted by others.

There are other reasons why anger management can become a problem for someone with Asperger's syndrome. For very young children and even some adults with Asperger's syndrome, aggression can have the function of achieving solitude. The pre-school-age child feels angry due to being interrupted by other children or having to play with them, and soon learns that offensive language and aggressive gestures and actions can keep other children at a distance. Such behaviour can continue throughout life. Doug, an adult with Asperger's syndrome who is concerned about his temper, said, 'Anger is a tool to push people away,' and Grant said, 'People leave me alone if I look imposing.'

In a conflict situation, typical young children will become angry and use acts of aggression to achieve possessions, dominance and control. Gradually, acts of aggression and threats are replaced by negotiation, compromise and cooperation, and the knowledge that one can sometimes get what one wants by being nice. These strategies may not be obvious to children with Asperger's syndrome, who tend to rely on immature, but sometimes effective, confrontation strategies and emotional blackmail. I have noted that some children with Asperger's syndrome can develop a conduct disorder in terms of using threats and acts of violence to control their circumstances and experiences. For example, they may threaten to hurt their mother if she insists on their going to school; or they may use violence to make her buy something associated with their special interest. It is interesting that such confrontational, oppositional and aggressive behaviour is usually not modelled on a member of the family. Indeed, the parents who are subjected to threats and acts of violence are often very meek people who may lack assertiveness in conflict situations.

Feelings of anger in response to what someone is doing can lead to acts of aggression as an effective means of making people stop. For example, if the child with Asperger's syndrome is being teased or bullied, he or she may have a relatively limited range of options to end the experience. The first option is to tell the person to stop, but if this does not work, and neither has ignoring the person, nor reporting the situation to an adult, then the only option remaining for the child with Asperger's syndrome is to engage in an act of explosive aggression to end the unbearable teasing and tormenting. I use the expression 'three strikes and you are out'. The child with Asperger's syndrome may several times ask the person teasing or tormenting them to stop. If this does not work, the only alternative known to the child that will stop the other person is to use violence. Although the child may be aware of the consequences of such unacceptable behaviour, he or she cannot continue to endure being tormented, and may not know what else to do.

In Chapter 1, reference was made to the four psychological responses a child can have to the recognition of being different to other children and having the profile of abilities and behaviour indicative of Asperger's syndrome. One of the reactions is to become arrogant, with high standards in expectations of self and others, and a tendency to feel very angry when confused or frustrated. Other people are perceived as being stupid or deliberately trying to confuse or annoy the child. Feelings of anger quickly become thoughts of retribution, destruction, punishment and physical retaliation.

A previous section of this chapter referred to a high incidence of depression in children and adults with Asperger's syndrome. In a typical depression, there is a lack of energy, low self-esteem and self-blame. The feelings are internalized. However, sometimes depression is externalized (blaming others) rather than internalized, and associated with periods of intense emotional energy. Clinicians will use the term 'externalized, agitated depression'. When I receive a referral for a child or adult with Asperger's syndrome who has problems with anger management, part of the assessment process is to determine whether signs of anger are actually signs of a clinical depression and should be treated as such.

There may be neurological reasons why there is a problem with emotion management in general and anger management in particular. We know that a part of the brain called the amygdala can be structurally and functionally abnormal in children and adults with Asperger's syndrome. The amygdala has many functions, including the perception and regulation of emotions, especially fear and anger. A metaphor to help understand the function of the amygdala is that of a vehicle being driven on a highway. The frontal lobes of the brain are the driver, who makes executive decisions on what to do, where to go, etc. The amygdala functions as the dashboard of the car, providing the driver with warning signals regarding the temperature of the engine, the amount of oil and fuel, and speed of the vehicle. In the case of people with Asperger's syndrome, the 'dashboard' is not functioning consistently. Information on the increasing emotional 'heat' and functioning of the engine (emotion and stress levels) are not available to the driver as a warning of impending breakdown.

This can explain why the child or adult does not appear to be consciously aware of increasing emotional stress, and his or her thoughts and behaviour are not indicative of deterioration in mood. Eventually the degree of emotion or stress is overwhelming, but it may be too late for the cognitive or thoughtful control of the emotion. There were no early warning signals of an emotional meltdown in observable behaviour that could be used by another person to repair the mood, or warning signals in the conscious thoughts of the person with Asperger's syndrome to enable him ore her to use self-control.

While a dysfunction of the amygdala is a plausible explanation of the difficulties in emotion communication and regulation, it is speculative, and it is important to state that impaired amygdala function should not be used as an excuse to avoid appropriate responsibilities and consequences. I do not want children to say that they couldn't help feeling angry and breaking something or hurting someone, and that it was his or her defective amygdala that was to blame.

Other reasons for problems with anger management include having a difficulty expressing feelings using words (alexithymia), and using physical acts to articulate the mood and release the emotional energy. Sometimes the anger is deliberately targeted at a person as a mood restorative. A girl with Asperger's syndrome was famous at school for her polite and compliant behaviour but notorious for the opposite when she returned home. She had contained her stress in the classroom and playground but on returning home was verbally and physically abusive to her younger sister. When I asked her why she was so mean to her sister when she came home from school, she looked at me as though the reason was obvious and replied, 'Because it makes me feel better.' The psychological term for such behaviour is negative reinforcement. Hurting her sister ended her own distress and was a powerful reinforcement for the aggressive behaviour.

Sometimes acts of aggression are pre-emptive strikes. The child with Asperger's syndrome has previous experience to suggest, or reason to believe, that a particular child will be deliberately mean to him or her. Without any provocation from the other child, the boy or girl with Asperger's syndrome anticipates conflict and makes the first strike: 'He was going to be mean to me, so I hurt him first.'

Unfortunately, feelings of anger and subsequent aggression further alienate the child with Asperger's syndrome from constructive interactions with peers. Since peers do not consider the child with Asperger's syndrome to be their friend, they can relinquish any responsibility to calm the child down when he or she is angry.

Managing rage

A subsequent section of this chapter will describe CBT programs for anger management (see page 151), but at this stage it is important for the reader to know what to do and what not to do when the person with Asperger's syndrome is feeling extremely angry and rapidly losing control, i.e. losing his or her temper and entering a state of rage.

We all feel angry sometimes, and I know children and adults with Asperger's syndrome who very rarely feel angry. However, when the feelings of anger are extremely intense and lead to an explosive rage, there is a diagnostic term that may be applicable to some people with Asperger's syndrome. Intermittent Explosive Disorder (IED) is included in the diagnostic manual DSM-IV, and is defined as follows:

> The person has several discrete episodes of failure to resist impulses that result in serious assault or destruction of property, the degree of aggression is grossly out of proportion to any precipitating psychosocial stressors and not accounted for by other mental disorders such as a personality disorder, psychotic disorder, conduct disorder or ADHD, or alcohol or drugs. (American Psychiatric Association 2000, p.667)

Thus, if a person with Asperger's syndrome has problems with the management of anger that is intermittent and extreme, there may be a relevant diagnostic category that should enable the person to access appropriate treatment.

When managing someone with Asperger's syndrome who is feeling angry, it is important to know that some actions can cause feelings of anger to increase; these include raising your voice, confrontation, sarcasm, being emotional and using physical restraint. Raising one's voice and confrontation (emphasizing punishments) will inflame the situation and cause the person with Asperger's syndrome to become more agitated and less flexible in thinking, which inhibits the ability to consider appropriate options to reduce the feeling of anger. Sarcasm will make the person with Asperger's syndrome more confused; and the other person becoming emotional, being angry, and sometimes even being affectionate, can be counterproductive and 'add fuel to the fire'.

When I was discussing with a child with Asperger's syndrome strategies to encourage him not to go into a rage, I asked him if a hug from his mother would help him feel better. He replied with an emphatic 'No! It makes me madder.' That was very useful information to know. Touch, and especially attempts at physical restraint, can increase the feelings of anger and energy levels. Sometimes asking the person 'What's the matter?' can also inflame the situation, because when experiencing severe emotional distress, the person's ability to articulate the cause of the anger can be significantly diminished and create further frustration.

I recommend that when the child or adult with Asperger's syndrome is in a rage, the person managing the situation uses a quiet and assertive voice, perhaps not enquiring about the cause of the agitation, but focusing on distraction or more constructive means of releasing the emotional energy. This can include suggesting access to the special interest, which can be mentally absorbing and extremely enjoyable, such that the angry feelings are excluded from the person's thoughts; solitude, to slowly calm down; or an energetic physical activity, such as a long run, to 'burn off' the destructive energy.

LOVE

We know that people with Asperger's syndrome have impaired or delayed Theory of Mind abilities that explain their difficulties conceptualizing the thoughts and feelings of other people, and conceptualizing their own thoughts and feelings. When a person with Asperger's syndrome is referred for the treatment of a mood disorder, the referral is almost invariably resulting from concerns regarding feelings of anxiety, sadness and anger. However, from my extensive clinical experience of children and adults with Asperger's syndrome, I would suggest that there is a fourth emotion that is of concern to the person with Asperger's syndrome in terms of his or her understanding and expression, and that is love.

Typical children enjoy and seek affection from their parents; they are able to read the signals when someone expects affection from them and recognize when to give affection to communicate reciprocal feelings of love, or to repair someone's feelings. Children less than two years old know that words and gestures of affection are perhaps the most effective emotional restorative for themselves and for someone who is sad. However, the person with Asperger's syndrome may not understand why typical people are so obsessed with expressing reciprocal love and affection. For a person with Asperger's syndrome, a hug can be experienced as an uncomfortable squeeze, and the young child with Asperger's syndrome may soon learn not to cry, as this will elicit a squeeze from someone.

Donna Williams eloquently explained in her autobiography:

> Anne screamed in terrified hysterics as one of the professionals sat on the bed beside her tucking a doll in next to her, which seemed to horrify her all the more. Oh, these symbols of normality, dolls, I thought. Oh, these terrifying reminders that one is meant to be comforted by people and if one can't one is meant at least to feel comforted by their effigies. (Williams 1998, p.171)

When considering the feeling of love, the person with Asperger's syndrome may enjoy a very brief and low-intensity expression of affection, and become confused or over-whelmed when greater levels of expression are experienced or expected. However, the reverse can occur for some children and adults with Asperger's syndrome, with the person needing frequent expressions of affection (sometimes for reassurance) and often expressing affection that can be overbearing for others. There may not be the varied vocabulary of affection expression that includes subtle, and for children, age-appropriate expressions. For some people with Asperger's syndrome the expression is excessive. An adult with Asperger's syndrome said to me, 'We feel and show affection but not often enough, and at the wrong intensity.'

In his autobiography, Edgar Schneider explains his confusion regarding love:

> At one point my mother, exasperated at me, said, 'You know what the trouble is? You don't know how to love! You need to learn how to love!' I was taken aback totally. I hadn't the faintest notion what she meant. I still don't. (Schneider 1999, p.43)

A psychoanalytic study of Asperger's syndrome suggests that such people do not fall in love readily (Mayes, Cohen and Klin 1993). I have conducted relationship counselling for couples where one partner has a diagnosis of Asperger's syndrome. A question that I ask each partner is his or her description of love. The following are the thoughts of women and men who do not share their partner's diagnosis of Asperger's syndrome:

Love is: Tolerance, non-judgemental, supportive.

Love is: A complex of beliefs that tap into our childhood languages and experiences; it is inspired when you meet someone that has a quality that maybe you admire, or do not have (admiration and respect) – or that they (someone you admire) reflect back to your ideal self – which is what you want to be or see yourself as.

Love is: Passion, acceptance, affection, reassurance, mutual enjoyment.

Love is: What I feel for myself when I am with another person.

The following are some of the descriptions given by their partners with Asperger's syndrome:

Love is: Helping and doing things for your lover.

Love is: An attempt to connect to the other person's feelings and emotions.

Love is: Companionship, someone to depend on to help you in the right direction.

Love is: I have no idea what is involved.

Love is: Tolerance, loyal, allows 'space'.

Love is: I don't know the correct answer.

Love is: Yet to be felt and experienced by myself.

In her book *Aspergers in Love*, Maxine Aston explains that:

> In relationships AS men are often very honest, loyal and hardworking, most will be faithful and remain with their chosen partner for life. They will give and offer love in the ways that they can. If their partners understand Asperger syndrome they will appreciate that this giving will often take a practical form. It is unlikely that an AS man will be able to offer emotional support or empathic feelings. Some women will not be able to live with the emptiness and loneliness that this can bring. (Aston 2003, p.197)

The person with Asperger's syndrome may have remarkable compassion for someone's physical suffering and be clearly moved by pictures of the results of a famine or natural disaster. However, I sometimes have to explain to a person with Asperger's syndrome that as much as blood trickling from a wound indicates physical pain, tears trickling down a face can indicate emotional pain, and there are practical actions that he or she could do to alleviate emotional pain in someone.

A child's rare use of gestures and words of affection can be lamented by the child's parents, and especially the child's mother. When she expresses her love for her child, with an affectionate hug, the child's body may become 'stiff' and the child may not always be soothed by demonstrative affection when distressed. A mother may wonder what she can do to console her child with Asperger's syndrome when an expression of love and affection is rejected or simply is not an effective emotional restorative.

The child with Asperger's syndrome may find confusing or misinterpret the expressions of love from his or her parents. For example, the mother of an anxious eight-year-old child with Asperger's syndrome would lie next to him in his bed as he fell asleep. This was an expression of her love for him, and ensured that, as he fell asleep, he would be next to someone who loved him. When I asked the child why his mother lay next to him, his reply was, 'She's tired and she said that my bed is the most comfortable bed.'

Teachers soon realize that the child with Asperger's syndrome may intensely dislike public praise that includes gestures or words of affection. The person with Asperger's syndrome has a limited tolerance of affectionate and sentimental behaviour in others. Chris explained that, 'I detest sentimentality, which I think is a wilful display of empty emotion over matters of no consequence, and it really should be avoided because it devalues the true expression of feeling' (Slater-Walker and Slater-Walker 2002, p.88).

While the person with Asperger's syndrome can enjoy and express low levels of the expression of love, there can be a problem when he or she develops a 'crush' on someone during adolescence and the early adult years. The expression of love and acts of affection can be too intense. Someone's kind act may be misinterpreted as having a more significant meaning than was intended. Due to impaired or delayed Theory of Mind abilities, the person with Asperger's syndrome may assume that the other person feels a reciprocal level of love, and may persistently follow around and try to talk to the other person. This can result in accusations of stalking.

While we have treatment programs and medication for the management of anxiety, depression and anger, clinicians are rarely asked to treat a typical person for 'love sickness'. However, specialists in Asperger's syndrome are recognizing that children and adults with Asperger's syndrome need education in the understanding and expression of affection and love, from liking someone and giving compliments, to being in love and appreciating the expectations a partner may have for sentimentality, romance and passion within the relationship. The education program on love and relationships needs to include an explanation, using a series of Social Stories™ or Social Articles (see p.69), of why typical people like affection and how it helps them; how to show you like someone and to know when they like you; and how to achieve a compromise between the level of affection enjoyed by a person with Asperger's syndrome, and the level expected by family members and friends.

For a partner and parent with Asperger's syndrome, therapy can include education in when and how to express love and affection, and with what frequency. Sometimes I use the strategies used in CBT, such as affective education, to help the person with Asperger's syndrome understand the concept and feelings of love; cognitive restructuring to change thinking and behaviour; and desensitization to reduce the anxiety, confusion and frustration often associated with feelings of love. The intention is to gradually increase the person's tolerance, enjoyment, and ability and confidence to express the range of feelings from like to love.

Temple Grandin explained that:

My brain scan shows that some emotional circuits between the frontal cortex and the amygdala just aren't hooked up – circuits that affect my emotions and are tied to my ability to feel love. I experience the emotion of love, but it's not the same way that most neurotypical people do. Does this mean my love is less valuable than what other people feel? (Grandin and Barron 2005, p.40)

COGNITIVE BEHAVIOUR THERAPY

When a mood disorder is diagnosed in a child or adult with Asperger's syndrome, the clinical psychologist or psychiatrist will need to know how to modify psychological treatments for mood disorders to accommodate the unusual cognitive profile of people with Asperger's syndrome. The primary psychological treatment for mood disorders is Cognitive Behaviour Therapy (CBT), which has been developed and refined over several decades. Research studies have established that CBT is an effective treatment to change the way a person thinks about and responds to emotions such as anxiety, sadness and anger (Graham 1998; Grave and Blissett 2004; Kendall 2000). CBT focuses on the maturity, complexity, subtlety and vocabulary of emotions, and dysfunctional or illogical thinking and incorrect assumptions. Thus, it has direct applicability to children and adults with Asperger's syndrome who have impaired or delayed Theory of Mind abilities and difficulty understanding, expressing and managing emotions. The theoretical model of emotions used in CBT is consistent with current scientific models of human emotions, namely becoming more consciously aware of one's emotional state, knowing how to respond to the emotion, and becoming more sensitive to how others are feeling (Ekman 2003). We now have published case studies and objective scientific evidence that CBT does significantly reduce mood disorders in children and adults with Asperger's syndrome (Bauminger 2002; Fitzpatrick 2004; Hare 1997; Reaven and Hepburn 2003; Sofronoff, Attwood and Hinton 2005).

CBT has several components or stages, the first being an assessment of the nature and degree of mood disorder using self-report scales and a clinical interview. The subsequent component is affective education to increase the person's knowledge of emotions. Discussion and activities explore the connection between thoughts, emotions and behaviour, and identify the way in which the person conceptualizes emotions and perceives various situations. The more someone understands emotions, the more he or she is able to express and control them appropriately. The third stage of CBT is cognitive restructuring to correct distorted conceptualizations and dysfunctional beliefs and to manage emotions constructively. The last stage is a schedule of activities to practise new cognitive skills to manage emotions in real-life situations.

I have designed two CBT programs, entitled *Exploring Feelings*, for children and adolescents with Asperger's syndrome, one to manage anger, the other to manage anxiety (Attwood 2004a, 2004b). A clinical psychologist usually implements a CBT program, but the *Exploring Feelings* programs are designed to be implemented by a psychologist (educational or clinical), psychiatrist, teacher, speech/language pathologist, occupational therapist or parent.

A previous section of this chapter has explained the assessment strategies that can be used with children and adults with Asperger's syndrome to measure the degree of mood disorder and identify specific situations that are associated with difficulties in managing emotions. The actual therapy begins with an opportunity to learn about emotions, described by psychologists as affective education.

Affective education

In the affective education component of CBT the person learns about the advantages and disadvantages of emotions and the identification of the different levels of expression in words and actions, within the person him- or herself and others. For children, this can be undertaken as a science project. A basic principle is to explore one emotion at a time, starting with a positive emotion before moving on to an emotion of clinical concern. The psychologist or therapist often chooses the first emotion, usually happiness or pleasure. The following are activities and strategies that can be included in the affective education component of CBT.

Creation of an emotions scrapbook

One of the first tasks is to create a scrapbook that illustrates the emotion. This can include pictures or representations that have a personal association with the emotion for the person with Asperger's syndrome: for example, if the emotion is happiness or pleasure, the book can include a photograph of a rare spider for the person who has a special interest in insects and spiders. It is important to remember that the scrapbook illustrates the pleasures in the person's life, which may not always be those more conventional pleasures of typical children or adults. I have noted that adults with Asperger's syndrome often include pictures in their pleasures book but the pictures are usually of scenes and animals without the presence of people.

Young children can cut out and place in the book pictures of happy people from magazine advertisements and pictures of enjoyable actions and events. Pictures may also be chosen to illustrate how what may appear to be insurmountable problems can be overcome; for example, one photograph may depict the child in the first stages of learning a skill, such as riding a bicycle. A note is made of the lack of competence at this stage, and the related emotions, such as anxiety or frustration. Adjacent to this photograph, another one is placed to illustrate the child's eventual success, and his or her enjoyment. The book can also include pictures and descriptions of favourite food, toys and people.

The education program also explores the sensations associated with the feeling, such as aromas, tastes and textures. These should be recorded in the scrapbook, which can also be used as a diary to include compliments that the person has received, records of achievement such as certificates, and memorabilia associated with enjoyable occasions. The scrapbook is regularly updated and can be used at a later stage in CBT to help change a particular mood and encourage confidence and self-esteem.

The happiness or pleasures scrapbook can also be used to illustrate different perceptions of a situation. For example, if the therapy is conducted in a group, the participants' scrapbooks can be compared and contrasted. It will become clear that one person's favourite topic is not necessarily another's – talking about trains may be an enjoyable experience for one participant, but perceived as remarkably boring by someone else. Part of the education, therefore, is to explain that while a certain topic may create a feeling of well-being for you, attempting to cheer up another person by using the same topic may not be a successful strategy.

Perception of emotional states

Another important aspect of affective education in CBT is to enable an individual to discover the salient cues that indicate a particular level of emotion in terms of his or her body sensations, behaviour and thoughts. These sensations can act as early warning signs of an impending escalation of emotion. In part, affective education is designed to improve the function of the amygdala in informing the frontal lobes of the brain about increasing stress levels and emotional arousal. Technology can be used to identify internal cues in the form of biofeedback instruments, such as auditory electromyography (EMG) and galvanic skin response (GSR) machines. The intention is to encourage the person to be more consciously aware of his or her own emotional state and to be able to manage an emotion before losing cognitive control.

The affective education includes information on how to read the emotional states of others. In her autobiography Nita Jackson explained that:

> I discovered that I couldn't comprehend people's facial expressions, what they said or the way in which they said it. Reminiscing on my early school days I realised how I used to laugh when someone cried because I thought the other person was laughing. I can't understand how I made this mistake – all I know is that I did this often. (N. Jackson 2002, p.20)

The extreme facial expressions for someone crying and laughing can be very similar. Both emotions can produce tears. The confusion for someone with Asperger's syndrome is quite understandable but can be misinterpreted by others. Children with Asperger's syndrome can become very distressed when someone laughs in response to something they have said or done. They may not know why someone would find the comment or actions amusing or know if the person is intending to laugh with them or to laugh at them. The affective education activities can include strategies to improve Theory of Mind abilities (see Chapter 5), including the abilities to read facial expressions and determine the intentions of others, especially whether an act was friendly, accidental or malicious.

Affective education includes information on the facial expression, tone of voice and body language that indicate the feelings of another person. The face is described as an 'information centre' for emotions. The typical errors include not identifying which cues are relevant or redundant, and misinterpreting cues. The therapist uses a range of games and resources to 'spot the message', and to explain the multiple meanings: for example a furrowed brow can mean anger, bewilderment, or be a sign of ageing skin; a loud voice does not automatically mean that the person is angry. Participants use pictures to compare the facial expressions of different emotions, and explore the combination of facial elements used in these expressions.

To learn how to identify mood from verbal cues, participants can listen to audio-tapes of someone's speech, and note the changes in prosody and emphasis. Another activity is for the same sentence to be repeated using a different tone of voice to indicate the person's mood: for example, 'Come here' can be whispered, shouted, accompanied with a sigh or said quickly, and has very different meanings (Pyles 2002). Tuition in gestural communication can be provided using a modified version of 'Charades', by requiring the person to mime an action to and simultaneously portray a particular mood. The other participants have to guess both the action and the emotion. For example, the action could be playing tennis while feeling confused, or cleaning the dishes while feeling relaxed.

The affective education activities are also designed to increase the person's vocabulary of emotional expression. What may often be missing are the subtle expressions of feelings, for example the states in between being mildly irritated and being in a rage, or feeling a little sad and wanting to end the suffering by suicide. Parents can be concerned that when agitated over what should be a relatively minor event, the child can have an extreme over-reaction. The child realizes that the jar of his favourite jam or jelly is empty, a replacement jar is not in the pantry and the shops are closed. His response can be overly dramatic, saying through his tears that it is his mother's fault and that his mother does not love him. To a parent this is a ridiculous and hurtful over-reaction but can be an example of a limited vocabulary of emotional response.

I saw a teenager with Asperger's syndrome whose mother was concerned that several times a week he would say he was going to kill himself. I immediately conducted an examination for the clinical signs of depression. There were none. I then explained to him the concept of an emotion thermometer to measure the intensity of emotions, and wrote on a small piece of paper the words he uses that had caused so much concern: 'I am going to kill myself.' The thermometer had a scale from zero to ten and I asked him to place the quotation at the point on the thermometer when he would say those words. He placed the quotation at level two. We discovered that he had an extremely limited vocabulary to express feelings of disappointment and sadness. He had remembered the words from a film when the actor was suicidal with grief, and assumed that was the way of communicating all levels of sadness.

An increase in the vocabulary of emotional expression can help when the person with Asperger's syndrome does not know what would be the appropriate emotional response. In his autobiography, Stephen Shore explained that:

> There are times when I find myself very interested in the study of feelings and emotions. This happens especially when I see someone experience a strong emotion or I sense that I don't seem to have an 'appropriate' emotion for a given situation...I find that music can serve as an amplifier of feelings. If I am in a particular mood I listen to, or run in my head, music expressing that feeling... Sometimes I think that I should be feeling a particular emotion but it just doesn't seem to be 'there' to feel... After my first girlfriend left to study in Sweden for a year, I played Gustav Mahler's Ninth Symphony. The last movement in particular, helped me deal with the sadness and loss relating to her departure. Added to that was the realization that our relationship as boyfriend and girlfriend was probably over. (Shore 2001, p.107)

Measuring the intensity of emotion

Once the key elements that indicate a particular emotion have been identified, it is important to use a measuring instrument to determine the degree of intensity. The therapist can use a model 'thermometer', 'gauge' or 'volume control', and a range of activities to define the level of expression. For example, a series of pictures of faces expressing varying degrees of happiness can be selected, and each placed at the appropriate point on the instrument. Alternatively, a variety of words that define different levels of happiness can be generated, and placed appropriately on the gauge.

Pictures of other emotions, such as sadness, anger or affection, can be less easy to find than those depicting happiness. I have used weekly news magazines to collect pictures of sad situations such as the human suffering from a natural disaster, or sports publications to obtain pictures of people expressing anger. Pictures of affection can be cut out of magazines of popular entertainers.

During therapy for emotion management it is important to ensure the child or adult with Asperger's syndrome has the same definition or interpretation of words and gestures as the therapist, and to clarify any semantic confusion. Clinical experience has indicated that some children and adolescents with Asperger's syndrome tend to use extreme statements when agitated. Affective education increases the person's vocabulary of emotional expression to ensure precision and accuracy in verbal expression, thereby avoiding extreme and offensive or hurtful expressions.

Stephen Shore teaches music. He explained to me that a child with Asperger's syndrome who is one of his music students had a problem with the gradation of emotional expression and Stephen taught him conducting to bring the concept of gradation into the physical realm. Stephen and his student would take turns conducting each other through the entire dynamic range which enabled the student to transfer this concept to emotions and other areas of his life where more than just an 'on' or 'off' approach is required.

Once the concept of a measuring instrument is established, it can also be used to determine the degree of emotional experience in particular situations. When exploring the dimension of a given emotion, questions can be asked, such as 'How happy/sad/angry would you feel if …?', requiring both a numerical rating on the 'instrument' and the associated words, facial expression, tone of voice and body language that represent that degree of expression.

This activity is particularly useful to determine the person's emotional response to specific situations that elicit anxiety, sadness or anger, and can be used to explore how the words and actions of others affect the feelings of the person with Asperger's syndrome. I have noticed how people with Asperger's syndrome have considerable difficulty recognizing how their own words and actions affect the feelings of others, a consequence of impaired Theory of Mind and empathy skills. Questions can be asked, such as 'How happy would your mother/partner feel if you said that you love him/her?' or 'How sad does he/she feel when you say…?' This can be quite an important discovery for both parties.

Photographs of emotions, reading material and computer programs

The affective education program can include the creation of a photograph album with pictures of the child and family members expressing particular emotions; or video recordings of the child expressing his or her feelings in real-life situations. This can be particularly valuable to demonstrate his or her behaviour when angry. Another activity, entitled 'Guess the message', can include the presentation of specific, less obvious cues such as a cough as a warning sign, or a raised eyebrow to indicate doubt.

Books on specific emotions can be a valuable part of the program. The literature on emotions will need to be appropriate for the reading level of the child. For example, young children can read the *Mr Men* books by Roger Hargreaves, as the titles include such characters as *Mr Happy* and *Mr Grumpy*. We now have age-appropriate literature on specific mood disorders, and fictional stories can be read to discover how the central character eventually understands and is able to control his or her emotions. Some of the books that I have used with children and adults with Asperger's syndrome to learn about emotions are included in the Resources section towards the end of the book.

An invaluable component of affective education programs for children and adults with Asperger's syndrome are computer programs that explain how to identify the thoughts and feelings of someone (Carrington and Forder 1999; Silver and Oakes 2001). Perhaps the most widely used is *Mind Reading: The Interactive Guide to Emotions* developed by Simon Baron-Cohen and colleagues (see Chapter 5 and the Resources section at the end of the book). There is also a new affective education resource kit specifically designed by myself and colleagues in Denmark for children and adults with Asperger's syndrome, the *CAT-kit*. Further information is available at www.cat-kit.com.

Incorporating the special interest in the affective education program

It is important to incorporate the person's special interest in the program to improve motivation, attention and conceptualization. For example, I have worked with adolescents whose special interest has been the weather, and have suggested that their emotions are expressed as a weather report. A field study for emotions for a child whose special interest is aircraft can be a visit to an airport to observe the emotions of passengers saying farewell, greeting friends and relatives, and waiting in the line for security screening. An interest in theme parks can be constructively used to explore emotions that range from the thrilling feelings of being on a roller coaster to the feeling of fear when riding the ghost train.

Alternative ways to express emotion

The person conducting the affective education program can also explore different ways of expressing feelings. I have noted that while the person with Asperger's syndrome can have considerable difficulty talking about emotions, there can be a greater eloquence and insight when expressing his or her emotions typing an e-mail, writing a diary or composing a poem; or perhaps choosing or playing music, drawing a picture that represents the emotions or recalling a scene from a movie.

Moving through the program

When an enjoyable or positive emotion such as happiness or affection and the levels of expression are understood, the next component of affective education is to use the same activities and procedures for a contrasting negative emotion such as anxiety, sadness or anger. When exploring the negative emotions of anxiety and anger, activities are used to explain the concept of fight, flight or freeze as a response to perceived danger or threat. The child explores how the negative emotions of anxiety and anger affect his or her body and thinking. Adrenalin causes increased heart rate, excessive perspiration and muscle tension, and affects perception, problem-solving ability and physical strength. Over many thousands of years, these changes have been an advantage in anxiety-provoking or life-threatening situations. However, in our modern society, we may experience the same intensity of physiological and psychological reaction to what we *imagine* or *misperceive* as a threat. It is also important to explain that when we are emotional, we can be less logical and rational and this affects our problem-solving abilities and decision making. To be calm and 'cool' will help the child in both interpersonal and practical situations.

From my clinical experience, some children and adults with Asperger's syndrome are extremely sensitive about exploring and expressing an emotion that they find very difficult to control or has caused considerable confusion or negative consequences. For example, the child may have been referred for problems with anger management but when I start to explore this emotion, the child is extremely reluctant to discuss even low levels of the expression of anger. In such circumstances I tend to start with another negative emotion that can be used to illustrate what can be achieved and to give the child confidence in being able to control other emotions before focusing on the clinically important emotion.

Cognitive restructuring

The cognitive restructuring component of CBT enables the person to correct the thinking that creates emotions such as anxiety and anger, or feelings of low self-esteem. The therapist helps the person change his or her thoughts, emotions and behaviour using reasoning and logic. CBT also encourages the person to be more confident and optimistic by using the recognized qualities of a person with Asperger's syndrome, namely logic and intelligence.

The first stage is to establish the evidence for a particular thought or belief. People with Asperger's syndrome can make false assumptions of their circumstances and the intentions of others due to impaired or delayed Theory of Mind abilities. They also have a tendency to make a literal interpretation, and a casual comment may be taken out of context or to the extreme. For example, another child at school may have strong feelings of anger directed at the child with Asperger's syndrome and in the 'heat of the moment' say, 'Tomorrow, when you come to school, I'm going to kill you.' The child with Asperger's syndrome can make a literal interpretation of what was said and fear that tomorrow he or she could be killed. Another example of misinterpreting feelings or intentions, this time for affection, is when a five-year-old girl with Asperger's syndrome came home from school, clearly worried about something, and started packing a suitcase, insisting she and her mother left town that evening. Eventually her mother dis-covered the reason for her desperation to leave town was that a little boy of the same age had come up to her and said, 'I'm going to marry you.'

An essential and effective component of cognitive restructuring is to challenge certain beliefs with facts and logic. Information can be provided that establishes the real intentions of others and that the statistical risk of a particular event is highly unlikely and not necessarily fatal. We are all vulnerable to distorted conceptualizations but people with Asperger's syndrome are less able to put things in perspective, to seek clari-fication or to consider alternative explanations or responses. In CBT the person is encouraged to be more flexible in his or her thinking and to seek clarification, using questions or comments such as 'Are you joking?' or 'I'm confused about what you just said.' Such comments can also be used when misinterpreting someone's intentions, such as 'Are you serious?' or 'Did you do that deliberately?', and to rescue the situation after the person has made an inappropriate response, with a comment such as 'I'm sorry I offended you' or 'Oh dear, what should I have done?' Stephen Shore uses questions such as 'I can see you have an expression on your face but I am unable to read it. Is there anything I said that is bothering you?'

Another aspect of cognitive restructuring is increasing the range of constructive responses to a particular situation. Unfortunately, children and adults with Asperger's syndrome usually have a limited range of responses to situations that elicit anxiety or anger. The therapist and child create a list of appropriate and inappropriate responses and the consequences of each response. Various options can be drawn as a flow diagram that enables the child to determine the most appropriate response in the long term for all participants.

Comic Strip Conversations

To explain alternative perspectives or to correct errors or assumptions, Comic Strip Conversations, developed by Carol Gray (see Chapter 5), can help the child or adult determine the thoughts, beliefs, knowledge and intentions of the participants in a particular situation. The strategy is to draw an event or sequence of events in storyboard form with stick figures to represent each participant, and speech and thought bubbles to represent their words and thoughts. The child and therapist use an assortment of fibre-tipped coloured pens, with each colour representing an emotion. As they write in the speech or thought bubbles, the child's choice of colour indicates his or her perception of the emotion and thoughts conveyed or intended. This can clarify the child's interpretation of events and the rationale for his or her thoughts and response. This technique can help the child identify and correct any misperception and determine how alternative responses will affect the participants' thoughts and feelings.

Comic Strip Conversations also allow the child to analyse and understand the range of messages and meanings that are a natural part of conversation and interaction. I have found that children with Asperger's syndrome often assume that other people are thinking exactly what they (the children) are thinking; or they assume other people think exactly what they say, and nothing else. The Comic Strip Conversations can then be used to show that each person may have very different thoughts and feelings and opinions about what to think and do in a particular situation. This technique can also be used to determine what someone is likely to think or do in response to the range of alternative reactions being explored by the client and therapist. The client can then choose what to think, say and do in order to achieve the best outcome for all concerned.

An Emotional Toolbox

From an early age, children will know a toolbox contains a variety of different tools to repair a machine or fix a household problem. I recently developed the concept of an

Emotional Toolbox, which has proved an extremely successful strategy for cognitive restructuring and in the treatment of anxiety and anger in children with Asperger's syndrome (Sofronoff *et al.* 2005). The idea is to identify different types of 'tools' to fix the problems associated with negative emotions, especially anxiety, anger and sadness. The range of tools can be divided into those that quickly and constructively release or slowly reduce emotional energy, and those that improve thinking. The therapist works with the child or adult with Asperger's syndrome, and the family, to identify different tools that help fix the feeling, as well as some tools that can make the emotions or consequences worse. Together they use paper and pens during a brainstorming session in which they draw a toolbox, and depict and write descriptions of different types of tools and activities that can encourage constructive emotion repair.

Physical tools

The emotion management for children and adults with Asperger's syndrome can be conceptualized as a problem with 'energy management', namely an excessive amount of emotional energy and difficulty controlling and releasing the energy constructively. Children and adults with Asperger's syndrome appear less able to release emotional energy slowly by relaxation and reflection, and usually prefer to fix or release the feeling by an energetic action.

I ask the person to list the types of tools found in a toolbox and use different categories of tools to represent different energy management strategies. A hammer can represent tools or actions that physically release emotional energy through a constructive activity. A picture of a hammer is drawn on a large sheet of paper and the person with Asperger's syndrome and the therapist devise a list of safe and appropriate physical energy release activities. For young children this can include bouncing on the trampoline or going on a swing. For older children and adults, going for a run, sports practice or dancing may be used to 'let off steam' or release emotional energy. One child with Asperger's syndrome nominated a game of tennis as one of his physical tools, as it 'takes the fight out of me'. Other activities may include cycling, swimming or playing the drums. Some household activities can provide a satisfying release of energy: these might include squeezing oranges or pounding meat in the kitchen; or adults may consider some aspect of gardening or household renovations.

Some children and adults with Asperger's syndrome may have identified that destruction is a physical tool that can be a very effective 'quick fix' to end unpleasant feelings of frustration. There are some household activities that provide a satisfying and constructive release of potentially destructive energy without causing the sort of damage that requires expensive repairs. For example, cans or packaging can be crushed for recycling, or old clothes torn up to make rags. This 'creative destruction' might be the repair mechanism of first choice for adolescents with Asperger's syndrome.

Relaxation tools

Relaxation tools help to calm the person, lower the heart rate and gradually release emotional energy. Perhaps a picture of a paintbrush could be used to illustrate this category of tools for emotional repair. Relaxation tools or activities could include drawing, reading and especially listening to calming music to slowly unwind thoughts and fears. People with Asperger's syndrome often find that solitude is a very effective means of relaxing. They may need to retreat to a quiet, secluded sanctuary as an effective emotional repair mechanism. There will need to be an emotionally restoring sanctuary at home, perhaps the child's bedroom, and a sanctuary at school – perhaps a secluded area of the classroom, or a secluded area of the playground that is safe from predatory children (see Chapter 4). Young children may relax by using gentle rocking actions or engaging in a repetitive action: this can include manipulating an object such as a stress ball, Rubik's cube or relaxing equivalent of worry beads. Repetition and predictability can induce relaxation and an adolescent or adult with Asperger's syndrome may listen to the same song again and again. However, this is not usually relaxing for anyone else.

Sean Barron explained that:

> I have no idea how many ways there are to deal with a level of fear so great that it hangs over you like a storm cloud. The three remedies I chose and that made the most sense to me in all areas of my life were repetition, repetition and repetition. (Grandin and Barron 2005, p.85)

For adults, a routine chore such as making the house clean and tidy or organizing belongings can be a repetitive action that results in satisfaction and relaxation when complete. Such routine chores may also be used by teachers in the classroom situation. For example, a teacher who notices that a child is becoming distressed may suggest a high-status responsibility that will enable the child to escape a stressful situation, such as leaving the class to take an important message or document to the school office; or he or she may distract the child with an activity that restores order and consistency, such as tidying the book cupboard and placing all the books in alphabetical order. An adult with Asperger's syndrome may nominate his or her own relaxation tools for use at work and at home.

The CBT program will include training in relaxation techniques that emphasize breathing, muscle relaxation and imagery to induce a feeling of being calm and in control of one's emotions. This is particularly valuable when the person with Asperger's syndrome is notorious for becoming extremely agitated when something is not working, or he or she cannot solve the problem. For children, I explain that if you remain calm, you remain smart. If you become agitated you become stupid. For adults I explain that if you become anxious about solving the problem, your IQ drops 30 points, and if you become angry, your IQ drops 60 points. When calm and in control of feelings, the solution will be less elusive and more easily discovered.

When a child with Asperger's syndrome is in an agitated state because the solution is not apparent, I ask his or her parent or teacher first to concentrate on helping the child calm down. Only when relaxed will the child be able to listen or be flexible enough in thought to consider your suggestion or find another solution.

Social tools

This category of tools uses other people or animals as a means of managing emotions. The strategy is to find and be with someone, or an animal, that can help repair the mood. The social activity will need to be enjoyable and without the stress that can sometimes be associated with social interaction, especially when the interaction involves more than one other person.

The supportive social contact needs to be someone who genuinely admires or loves the child, gives compliments (not criticism) and manages to say the right words to repair the feelings. The social emotional restorative can be a family member, friend, or member of staff at school, who has time to be patient with the child, listen (without judgement), validate feelings and be understanding. For young children, the person who is the most able emotional restorative may be a grandparent. I sometimes suggest that the grandparent record soothing comments about the child that he or she can listen to at times of stress and when the child needs to relax, for example to fall asleep.

Sometimes the best friend may be a pet. Despite the negative mood or stressful events of the day, dogs are delighted to see their owner, show unconditional adoration and clearly enjoy the person's company, as demonstrated by the wagging tail. Time spent in the company of animals can be a very effective emotional restorative for children and adults with Asperger's syndrome. Pets are the best non-judgemental listeners and more forgiving than humans.

For adolescents, Internet chat lines can be a successful social activity that can be an emotional repair mechanism. People with Asperger's syndrome may have greater eloquence and insight in disclosing their thoughts and feelings by typing rather than talking. One does not need skills with eye contact, or to be able to read a face or understand changes in vocal tone or body language when engaged in a 'conversation' on the Internet. The chat line can include other people with Asperger's syndrome who have genuine empathy and may offer constructive suggestions to repair a mood or situation. I have known several mature adults with Asperger's syndrome who have provided wise support and advice on emotion management for younger members of the 'Asperger community' using the Internet.

Another social tool or activity that can repair feelings of despair is the act of helping someone and being needed – an altruistic act. I have noted that some children and, especially, adults with Asperger's syndrome can change their mood from self-criticism and pessimism to a feeling of self-worth and enthusiasm when helping others. This can include activities such as helping someone who has difficulties in an area of the child's talents or expertise: for example, helping an adult fix a problem with a computer, or guiding another classmate who does not have the child's ability with a subject such as mathematics. Adults with Asperger's syndrome can enjoy and benefit emotionally from voluntary work, particularly with the elderly, very young children and animals. Being needed and appreciated is a significant emotional repair mechanism for all of us, including those with Asperger's syndrome.

Thinking tools

The child or adult can nominate another type of implement, such as a screwdriver or wrench, to represent a category of tools that can be used to change thinking or knowledge. The person is encouraged to use his or her intellectual strength to control feelings using a variety of techniques. We can control feelings and behaviour by talking to ourselves – an internal dialogue – and self-talk is a valuable emotion management strategy. The person is encouraged to use thoughts, or 'inner speech', such as 'I can control my feelings' or 'I can stay calm,' when under stress. The words are reassuring and encourage self-esteem.

Evan, a young man with Asperger's syndrome, developed his own form of thinking tools and created his 'antidotes to poisonous thoughts'. The procedure is to think of a comment that neutralizes or is an antidote to negative (poisonous) thoughts. For example, the negative thought 'I can't do it' (poisonous thought) can be neutralized by the antidote 'Asking for help is the smart way to fix the problem,' or 'I'm a loser' can be neutralized by the antidote 'but I'm a winner at chess'. A list is created of the person's negative or poisonous thoughts and the therapist and client create a personalized antidote to each thought. Evan carried everywhere with him a list of antidotes to his poisonous thoughts, which were 'administered' or remembered when needed. The antidotes are based on the person's abilities and thoughts that are logical and reasonable.

Another thinking tool is to put the event in perspective: a reality check. The approach is to use logic and facts with a series of questions such as 'Is there another shop where I could buy that computer game?' or 'Will children teasing me about my interest in astronomy prevent me from being an astronomer?'

Temple Grandin explained that:

> When I was in my twenties, my Aunt Anne successfully used cognitive therapy on me. When I was depressed and complaining, she gave me objective reasons why I should be happy. She said, 'You have a nice, new truck and I have an old, crummy one.' She also gave me other examples of things that were positive or were going right in my life. It perked me up when I compared the pictures in my head of the two trucks. It concretely helped me understand that some of my thoughts were illogical and not based on fact. Emotions can do that; they confuse thinking. (Grandin and Barron 2005, p.110)

Nita Jackson explained how she now sees in perspective a problem that previously caused feelings of intense anger.

If things anger me now I don't charge around the room fuming, red in the face, with steam shooting out of my ears and nostrils. Instead, I apply the tactics my best friend and mentor Jodie taught me – to distract my anger by concentrating on something else for a minute, for example my studies, my music or my novels, and then returning to the problem and trying to solve it. It's honestly true that after this, the problem doesn't seem half as bad as it did before because I can put it in perspective. (N. Jackson 2002, p.91)

One thinking tool that can be used by children with Asperger's syndrome to improve mood and self-esteem is achieving academic success, which is often not the emotion repair mechanism of other children. When a child with Asperger's syndrome is agitated, the teacher may instruct the child to complete a school activity that he or she enjoys and for which the child has a natural talent, such as solving mathematic problems or spelling. This is in contrast to other children, who would probably try to avoid academic tasks when stressed.

Cue-controlled relaxation is also a useful thinking tool. The strategy is for the child to have an object in his or her pocket that symbolizes relaxation, or to which, through classical conditioning or association, he or she responds by feeling relaxed. For example, Caroline, a teenage girl with Asperger's syndrome, was an avid reader of fiction, her favourite book being *The Secret Garden*. She kept a key in her pocket to metaphorically 'open the door to the secret garden', an imaginary place where she felt relaxed and happy. A few moments touching or looking at the key helped her to contemplate a scene described in the book and consequently to relax and achieve a more positive state of mind. Adults can have a special picture in their wallet, such as a photograph of a woodland scene, which reminds them of solitude and tranquillity.

Special interest tools

Children and adults with Asperger's syndrome can experience intense pleasure when engaged in their special interest (see Chapter 7). The degree of enjoyment may be far in excess of other potentially pleasurable experiences and can be a very effective emotional restorative. The interest can sometimes appear to be mesmerizing and dominating all thought, but this can effectively exclude negative thoughts such as anxiety and anger, and is, in effect, a form of 'thought blocking'. The interest can be a source of intense enjoyment and relaxation, and act as an 'off switch' when agitated.

We know that in the general population, routines, rituals and repetition are calming activities, and one of the characteristics of the special interests of children and adults with Asperger's syndrome is the repetitive, routine and ritualistic nature of the activities associated with them. An adolescent with Asperger's syndrome had a great interest in Japanese culture, and performed the elaborate and ritualized tea ceremony whenever she felt anxious. The activity was clearly very soothing for her. Luke Jackson (2002), a teenager with Asperger's syndrome with remarkable ability with computers, describes the cataloguing of the examples of his interests as a means of 'personal defrag'. The activity creates a sense of comfort and security.

I have observed that the degree of motivation and duration of time spent on the interest is proportional to the degree of stress, anxiety or agitation. The more the person experiences worries, confusion and agitation, the more the interest becomes obtrusive in thinking or dominant in the person's daily life. If the child or adult with Asperger's syndrome has few means of enjoyment and relaxation, i.e. few emotional repair tools in the toolbox, what may have started as a source of pleasure and relaxation, under conditions of extreme stress can become a compulsive act reminiscent of an Obsessive Compulsive Disorder. If the special interest is the exclusive source of relaxation or mental escape, then access to the interest can become irresistible, a compulsion. Being prevented from achieving uninterrupted access to such a powerful emotional restorative creates even more stress.

A program of controlled or timed access can be introduced to ensure the time spent on the interest is not excessive. Unfortunately, from the child's point of view, time goes quickly when one is enjoying oneself. There may need to be some negotiation and compromise regarding the duration of access.

When a child with Asperger's syndrome is extremely agitated, the range of emotion repair tools becomes limited and is often reduced to three tools: physical release of energy, solitude or having access to the special interest. The interest is not only pleasurable, but also becomes mesmerizing and no negative thoughts can intrude on the fixation. I have found that an effective 'off switch' can be access to the special interest. For example, if the adolescent has a special interest in soccer teams and the results of matches and the league table, suggesting writing out the results from the games played last Saturday can have a remarkably calming effect. This is not rewarding inappropriate behaviour. In an emotional emergency, it is finding a quick way of preventing further agitation in a situation where the toolbox has no other tools.

Medication

Medication is often prescribed for children and adults with Asperger's syndrome to manage emotions. If the child or adult is showing clear signs of a mood disorder then medication is recommended as an emotion management tool. Clinical experience has confirmed the value of medication for the treatment of anxiety, depression and anger in children and adults with Asperger's syndrome but there are some concerns often voiced by parents and those with Asperger's syndrome. One concern of parents and physicians is that, at present, we do not have longitudinal studies of the long-term effect of psychotropic medication on young children with Asperger's syndrome. However, there is evidence that low doses of such medication can benefit some adults with Asperger's syndrome (Alexander, Michael and Gangadharan 2004).

Another concern for parents, teachers and especially the child and adult with Asperger's syndrome is the effect on the person's clarity of thought. Many children and adults with Asperger's syndrome report that medication slows their thinking and hinders their cognitive skills. People with Asperger's syndrome often value their clarity of thought: one adult described his reaction to medication: 'It was like I was locked out of my own home.' Several adults with Asperger's syndrome who have taken anti-psychotic medication to manage anger have explained to me that the medication does not change the inner experience but reduces the energy to express the feeling.

Some mood disorders are so severe that psychotherapy such as CBT does not have the 'strength' to help the person manage the intense emotions. When medication has 'lifted' the mood or reduced the intensity of the emotion, other strategies can become more effective and may eventually replace the need for medication. However, there are those with Asperger's syndrome whose ability to manage emotions and quality of life has been greatly enhanced by the long-term use of a relatively low dosage of medication to alleviate feelings of anxiety and depression.

While medication for emotion management can be a very valuable tool in the Emotional Toolbox, my personal concern is when medication is the only tool added to the toolbox because it is relatively cheap and easy to administer. It is important to establish why specific feelings occur and to address the cause of the emotion.

Other tools in the toolbox

Other potential tools for the Emotional Toolbox are enjoyable activities such as watching a favourite comedy. Sometimes a good laugh can be a very effective emotional restorative. Another tool is to read the autobiographies (of which there are several) of adolescents and adults with Asperger's syndrome for inspiration, encouragement and advice.

There is one important category of tool that is used by the CBT therapist, namely education to change the knowledge and attitude of people who interact with or supervise the person with Asperger's syndrome. Tools that change attitudes can prevent situations that can cause considerable emotional distress. At a conference I attended in the United States, a teenager with Asperger's syndrome had the following words printed on the front of his T-shirt: 'People like you are the reason people like me have to take medication.'

A tool that can encourage self-control is the suggestion of a prize or reward. The reward can be to earn access to preferred activities, the special interest or even money. I have noted that some children with Asperger's syndrome are natural capitalists. Unfortunately, the subsequent problem can be inflation and manipulation of the economy.

Another category of tools, which could be described as sensory tools, involves assessing the person's ability to cope with the sensory world and identifying strategies to avoid specific sensory experiences (see Chapter 11). For example, the position of the child's desk in class or the adult's workstation may be changed to reduce the general level of noise, light intensity and proximity to aromas such as cleaning products.

Chapter 9 on cognitive abilities explains other strategies to reduce confusion and frustration when teaching academic tasks.

When a situation is known to cause a child with Asperger's syndrome to become extremely distressed, it may be wise to avoid that situation if possible. For example, if the young child is almost certainly going to become extremely anxious if his or her teacher is away for a day and there will be a temporary replacement, a Social Story™ could prepare the child for the changes in routine, class atmosphere and changes in behaviour of the other children. If this is not an effective strategy to prepare for the event, then parents can suggest that the child completes the assignments of the day at home.

Sometimes the degree of stress and emotional exhaustion from coping with school can have a detrimental effect on the child's mental health. Information from the rising emotional temperature using the thermometer and mood diary can indicate an imminent 'meltdown', and parents, therapist and teacher may determine whether the child would benefit from a short break from school. If the child was ill with a typical childhood illness, he or she would be expected to have time at home to recover. The same can occur for an emotional illness. However, parents and teachers will need to be vigilant that the child genuinely needs the break away from being at school and is not trying to manipulate the situation to his or her advantage.

Inappropriate tools

When explaining the concept of an Emotional Toolbox, the therapist and client discuss inappropriate tools (noting that one would not use a hammer to fix a computer) in order to explain how some actions, such as violence, thoughts of suicide and engaging in retaliation, are not appropriate tools or emotional repair mechanisms. Another emotional repair strategy that could become inappropriate is the retreat into a fantasy world. The use of fantasy literature and games as a means of escape can be a typical tool for ordinary adolescents but is of concern when this becomes the dominant or exclusive coping mechanism. The border between fantasy and reality may become unclear, leading to concern regarding the development of signs of schizophrenia. The therapist also needs to assess whether teenagers or adults with Asperger's syndrome are using illegal drugs and alcohol to manage stress levels and mood, and, if so, whether prescription medication would be more effective, and safer. Other inappropriate tools could include taking stress out on someone else through violence, self-injury or the destruction of something valuable or precious.

It is also necessary for the therapist to evaluate emotional repair tools used by parents, family members and teachers and to remove from the toolbox those that may be inappropriate or counterproductive. Children and adults with Asperger's syndrome are often confused by certain emotions and this can be the case with the expression of affection, which can be the cause of more agitation or confusion. A teenage boy with Asperger's syndrome was describing how sometimes he feels very sad, but pointed out, 'I get angry when someone tries to cheer me up.' Retaliation by sarcasm will increase the confusion and agitation of a person with Asperger's syndrome, and threats could escalate the situation. One of the reasons why CBT is so effective with people with Asperger's syndrome is that the strategies are based on logic, not punishment. From my extensive clinical experience, punishment rarely changes the emotions and behaviour of a person with Asperger's syndrome. Punishment may be a tool used by parents and teachers and, when clearly not working, should be removed from the Emotional Toolbox.

Finally, the concept of a toolbox can be extremely helpful in enabling people with Asperger's syndrome to repair their own feelings but also to repair the feelings of others. They often benefit from tuition in learning what tools to use to help friends and family, and which tools others use, so that they may 'borrow' tools to add to their own emotional repair kit.

Putting the Emotional Toolbox into practice

When the child has a list of emotion repair tools, the therapist can make a 'toolbox' out of, for instance, an index card box, with each card representing a category of tools. Each card can have a picture of the type of tool, for example a hammer or screwdriver, and the list of tools or strategies that belong in that category. As the therapy evolves, new tools can be discovered and added to the list. A parent may have the emotion thermometer on the fridge door to be easily accessible. In this way, the child can point to the degree of emotion or stress he or she is experiencing, for example when returning home from school in the afternoon, and decide which are the tools of first choice to lower the emotional temperature. Adults can use an alternative to the card box, such as a credit card wallet, with each category of tool written as a different card, and stored in the wallet for easy access.

The practical application of the Emotional Toolbox can be described in a Social Story™. The following unpublished Social Story™ was written by Carol Gray and me for a teenager with Asperger's syndrome.

Using the Toolbox to stay calm and in control

As teenagers go through each day there will be times when they feel sad, anxious, confused or frustrated. There are also times when they feel confident, calm and in control. The art and science of emotion management is learning to draw upon positive emotions and strategies to keep moving through the tough times.

Staying calm and in control is the smart thing to do.

As people grow older they learn to use their intelligence to keep their emotions in control. That way, everyone around them feels comfortable. Keeping negative feelings in control is important in a friendship and when working with others. Each person is accountable for how his or her emotions impact on others. The first step to staying in control is to know when emotions are becoming more intense. Each person has his or her own signals that their emotions are on the rise. Mine are: (list)

When emotions become stronger, each person learns to stay in control by using a personal emotion repair toolbox. My tools include: (list)

When other people know about my toolbox and how I am feeling, they can help me stay in control.

Practising CBT strategies

Once the child or adult with Asperger's syndrome has improved his or her intellectual understanding of emotions and identified strategies (or tools) to manage emotions, the next stage of CBT is to start practising the strategies in a graduated sequence of assignments. The first stage is for the therapist to model the appropriate thinking and actions in role-play with the child or adult with Asperger's syndrome, vocalizing thoughts to monitor cognitive processes. A form of graduated practice is used, starting with situations associated with a relatively mild level of distress or agitation. A list of situations or 'triggers' that precipitate specific emotions is created from the emotion assessment conducted at the start of the therapy, with each situation written on a small card. The child or adult uses the thermometer or measuring instrument originally used in the affective education activities to determine the hierarchy or rank order of situations. The most distressing are placed at the upper level of the thermometer. As the therapy progresses, the person works through the hierarchy to manage more intense emotions.

After practice during the therapy session, the child or adult has a project to apply his or her new knowledge and abilities in real-life situations. Successful exposure exercises are an essential aspect of CBT. The therapist will obviously need to communicate and coordinate with those who will be supporting the person in everyday circumstances. After each practical experience there is a discussion of the degree of success, using activities such as Comic Strip Conversations to debrief; reinforcement for achievements, such as a certificate of achievement; and a 'boasting book' or the writing of a Social Story™ to record emotion management success.

One of the issues during the practice stage of CBT will be generalization. People with Asperger's syndrome tend to be quite rigid in terms of recognizing when the new strategies are applicable in a situation that does not obviously resemble the practice sessions. It will be necessary to ensure that strategies are used in a wide range of circumstances and no assumption made that once an appropriate emotion management strategy has proved successful, it will continue to be used in all settings.

The duration of the practice stage is dependent upon the degree of success and list of situations. Gradually the therapist provides less direct guidance and support, thus encouraging confidence in independently using the new strategies. The goal is to provide a template for current and future problems, but it will probably be necessary to maintain contact for some time to prevent relapse.

SUMMARY AND CONCLUDING THOUGHTS

People with Asperger's syndrome clearly have problems understanding emotions within themselves and others, and expressing emotions at an appropriate level for the situation. We now have strategies to help people with Asperger's syndrome to learn about emotions, and effective psychological treatment for any secondary mood disorder. Unfortunately, typical people have difficulty empathizing with such experiences, and can only imagine what it must be like to live in a world of powerful emotions that are confusing and overwhelming. Liliana, an adult with Asperger's syndrome, explained one of the reasons people with Asperger's syndrome may lead an emotionally reclusive life when she said to me, 'We don't have emotional skin or protection. We are exposed, and that is why we hide.'

KEY POINTS AND STRATEGIES

- A qualitative difference in the understanding and expression of emotions, originally described by Hans Asperger, is acknowledged in the diagnostic criteria for Asperger's syndrome.

- The emotional maturity of children with Asperger's syndrome is usually at least three years behind that of their peers.

- There can be a limited vocabulary to describe emotions and a lack of subtlety and variety in emotional expression.

- There is an association between Asperger's syndrome and the development of an additional or secondary mood disorder, including depression, anxiety disorder, and problems with anger management and the communication of love and affection.

- About 25 per cent of adults with Asperger's syndrome also have the clear clinical signs of Obsessive Compulsive Disorder.

- People with Asperger's syndrome appear vulnerable to feeling depressed, with about one in three children and adults with Asperger's syndrome having a clinical depression.

- We do not know how common anger management problems are with children and adults with Asperger's syndrome, but we do know that when problems with the expression of anger occur, the person with Asperger's syndrome and family members are very keen to reduce the frequency, intensity and consequences of anger.

- A person with Asperger's syndrome may enjoy a very brief and low-intensity expression of affection, and become confused or overwhelmed when greater levels of expression are experienced or expected.

- The primary psychological treatment for mood disorders is Cognitive Behaviour Therapy (CBT). We now have published case studies and objective scientific evidence that CBT does significantly reduce mood disorders in children and adults with Asperger's syndrome.

- In the affective education component of CBT the person learns about the advantages and disadvantages of emotions and the identification of the different levels of expression in words and actions, within the person him- or herself and others.

- The cognitive restructuring component of CBT enables the person to correct the thinking that creates emotions such as anxiety and anger, or feelings of low self-esteem.

- The emotion management for children and adults with Asperger's syndrome can be conceptualized as a problem with 'energy management', namely an excessive amount of emotional energy and difficulty controlling and releasing the energy constructively.

- The strategy of the Emotional Toolbox is to identify different types of 'tools' to fix the problems associated with negative emotions, especially anxiety, anger and sadness.

CHAPTER 7

Special Interests

> Another autistic child had specialized technological interests and
> knew an incredible amount about complex machinery. He
> acquired this knowledge through constant questioning, which it
> was impossible to fend off, and also to a great degree through his
> own observations.

> *– Hans Asperger ([1944] 1991)*

Although people with Asperger's syndrome have difficulties with the interpersonal
aspects of life, most have remarkable ability in a chosen area of expertise. Hans Asperger
described some of the characteristics of the special interests:

> We know an autistic child who has a particular interest in the natural sciences. His
> observations show an unusual eye for the essential. He orders his facts into a
> system and forms his own theories even if they are occasionally abstruse. Hardly
> any of this he heard or read, and he always refers to his own experience. There is
> also a child who is a 'chemist'. He uses all his money for experiments which often
> horrify his family and even steals to fund them. Some children have even more
> specialized interests, for instance, only experiments which create noise and smells.
> Another autistic boy was obsessed with poisons. He had a most unusual knowl-
> edge in this area and possessed a large collection of poisons, some quite naively
> concocted by himself. He came to us because he had stolen a substantial quantity
> of cyanide from the locked chemistry store at his school. Another, again, was pre-
> occupied by numbers. Complex calculations were naturally easy for him without
> being taught. (Asperger [1944] 1991, p.72)

An essential component of the interest is the accumulation and cataloguing of objects or
the accumulation of facts and information about a specific topic. The special interest is
more than a hobby and can dominate the person's free time and conversation. The

Gillbergs' criteria (Gillberg and Gillberg 1989) for Asperger's syndrome include the presence of narrow interests that have at least one of the following characteristics:

- exclusion of other activities

- repetitive adherence

- more rote than meaning.

Criterion B in the DSM-IV diagnostic criteria for Asperger's syndrome describes the characteristics of the special interests that are used to confirm a diagnosis:

> Restricted, repetitive and stereotyped patterns of behaviour, interests, and activities, as manifested by at least one of the following:
>
> 1. encompassing preoccupation with one or more stereotyped and restricted patterns of interest that is abnormal either in intensity or focus
>
> 2. apparently inflexible adherence to specific, non-functional routines or rituals
>
> 3. stereotyped and repetitive motor mannerisms (e.g. hand or finger flapping or twisting, or complex whole-body movements)
>
> 4. persistent preoccupation with parts of objects. (APA 2000, p.84)

One of the distinguishing characteristics between a hobby and a special interest that is of clinical significance is an abnormality in the intensity or focus of the interest. The clinician makes a subjective judgement regarding the intensity, based on the amount of time typical children or adults would engage in the same activity: for example, playing with or talking about trains or horses, or collecting old records, or watching science-fiction movies. When the focus of the interest is eccentric, for example a child who avidly reads lawn-mower catalogues, initiates long monologues on lawn mowers and has a collection of several old lawn mowers in the garage, then the interest could be considered unusual and of clinical significance in an eight-year-old girl.

The DSM criteria refer to the development of non-functional routines and rituals, and the Gillbergs' criteria for Asperger's syndrome (Gillberg and Gillberg 1989) have a separate criterion that refers to repetitive routines, with the routines being imposed in all or almost all aspects of ordinary life.

It is difficult to determine whether the imposition of routines and rituals is a core characteristic of Asperger's syndrome or a characteristic of someone who is anxious. The imposition of routines and rituals can be a characteristic associated with anxiety disorders, and children and adults with Asperger's syndrome are prone to having high levels of anxiety. The routines may also develop as a coping mechanism for the unusual profile of cognitive abilities associated with Asperger's syndrome. Routines may be imposed to make life more predictable and to impose order, as surprises, chaos and uncertainty are not easily tolerated by children and adults with Asperger's syndrome (see Chapter 9). Theresa Jolliffe described how:

> Reality to an autistic person is a confusing, interacting mass of events, people, places, sounds and sights. There seems to be no clear boundaries, order or meaning to anything. A large part of my life is spent trying to work out the pattern behind everything. Set routines, times, particular routes and rituals all help to get order into an unbearably chaotic life. Trying to keep everything the same reduces some of the terrible fear. (Jolliffe *et al.* 1992)

The stereotyped and repetitive motor mannerisms such as hand or finger flapping can be an immature expression of excitement (much as very young typical children will 'jump for joy'), or a motor tic that could be a sign of a dual diagnosis of Tourette's disorder (see Chapter 10). Complex whole-body movements may also be associated with a specific emotion, such as gently rocking when agitated as a means of relaxation, or a sign of Tourette's disorder. From my clinical experience, motor mannerisms such as hand flapping when excited or agitated, and the persistent preoccupation with parts of objects, are more characteristic of very young children with Asperger's syndrome, and by middle childhood these characteristics have often disappeared, although may sometimes be observed in adults with Asperger's syndrome (South, Ozonoff and McMahon 2005).

The diagnostic criteria of Peter Szatmari and colleagues do not make reference to the presence of a special interest and clinical experience suggests that a small proportion of children (especially very young children) and adults, who fulfil all the other diagnostic criteria, do not have a current special interest (Szatmari *et al.* 1989b). Research has indicated that the percentage of children and adults who have all the other characteristics of Asperger's syndrome, but do not have a special interest, ranges from 5 to 15 per cent (Bashe and Kirby 2001; Hippler and Klicpera 2004; Kerbeshian, Burd and Fisher 1990; Tantam 1991). Thus I would not automatically exclude the possibility of a diagnosis of Asperger's syndrome in the absence of a current special interest.

If a clinician wants to examine the repetitive behaviour or special interest in greater depth, there are two measures that can provide more information. The Repetitive Behaviour Interview (Turner 1997) can be used to explore the nature of any unusual motor movements, use of objects and the insistence on rigid routines. The Yale Special Interest Interview (South, Klin and Ozonoff 1999) can be used to explore the qualitative aspects of the special interest.

We know that the amount of time and resources dedicated to the special interest can cause considerable disruption to the daily life of the person with Asperger's syndrome and his or her family, and that this characteristic is also remarkably stable over time (Piven *et al.* 1996; South *et al.* 2005). However, the special interest can also provide a valuable source of intellectual enjoyment and can be used constructively to facilitate friendships and employment.

THE DEVELOPMENT OF SPECIAL INTERESTS

Unusual or special interests can develop as early as two to three years of age (Bashe and Kirby 2001), and may commence with a preoccupation with parts of objects: spinning the wheels of toy cars, or manipulating electrical switches, for example. The next stage may be a fixation on something neither human nor toy (Pyles 2002), or a fascination with a specific category of objects and the acquisition of as many examples as possible. Sometimes the collections comprise items of interest to other children, such as stones and bottle tops, but some can be quite eccentric, such as spark plugs and yellow pencils. The child with Asperger's syndrome eagerly seeks any opportunity to gain new additions to the collection and much of his or her free time is spent on the search for a new example or 'trophy'.

The attachment to the objects can be remarkably intense with considerable distress if one is missing, and visible delight when it is found. The attachment or 'affection' for the objects can appear to be more intense than for family members. The research literature on Theory of Mind skills has established that children with Asperger's syndrome have considerable difficulty understanding and responding to the thoughts and feelings of others. The social and interpersonal world is confusing, such that the child finds objects and machinery easier to understand. They are also more reliable than people, not changing their mind, or becoming distracted or emotional. My sister-in-law has Asperger's syndrome and in her autobiography (unpublished) she wrote:

> It's easy to bestow love onto objects rather than people because although they can't love back they can't rebuke either. It is a very safe form of idolization where no one can get hurt.

The young child's play can also be somewhat eccentric in that he or she can pretend to be the object of interest rather than a person, super-hero or an animal, which would be the usual choice of pretend play for young children. For example, it was 'dressing up day' at school and children were expected to arrive at school in costume. There were many costumes based on characters from children's literature, popular films or television programmes. However, Joshua, who has Asperger's syndrome, chose to go as his special interest – a washing machine. Another young child with Asperger's syndrome would find a secluded area of the playground and adopt an unusual posture, declaring herself to be a blocked toilet. Her special interest was toilets.

In a letter, a grandmother described to me the unusual behaviour of her grandson with Asperger's syndrome:

> Jacob requires time alone in his room, particularly upon arriving home from school. He closes the door and plays a very rowdy and physical game involving running round the room, throwing himself on the bed, against the closet door, etc. Once he allowed me to observe and reluctantly told me he was playing soccer, chess, hockey, baseball, etc. in a specific order. He demonstrated, and I had no idea what was happening until he explained he was the ball or the chess piece.

In her biography of her son Ben, who has Asperger's syndrome, Barbara LaSalle described an unusual aspect of his imaginative play with his peers:

> I am remembering kindergarten and the dress up corner and the girl asking, 'Ben, will you be the daddy?' No, Ben would definitely not be the daddy, but he would be the radio. To be daddy you have to improvise – an actor without a script. Whereas to be the radio you have a script – the weather man's script, the sports caster script, the traffic reporter's script. (LaSalle 2003, pp.233–4)

While the first interest may be a fascination with unusual objects, a subsequent stage can be the collection of facts and figures about a specific topic. These may be age-appropriate interests, but their intensity and duration can be unusual. Many typical pre-school children have an interest in television programmes such as *Thomas the Tank Engine*, but as they grow older, the interest is replaced with other popular programmes with associated marketing. However, a child with Asperger's syndrome may continue an interest in *Thomas the Tank Engine* into his or her teen years.

The topic may not be age appropriate and be somewhat unusual for a young child. Stephen Shore explained that in his childhood:

> Catalogues and manuals were always of great interest and comfort as they were predictable. Often I compared different sizes and versions of products offered in the catalogues. Air conditioner capacities as expressed in British thermal units caught my fancy one day, so in every catalogue I would seek the highest capacity air conditioner that ran on 115 volts alternating current. (Shore 2001, p.54)

Stephen has sent me a further comment regarding the quotation in that the considerable knowledge he originally acquired as a child about air conditioners has been very useful when advising his family, friends and colleagues on air conditioners. He speculates that one reason air conditioners may have become a special interest is that, like many other children and adults on the autism spectrum, he is intolerant of high heat and humidity (see Chapter 11).

Some of the topics would not usually be expected choices for children with Asperger's syndrome. For example, there can be an interest in sport, which would not be anticipated when one considers the motor clumsiness of many children with Asperger's syndrome. However, the interest may be collecting and memorizing sporting statistics and sporting records rather than participation in the sport itself. There are exceptions, and some children with Asperger's syndrome can develop an interest and ability in solitary rather than team sports. To achieve competence, these sports require solitary practice, accuracy, timing and stoicism such as golf, swimming, snooker, rock climbing and marathon running. The single-minded determination of people with Asperger's syndrome and time dedicated to practice can lead to outstanding sporting success.

Much of the knowledge associated with the interest is self-directed and self-taught. The interest is chosen because of some aspect that is appealing or important to the child with Asperger's syndrome and not because the activity is the latest craze and the child must have the 'currency' of popularity. The interest is often a solitary and intuitive activity, pursued with great passion, but often not shared with family members or peers. The degree of expertise and talent can be extraordinary and lead to success in school or national competitions for spelling or mathematics, for example, and the genuine admiration of others.

The interest can be in the creative arts, such as an amazing ability in drawing, sculpture or music. The attention to detail, photographic realism and use of colour can be outstanding. The art works are usually associated with the interest, for example oil paintings of steam trains. There may be rare qualities such as singing with perfect pitch, or an ability to communicate emotions in musical compositions and performances, which appears to be such a contrast to the difficulties the person has with the communication of emotions using speech and body language.

In the pre-teenage and teenage years the interests can evolve to include electronics and computers, fantasy literature, science fiction and sometimes a fascination with a particular person. All of these mirror the interests of peers but the intensity and focus is again unusual.

Nita Jackson, a teenager with Asperger's syndrome, describes her progression from an interest in objects to an interest in specific individuals:

> My preferences began with plastic objects such as bottles, My Little Ponies (I collected 44 in total – lining them up along my windowsill in alphabetical order) and Barbies. I then progressed to people. Between the ages of 8 and 12 I obsessed about women who I admired and desperately wanted to emulate, whether fictitious or not. One particular character was Hewlett and Martin's Tank Girl – a feisty Australian comic book bitch-heroine who could kick the living daylights out of anyone who dared cross her path. She had a punk lad/kangaroo hybrid called Booga as a boyfriend, and a rowdy crew of friends consisting of men, women, other similar lad/kangaroos, a brilliantly hilarious fashion-conscious talking koala, Camp Koala, and an aardvark – Mr Precocious – among various others. I was totally infatuated with her because she was everything that I was not – tall, attractive, hard-talking, hard-hitting, tough, popular, independent and in demand. I read Hewlett and Martin's comic books religiously until I could recite them word for word. I must have looked ridiculous, spouting Tank Girl phraseology mid-conversation, when it bore no relevance to anything. A typical example could be:
>
> Mum: What did you do at school today?
>
> Me: Who the hell is David Essex anyway Booga? And by the way, Camp Koala says you're batting first. (N. Jackson 2002, p.37)

There can be a fascination with a particular character, mythical, historical or real. The interest that is focused on a real person can be interpreted as a teenage 'crush', but the intensity can lead to problems with accusations of stalking and harassment and the misinterpretation of intentions. The interest in fantasy literature and fantasy figures and figurines can be so intense that the person develops his or her own role-play games and detailed drawing skills based on the special interest.

Some teenagers and adults with Asperger's syndrome seem to have a natural ability to understand computer languages and computer graphics, and often have advanced computer-programming skills. The interest is appreciated by peers and there is a distinct teenage culture for experts in computers. Such individuals would have previously been considered as nerds and despised by peers but are now popular as they can access cheat codes, solve computer problems and may be portrayed as the hero, not the 'fall guy', in popular films and television programmes.

Adults with Asperger's syndrome are more likely to read than talk about their interest, which can become a hobby or even a source of employment. The adult is regarded as an expert in a specialized subject that may be recognized within a hobby or interest group, or he or she can be employed to provide information or advice on this specialized area. People with Asperger's syndrome are natural experts.

CATEGORIES OF INTERESTS

There appear to be two main categories of interest: collection and the acquisition of knowledge on a specific topic or concept.

Collections

Hans Asperger first described the tendency of children with autistic personality to be avid collectors:

> Very often, the relationship of autistic children to things is limited to collecting, and here again, instead of the harmonious order and richness of a normally balanced affective life, we find deficiencies and empty spaces, in which singular areas develop to an excessive extent. The collections that are favoured by autistic children appear like soulless possessions. The children accumulate things merely in order to possess them, not to make something of them, to play with them or to modify them. Thus, a six-year-old-boy had the ambition to collect 1000 match-boxes, a goal which he pursued with fanatical energy. (Asperger [1944] 1991, pp.81–2)

The collection of unusual objects can also occur in adults with Asperger's syndrome. Robert Sanders describes in his autobiography his preoccupation with collecting old telephones:

> To demonstrate one example of uniqueness in my collecting old telephones, when I was in New Zealand in 1986, I noticed that a lot of the small towns at that time (not anymore) had manual exchanges with operators to connect all calls. To be specific, Kaikoura with 3000 people had a manual exchange with 9 operators. The telephones were made of black bakelite, and each one had a crank handle. Early the next year, I wrote the New Zealand Post Office (their phone company) and

requested the possibility of selling me some of those crank phones. The postmaster wrote me back and said that Kaikoura had converted to automatic on October 15, 1986, and they were selling the old instruments for NZ $2 each. I wrote back and sent cash to purchase 3 of them, which including postage added up to around US $60. Upon receiving my money, he sent them in the mail to me by surface mail.

Several years later, I was travelling over New Zealand again, and when going through Kaikoura, I talked to the Post Office. The postmaster was still there, and I thanked him for accommodating me by selling me and sending me those crank phones and that they were well appreciated. He surprised me by telling me that I was the *only* American who had corresponded with him and ordered crank phones.

The only one?! I had a moment of realization about how unique I am, well, how unique a lot of people are in this world. I just assumed that there would have been at least 10 or 20 Americans, including phone collectors, who would certainly have ordered crank phones from Kaikoura. (Sanders 2002, p.54)

As the number of accumulated objects increases, there is a need to develop a cataloguing or 'library' system. The system has to be logical but can be idiosyncratic. When Gisela and Chris were married, they shared an interest in classical music and combined their record collection. Chris has Asperger's syndrome, a diagnosis not shared by his wife. He completed the cataloguing and sorting of the combined record collection based on the date of birth of the composer rather than alphabetical order (Slater-Walker and Slater-Walker 2002). His cataloguing system is logical and possibly intellectually and functionally superior to an alphabetical system that has Bach adjacent to Bartok, two very different composers. Using the date of birth of the composer, the linear collection of records also represents the evolution of music styles. However, most typical people do not know the date of birth of a composer to help them find a particular record in the collection.

When the objects are displayed, there can be the creation of a specific ordering system and a fascination with symmetry. If someone should accidentally or deliberately move any item out of sequence, the person with Asperger's syndrome can become extremely agitated and determined to restore the symmetrical sequence.

The acquisition of knowledge and expertise

The collection of objects can mature into a collection of facts about a specific topic or concept, with the person becoming an expert in the special interest. The child can bombard adults with questions about the topic, usually unaware of the adult's signs of boredom or irritation at having to answer incessant questions. The non-verbal signs and context that would be obvious to other children are not perceived by the person with Asperger's syndrome, who appears to be in a trance-like state of enthusiasm.

The child or adult can accumulate an encyclopaedic knowledge of facts. Carolyn, an adult with Asperger's syndrome, wrote in an e-mail to me that 'facts are important to us because they "secure" us in what is otherwise a very unstable world. Hard cold facts give comfort and security.' The child or adult can record the facts in lists and eventually memorize facts and figures. The person is similar to a scientist collecting data, but the facts can be eccentric, such as registration numbers or the location of radio transmitters in a state or country.

An evaluation of the children seen by Hans Asperger at his clinic in Austria from 1950 to 1980 indicates that there are certain topics that are very appealing for a child with the syndrome (Hippler and Klicpera 2004). The most common interest was animals and nature, which can commence with an interest in dinosaurs, typical of many young children, though the depth of knowledge and the dominance of dinosaurs in the child's conversation and free time can be unusual. The interest in animals can progress to a special interest in specific classifications of animals, such as arachnids (spiders) or desert reptiles. The second most common interest is technical and scientific and can include technical specifications of particular vehicles such as BMW cars or Deltic trains, or an interest in a branch of science such as geography and volcanoes, astronomy and the planets, mathematics and prime numbers, chemistry and the periodic table. The third most common interest is public transport systems. This can include memorizing all the stations on a subway system, restoring old vehicles and travelling on obscure railways. Other interests can be drawing, often based on a particular theme or comic book, or drawing animals with photographic realism; and music, as a listener, player or collector of recordings (Mercier, Mottron and Belleville 2000).

A recent survey completed by parents of children with Asperger's syndrome confirms the consistent themes or focus of the special interests originally identified by Hans Asperger (Bashe and Kirby 2001). However, the survey by Bashe and Kirby reflects current interests that were not available when Hans Asperger was a clinician, and includes interests in computer games and Japanese animation as well as science-fiction films.

The child's 'encyclopaedic' knowledge can become quite remarkable and he or she is perceived as a 'little professor', eager to read about the interest, ask adults questions related to the interest, and instruct peers about the interest (in a manner more resembling a teacher than a peer). There can be an impression that the child is a potential genius but teachers note that, though the child's attention span and attention to detail are quite impressive when engaged in the special interest, the same degree of motivation, attention and ability are conspicuously absent when the child is engaged in other classroom activities, especially those that would be of interest to his or her peers.

The focus of the interest invariably changes, but at a time dictated by the child, and is replaced by another special interest that is again the choice of the child, not a parent. The complexity and number of interests vary according to the child's developmental level and intellectual capacity. Over time there is a progression to multiple and more abstract or complex interests such as periods of history, specific countries or cultures. Some children develop two or more simultaneous interests and the number of simultaneous interests increases with maturity (Bashe and Kirby 2001).

THE INTERESTS OF GIRLS AND WOMEN

Girls and boys with Asperger's syndrome may enjoy the same special interests, for example becoming an expert on the *Titanic* or avidly collecting Pokémon cards. However, I have noticed some differences between the interests of boys and girls with Asperger's syndrome. A girl with Asperger's syndrome may have a special interest typical of the interests of girls in general, such as collecting Barbie dolls, but the girl with Asperger's syndrome may have a collection of many more dolls than her peers, the dolls are arranged in a particular order and she usually does not share her play Barbies with a friend. She may use the dolls as figures to represent real people in her life, re-enacting events to improve her comprehension of social situations, much as replaying a video can help to interpret what is happening in a complex scene in a film. The dolls can also be used to rehearse what to say in prospective situations, and can become alternative friends who, perhaps unlike real girls in her life, are supportive, inclusive and kind. The interest is solitary and functional.

Both boys and girls can acquire facts on an area of interest, often a scientific interest, and the most popular reading material can be encyclopaedias and record books. However, I have noticed that some girls with Asperger's syndrome can develop a special interest in fiction rather than facts. The interest in fiction can include collecting and reading many times the novels of an author such as J.K. Rowling; or there may be a fascination with classical literature such as Shakespeare's plays, or the stories of Charles Dickens, or Roald Dahl. This is not in order to achieve success at school in English literature, but from a genuine interest in the great authors and their works. The girl can escape into an alternative world and may consider writing fiction herself. This can be the starting point for a career as an author. Reading and writing fiction can also be an indirect remedial activity to learn more about the inner thoughts of other people, assisting with the development of Theory of Mind abilities.

Sometimes the special interest is animals but can be to such an intensity that the child acts being the animal, and if the interest is horses, for example, she may want to sleep in a stable. Animals can intuitively recognize someone who likes them and intends no harm and a relationship can develop that can be a substitute for human friends. Animals do not deceive, tease or behave in as fickle a way as occurs with humans, and are non-judgemental when listening to the person describing the events of the day.

During adolescence, some girls (and sometimes boys) with Asperger's syndrome can develop a special interest in fantasy worlds. The interest can be in science fiction and fantasy but also fairies, witches and mythical monsters. An intense interest in the supernatural could be confused with some of the characteristics associated with schizophrenia, and the clinician needs to be aware of the qualitative and functional differences between a special interest in the supernatural and the early signs of schizophrenia.

A constructive way that girls and women with Asperger's syndrome can learn about social relationships and expectations is to watch television soap operas avidly. The unfolding drama provides a voyeuristic insight into interpersonal relationships and a potential script for real-life encounters. The special interest in soap operas has value in being a window to the social world. This activity also provides a 'safe' vantage point from which to observe and absorb knowledge on friendships and more intimate relationships. However, the role models and screenplay may be over-dramatized and inappropriate if the person with Asperger's syndrome uses the script in real-life situations.

As an adult, an intense interest in literature can lead to reading popular 'psychology' books that provide practical and much-needed advice on relationships. Liane Holliday Willey, who has Asperger's syndrome, and whose academic career has been based upon her love of language and literature, has found that by reading books on normal child development she has been better able to understand her own children (Willey 2001). When presented with a problem, people with Asperger's syndrome seek knowledge when intuition is unreliable.

THE FUNCTION OF THE SPECIAL INTEREST

There is very little research on the origins and function of the special interests associated with Asperger's syndrome, but from my extensive clinical experience and reading the autobiographies of adults with Asperger's syndrome, there are several functions.

To overcome anxiety

An intelligent and practical way of reducing fear is to learn about the cause of the anxiety: for all people, knowledge is an antidote to fear. Lisa Pyles, the mother of a son with Asperger's syndrome, wrote in her biography of her son that the interest can help the child control his or her fears. Her son's interest in witches was his way of coping with his fear of them (Pyles 2002). Several parents have described to me how something that is feared can develop into a special interest. A fear of the sound of a flushing toilet can evolve into a fascination with plumbing; an acute auditory sensitivity to the noise of a vacuum cleaner can lead to a fascination with the different types of vacuum cleaners, how they work and their function. I know of several girls with Asperger's syndrome who have had an intense fear of thunder and developed an interest in weather systems to predict when a thunderstorm was imminent. Liliana, an adult with Asperger's syndrome, described how, in her childhood, she was initially scared of spiders but decided to overcome her fear by reading all the books she could find on spiders and actually searching for spiders to study them. Matthias explained to me in an e-mail that 'If I am full of fear or chaotized I tend to talk about security systems, one of my special interests.'

Typical children may resolve their fears by reassurance and affection from parents and friends, but this method of overcoming anxiety may not be as effective for children with Asperger's syndrome. However, their relative strength is in the ability to acquire knowledge and facts and this can be their way of reducing anxiety.

A source of pleasure

Some interests commence by association with a pleasurable experience. The interest is commemorative, linked to a memory of a happier or simpler time (Tantam 2000a). One of my sister-in-law's early interests (that actually lasted for several decades) was trains: to be more specific, a particular type of diesel engine known as a Deltic. The opening paragraphs of my book *Asperger's Syndrome*, published in 1998, described a fictitious but representative description of my sister-in-law and her propensity to talk enthusiastically to strangers about Deltic trains. She recently sent me her brief autobiography (unpublished), in which she wrote:

> Most of the happier times were during vacations which is why I love ships and trains (the only times when we would experience these things). These occasions were more secure and stable for me.

An association with pleasure is illustrated by the example of a young child with Asperger's syndrome who visited a theme park and was taken on his first roller-coaster ride. The emotional experience of acceleration and falling was extremely exhilarating for him and he insisted that he spent most of the day at the front of the roller coaster, screaming, not with fear but pleasure. Whenever he subsequently saw pictures of roller coasters, read about them or talked about them, he experienced a 'ghosting' of the euphoria he had experienced on his first roller-coaster ride. He subsequently developed a special interest in roller-coaster rides and, when we met, gave me a fascinating and detailed 'lecture' on the history and different types of roller coasters. He was only eight years old.

In his guidebook for teenagers with Asperger's syndrome, Luke Jackson explained that:

> If I am focused on my fascination, whether it is dinosaurs (when I was little I hasten to add), Pokémon, a particular PlayStation game, computers – this has always been an everlasting obsession for me – or anything else, I feel an overwhelming excitement in me that I cannot describe. (L. Jackson 2002)

The interest can be a source of humour. Grace, a young woman, has a fantasy world and draws imaginary machines with idiosyncratic names, such as the 'Turbo Fan Cuddle Cubicle' and the 'Glinker Flinker Macho Machine'. Neologisms (new words) and imaginary worlds are a feature of Asperger's syndrome and Grace incorporates her interest in her fears and pleasures. Grace has a hatred of corduroy trousers, and has invented the 'corduroytrousersnatcher'. Her puns or jokes are based on her interest and are not intended to be humorous to others for shared enjoyment (Werth *et al.* 2001).

When I assess and discuss the pleasures in the life of an adult with Asperger's syndrome, as part of the Cognitive Behaviour Therapy treatment program, the pleasures associated with the special interest are greatly superior to many other pleasures in life.

Indeed, the discovery of an extremely rare item to be added to the collection can be perceived as an intellectual or aesthetic 'orgasm' that outranks any other pleasurable interpersonal experience.

The pleasure or enjoyment can also be due to mastering a particular skill, and may provide a means of personal validation and personal growth (Mercier *et al.* 2000). The ability can achieve commendations from family members, result in genuine friendships, and can be a form of compensation and boost to self-esteem, especially if the person has little success in the social and interpersonal aspects of life.

A means of relaxation

Repetitive activities can help a person reduce feelings of stress and relax in the predictability of routine. Clinical experience of people with Asperger's syndrome has indicated that the degree or dominance of the interest in the person's daily life is proportional to the degree of stress: the greater the stress, the more intense the interest. In psychological terms, the interest acts as negative reinforcement, i.e. it ends an unpleasant feeling. The interest can also act as a form of thought blocking: no anxious, critical or depressive thoughts intrude into conscious thought when the person is mesmerized by the special interest. The perception of time is also altered, and the teenager who is informed that he or she has spent five hours on the computer complains that it has not been long enough and feels as though it has been only five minutes. Time goes faster when one is having fun.

One of my clients is a very successful rock musician. He is an extremely nervous and shy person. During his high-school years he would return home from school, mentally exhausted and agitated, and would retreat to his bedroom and listen intently to rock music. His special interest became the rock and popular music of a specific year, some years before he was born. Listening to the music was his form of relaxation, but he also developed the ability to express his thoughts and feelings in the creation of original music that was more eloquent and effective than his ability to communicate his thoughts and feelings using conversational speech. With the formation of a rock group, his songs became extremely popular and he toured the world with his group. I asked him how, as such a shy person, he coped with performing in front of tens of thousands of people. He replied, 'My music protects me.' But when the music stops, he has to exit the stage as fast as he can.

In her autobiography, Liane Holliday Willey explains how one of her interests is a source of relaxation and pleasure:

> To this day, architectural design remains one of my most favored subjects and now that I am older I indulge my interest, giving in to the joy it brings me. In many ways it is the perfect elixir for whatever ails me. When I feel tangled and tense, I get out my history of architecture and design books and set my eyes on the kinds of spaces and arenas that make sense to me; the linear, the straight lines and the level buildings that paint pictures of strong balance. When I feel blighted by too

many pragmatic mistakes and missed communications, I find my home design software programs and set about building a perfect sense home. (Willey 1999, p.48)

An attempt to achieve coherence

The routines that are imposed in daily life and that can be part of the special interest ensure greater predictability and certainty in life. The person develops a cataloguing or ordering system based on logic and symmetry that is reassuring and calming. People with Asperger's syndrome often have difficulty establishing and coping with the changing patterns and expectations in daily life. The interests tend to involve order, as in cataloguing information or creating tables or lists.

A psychological theory developed by Uta Frith and Francesca Happé (1994) may help to explain some aspects of the special interests and the imposition of routines and rituals. They suggest that children and adults with Asperger's syndrome have a different system of information processing, focusing on the details of the environment rather than the 'gestalt' or 'big picture', and tend to get 'lost' in the detail. The person may not perceive the wider context or meaning and have problems with 'central coherence'. Due to the person's having *weak central coherence*, the psychological term originally suggested by Frith and Happé, the interests are an attempt to achieve an elusive coherence.

When the person with Asperger's syndrome has discovered or imposed a taxonomy for the interest, such as the different classifications of insects or the periodic table, or developed a cataloguing system, he or she achieves an understanding and predictability that is extremely satisfying. Thus, the interests can be an attempt to make order out of apparent chaos.

An interest in trains could be attributable to a fascination with order (the carriages are linked in a line), and predictability of outcome (the train must follow the tracks). An interest in symmetry or patterns is also a factor in terms of the parallel track and sleepers or ties.

Luke Jackson wrote that:

> I would say that collecting something is a pretty harmless way of feeling secure and no one should stop anyone from doing so. Organizing something is a wonderful way of shaking off the feeling of chaos that comes from living in such a disorganized world. (L. Jackson 2002, p.50)

For adolescents and adults, the search for the pattern or rules of life can include a fascination not only for the laws of science but the rules of law, leading to a career in the legal profession, and religious laws with a subsequent interest in the Bible and fundamental religions. This can also provide access to a peer group who share the same beliefs and a community with similar values. However, one must be careful that as a consequence of social vulnerability the person with Asperger's syndrome is not unwittingly recruited into extreme organizations. This can occur when the interest is politics, and the person expresses and acts upon 'black and white', or extreme, views.

Understanding the physical world

The person with Asperger's syndrome has a natural ability with the physical rather than the interpersonal world and this is reflected in the choice of interests (Baron-Cohen and Wheelwright 1999). While other children are exploring the social world, children with Asperger's syndrome are exploring objects, machines, animals and scientific concepts. We use the term 'the life-long search for the pattern or meaning of life': those with Asperger's syndrome seem to have a natural ability to determine the function of objects, and an innate interest in what physically influences life, such as science (especially the weather and geography), and the patterns or formulae of life determined by history, biology and mathematics. The autobiographies of adults with Asperger's syndrome often describe how chaotic and unpredictable they perceive their daily lives to be. A special interest in aspects of the physical world can therefore provide great benefit to such individuals, enabling them to find the pattern and predictability they crave.

The creation of an alternative world

The interest may be valuable to the person with Asperger's syndrome as an alternative world in which he or she is happy, successful and popular. My sister-in-law wrote in her unpublished autobiography that:

> When I was about seven, I probably saw something in a book, which fascinated me and still does. Because it was like nothing I had ever seen before and totally unrelated and far removed from our world and our culture. That was Scandinavia and its people. Because of its foreignness it was totally alien and opposite of any one and anything known to me. That was my escape, a dream world where nothing would remind me of daily life and all it had to throw at me. The people from this wonderful place look totally unlike any people in the 'real world'. Looking at these faces, I could not be reminded of anyone who might have humiliated, frightened or rebuked me. The bottom line is I was turning my back on real life and its ability to hurt, and escaping.

She developed a special interest in Scandinavia, particularly the Vikings. She insisted that her mother make her a Viking outfit, which included an upturned pudding basin, with 'horns' attached, as a helmet. As an eight-year-old, she wandered around her home village in England pretending to be a Viking. Fortunately the role-play did not extend to the actions of real Vikings a thousand years ago, namely stealing of cattle or extorting money.

The interest can be periods of history such as ancient Egypt; other countries, especially Japan (a country renowned for its fascination with technology, and the creation of cartoon characters); and science fiction. The search is for a different world, in the past, present or future, that is an alternative to the world experienced by the person with Asperger's syndrome, whose real life is often associated with a lack of success with social integration and friendships.

Daniel Tammet has Asperger's syndrome, and has developed a remarkable ability in mathematics, which became a special interest when he was a child. He explained in an interview that at primary school he would wander around the playground and count the number of leaves on the trees rather than mingle with his peers (*Metro* 2006, p.10). When experiencing feelings of anxiety he would count to himself in powers of two. He regards numbers as friends and has described his attachment to them as emotional rather than purely intellectual. He cares for numbers 'in the same way a poet humanizes a river or tree through metaphor' (Sunday Mail 2005, p.69).

An escape into an imaginary or alternative world can have distinct advantages for the person with Asperger's syndrome. However, this may be of some concern when the contrast between the real and the fantasy world becomes too great, and the person retreats into the alternative world for a disproportionate amount of time. Sometimes there is a blurring of the line between fantasy and reality, and the person begins to exclude other important activities from his or her life.

A sense of identity

Young children with Asperger's syndrome can become increasingly aware of not being popular and successful in social situations and can develop low self-esteem and sadness due to being different; they perceive themselves as having low status and value within their peer group. An interest in and role-playing of super-heroes, such as Spiderman, can be a way of achieving social success and admiration. Often the super-hero is someone who has two identities, a timid and often meek and unsuccessful person who is able to transform himself into someone with special abilities, able to conquer adversity. Instead of being a 'loser', he or she becomes the hero. Thus, the super-hero provides a missing aspect of the child's life, an alter-ego.

In an e-mail I received from Jennifer McIlwee Myers, an adult who has Asperger's syndrome, she explained that:

> Morbid and gruesome topics become a way to deal with one's own otherness, as well as with the constant well-founded fear of pain and rejection. Examples: An interest in 'freaks' provides a forum for mentally dealing with one's own otherness; the works of Edgar Allen Poe and H.P. Lovecraft provide an outlet for both feelings of paranoia and otherness; identifying with inevitability and dangerously misunderstood monsters (such as Frankenstein, the Wolf man, and the Phantom of the Opera) allows one to deal with the very difficult and painful feelings of being an outsider. If an interest serves a legitimate purpose, it should be tolerated even when it is strange or distasteful.

One of the 'triggers' to a special interest can be reading about someone who is different, an outcast such as Harry Potter in the books by J.K. Rowling. The child with Asperger's syndrome is able to identify with the adversity faced by the hero of the story, and wishes that perhaps he or she could have the special abilities that are eventually recognized in the character of the triumphant hero.

The special interest is also important in helping to create a sense of personal identity in adults. In conversation, adults with Asperger's syndrome often describe themselves in terms of their interests rather than personality. The collection of objects provides a sense of both security and identity. Although new interests may occur, the person with Asperger's syndrome is usually extremely resistant to any suggestion that the previously treasured items that have now become space-occupying clutter should be deposited in the garbage. His or her sense of identity and personal history are defined by the collections and to suggest their disposal is almost equivalent to suggesting a finger is amputated.

To occupy time, facilitate conversation and indicate intelligence

How else does one spend one's time, if it is not spent socializing? The special interest is an enjoyable recreational activity for the person with Asperger's syndrome that increases knowledge and may be of practical value, for example writing computer programs or restoring old vehicles.

In social situations, if the person with Asperger's syndrome is not a good conversationalist, has little idea about 'small talk' or social 'chit chat', and is unsure of the contextual cues that indicate an appropriate topic of conversation, then there is a comfortable assurance and fluency if the conversation (or monologue) is about the special interest. The words tumble out with an ease and eloquence that has been practised in many similar interactions. The person with Asperger's syndrome may assume that the other person shares an equivalent fascination for the topic or might become 'infected' with the same degree of enthusiasm.

A common aspiration for people with Asperger's syndrome is to avoid appearing stupid, and there can be a compensatory intellectual arrogance and vanity when the person realizes that he or she is not as able as peers at socializing. One way to indicate intelligence and to impress people with one's knowledge is to deliver a monologue that includes technical terms unfamiliar to the listener. If the person with Asperger's syndrome is a professor or has a profession notorious for using restrictive terminology (such as a lawyer, academic or medical specialist), then the other person may just assume that he or she is simply a typically eccentric member of that profession, and tolerate or admire the obscure knowledge, especially if the listener can benefit from that knowledge.

PARENTS' PERSPECTIVE

From the perspective of the parents of the child with Asperger's syndrome, the special interest presents a number of problems. Parents have to try to quench the almost insatiable thirst for access to the interest. A survey of parents found that they frequently had to make a special trip to replace or purchase an item related to the interest, had been late for appointments for reasons due to the particular interest, and driven out of their way or scheduled unusual vacations to accommodate access to the interest (Bashe and Kirby 2001).

The duration and dominance of the interest in the child's play can have other consequences. The play date arranged by the parents might collapse as the child dominates the play with a conspicuous lack of reciprocity in the chosen play activities or conversation. However, there may be fewer problems in determining what the child would like as a birthday or Christmas present or what book to read at bedtime.

The propensity to talk endlessly about a particular topic can test the patience of parents and family members, especially if the child or adult gives a monologue and does not appear to be interested in the other person's thoughts, opinions and experiences. In her autobiography, Donna Williams described how her monologues were not an attempt at a dialogue but more a vocalization of thinking and problem solving.

> When I was in a talkative mood, I would often talk on and on about something which interested me. The older I got, the more interested I became in things and the longer I would go on about them. I really was not interested in discussing anything; nor did I expect answers or opinions from the other person, and would often ignore them or talk over them if they interrupted. The only thing that was important to me was to talk in an effort to answer *my own* questions, which I often did. (Williams 1998, p.49)

Unfortunately, the determination to maintain access to the interest can lead to more problems as the child becomes a teenager. Access to the interest may occur without careful planning with regard to the consequences. I have known of adolescents with Asperger's syndrome who have been interested in trains and undertaken journeys without consideration of how they are to return, or without informing parents of their journey and destination. They are completely unaware of how distressed parents can be not knowing where their son or daughter is and how he or she is. The person's financial planning can also be affected by spending a disproportionate amount of his or her income on the interest; this, in turn, can affect the family, who has to suffer the economic consequences or arrange extra funds.

Being thwarted in gaining access can also lead to anger. In his autobiography, Luke Jackson describes, 'I feel an overwhelming excitement in me that I cannot describe. I just have to talk about it and the irritation of being stopped can easily develop into raging fury' (L. Jackson 2002, p.44). Parents can be concerned that interrupting the activity can result in extreme agitation.

Denial of access to the source material can cause the person with Asperger's syndrome to be in conflict with the law (Chen *et al.* 2003). Adults with Asperger's syndrome are usually very concerned that others obey the law, but they can be tempted themselves to commit criminal offences to obtain money to achieve access to their special interest (see Chapter 15, p.334).

The class teacher may be concerned that at school the child's monologues about the special interest can make the child appear eccentric and thus prone to teasing by other children who think that the child with Asperger's syndrome is boring, pedantic, self-centred and rude. The interest thus becomes a barrier to social inclusion. The determination to talk about or read about the interest can interfere with the child's ability to attend to other activities. The amount of time dedicated to the interest may inhibit the learning of new skills (Klin, Carter and Sparrow 1997).

An interest in weapons and firearms, together with a tendency not to reflect on the consequences of what might be said in 'the heat of the moment' (and this can include threats that others perceive as likely to be carried out), could lead to school suspension or exclusion, or sometimes to the involvement of law enforcement officers.

THE CLINICIAN'S PERSPECTIVE

The special interest can provide considerable information for the clinician. During a diagnostic assessment, teenagers or adults may interact with the clinician in a guarded manner, thinking before giving a response and being somewhat hesitant and reluctant to talk. This is due to their being unsure of the conversational 'script' in a situation with someone they do not know well, and who is observing and analysing their behaviour and abilities. However, their character can change quite dramatically when one broaches the topic of their particular interest. They visibly relax, showing enthusiasm and energy as well as a delight in impressing the clinician with their knowledge. The contrast between the two 'personas' can be one of the positive indicators of Asperger's syndrome.

The focus of the interest can also be of clinical value. A change of preoccupation to a morbid or macabre topic such as death can be indicative of a clinical depression and an interest in weapons, the martial arts and revenge a possible indication of bullying at school (see Chapter 4).

The child or adult may collect information on a topic that is causing emotional distress or confusion, as a means of understanding a feeling or situation. This can include death and mortality. An example is a child with Asperger's syndrome who had a very close relationship with his grandfather. The two would often walk around the family farm, deep in conversation about animals and farm machinery. On one walk, the grandfather had a cardiac arrest and died. The child did not appear to mourn the death of his grandfather in conventional ways but began a special interest in cardiac disease, and read as many books as he could find on heart disorders. He wanted to know exactly why and how his much-loved and admired grandfather died.

The interest can become so intense and so dominating in the person's life that a clinician may be concerned that it is no longer pleasurable or of intellectual or psychological value, but has become irresistible and unwanted. The inability to control the amount of time devoted to the special interest can be indicative of the development of an Obsessive Compulsive Disorder (Baron-Cohen 1990). Luke Jackson in his autobiography explained that: 'I cannot begin to explain the feeling if something wasn't performed. This was when I felt like my whole body was going to burst' (L. Jackson 2002, p. 56). If the special interest crosses the psychological 'border' and becomes unwanted or has a detrimental effect on the person's quality of life, then the person may need to seek professional help for an anxiety disorder (see Chapter 6). The special interest can also be associated with a delusional disorder (Kurita 1999). This can occur if the interest is fantasy literature and super-heroes, and the person acts as his or her hero in an attempt to be successful and respected in social situations with peers. This characteristic, or adaptation to having Asperger's syndrome, can be of clinical significance when the person cannot separate from the alternative persona and may consider him- or herself to have special or magical powers and omnipotence.

Some aspects of the special interest can be indicative of impaired executive function (see Chapter 9). One of the roles of the 'executive' or frontal lobes of the brain is the cognitive or thoughtful control of what you do or say, especially the ability to change and inhibit thoughts and actions. When a person with Asperger's syndrome engages in or talks about the special interest, there may be evidence of perseveration and being 'stuck in set', with considerable difficulty changing thinking or conversational focus to another topic (Turner 1997). The person seems to have a 'one-track' mind, with an irresistible determination to complete the activity or monologue. Children and adults with Asperger's syndrome often say how the special interest dominates their thinking and how difficult it is to stop part-way through the thought or activity and to do something else. It is almost as if once the person has started there is a compulsion for completion. The person cannot be interrupted or distracted, or close the thought before the natural conclusion.

We do not have a biological model for the development of special interests but a recent study of four-year-old, typically developing children has indicated that restricted interests in boys and girls is positively correlated with foetal testosterone (Knickmeyer *et al.* 2005). However, while this may be one of the factors that can influence the development of special interests, there are many more factors described above that also influence their development in children and adults with Asperger's syndrome.

We recognize that the special interest can provide a source of extreme pleasure for the person with Asperger's syndrome. However, several adults who have been prescribed medication to treat anxiety, depression or problems with anger management have described how the medication has 'lifted' their mood, but 'flattened' their enjoyment of the special interest. The clinician may need to consider and explain the advantages and side effects of medication on mood in general, including its effect on the pleasure gained from engaging in the special interest.

The clinician is often asked by the person with Asperger's syndrome, or his or her family, for strategies to manage, adapt, reduce, diversify or constructively use the person's special interests. Fortunately we have some suggestions.

Reducing, removing or constructively using the special interest

While the motivation for the child with Asperger's syndrome is to increase his or her time engaged in the interest, the motivation for parents and teachers is to reduce the duration and frequency of access to the interest. This is to enable the child to engage in a wider range of activities, which is particularly important when the time devoted to the interest appears to virtually exclude social interaction with family members at home and peers at school and affects the completion of homework assignments. What are the strategies that can reduce the time spent engaged in the interest, should some interests be ended, or can they serve a constructive purpose?

Controlled access

The problem may not be the activity itself but its duration and dominance over other activities. Some success can be achieved by limiting the time available using a clock or timer. When the allotted time is over, the activity must cease and the child can be actively encouraged to pursue other interests or priorities, such as social contact and completing chores or assignments. The child can be reassured that there will soon be another scheduled time to enjoy his or her special interest. It is important that the alternative activity is out of sight of the resource material for the interest. The temptation to continue the interest will be quite strong so the new activity could be in another room or outside. The replacement activity may need to be something the child enjoys, even if it is not as enjoyable as the special interest. The approach is to ration access, and actively to encourage a wider range of interests. The 'pleasures book', described in Chapter 6, can provide some suggestions for alternative activities (see page 152).

Part of the controlled access program can be to allocate specific social or 'quality' time to pursue the interest as a social activity. In this instance, the parent or teacher has a schedule of regular times to talk about or jointly explore the interest. The adult ensures that they are not going to be distracted and both parties view the experience as enjoyable. I have found that such sessions, often at the end of a clinic appointment, can be an opportunity to improve my knowledge of such interesting topics as *The Guinness Book of Records*, butterflies, the *Titanic*, or weather systems. I am then able to talk with some authority and achieve respect from other children I meet with Asperger's syndrome who share the same interest as the child who became my teacher. The conversation can become reciprocal if you, as an adult, explain what you are interested in and the two of you can spend time exploring each other's interests.

Modifying or removing unacceptable interests

If the interest is potentially dangerous, illegal or likely to be misinterpreted, such as an interest in fires, weapons or pornography, steps can be taken to terminate, or at least modify, the interest, although clinical experience suggests that this is not an easy task. You must explain why the interest is not acceptable to other people, perhaps using Social

Stories™ to explain the social conventions. You may also need to explain any relevant legislation, and to explore some modifications to the current interest (Gray 1998). For example, an interest in pornography can be a way of trying to understand about relationships and sexuality. The interest becomes unacceptable when the adolescent or adult with Asperger's syndrome considers that the photographs are realistic representations of typical people and the sexual activities provide a guide to behaviour on a first date. Fortunately we now have programs specifically to inform adolescents and adults with Asperger's syndrome about appropriate levels of intimacy and sexuality (Hénault 2005).

Comic Strip Conversations (drawing a situation using stick figures and thought and speech bubbles), also developed by Carol Gray (1998), can help the child understand the perspectives of other people. The drawings include the depiction of the child's thoughts but also the thoughts, emotions and perspectives of family members, other adults, the community perspective, and possible consequences. An appeal is made to the self-image of the child in that the logical, mature and wise decision is to modify the focus of the interest; for example an interest in poisons may be modified to an interest in the digestive system, or carnivorous plants.

The alternative option is to end the interest. A replacement interest that is mutually acceptable can be actively sought and encouraged. However, you must acknowledge that the choice must be based on the child's character and previous types of interests and the function of that interest. For example, if the interest is weapons and retaliation for being bullied at school, then steps must be taken to end the bullying.

Constructive application

Sometimes it is wiser to work with rather than against the motivation to engage in the special interest. The interest can be a source of enjoyment, knowledge, self-identity and self-esteem that can be constructively used by parents, teachers and therapists.

Motivation and learning

Typical children are usually motivated to please their parents or teacher, to impress the other children or to imitate or be included in the activities of their peers. These conventional desires or motivations are not as powerful for children with Asperger's syndrome. In contrast, they usually have a greater motivation to engage in their special interest than to please others. A constructive application is to increase motivation for non-preferred activities by incorporating the interest, or to use access to the interest as an encouragement. For example, if the young child with Asperger's syndrome has an interest in Thomas the Tank Engine, there is a wide range of merchandise that incorporates the engines in reading books for different reading ages, mathematical activities, and writing and drawing. The child is more likely to be motivated to read a book about his or her favourite character than a book about someone in whom he or she is not interested.

If the interest is in geography, and flags in particular, the child could count flags rather than the conventional items being counted by his or her peers in the classroom or for homework. Indeed, one of the problems encountered by parents is the child's motivation for homework. If the homework assignment involves an aspect of the special interest, there are fewer issues with the completion of homework assignments (Hinton and Kern 1999).

Access to the interest is a remarkably potent incentive (Mercier *et al.* 2000). Completion of allocated tasks in class results in free time to pursue the interest. For example, if the child solves ten mathematical problems within ten minutes, he has earned ten minutes of free time on the computer. For older children, a special interest in a branch of science can lead to knowledge of scientific methodology, and success in science competitions, which can be self-rewarding and improve self-esteem. The strategy of incorporating the interest in the curriculum does require the teacher to be more flexible in the presentation of the class activities and encouragement systems. However, the benefits can be improved abilities and concentration.

Some parents have used the removal of access to the interest as a punishment for misbehaviour or tasks not completed. While this strategy can be an effective component of a home-based behaviour management program, it could become a trigger to agitated behaviour if the child cannot tolerate denied access. I recommend that there is some caution regarding removal of access to the interest as a punishment, as other strategies may be more successful, and the interest should remain a positive aspect of the person's daily life. Preventing access to one of the few pleasures in the person's life will invariably be resisted.

Elisa Gagnon has developed the concept of Power Cards (Gagnon 2001). The strategy is to use the interest to increase motivation and aid learning. This strategy can be used in the classroom and at home, and involves creating a card (the size of a business or trading card) that provides an explanation of, and advice that incorporates scenes or characters associated with, the special interest. The text is written in a similar style to a Social Story™, and can include pictures and characters associated with the interest. For example, a girl with Asperger's syndrome was unpopular for her direct and sometimes personal comments about her peers. She would loudly say comments such as 'You have bad breath.' She needed to learn to inhibit such comments, or say them in a more tactful way. Because she had a great interest in the popular singer Britney Spears, a Power Card was written with a picture of Britney and a text which included Britney's 'advice' to her on what to say to the other children in her class. The inclusion of the interest can focus the child's attention and the recommendations are thus more likely to be remembered and used.

Employment

Some interests eventually become a source of income and employment. One teenager with Asperger's syndrome has an amazing knowledge of fishing, especially the different types of fish and fishing equipment. His high school had a vocational experience scheme such that at the end of the school year each student was allocated to an employment situation for a day of work experience. The teachers had some discussion as to what work experience he should have. Eventually the suggestion was made that he could work for a day at the local fishing tackle shop. He went for the day, but never returned to school: he was employed by the end of the day, as the shop owner recognized that his knowledge and enthusiasm would make him a valued employee.

An interest in the weather could lead to employment as a meteorologist; an interest in maps, a job as a taxi driver or truck driver; an interest in different cultures and languages, a job as a tour guide or translator. Stephen Shore enjoyed making bicycles and cycling and explained to me that he got a job as a mechanic in a bicycle shop using his customized bicycle that he built himself as a 'work portfolio' equivalent. While he demonstrated and described his customized bicycle, Stephen mentioned he knew how to build bicycle wheels, which was a rare and valued skill at the time. The manager initially hired him to build ten bicycle wheels; he was subsequently hired for more hours, and eventually became manager of the shop.

Parents may consider private tuition to develop, in an adaptive way, those interests that could become a source of income or employment, such as a natural ability with computers. I think that computers were designed by and for people with Asperger's syndrome, and in the twenty-first century computer skills are required in many occupations. An interest in books and cataloguing systems can become the skills necessary to be a successful librarian, or an interest in animals lead to a career in veterinary science.

Temple Grandin, who has a diagnosis of High Functioning Autism or Asperger's syndrome, has advocated that those with autism and Asperger's syndrome should consider developing a level of expertise in a given subject, such that others seek their knowledge, rather than their having to acquire the social ability to gain entry into employment. A work portfolio of examples of their abilities and knowledge can compensate for their difficulties in the social skills required in a job interview.

Since one of the characteristics of the interest is the accumulation of knowledge and expertise, an academic career could be a constructive application of a special interest. A professor with Asperger's syndrome from a university in California wrote to me that: 'The best thing about academia is that we get paid to talk about our favorite topic and students take note and feed back our words of wisdom at exams.'

Adults with Asperger's syndrome may congregate in working environments that need expertise in those special interests associated with Asperger's syndrome. Companies that employ engineers and computer specialists may have more employees with Asperger's syndrome than one would expect when considering the prevalence figures in the general population. These employers may create an 'Asperger friendly and appreciative' community. The same can occur in artistic communities, where there is often an acceptance of each unusual or eccentric character because of his or her expertise, perhaps as a writer or artist (Fitzgerald 2005).

A component of a Cognitive Behaviour Therapy program

The primary psychological treatment for mood disorders is Cognitive Behaviour Therapy (CBT). I have developed several modifications to CBT to accommodate the unusual profile of cognitive and social skills associated with Asperger's syndrome (Sofronoff *et al.* 2005). One of these modifications is the concept, or metaphor, of a 'toolbox' that contains a variety of tools to 'repair' an emotion (see Chapter 6, p.159). Since one of the attributes of the special interest is that it provides a source of pleasure and relaxation, one of the tools in the toolbox can be access to the interest as an emotional restorative. Distraction, consolation and conversation may be unsuccessful in emotion management, while time engaged in the special interest may provide a means of relaxation, pleasure and thought blocking to prevent a further deterioration in mood.

The interest can also be incorporated in the cognitive restructuring component of the CBT program. For example, one adolescent, who had a dual diagnosis of Asperger's syndrome and Obsessive Compulsive Disorder, had a fear of contamination by bacteria. His special interest was the television programme *Doctor Who*, about space and time travel. A therapy activity was designed whereby the client was encouraged to imagine himself as Dr Who, marooned on a planet with an invisible monster that creates and thrives on fear. I, a clinical psychologist, could be imagined by the adolescent as a scientist who has studied the behaviour of the monster. Working as a team, Dr Who and the scientist developed strategies to overcome the monster and escape from the planet. This theme was typical of many of the television adventures of Dr Who, and provided a role and conceptualization and structure that was appealing to the adolescent and contributed to the clinical success of the therapy.

In the affective education component of CBT, designed to improve the person's knowledge of emotions and how emotions affect thoughts, feelings and behaviour, the special interest can again be used as a metaphor. For example, a girl with an interest in the weather was able to develop a 'barometer' to forecast changes in mood, expressing thoughts as weather features (for example, confusion described as fog), and to explain her emotions and thoughts as a weather report.

A means of making friends

Can the special interest actually encourage friendships for children with Asperger's syndrome? One of the common replies of typical children and adults to the question 'What makes a good friend?' is 'We like the same things'; shared interests can be the basis of friendship. Parents can consider some social engineering using the child's special interest, to encourage prospective friendships. Local parent support groups can include the names and addresses of group members, but also the special interests of their son or daughter for the possibility of an arranged but potentially successful friendship. However, I have noted that when the shared interest ends for one partner, the friendship may also end. Adults with Asperger's syndrome can meet like-minded individuals and prospective friends at special clubs and gatherings, such as train-spotters clubs or *Star Trek* conventions, a favourite opportunity for a social reunion of people with Asperger's syndrome.

The interest itself can be used to facilitate friendship with typical peers, though not always successfully. My sister-in-law has an outstanding ability in art, drawing with photographic realism. She wrote in her unpublished autobiography that at school: 'Longing to make friends, when someone complimented a drawing I had done, I started giving people drawings until someone accused me of bragging – a rebuke I never forgot. I was only trying to win friendship.'

An interest in computers can be popular with peers and there can be great delight in being sought after for advice or ability to repair a computer 'crash', or to develop a new computer program or graphic. This can provide a rare moment of being genuinely needed and valued by others. A small group of friends can form at school, based on a common interest in computers, and within this group the person can make genuine friends.

Sometimes the friendship based on a common interest can develop beyond the platonic stage and become a more significant relationship. During conversations with partners of adults with Asperger's syndrome, I have often listened to how their partner's special interests were initially viewed as endearing and an attractive quality. This opinion can change when the adult with Asperger's syndrome has to decide his or her priorities as a partner or parent. The non-Asperger's syndrome partners can later complain that too much in the way of time and resources is spent on the interest.

The interest itself can lead to finding a friend who eventually becomes a life-long partner. I was describing at a conference how an interest in insects can lead to a career as an entomologist, that this may be a way of making friends with fellow entomologists, and that a fellow entomologist could even become a partner. This was a hypothetical point, but during one of the breaks a woman approached me and said that indeed she and her husband were both entomologists and that she had only recently recognized that not only did her son have Asperger's syndrome, but that her husband probably had the same diagnosis. Her husband's abilities as an entomologist were some of the attributes that changed feelings of admiration to feelings of love.

LEARNING WHEN TO TALK ABOUT THE INTEREST

If a conversation includes talking about the special interest, the child or adult with Asperger's syndrome usually has to learn the relevant cues and responses to ensure the conversation is reciprocal and inclusive. Activities can be undertaken to 'spot the message' that indicates that the listener is bored, embarrassed or annoyed. The person with Asperger's syndrome may have to be reminded to make regular checks on the other person's perception of the conversation and his or her potential contribution, looking for nods of approval and signs of being genuinely interested. If the person with Asperger's syndrome is unsure about the signals, he or she needs to learn to seek information by comments or questions such as 'I hope that this isn't boring you' or 'and what are your thoughts and opinions on this?' The person with Asperger's syndrome also seems to have a different time perception when talking about the interest and needs to be aware of how long the monologue has dominated the conversation. As previously noted, time goes quickly when one is having fun.

Sometimes parents or teachers have a 'secret sign' for the child with Asperger's syndrome that indicates that he or she needs to recognize and respond to the subtle signals from the other child, and to incorporate the friend's knowledge and suggestions, or switch the topic to the other child's interests. The child with Asperger's syndrome may also need explicit information on who may or may not be an appropriate person to engage in a conversation about the interest. One can use the concept of concentric circles of relationships, whereby for those people within the inner circles, such as the family, relatives and close friends, the topic could be appropriate. However, for people who are less well known, the person with Asperger's syndrome may need to be more aware of the context and social cues before engaging in a conversation about the special interest.

A teenager with Asperger's syndrome was aware that, when starting a conversation with a stranger, he should wait a while before talking about his special interest. He wanted my advice on how soon it would be appropriate for him to tell an attractive teenage girl about his interest in visiting cemeteries, and recording the inscriptions on gravestones. He did at least recognize the importance of just a few minutes before embarking on an enthusiastic description of all the cemeteries in the city.

SPECIAL INTERESTS: A PROBLEM OR A TALENT?

Hans Asperger had a very positive attitude to special interests, and considered the abilities demonstrated in the interests to be a special gift. In his first published paper that described (to use his original term) autistic personality, he stated that:

> We claim – not from theoretical reasons, but from experiences with many children – that this boy's positive and negative features are two naturally necessary, connected aspects of one really homogeneously laid out personality. We can also express it like this: the difficulties, which this boy has with himself as well as with his relationship to the world, are the price he has to pay for his special gifts. (Asperger 1938, p.2)

The interest can be either a barrier or bridge to social contact, but can also be used constructively at school and in psychological therapies or become the basis of a successful career. When one considers the attributes associated with the special interests, it is important to consider not only the benefits to the person with Asperger's syndrome, but also the benefits to society. There have been suggestions that successful individuals in the sciences and arts have personalities that resemble the profile of abilities associated with Asperger's syndrome (Fitzgerald 2005; Ledgin 2002; Paradiz 2002).

Hans Asperger considered that:

> It seems that for success in science or art, a dash of autism is essential. For success, the necessary ingredient may be an ability to turn away from the everyday world, from the simply practical, an ability to re-think a subject with originality so as to create in new untrodden ways, with all abilities canalized into the one specialty. (Asperger 1979, p.49)

Different societies and cultures will have varying perceptions of the special interest. In some societies the interest would be considered as pathological and indicative of someone who needs psychiatric treatment, or to 'get a life'. But in some cultures, notably the British, the person is just considered as a benign eccentric and the special interest could be the theme of a popular television programme with the audience appreciating the person's abilities and personality. I have watched the British television programme *Antiques Roadshow* and enjoyed the enthusiasm of avid collectors who seem to have signs of Asperger's syndrome. As a culture, the British have always accepted and admired eccentric people. In conclusion, I endorse the comment of Jennifer McIlwee Myers, who has Asperger's syndrome, who, in an e-mail to me, wrote 'Don't treat the special interest as a toxin to be purged but as a trait to be managed.' In my opinion, it is a trait that can be a great advantage to society.

KEY POINTS AND STRATEGIES

- One of the characteristics that distinguishes between a hobby and a special interest that is of clinical significance is an abnormality in the intensity or focus of the interest.

- Unusual or special interests can develop as early as age two to three years and may commence with a preoccupation with parts of objects such as spinning the wheels of toy cars, or manipulating electrical switches.

- The next stage may be a fixation on something neither human nor toy, or a fascination with a specific category of objects and the acquisition of as many examples as possible.

- A subsequent stage can be the collection of facts and figures about a specific topic.

- Much of the knowledge associated with the interest is self-directed and self-taught.
- In the pre-teenage and teenage years the interests can evolve to include electronics and computers, fantasy literature, science fiction and sometimes a fascination with a particular person.
- There appear to be two main categories of interest: collections, and the acquisition of knowledge on a specific topic or concept.
- Some girls with Asperger's syndrome can develop a special interest in fiction rather than facts.
- Sometimes the special interest is animals but can be to such an intensity that the child acts being the animal.
- The special interest has several functions:
  - to overcome anxiety
  - to provide pleasure
  - to provide relaxation
  - to ensure greater predictability and certainty in life
  - to help understand the physical world
  - to create an alternative world
  - to create a sense of identity
  - to occupy time, facilitate conversation and indicate intellectual ability.
- Parents have to try to quench the almost insatiable thirst for access to the interest.
- The special interest can provide considerable information for the clinician.
- A change of preoccupation to a morbid or macabre topic such as death can be indicative of a clinical depression, and an interest in weapons, the martial arts and revenge a possible indication of bullying at school.
- The child or adult may collect information on a topic that is causing emotional distress or confusion, as a means of understanding a feeling or situation.
- The inability to control the amount of time devoted to the special interest can be indicative of the development of an Obsessive Compulsive Disorder.
- The problem may not be the activity itself but the duration and dominance over other activities. Some success can be achieved by limiting the time available using a clock or timer.
- Part of the controlled access program can be to allocate specific social or 'quality' time to pursue the interest as a social activity.

- If the interest is potentially dangerous, illegal or likely to be misinterpreted, steps can be taken to terminate, or at least modify, the interest, although clinical experience suggests that this is not an easy task.

- Sometimes it is wiser to work *with* rather than *against* the motivation to engage in the special interest.

- The interest can be a source of enjoyment, knowledge, self-identity and self-esteem that can be constructively used by parents, teachers and therapists.

- Parents may consider private tuition to develop, in an adaptive way, those interests that could become a source of income or employment, such as a natural ability with computers.

- The special interest can be integrated within a Cognitive Behaviour Therapy program to understand and manage emotions.

- The interest can be used to facilitate friendships with typical peers and people with Asperger's syndrome who share the same interests.

- If a conversation includes talking about the special interest, the child or adult with Asperger's syndrome usually has to learn the relevant cues and responses to ensure the conversation is reciprocal and inclusive.

- When one considers the attributes associated with the special interests, it is important to consider not only the benefits to the person with Asperger's syndrome, but also the benefits to society.

CHAPTER 8

Language

They all have one thing in common: the language feels unnatural.

– Hans Asperger ([1944] 1991)

Hans Asperger eloquently described an unusual profile of language abilities that included problems with conversation skills, the 'melody' or flow of speech, and an unusual developmental history for language such as the early or late development of speech. He also described a tendency for some young children to talk like an adult with an advanced vocabulary and to use quite complex sentences. Asperger wrote that: 'if one listens carefully, one can invariably pick up these kinds of abnormalities in the language of autistic individuals, and their recognition is, therefore, of particular diagnostic importance' (Asperger [1944] 1991, p.70).

The diagnostic criteria of Christopher Gillberg acknowledge an unusual profile of language skills, with at least three of the following speech and language peculiarities being required for a diagnosis of Asperger's syndrome (Gillberg and Gillberg 1989):

- delayed speech development
- superficially perfect expressive language
- formal pedantic language
- odd prosody, peculiar voice characteristics
- impairments of comprehension including misinterpretations of literal/implied meanings.

The diagnostic criteria of Peter Szatmari and colleagues also recognize odd speech characteristics and require at least two of the following (Szatmari *et al.* 1989b):

- abnormalities in inflection
- talking too much

- talking too little
- lack of cohesion to conversation
- idiosyncratic use of words
- repetitive patterns of speech.

These diagnostic criteria incorporate both the original descriptions of Hans Asperger and those characteristics in language ability recognized by clinicians conducting a diagnostic assessment. The American Psychiatric Association's diagnostic criteria for Asperger's disorder in DSM-IV and the World Health Organization criteria in ICD-10 briefly refer to language abilities, but state that 'there is no clinically significant general delay in language' (APA 2002, p.84). Unfortunately, this may be interpreted as an absence of any unusual qualities in language skills. By the age of five years, the child with Asperger's syndrome does not have a general delay in language, but research studies, clinical experience and the descriptions of parents indicate that the child or adult is unusual with regard to specific and more subtle aspects of language.

The accompanying text to the diagnostic criteria in the DSM-IV refers to the way in which the language may be abnormal in terms of the individual's preoccupation with certain topics, verbosity and failure to appreciate and utilize conventional rules of conversation, and the fact that the child may have a vocabulary that would be typical of an adult. Unfortunately these characteristics are not included in the DSM diagnostic criteria. In my opinion, unusual language abilities are an essential characteristic of Asperger's syndrome and should be included in future revisions of the DSM criteria.

THE ASSESSMENT OF LANGUAGE ABILITIES

The standardized tests to measure receptive and expressive language may not be sensitive to the specific language characteristics of children and adults with Asperger's syndrome. In general, the surface structure can be age appropriate in terms of the development of vocabulary and the ability to say quite complex sentences. However, formal assessment, using tests such as the Clinical Evaluation of Language Fundamentals IV, or CELF-IV, can indicate problems with receptive language abilities, especially specific aspects of language comprehension such as understanding figures of speech and the interpretation, recall and execution of increasingly complex oral directions (Koning and Magill-Evans 2001).

This may explain a problem that is often reported by parents and teachers, namely that of a child who can say quite complex sentences, sometimes more typical of an adult than a child, but who is confused when an adult asks the child to complete a sequence of requests that should be understood by a typical child of the same age. His or her tendency to use complex sentences does not automatically mean that the child with Asperger's syndrome can fully understand your complex instructions.

The child's language profile can include highly developed syntax, grammar and vocabulary such that the child may be considered ineligible for speech therapy services (Paul and Sutherland 2003). However, parents and teachers often need guidance regarding how to encourage the child to have a reciprocal conversation (Linblad 2005), and problems with conversation skills can inhibit the child's successful integration with peers in the classroom and playground. The formal assessment of language abilities of children with Asperger's syndrome should include the administration of tests to examine the pragmatic aspects of language or the 'art of conversation' (Bishop and Baird 2001), as well as aspects of prosody such as the use of stress on key words or syllables, and the fluency and tone of speech. The assessment should consider a broad view of language and include an evaluation of the ability to understand figures of speech, written language, narrative ability (the ability to tell a story), and aspects of non-verbal communication such as body language and the communication of emotions. The assessment should also examine whether there are characteristics such as pedantry or creativity in the use of language.

There is often a significant difference between language knowledge and practice. The child may demonstrate linguistic ability in a formal testing situation with a speech pathologist but have considerable difficulties with the speed of language processing needed in real-life situations such as when playing with peers, and with hearing and understanding someone's speech when there are other distractions and background noise.

The assessment should also examine the person's ability to communicate thoughts and feelings using means of communication other than speech. I have observed that one of the interesting language abilities of people with Asperger's syndrome is that they may have difficulty explaining a significant emotional event by talking about it in a face-to-face conversation, yet show eloquence and insight expressing their inner thoughts and emotions by typing an account in a diary on a computer, or by sending an e-mail. Their written or typed language is often superior to their spoken communication (Frith 2004).

LANGUAGE QUALITIES AND DIFFICULTIES

The language of a child with Asperger's syndrome can include some areas of conspicuous ability. The child may develop an impressive vocabulary that includes technical terms (often related to a special interest) and expressions more often associated with the speech of an adult than a child. The child can sometimes speak like a 'little professor' and entrance someone with a well-practised monologue on a favourite topic. However, when this characteristic occurs in an adolescent it can be a contributory factor for social exclusion. There can be a natural curiosity about the physical world and how things work, and a tendency to ask questions and provide fascinating facts. I enjoy the intellectual exchange of information when engaged in a conversation with someone with

Asperger's syndrome, and have found that such individuals (especially adults), whose knowledge exceeds mine, can be remarkably patient in explaining particular concepts – extremely important when assisting me with a computer problem and preventing me from having an emotional 'meltdown'.

Some young children who subsequently have a diagnosis of Asperger's syndrome can be delayed in the development of speech but the first spoken words can be an utterance comprising several words or sentences. My sister-in-law has Asperger's syndrome, and did not speak until she was over three years old, but her first words were quite remarkable. She was about to kiss her father on his cheek when she suddenly recoiled, saying 'No wanna kissa da Daddy till Daddy usa da Hoover.' A Hoover is type of vacuum cleaner and she recoiled because he had not had a shave. This incident also illustrates an imaginative use of words – a shaver was conceptualized as a vacuum cleaner for facial hair.

The child's articulation can be age appropriate but can be unusual in being almost over-precise. The word may be pronounced as it is written rather than spoken: the child learned language more by reading than from listening. There may be stress on specific syllables that changes the expected pronunciation. I have observed that for some young children with Asperger's syndrome, the development of language appears to rely less on conversation with family and peers and more on what is absorbed from television programmes and films. Often the young child with Asperger's syndrome pronounces the word with the accent of the person whom he or she heard first say the word. This explains the tendency for some young children with Asperger's syndrome in the United Kingdom and Australia to speak with an American accent. Their vocabulary and pronunciation of words was developed by watching television rather than talking to people and especially by watching cartoons and films that use American actors and voices. This characteristic can be quite conspicuous when other family members have the local accent, but the child with Asperger's syndrome talks as though he or she is a foreigner.

The child with Asperger's syndrome may also create his or her own words or neologisms (Tantam 1991; Volden and Lord 1991). One child created the word 'snook' to describe a flake of chocolate in an ice block, and the word 'clink' for a magnet. Another child was asked why he was not interested in his baby brother and replied, 'He can't walk, he can't talk – he's broken.' When making his bedroom untidy, with toys strewn all over the floor, another child explained he was 'tidying down' (the opposite of tidying up). My sister-in-law described her ankle as the 'wrist of my foot', and ice cubes as 'water bones'.

Sometimes the sound or meaning of a particular word provokes great laughter or giggling in the child. He or she may repeatedly say the word aloud and laugh, with no intention of sharing the enjoyment or explaining why the word is so fascinating or funny. The humour is idiosyncratic to the child and can be very puzzling to a teacher or parent. This ability to provide a novel perspective on language is fascinating, and one of the endearing and genuinely creative aspects of Asperger's syndrome. Perhaps the child could be given a creativity prize for the lateral thinking that produces such novel words, phrases or descriptions, and be encouraged to incorporate them in his or her writing.

Although there can be positive qualities in the profile of linguistic skills, there are specific difficulties. The most conspicuous is the inability to modify language according to the social context. Typical school-age children can engage in a reciprocal or 'balanced' conversation, aware of the knowledge, interests and intentions of the other person and the social conventions that determine what to say, how to say it and how to listen attentively. Speech pathologists describe the modification and use of language in a social context as the *pragmatic aspects* of language, and a subsequent section of this chapter will describe the difficulties in this area of language in more detail and provide remedial strategies for parents and teachers.

The prosody and especially the vocal tone of speech can be unusual, with some children and adults with Asperger's syndrome having a 'flat' vocal tone that is perceived as monotonous. The speech characteristics can include problems with volume, being too loud or too quiet for the context. Speech that is too loud can be extremely irritating for family members and especially difficult for teachers who are trying to encourage less noise in the classroom. The person's speech may also be unusually high-pitched or have a 'nasal' quality that is quite distinct and distracting for the listener. The fluency or delivery of speech can sometimes be too rapid, particularly when the person is excited or talking about a special interest. In contrast, speech may be unusually ponderous when the person has to think what to say, especially if the reply requires understanding what someone is thinking or feeling during a social conversation.

Conversation with a person with Asperger's syndrome can include moments when there appears to be a breakdown in the communication 'transmission'. The person is deep in thought, deciding what to say and, to ensure total concentration, avoids looking at the face of the other person. Unfortunately, the temporary loss of conversational momentum and eye contact can be confusing to the other person, who expects an immediate response and is unsure whether to interrupt the person with Asperger's syndrome to re-establish the dialogue. I usually wait patiently, knowing that some adults with Asperger's syndrome prefer not to be interrupted as an interruption can cause the person to start the whole thinking process again.

While someone with Asperger's syndrome can dislike being interrupted, that same person may be notorious for interrupting or talking over the speech of other people. Teachers can complain that the child hates being interrupted when he or she is talking or working but seems oblivious to the signals of when not to interrupt other people. A frequent request to speech pathologists and psychologists is for advice on how to stop the child continually interrupting the teacher.

During a conversation, the person with Asperger's syndrome may frequently change topics, unaware that the logical link between the topics is not obvious to the listener. Such conversations or monologues appear to be without structure and are perceived as a stream of thoughts and experience that lack coherence or relevance to the context. The person fails to acknowledge the perspective of the listener, who is trying to follow the logic and wondering what the ultimate point will be and also whether he or she will have an opportunity to contribute to the conversation. There can be a conspicuous lack of inclusive comments such as 'What do you think of that suggestion?' or 'Have you had a similar experience?'

Another characteristic of children and some adults with Asperger's syndrome is to vocalize their thoughts, commenting on their own actions or giving monologues without needing a listener (Hippler and Klicpera 2004). A characteristic of all young children is to vocalize their thoughts as they play alone or with others. By the time they start school, however, they have learned to keep their thoughts to themselves. Eventually, talking to oneself is considered by some members of the public as a sign of mental disturbance. Children with Asperger's syndrome may continue to vocalize their thoughts many years after one would expect them to internalize them. This often disrupts the attention of other children in the class, and may lead to their being teased when they talk to themselves while alone in the playground. The child may also fail to hear the instruction of the teacher because he or she is too engrossed in a personal 'conversation'.

There may be several reasons for this behaviour. First, the child may be less influenced by peers to be quiet, or less concerned at appearing different. The vocalizations may also have a constructive purpose or be reassuring. For example, an adolescent with Asperger's syndrome described how 'talking to myself helps me figure out and practise how to express ideas well', while another explained that:

> You know I like the sound of my own voice because it keeps me from feeling lonely. I think there is also a little fear that if I don't talk a lot I may lose my voice. I didn't talk until I was almost five, you know. (Dewey 1991, p.204)

Another reason may be that the person is rehearsing possible conversations for the following day, or repeating previous conversations to try to understand them. Sometimes children and adults with Asperger's syndrome, who are prone to being anxious, talk to themselves as a form of self-comfort and reassurance. The person is externalizing the reassuring comments that typical people keep to themselves.

It is important to find out why the person talks to him- or herself. It could simply be developmental delay, or a means of organizing his or her thoughts, improving comprehension and providing comfort. Should this aspect of language become a problem, then encourage the child to whisper rather than speak, and to try to 'think it, don't say it' when near other people. I have noticed that when some adults with Asperger's syndrome are deep in thought, their lips can move as though the person has difficulty disengaging mind and mouth.

There are secondary social consequences of having the unusual profile of language skills associated with Asperger's syndrome. Other children may withdraw from playing or talking with the child due to his or her problems with conversation skills and the child could be prone to being teased and ridiculed for his or her strange accent. Hans Asperger said that the language was 'often like a caricature, which provokes ridicule in the naïve listener' (Asperger [1944] 1991, p.70). Thus, therapy programs to improve language abilities are an essential component of services for children with Asperger's syndrome.

THE ART OF CONVERSATION

When listening to the speech of a child with Asperger's syndrome, you can be impressed with the child's use of complex sentences and extensive vocabulary of technical terms. However, the overall impression of the conversation is that, in contrast to evidence of linguistic ability, there are specific errors in the ability to have a natural conversation.

The person with Asperger's syndrome may not follow the conventional conversational rules regarding how to initiate, maintain and end a conversation. He or she may start the interaction with a comment irrelevant to the situation, or by breaking the social or cultural codes. For example, the young child may approach a stranger in the supermarket and strike up a conversation by saying 'Do you have a cylinder mower?' and then proceed to give a monologue demonstrating an encyclopaedic knowledge of garden machinery. Once the conversation has begun there seems to be no 'off switch', and it only ends when the child's predetermined and practised 'script' is completed. Sometimes the parents can predict exactly what the child is going to say next in a well-practised conversational script.

The child with Asperger's syndrome usually appears unaware of the effect of the monologue on the listener, oblivious to signs of embarrassment, confusion or desire to end the interaction. One has the impression that the child is talking, but not listening, and is unaware of the subtle non-verbal signals that should regulate the flow of conversation. During the conversation there can be a lack of recognition or appreciation of the context, social hierarchy and conventions, and little attempt to incorporate the other person's comments, feelings or knowledge in the conversation.

In contrast to engaging in a conversation 'monologue' there can be times when the person with Asperger's syndrome can be very reluctant to participate in a conversation at all. The person may be notorious for being verbose when interested in the topic, but reluctant to maintain a conversation when the subject matter is of little personal interest or has been introduced by another person (Paul and Sutherland 2003). I have the impression that many people with Asperger's syndrome consider a conversation to be primarily an opportunity to exchange information, to learn or inform, and if there is no practical information to exchange, why waste time talking?

Another example of impaired conversation skills is knowledge on how to repair a conversation. When a conversation becomes confusing, perhaps because the other person is imprecise or the reply is unclear, the natural reaction of most people is to seek clarification in order to maintain the topic of conversation. When in doubt as to what to say, the person with Asperger's syndrome can lack the confidence to admit 'I don't know' or 'I'm confused' and, rather than saying 'I'm not sure what you mean by that,' 'This is not easy to talk about,' or 'I'm lost for words,' can take a considerable length of time to think of his or her reply, or may suddenly change the conversation to a topic he or she is familiar with. The conversation can lack flexibility of themes and thought and there may be problems generating relevant ideas (Bishop and Frazier Norbury 2005). Thus, the conversation can include abrupt changes of topic and tangential responses (Adams *et al.* 2002; Fine *et al.* 1994). An unfortunate characteristic of some conversations with a person with Asperger's syndrome is that the conversation eventually reverts to the person's special interest, or is characterized by 'and now for something completely different.'

When the conversational partner is confused, the person with Asperger's syndrome often lacks the mental flexibility to provide an explanation using other words, or to facilitate understanding by using gestures or metaphor. When a child with Asperger's syndrome is asked a question or is expected to reply to a comment, there can be a tendency to avoid responding or offering new or relevant information (Capps, Kehres and Sigman 1998). This is not necessarily indifference or insolence but another example of a genuine difficulty repairing and maintaining a conversion.

Another unusual feature of conversations is a tendency to make what appear to be irrelevant comments. A statement or question can be made that is not obviously linked to the topic of conversation. These utterances can be word associations, fragments of the dialogue of previous conversations or seemingly quite bizarre utterances. It appears that the child says the first thought that comes to mind, unaware how confusing this can be for the other person. The reason for this feature remains elusive but may be associated with a tendency to be impulsive and less able to formulate a logical structure or sequence for the statement or description, and an inability to consider the perspective of the other person. When this occurs, you are unsure whether to respond to the irrelevant comment or continue the conversation as if it had not occurred. I tend to ignore such comments and focus on the central theme of the conversation.

There can also be a tendency for children and adults with Asperger's syndrome to interrupt or talk over the speech of others. Temple Grandin describes how:

> During the last couple of years, I have become more aware of a kind of electricity that goes on between people. I have observed that when several people are together and having a good time, their speech and laughter follow a rhythm. They will all laugh together and then talk quietly until the next laughing cycle. I have always had a hard time fitting in with this rhythm, and I usually interrupt conversations without realizing my mistake. The problem is that I can't follow the rhythm. (Grandin 1995, pp.91–2)

Such interruptions can be infuriating and imply that the person with Asperger's syndrome is being very rude. The conversational partner needs to recognize that this is a characteristic of Asperger's syndrome and not due to a lack of respect.

During a typical conversation there is the expectation that the person listening will show clear signs of paying attention to the speaker, and communicate signs of listening by nodding the head and making sympathetic facial expressions, or vocalizations such as 'uh huh' or 'yes'. These behaviours confirm a sense of rapport and being 'in tune' with the speaker. There should also be a synchrony of gestures and movements, especially when there is a positive relationship between the two people. These signals can be less apparent when one of the conversational partners has Asperger's syndrome. Although signs of disagreement may be clear, signs of agreement, attentive listening and sympathy may not be as conspicuous as one would expect. The person with Asperger's syndrome is often perceived as a poor listener. This may not be too much of a problem for a casual acquaintance, but is of concern to a partner, close relative, friend or colleague.

Sometimes the person with Asperger's syndrome can be criticized for being tactless or socially naïve during a conversation, perhaps saying something that is true but would hurt someone's feelings, or is inappropriate for the context. From early childhood, typical children modify the topic of conversation according to whom they are talking to. Such modifications are based on an understanding of social hierarchies and conventions and the need to inhibit certain comments when taking into account the other person's thoughts and feelings. Due to impaired or delayed Theory of Mind abilities (see Chapter 5) the conversation can be a social 'minefield', with a tendency for the conversational partner to be offended by the comments, criticisms and value judgements of the person with Asperger's syndrome. However, being offensive is not usually the intention of the person with Asperger's syndrome, who tends to speak his or her mind and unfortunately has a greater allegiance to facts and the truth than to someone's feelings.

Sometimes the problem is not what was said by the person with Asperger syndrome, but the way he or she said it. This can give the impression that the person is overly critical, grudging with compliments, abrasive, argumentative and impolite. Other people will know when to think rather than say something and how to avoid or subtly modify comments that could be perceived as offensive. Once again, it is important to recognize that there may be no malicious intent.

Impaired or delayed Theory of Mind skills can also explain another characteristic of impaired pragmatic aspects of language. That is, the person with Asperger's syndrome can be unsure what the other person knows, or wants to know. When the mother of a typical child asks 'What did you do today at school?' the child has some idea of what his or her mother would like to know. The child with Asperger's syndrome, however, can be dumbfounded in that the question is not precise. Does she want to know who I talked to, what I learned, where I went, who I played with, whether I was happy, whether someone teased me, or what the teacher said and did? The response can be to avoid answering altogether, or to embark on a detailed description of the day in the hope that something that is said will provide the right answer.

When asked to describe an event (that is, provide a 'narrative discourse'), the child with Asperger's syndrome may have significant difficulty providing an organized and coherent framework for the story (Abele and Grenier 2005). At about six years of age, a typical child can organize a story into a narrative structure that is easily understood by the listener. There is a clear framework and logical sequence with an emphasis on key events, thoughts and consequences (Landa 2000). When asked what he or she did over the weekend, the typical child will analyse all the available information in order to determine which aspects are relevant and would be interesting to the listener, and will give consideration both to the time needed to impart these facts and the amount of time available to tell the story. The child (and some adults) with Asperger's syndrome can have significant developmental delay in the narrative discourse aspects of a conversation. There may be no clear beginning to the story, too much or too little information provided for the listener, an absence of key information, and a tendency to be side-tracked with irrelevant information. There can also be a difficulty summarizing and getting to the point, which can be boring or irritating to the listener who expects a shorter and more coherent story. The facts may be there, but logical structure and the thoughts and feelings of the participants are often missing. The errors in the pragmatic aspects of language can cause other people to assume that the person with Asperger's syndrome is being deliberately obtuse and uncooperative, and thus there may be a reluctance to engage in subsequent conversations.

STRATEGIES TO IMPROVE CONVERSATIONAL SKILLS

The person with Asperger's syndrome will need guidance in the art of conversation. This should include explanations of the social context and conventions using Social Stories™ (Gray 1998), the opportunity to learn and practise conversations, and activities to improve the maturity of Theory of Mind abilities.

The strategies to improve social understanding described in Chapter 3 will be relevant to improving the person's pragmatic language skills. Social Stories™ can be used to aid understanding of the social context and conventions, expectations, thoughts and feelings of each participant in a conversation. They can also provide guidance as to when to use conversational repair mechanisms. The first Social Stories™ need to be written to record the child's existing conversational abilities. Subsequent Social Stories™ should have a balance between stories to record ability and stories to learn new information. Social Stories™ or Social Articles can also be written for adolescents and adults; for example, a Social Workbook has been developed by Carol Gray as a guide to making and understanding compliments for young adults with Asperger's syndrome (Gray 1999).

While Social Stories™ can improve social cognition or knowledge, it is also important to practise new skills in a controlled and supportive environment. Speech pathologists, teachers and psychologists can organize social skills programs that include activities to improve conversational skills (Abele and Grenier 2005; Chin and Bernard-Opitz 2000).

The first stage in organizing the program is to identify the pragmatic abilities and errors of the child or adult with Asperger's syndrome. There can be different errors according to the context; for example, the child may be able to engage in a reasonable conversation with an adult but make conspicuous errors in the pragmatic aspects of language when playing with peers, and may not know when to be formal or informal. A teenager with Asperger's syndrome may not know the colloquial vocabulary and topics of interest of adolescent peers. An adult may be able to engage in a conversation about practical matters but have considerable difficulty with social chit chat or the language of courtship.

The next stage is to improve cognition or knowledge using Social Stories™ or Social Articles. This can be followed by individual or group education and discussion to identify those social cues or signals that indicate there needs to be some modification to the conversation. Participants practise new responses and abilities with guidance and encouragement and finally apply the new conversational skills in real situations. For children with Asperger's syndrome, the new skills can be learned and practised using games and role-play activities (Schroeder 2003). An appeal can be made to the child's genuine concern for others and motivation to be a good friend by explaining that sometimes talking about what somebody else wants to talk about is an act of kindness and friendliness. It is also important to teach exit or conversation closure strategies to prevent the person continuing the 'conversation' indefinitely.

To avoid the child with Asperger's syndrome feeling incompetent and thereby reluctant to participate, the adult can act as the person who makes pragmatic or conversation errors, asking the child to identify what he or she did that was not a good conversation technique. The child will then be asked to recommend what the adult could do to improve his or her conversation skills. The child can then model the ability in response to the request, 'Well, you show me what I should have said.' If the child is unsure what to say or do during a practice conversation, an adult can whisper instructions into his or her ear.

The child with Asperger's syndrome will need to know the cues that indicate a change of 'script'. For example, if during a conversation about a recent shopping expedition we learn that someone has had an unfortunate experience such as losing money, we tend to modify the script and offer sympathetic comments. The conversations of people with Asperger's syndrome have fewer examples of spontaneous sympathetic comments. However, when an adult models an appropriate statement, children with Asperger's syndrome can use this as a cue to provide their own sympathetic comments (Loveland and Tunali 1991). So, although the significance of some cues may not be recognized, the child can be encouraged to make an appropriate response if a parent or teacher models this first.

The child or adult with Asperger's syndrome may need to learn 'rescue' questions and comments that can be used to repair a conversation or to seek clarification. Examples of rescue or repair questions can be 'I'm confused, can you please explain what you mean?', 'Are we understanding each other?' or comments such as 'I am interested in your thoughts.'

Other features of the art of conversation are to seek or comment on the opinions, abilities and experience of the other person, to offer sympathy, agreement and compliments, to know how to make the topic interesting, and to know how and when to listen to and look at the other person. These are remarkably complex and advanced skills that may be elusive for the child or teenager with Asperger's syndrome. An activity for young children, designed to encourage such skills, is to sit the child with Asperger's syndrome next to a tutor (a teacher, therapist or parent) and facilitate a conversation with another child or adult. The idea is that the conversation tutor whispers in the ear of the child what to say or do and when to say it. The tutor identifies the relevant cues and suggests or prompts appropriate replies, gradually encouraging the child to initiate his or her own dialogue. An example is (whispering) 'Ask Jessica what is her favourite television programme,' or 'Say, "I like that programme, too,"' so that the conversation is not restricted to a series of questions.

A classroom activity to encourage conversation is to arrange for the children to work in pairs. Each participant practises how to start and maintain a conversation with a friend. The class will have previously identified a range of conversational openers such as 'How are you today?' or 'What do you think of the weather?', or a topical item in the news. Each child has also to identify and remember information about his or her conversational partner and think of relevant questions, comments or topics of conversation, for example 'Is your grandmother feeling better?', 'I really like your new glasses' or 'That new *Simpsons* programme last night was really funny.' Another activity is to try to discover through conversation interests they have in common, and shared opinions that could form the basis of a friendship.

The program to improve conversation ability includes instruction and activities to enhance:

- listening skills

- the ability to give and receive compliments and criticism

- awareness of when and how to interrupt

- the ability to make connecting comments to introduce a change of topic

- the ability to use repair comments

- knowledge of how to ask questions when confused as to what to say or do.

There may also need to be guidance and practice on the choice of topic, when to relinquish control of the conversation, and closure. The program can use video recordings of the activities to identify conversational errors and successes, and sections of television programmes and films that illustrate a breakdown in conversation skills. Activities can be undertaken to practise the ability to tell a story, to mentally highlight important information and to create a clear and coherent structure. For young children this can be telling the story using a picture book with no words, and for older children there can be practice in the preparation of the story before an anticipated conversation occurs. For example, a parent may say to the child, 'Grandma is probably going to ask you how your birthday party went. Let's practise what you are going to say.' Throughout the program, the emphasis is on discovering new skills and not feeling incompetent, and any improvement in abilities is recognized and applauded.

Teenagers with Asperger's syndrome may be reluctant to participate in a conversation group, but guidance in conversation skills may be accepted when integrated into a drama class at high school. Attending a drama class is more likely to be acceptable to peers and to the self-image of the adolescent with Asperger's syndrome. The director, rather than therapist, provides a potential script, and coaching in body language, tone of voice and emotions. There is also guidance and practice in identifying what to say and how to say it when acting everyday situations. Eventually the script and new skills can be applied in reality rather than on stage. The person with Asperger's syndrome can be encouraged to observe peers who have good conversational skills, and to absorb and imitate those abilities. Sometimes the acting can be so convincing, the conversational partner has no idea how the conversation skills were acquired and who was the role model.

Comic Strip Conversations, also originally developed by Carol Gray (1998), can be used to explain what someone may be thinking and feeling in a conversation. Stick figures can be drawn to represent conversational partners, and speech, thought and emotion bubbles used to identify someone's inner thoughts. Speech bubbles can be drawn in a variety of ways to convey emotion – for example, sharp edges to indicate anger or wavy lines to indicate anxiety. Colours can also be used. Happy or positive statements could be written in a particular colour (chosen by the child) while unpleasant thoughts could be written using another colour. A whole colour chart can be developed, for example embarrassed comments written with a pink marker, or sad feelings written in blue. These can then be translated into relevant aspects of the person's tone of voice or body language.

When the person with Asperger's syndrome is notorious for interrupting, a Social Story™ can explain the effects of interrupting on the thoughts and mood of someone; but a picture is worth a thousand words, and Comic Strip Conversations can provide a pictorial representation, as shown in the Comic Strip Conversation for interrupting illustrated in Figure 8.1.

Guidance and role-playing activities can be used to identify the cues for when to start talking, such as the natural closure of a topic or conversational 'paragraph', or when someone gives eye contact that communicates 'your turn to speak'. The person with Asperger's syndrome will also deserve some commendation when he or she speaks in response to the appropriate 'green-light' signals.

Comic Strip Conversations are extremely valuable as a means of exploring and explaining the range of messages and meanings that are a natural part of conversation or play. Many children with Asperger's syndrome are confused and upset by teasing or sarcasm. The speech and thought bubbles, as well as choice of colours, can illustrate the hidden messages and enable the child to understand how other children perceive his or her speech and conversation abilities.

Interrupt: when my words bump into words from other people

Figure 8.1 **Comic Strip Conversation for interrupting**

A young child with Asperger's syndrome often assumes that other people are thinking exactly what he or she is thinking; or the child assumes that other people's words match their thoughts. The Comic Strip Conversations can then be used to show that each person may have very different thoughts and feelings in the same situation, and that what people say may not always correspond with what they are thinking. Another advantage of this technique is that it can be used to represent the sequence of events in a conversation and illustrate the potential effects of a range of alternative comments or actions.

A number of activities to teach Theory of Mind skills, as described in Chapter 5, are also designed to improve conversation abilities. The interactive DVD *Mind Reading: The Interactive Guide to Emotions* (2004) is valuable in helping to identify the changes in facial expression and tone of voice that can be used to modify conversation. The DVD can be used by both children and adults with Asperger's syndrome, as the emotions are graded according to difficulty (see the Resources section towards the end of the book). Adults with Asperger's syndrome can also read self-help books that provide guidance in the art of conversation (Gabor 2001).

The last stage of the program is to apply the new skills in real situations. It may be necessary to inform peers and family members of the new conversation abilities to ensure that they are used successfully, in order to encourage motivation and self-esteem. It is extremely important that the person with Asperger's syndrome is commended for successful conversations, that what he or she said that was appreciated is identified, and that there is progress with improving conversational skills. With increased maturity, new conversation skills are expected, and may have to be explained and practised. Tuition in the art of conversation can be a life-long program.

LITERAL INTERPRETATION

The person with Asperger's syndrome tends to make a literal interpretation of what the other person says, being greatly confused by idioms, irony, figures of speech, innuendo and sarcasm. An example of a relatively simple literal interpretation of what someone says was when a young man was asked by his father to make a pot of tea. Some time later his father was concerned that he had not received his refreshment and asked his son, 'Where's the tea?' His son replied, 'In the pot, of course.' His son was unaware that the original request implied not just the preparation of the tea, but the presentation of a cup of tea for each person. The person with Asperger's syndrome is not being deliberately lazy, obtuse or defiant, but responding to the literal, not the implied, meaning.

During a diagnostic assessment, I asked a young girl with Asperger's syndrome 'Can you count to ten?' to which she replied 'Yes', and she silently continued with her play. There can also be a literal interpretation of pictures. A child with Asperger's syndrome was watching a 'Road Runner' cartoon, where the coyote fell from a cliff and suddenly produced an umbrella to substitute for a parachute. The confused child commented, 'Why would he do that if it wasn't raining?'

The person is not being deliberately annoying, or stupid. Rather, he or she is less aware of the hidden, implied or multiple meanings. This characteristic also affects the understanding of common English phrases, idioms or metaphors such as:

- Has the cat got your tongue?
- You're pulling my leg.
- A flat battery.
- I caught his eye.
- Looks can kill.
- Your voice is breaking.
- Keep your eye on the ball.
- Pull yourself together.
- I've changed my mind.

I have observed that each of these comments has caused some confusion for children with Asperger's syndrome, and you have to explain precisely the meaning of many figures of speech. Fortunately, the problem of making a literal interpretation has been recognized by parents and psychologists, and two books, one for children and the other for adults, provide an illustrated guide to understanding metaphors and everyday expressions (Stuart-Hamilton 2004; Welton and Telford 2004).

Social Stories™ can also be applied to help understand figures of speech, such as idioms. Carol Gray used the following example of a Social Story™ to explain one of the above phrases:

> Sometimes a person says, 'I've changed my mind.'
>
> This means they had one idea, but now they have a new idea.
>
> I will try to stay calm when someone changes their mind.
>
> When someone says, 'I've changed my mind', I can think of someone writing something down, rubbing it out and writing something new. (Quoted in Attwood 1998, p.77)

Children can nominate a phrase they have found confusing such as 'chill out' or 'catch you later', and guess the meaning of the statement. A story can be composed to explain its meaning and describe those situations when the phrase may be used.

People with Asperger's syndrome are often very confused by teasing, irony and sarcasm. Research has confirmed that the understanding of idioms is less advanced than one would expect considering the child's intellectual and linguistic abilities (Kerbel and Grunwell 1998). Other children, and sometimes teachers, can have great fun exploiting this naïvety. Ironic remarks are more likely to cause the person with Asperger's syndrome to assume the person is lying (Martin and McDonald 2004). The hidden meaning is elusive. The person with Asperger's syndrome may also not have the flexibility of thought to understand an alternative meaning, and relies on logic rather than symbolism, and the assumption that the other person is saying exactly what he or she means. Figures of speech are perceived as illogical and yet another example of how typical people fail to make their intentions clear.

Making a literal interpretation can also lead to the assumption of behaviour or conduct problems. For example Donna Williams, in her autobiography, refers to how:

> The significance of what people said to me, when it sank in as more than just words, was always taken to apply only to that particular moment or situation. Thus, when I once received a serious lecture about writing graffiti on Parliament House during an excursion, I agreed that I'd never do this again and then, ten minutes later, was caught outside writing different graffiti on the school wall. To me, I was not ignoring what they said, nor was I trying to be funny: I had not done *exactly* the same thing as I had done before. (Williams 1998, p.64)

Parents, teachers and family members need to be aware of the child's propensity to make a literal interpretation, and to stop and think how the comment or instruction could be misinterpreted or cause confusion. Whenever a literal interpretation occurs, it is important always to explain the hidden intention or full meaning. This occurred with my sister-in-law when she was a teenager. She answered the telephone and was asked by the caller, 'Is Sarah there?' Sarah is her sister. As Sarah was not in the room, she replied 'No' and promptly hung up the receiver. In this instance the caller was me, and I was aware of her tendency to be literal. I phoned again and explained that if Sarah was not there, I would like her to find Sarah and ask her to come to the telephone so that I could talk to her.

PROSODY

When listening to the speech of a person with Asperger's syndrome, you can become aware of unusual aspects of pitch, stress and rhythm, i.e. the prosody or melody of speech (Fine *et al.* 1991; Paul *et al.* 2005; Shriberg *et al.* 2001). There can be a lack of vocal modulation such that speech has a monotonous or flat quality, an unusual stress pattern, or over-precise diction with stress on almost every syllable.

There are three levels of prosodic function: grammatical, pragmatic and affective. The *grammatical* function is to communicate aspects such as whether the utterance was a question (with a rising pitch), or a statement (with a falling pitch), or whether the word used is intended as a noun or a verb. This aspect of prosody appears to be the least affected in children and adults with Asperger's syndrome. The *pragmatic* function is to provide social information for the listener, using emphatic or contrastive stress to communicate thoughts, opinions and intentions, or to draw the listener's attention to information that is new to the conversation. This is the vocal equivalent of using a highlighter pen when reading.

Affective prosody functions as a means of communicating feelings and attitudes. For example, the simple request 'Come here' could be said with a tone of voice that would indicate the person has found something interesting and is happy; is anxious and needs reassurance; or is perhaps angry and about to administer an expected consequence (Pyles 2002). Research has confirmed the impressions of parents and clinicians, that the prosody of children and adults with Asperger's syndrome can be unusual, especially with regard to pragmatic and affective prosody (Shriberg *et al.* 2001). The person's speech may not convey the amount of social and emotional information that one would expect.

The prosody for some children and adults with Asperger's syndrome can also be perceived as dysfluent in terms of the frequency of word repetitions, fewer pauses than would occur with a typical speaker of that age, and distortion or unusual pronunciation of a word. There can also be problems with the volume, which is often overly loud, and there is sometimes a nasal and/or high-pitched quality that was first described by Hans Asperger and confirmed by subsequent studies of prosody (Shriberg *et al.* 2001).

The child or adult with Asperger's syndrome may also have difficulty understanding the relevance of the change in tone, inflection or emphasis on certain words when listening to the speech of the other person (Koning and Magill-Evans 2001). These subtle cues are extremely important in identifying the different intentions, thoughts and emotions. The following example is taken from Andrew Matthews' book *Making Friends*, and illustrates how the meaning changes when the emphasis is put on a different word (Matthews 1990, p.129).

I didn't say she stole my money.

I didn't say she stole my money [but *someone* said it].

I *DIDN'T* say she stole my money [I *definitely* didn't say it].

I didn't *say* she stole my money [but I *implied* it].

I didn't say *she* stole my money [but *someone* stole it].

I didn't say she *stole* my money [but she did *something* with it].

I didn't say she stole *my* money [she stole *someone else's*].

I didn't say she stole my *money* [she stole *something else*].

There are seven different meanings achieved simply by changing the emphasis of each word in the sentence.

The person with Asperger's syndrome who has problems with prosody, in terms of both production and perception, will require guidance in understanding the messages conveyed by prosody. Role-plays, listening to audio recordings, and drama activities can be used to explain how and why the emphasis changes. Stress on a particular word can be conceptualized as similar to using a highlighter pen, with consideration as to which words need to be highlighted to convey thoughts, feelings and information that are important to the listener. A game of 'Spot the hidden message' can be used to identify the speaker's thoughts and feelings when listening to an audio recording. The DVD *Mind Reading: The Interactive Guide to Emotions* includes audio recordings of dialogue that convey particular emotions (see Resources section towards the end of the book). These can be used to identify feelings and as a model to practise expressing a particular emotion. Some of the emotion communication activities described in Chapter 6 can be used to improve the understanding and use of the prosodic aspects of language.

It is also important that children with Asperger's syndrome understand how their volume, speed of speech, intonation and so on affect the listener's ability to understand what they are saying. An audio recording can provide valuable insight, and strategies can be used to encourage comprehension of their speech, such as 'Your train of thought is going too fast for me to jump on board.'

PEDANTIC SPEECH

The speech of children and adults with Asperger's syndrome can be perceived as being pedantic, overly formal and pretentious (Ghaziuddin and Gerstein 1996; Ghaziuddin *et al.* 2000; Kerbeshian *et al.* 1990). The characteristics include providing too much information, an emphasis on rules and minor details, a tendency to correct errors in the previous utterance of the other person, the use of overly formal sentence structures, and making a rigid interpretation of what someone says that could be perceived as being argumentative rather than corrective. The person with Asperger's syndrome is often characterized as being a pedant, a comment which is not intended as a compliment.

An example is a teenager, when helping his father in his job as an after-hours office cleaner, was asked to empty all the bins. A while later, the father was annoyed that several bins had obviously not been emptied. When he asked his son why, he replied, 'Those aren't bins, they're wicker baskets.' The characteristic of being pedantic could be perceived as offensive, as in the example of my conversation with a young man in the United States who was fascinated by the potential maximum speed of different makes of vehicles and the speed limits in various countries. I live in Australia and the conversation progressed quite amiably until I mentioned the value of low speed in conserving petrol. The young man suddenly became agitated, protesting vehemently that the word is 'gasoline', not 'petrol'.

The choice of words for children with Asperger's syndrome can be overly formal, as in the example of a five-year-old girl who, when collected from school by her older sister, asked, 'Is my mother home?' The older sister's reply was 'No, Mum's not home yet.' Clearly, the family used the word 'Mum', but the girl with Asperger's syndrome used an unusually formal way of referring to her mother. People may be addressed by their full name and title; instead of saying 'Hello, Mary', the child may say 'Hello, Mrs Mary Smith.'

Sometimes the child's choice of words and phrases would be more appropriate for an adult than a child. The child's language style has been absorbed and imitated from listening to and preferring to interact with adults rather than peers. Adults, rather than other children, may be the more important influence in the developing speech patterns of school-age children with Asperger's syndrome. For example, the child's accent may not be consistent with local children, perhaps maintaining his or her mother's accent (Baron-Cohen and Staunton 1994). We usually expect a typical school-age child's accent to change to that of his or her peer group at school, which is noticeable when the family has moved to an area with a different accent. The child with Asperger's syndrome is less likely to change his or her accent to that of other local children. Once the child with Asperger's syndrome has heard a particular word or phrase, the original enunciation will be continued such that the experienced listener may be able to identify whose accent is being echoed.

Another characteristic of being pedantic is that during a conversation with someone with Asperger's syndrome, the conversational partner soon recognizes that abstractions and a lack of precision are rarely tolerated. Family members have learned to avoid comments or replies using words such as 'maybe', 'perhaps', 'sometimes' or 'later'. For example, Therese Jolliffe explains how:

> Life is such a struggle; indecision over things that other people refer to as trivial results in an awful lot of inner distress. For instance, if somebody at home says, 'We may go shopping tomorrow', or if somebody says, 'We will see what happens', they do not seem to realise that the uncertainty causes a lot of inner distress, and that I constantly labour, in a cognitive sense, over what may or may not occur. The indecision over events extends to indecision over other things, such as where objects are to be put or found and over what people are expecting from me. (Jolliffe *et al.* 1992, p.16)

When anxious, the person with Asperger's syndrome can become increasingly pedantic. Sometimes a child with Asperger's syndrome will incessantly bombard a parent with questions seeking reassurance about when an event will occur. To avoid ambiguity and reduce anxiety, the parent may become as pedantic as the child.

AUDITORY PERCEPTION AND DISTORTION

Several autobiographies of people with Asperger's syndrome have included reference to problems with focusing on one person's voice when several people are talking, or distorted perceptions of other people's speech. For example, from my clinical experience, I remember a child with Asperger's syndrome who was in an open-plan classroom that comprised two classes. The teacher of his class was reading out a maths test while the teacher in the other class was reading out a spelling test. When his teacher marked his test paper, she noted he had written the answers to both tests.

Candy described how 'many voices make speech difficult to understand', and the child can be very confused when too many people are talking at the same time, especially if they are all talking about the same topic, as occurs in the background chatter in a classroom. We now have research evidence to confirm significant problems for children and adults with Asperger's syndrome in their ability to understand what someone says when there is background speech or noise (Alcantara *et al.* 2004) and perceive, discriminate and process auditory information (Jansson Verkasalo *et al.* 2005).

Most people use moments when the background noise briefly subsides to work out the gist of the conversation, i.e. to 'fill in the gaps' in order to understand what someone is saying. People with Asperger's syndrome are not very good at this ability. This is invaluable information for parents and especially teachers. To help auditory perception and understanding, it is important to minimize background noise and chatter. The child should be positioned as close to the teacher as possible, so that he or she can hear the teacher more clearly, and may have the confidence to say whether or not an instruction was audible. The problem is one of auditory perception, not necessarily inattention.

The distortion of someone's speech is explained by Darren White:

> I was sometimes able to hear a word or two at the start and understand it and then the next lot of words sort of merged into one another and I could not make head or tail of it. (White and White 1987, p.224)

I was often lazy at school because sometimes my ears distorted the teacher's instructions or my eyes blurred to stop me seeing the blackboard properly and the teachers would say 'On with your work, Darren.' (White and White 1987, p.225)

Donna Williams describes how:

Anything I took in had to be deciphered as though it had to pass through some sort of complicated checkpoint procedure. Sometimes people would have to repeat a particular sentence several times for me as I would hear it in bits and the way in which my mind had segmented their sentence into words left me with a strange and sometimes unintelligible message. It was a bit like when someone plays around with the volume switch on the TV. (Williams 1998, p.64)

Temple Grandin also refers to how:

Even now, I still have problems with tuning out. I will be listening to my favourite song on the radio and then notice that I missed half of it. My hearing shuts off unexpectedly. In college I had to constantly keep taking notes to prevent myself from tuning out. (Grandin 1990, p.61)

Should such problems become apparent, perhaps appearing as 'selective deafness', then it is important for a speech pathologist or audiologist to assess the child's skills with the cortical processing of auditory information. This is not strictly a hearing problem but a problem with how the brain processes someone's speech.

The child should be encouraged to ask the person to repeat what he or she said, simplify the comment or instruction or put it into other words. Unfortunately, children with Asperger's syndrome can be reluctant to seek help because of a fear of being considered stupid or annoying the adult. A strategy to be sure the child perceived and understood the instruction is to ask the child to repeat aloud what you said, or ask 'Can you tell me what you've got to do?'

It may also help to pause between each sentence to allow the person time to process what you have said, and to use written instructions. The advantages of these techniques are explained by Therese Jolliffe in the following quotation:

But when somebody talks to me I have to really try and listen carefully, if I am going to stand any chance of working out what the words are. At school and during my first degree I was helped by the fact that I could read up topics in advance, things were also written down on the blackboard, the work tended to follow a logical progression and because new material was being put across to students, teachers could not talk too fast, rather they seemed to leave gaps of a second or two between each sentence which enabled me to guess more accurately what I had heard. When I read books the problem of deciphering what the words actually are does not exist because I can see immediately what they are meant to be. (Jolliffe et al. 1992, p.14)

Thus, the person with Asperger's syndrome is more likely to understand if he or she has to focus on only one voice, there is a brief silence between each instruction and the instructions can also be read. An example of the value of reading rather than listening to understand what to do is a young adult with Asperger's syndrome who was successful in his job, as his line manager would provide a written summary of what to do, as well as spoken instructions. When a new line manager was appointed, he refused to spend time writing his instructions for the employee with Asperger's syndrome. This young man then had considerable difficulty following the complex spoken instructions on the factory floor, and became extremely anxious that he did not know exactly what to do, and, indeed, his work performance deteriorated. Eventually the new line manager acknowledged the wisdom of writing instructions for this particular employee.

Some children with Asperger's syndrome develop precocious reading abilities (see Chapter 9) in terms of their ability to decode print, but their level of understanding is limited by their level of language development. The child may be able to read aloud complex words that would be very difficult for other children of that age to say correctly. However, an assessment of the child's reading ability usually indicates relatively advanced reading accuracy but reading comprehension consistent with his or her language abilities. Thus, the printed or written instructions for a child with Asperger's syndrome will need to be consistent with the child's level of language comprehension rather than based on his or her ability to say or read complex words.

VERBAL FLUENCY

One of the language characteristics of the child with Asperger's syndrome is that he or she may talk too much or too little. Sometimes the child's genuine enthusiasm for the special interest leads to garrulous speech and questions, a never-ending 'babbling brook' (another example of a potentially confusing figure of speech) which can be quite endearing – if occasionally tedious. The child is keen to develop and demonstrate his or her knowledge with a remarkable verbal fluency, but may have to learn the cues that indicate when to be quiet.

In contrast, some children with Asperger's syndrome may have periods when they are genuinely 'lost for words' or even mute. Clinical experience has identified children with Asperger's syndrome who will talk only to their parents and are electively mute with other adults or in the classroom (Gillberg and Billstedt 2000; Kopp and Gillberg 1997). Verbal fluency is affected by anxiety, as explained by Therese Jolliffe:

> One of the most frustrating things about autism is that it is very difficult to explain how you are feeling; whether something hurts or frightens you or when you are feeling unwell and you cannot stick up for yourself. I take Beta Blockers sometimes to reduce the physical symptoms of fear and although I can now tell people if something frightens me, I can never actually tell them while the event is occurring. Similarly, on several occasions when I have been asked what my name is by a stranger I cannot always remember it and yet when I am more relaxed I can remember phone numbers and formulae after just hearing them once. When I am

very frightened by somebody or something, or I am in pain, I can often make motor movements and a noise, but the words just do not come out. (Jolliffe *et al.* 1992, p.14)

Thus, being lost for words or even mute may be due to a high level of anxiety. Certainly some adults with Asperger's syndrome are prone to stuttering when anxious. Here the problem is not strictly impairment in language skills, but the effect of emotion on the ability to speak. Should this problem become apparent, there is a range of strategies to help the person with Asperger's syndrome cope with anxiety (described in Chapter 6).

ASPERGERESE

Over many years, I have been able to achieve a greater understanding of the cognitive, social and linguistic abilities of people with Asperger's syndrome, and have engaged in countless conversations with such individuals. I have developed a conversation style I describe as 'Aspergerese', which involves a careful consideration of what to say and how to say it. When engaged in a conversation with someone with Asperger's syndrome, communication may be enhanced by the typical person avoiding figures of speech, due to the tendency of those with Asperger's syndrome to make a literal interpretation of what other people say. If the conversation concerns social conventions, or thoughts and feelings, then I introduce a momentary pause between each statement to enable the person with Asperger's syndrome to process the information using intellectual rather than intuitive abilities. Temple Grandin has explained to me that people tend to talk too fast for her to process all the channels of communication that include the spoken words, prosody, body language and facial expressions.

When speaking 'Aspergerese', the typical person also needs to make his or her intentions clear, avoiding ambiguity or unnecessary subtlety. It is important to allow the person with Asperger's syndrome some time to collect his or her thoughts before anticipating a response to a question, and not to feel uncomfortable with momentary silences and a lack of eye contact. Intentions to express gestures of affection need to be explained before making the action, so that a touch on someone's arm as an indication of compassion, or a kiss as a response to receiving a present, do not come as unexpected and unpleasant surprises.

Facial expressions need to be clear and consistent with the topic of conversation; teasing and sarcasm are often best avoided. The person with Asperger's syndrome may need greater reassurance that you understand what he or she is saying and you may need to be aware that the person may be unsure how to respond to praise and compliments. If possible, ensure background noise and chatter is minimized, perhaps moving to a quieter area. Increased stress levels, especially when trying to engage in a conversation in a crowded area, can affect the language comprehension and verbal fluency of the person with Asperger's syndrome. It is also important not to be offended by the direct honesty of the person with Asperger's syndrome, and to be aware that the person is not naturally talented in the art of conversation.

FOREIGN LANGUAGES

The previous chapter provided an explanation of the tendency of many people with Asperger's syndrome to develop a special interest. Sometimes the person with Asperger's syndrome can have a natural talent and special interest in foreign languages. The person can acquire the ability to speak many languages without the pronunciation errors expected when a typical person from a specific home country learns that language. For example, when an Englishman learns French, a native of France can easily detect that the speaker's first language is English. When a person with Asperger's syndrome learns a foreign language, there can be a remarkable ability to pronounce the words as spoken by a native speaker. This can lead to a successful career in languages, such as a translator or interpreter. However, the one universal language that is invariably difficult for people with Asperger's syndrome to learn is the social language. As Geoff said to me, 'When there is a social conversation, it's like a different language.' If we consider social language to be rather like a foreign language to people with Asperger's syndrome, then we may find that if we teach and encourage social language at an early age, children with Asperger's syndrome may eventually speak this 'second language' like a native.

KEY POINTS AND STRATEGIES

- Unusual language abilities are an essential characteristic of Asperger's syndrome.

- The standardized tests to measure receptive and expressive language may not be sensitive to the specific language characteristics of children and adults with Asperger's syndrome.

- The child's tendency to use complex sentences does not automatically mean that he or she can fully understand your complex instructions.

- The child may demonstrate linguistic ability in a formal testing situation with a speech pathologist but have considerable difficulties with the speed of language processing needed in real-life situations.

- Some young children who subsequently have a diagnosis of Asperger's syndrome can be delayed in the development of speech but the first spoken words can be an utterance comprising several words or sentences.

- The person with Asperger's syndrome may not follow the conventional conversational rules regarding how to initiate, maintain and end a conversation.

- Social Stories™ can be used to understand the social context and conventions, expectations, thoughts and feelings of each participant in a conversation.

- New conversation skills can be learned and practised using interactive games and role-play activities.
- An adult can act the person who makes pragmatic or conversation errors, asking the child to identify what he or she did that was not a good conversation technique.
- The child or adult with Asperger's syndrome may need to learn 'rescue' questions and comments that can be used to repair a conversation or to seek clarification.
- An activity for young children is to sit the child next to an adult who facilitates a conversation with another child (or adult) and the conversation tutor whispers in the ear of the child what to say or do and when to say it.
- A program to improve conversation abilities needs to include instruction and activities to enhance:
  ○ listening skills
  ○ the ability to give and receive compliments and criticism
  ○ awareness of when and how to interrupt
  ○ the ability to make connecting comments to introduce a change of topic
  ○ the ability to use repair comments
  ○ knowledge of how to ask questions when confused as to what to say or do.
- The program can use video recordings of the activities to identify conversational errors and successes.
- Teenagers with Asperger's syndrome may be reluctant to participate in a conversation group but guidance in conversation skills may be accepted when integrated in a drama class at high school.
- Comic Strip Conversations can be used to explain what someone may be thinking and feeling in a conversation.
- It is extremely important that the person with Asperger's syndrome is commended for successful conversations, and that what he or she said (or did not say) that was appreciated is identified.
- The person with Asperger's syndrome tends to make a literal interpretation of what the other person says, being greatly confused by idioms, irony, figures of speech, innuendo and especially sarcasm.
- Figures of speech are perceived by people with Asperger's syndrome as illogical and yet another example of how typical people fail to make their intentions clear.

- The child or adult with Asperger's syndrome may have difficulty understanding the relevance and information conveyed by the change in tone, inflection or emphasis on certain words when listening to the speech of the other person.

- Role-plays, listening to audio recordings, and drama activities can be used to explain how and why the tone, inflection and emphasis change to convey hidden messages.

- Abstractions and a lack of precision are rarely tolerated by the person with Asperger's syndrome. Family members have learned to avoid comments or replies using words such as 'maybe', 'perhaps', 'sometimes' or 'later'.

- Several autobiographies of people with Asperger's syndrome have included reference to problems with focusing on one person's voice when several people are talking, or distorted perceptions of other people's speech.

- To help auditory perception and understanding, it is important to minimize background noise and chatter.

- Printed or written instructions for a child with Asperger's syndrome will need to be consistent with the child's level of language comprehension rather than based on his or her ability to say or read complex words.

- I have developed a conversation style I describe as 'Aspergerese' which involves a careful consideration of what to say and how to say it when engaged in a conversation with a person with Asperger's syndrome.

- When speaking 'Aspergerese', the typical person needs to make his or her intentions clear, avoiding ambiguity or unnecessary subtlety. It is also important to allow the person with Asperger's syndrome some time to consider his or her thoughts before anticipating a response to a question, and not to feel uncomfortable with momentary silences and a lack of eye contact.

- Do not be offended by the direct honesty of the person with Asperger's syndrome, and be aware that the person is not naturally talented in the art of conversation.

- If social language is considered to be rather like a foreign language to those with Asperger's syndrome, then by being taught from an early age, children with Asperger's syndrome may eventually learn to speak this 'second language' like a native.

CHAPTER 9

Cognitive Abilities

Where it is about logical thinking, where the issue is meeting their special interests, they are ahead, surprise their teachers with their clever answers; where it is about more or less mechanical learning by heart, where concentrated learning is demanded (copying, spelling, methods of arithmetic) these 'clever' children fail in a severe kind of way, so that they often are on the brink of failing their exams.

– Hans Asperger (1938)

Children and adults with Asperger's syndrome have an unusual profile of cognitive (i.e. thinking and learning) abilities. Some young children with Asperger's syndrome start school with academic abilities above their grade level. Such advanced literacy and numeracy may have been self-taught from an early age through watching educational television programmes such as *Sesame Street*, tuition from educational computer programs or avidly looking at books and reading about a special interest. Some young children with Asperger's syndrome appear to easily 'crack the code' of reading, spelling or numeracy; indeed, these subjects may become their special interest. In contrast, some children with Asperger's syndrome have considerable delay in these academic skills and an early assessment of cognitive abilities suggests specific learning problems. There seem to be more children with Asperger's syndrome than one might expect at the extremes of cognitive ability.

At school, teachers soon recognize that the child has a distinctive learning style, being talented in understanding the logical and physical world, noticing details and remembering and arranging facts in a systematic fashion (Baron-Cohen 2003). However, the child can be easily distracted, especially in the classroom, and when problem solving appears to have a 'one-track mind' and a fear of failure. As the child progresses through the school grades, teachers identify problems with organizational abilities, especially with regard to homework assignments and essays. They also observe that the child appears not to follow advice or learn from mistakes. End-of-year school reports often describe a conspicuously uneven profile of academic achievement with areas of excellence and areas that require remedial assistance.

It is extremely important that teachers and parents know how a particular child with Asperger's syndrome thinks and learns in order to improve his or her cognitive abilities and academic achievement. This is especially important as children usually have two reasons to attend school – to learn and to socialize. If the child with Asperger's syndrome is not successful socially at school, then academic success becomes more important as the primary motivation to attend school and for the development of self-esteem.

The diagnosis of Asperger's syndrome itself gives limited information on a specific child's expected profile of cognitive abilities, but valuable information can be obtained from formal testing using a standardized test of intelligence and tests of academic achievement.

PROFILE OF ABILITIES ON INTELLIGENCE TESTS

Standardized tests of intelligence have at least ten sub-tests that measure a range of intellectual abilities. Some sub-tests measure specific components of verbal reasoning, while others measure components of visual reasoning. The psychological term for visual reasoning is Performance and a person's Intelligence Quotient or IQ is usually divided into Verbal IQ, Performance IQ and an overall or Full Scale IQ. The Full Scale IQ is usually calculated from four separate factors: verbal comprehension, perceptual reasoning, working memory and processing speed. While the Verbal, Performance and Full Scale IQ of children with Asperger's syndrome are within the normal range, i.e. an IQ over 70, clinicians are more interested in whether there is a discrepancy between Verbal IQ and Performance IQ, and the child's profile of cognitive abilities on the sub-tests. The profile provides information on how the child learns academic concepts and on areas of cognitive difficulties, which can be valuable information for a teacher.

Elizabeth Wurst, a colleague of Hans Asperger, was the first to identify the variation in the profile of cognitive abilities associated with Asperger's syndrome. She and Hans Asperger noted that many of the children they saw at the children's clinic in Vienna had a Verbal IQ significantly greater than their Performance IQ. A subsequent review of the cases seen by Asperger and his colleagues over three decades confirmed that 48 per cent of the children had a significantly higher Verbal IQ than Performance IQ (Hippler and Klicpera 2004). The percentage of children having no significant difference between Verbal IQ and Performance IQ was 38 per cent, but 18 per cent of children with Asperger's syndrome demonstrated the opposite pattern, namely a Performance or visual reasoning IQ significantly greater than Verbal IQ.

A similar discrepancy between Verbal IQ and Performance IQ for children with Asperger's syndrome has now been confirmed by several studies (Barnhill *et al.* 2000; Cederlund and Gillberg 2004; Dickerson Mayes and Calhoun 2003; Ehlers *et al.* 1997; Ghaziuddin and Mountain Kimchi 2004; Klin *et al.* 1995; Lincoln *et al.* 1988; Miller and Ozonoff 2000). Children with a much higher Verbal IQ than Performance IQ and a particular profile of cognitive abilities are described as having Non-Verbal Learning Disability or NLD (Rourke 1989). Strategies to facilitate learning designed for children with NLD can be applied to children with Asperger's syndrome who have the same profile of cognitive abilities (Brown Rubinstein 2005; Russell Burger 2004; Tanguay 2002).

It is interesting that there have been studies that have not identified a clear superiority of Verbal IQ over Performance IQ in the majority of children with Asperger's syndrome, especially in children who are intellectually very able (Manjiviona and Prior 1999; Szatmari *et al.* 1990). A recent study has also suggested that the gap between Verbal IQ and Performance IQ closes as age increases (Dickerson Mayes and Calhoun 2003). Thus, there is no unique cognitive profile on an intelligence test that can be used to confirm a diagnosis of Asperger's syndrome. What we can say is that the overall profile of abilities on the intelligence test of a child with Asperger's syndrome tends to be conspicuously uneven, so one must exercise extreme caution in using a single IQ figure to represent the cognitive abilities of the child. The profile or pattern of intellectual abilities is more important than the overall or Full Scale IQ.

About 50 per cent of children with Asperger's syndrome have relatively advanced verbal reasoning skills, and may be colloquially described as 'verbalizers'. If such a child has difficulty acquiring a particular academic ability in the social 'theatre' of the classroom, then his or her knowledge and understanding may be improved by reading about the concept or engaging in a one-to-one discussion. If the child with Asperger's syndrome has relatively advanced visual reasoning skills (a 'visualizer' – about one in five children with Asperger's syndrome), then learning may be facilitated by observation and visual imagery. The phrase 'a picture is worth a thousand words' is very applicable to such children. The 'verbalizers' may eventually be successful in careers where verbal abilities are an advantage, for example journalism or the legal professions, and 'visualizers' may be successful in careers such as engineering or the visual arts.

When analysing a child's IQ assessment results, the clinician may find considerable value in an analysis of the profile of cognitive abilities based on the child's performance on the sub-tests of the intelligence scale. The research on IQ profiles indicates that children with Asperger's syndrome have good factual and lexical (or word) knowledge. Their highest scores are often on the sub-tests that measure vocabulary, general knowledge and verbal problem solving. Such children have an impressive vocabulary and their recall of facts can make them popular in a Trivial Pursuit team. In the Performance or visual reasoning sub-tests, children with Asperger's syndrome can achieve relatively high scores on the Block Design test. The child has to copy an abstract pattern using coloured cubes within a time limit. Such children are often good at breaking a large geometric pattern into small segments. This can explain the child's ability to look at a picture of a completed Lego model and very quickly complete the Lego construction. Children with Asperger's syndrome are also good at finding an embedded figure in a complex geometric pattern (Frith 1989). They can be very good at 'finding a needle in a haystack'. However, some teachers may dispute this when the child cannot find his textbook in his desk.

Their lowest performance tends to be on tests that require the mental manipulation of information (i.e. 'multi-tracking'), or in tasks in which the child is vulnerable to being distracted, or those which are affected by the child's being a ponderous perfectionist, namely the digit span, arithmetic, and coding (digit symbol) sub-tests. In these tests the child has to remember a sequence of numbers, complete mental arithmetic tasks and use a pencil to copy a series of shapes within a specified time limit. Children with Asperger's syndrome can also have relative difficulty with tests that require sequential reasoning, as in the picture arrangement test. A series of pictures that represent a story are mixed up and the child has to understand the story to arrange the pictures in the correct order.

The psychologist who administers the intelligence test can provide the class teacher or parent with an explanation of the cognitive strengths and weaknesses of the child, in order that they may understand why the child is achieving less success than might be expected in certain aspects of the school curriculum. The psychologist may also suggest alternative strategies to assist the child in achieving particular academic abilities based on his or her cognitive strengths. The relative delay in acquiring a particular ability may be due to a genuine difficulty understanding the concept – a problem with the 'hard wiring of the brain' – and a change in the method of instruction, based on knowledge acquired from the results of the assessment of intellectual abilities, may achieve greater success.

Having an IQ assessment can provide valuable information on cognitive abilities but Hans Asperger noted that most intelligence tests deliberately avoid testing school knowledge and exclude tasks where learning and environment play a role. He wrote that:

> The difficulties of these children will, however, be revealed in tests involving learning. We therefore use learning tests to tell us not only about the scholastic knowledge of these children, but also about their methods, attention, concentration, distractibility and persistence. (Asperger [1944] 1991, p.76)

A comprehensive assessment of cognitive abilities needs to include tests of scholastic knowledge and the grade level at which the child is functioning for school subjects.

PROFILE OF LEARNING ABILITIES AT SCHOOL

The child with Asperger's syndrome may have an IQ that suggests the intellectual potential to achieve good grades in school work, but some children have an unusual profile of learning abilities that can include specific learning difficulties and lower than expected grade levels (Manjiviona 2003). Teachers and parents agree that the child is smart but school work is not as good as one would expect. This can have a very detrimental effect on the child's self-esteem.

There are several reasons, the main explanation being that children with Asperger's syndrome often have problems with attention and *executive function*. Perhaps the best way to understand the concept of executive function is to think of a chief executive of a large company, who has the ability to perceive the 'big picture', can consider the potential outcomes of various decisions, is able to organize resources and knowledge, plan and prioritize within the required time frame, and modify decisions based on results. Such executive function skills may be significantly delayed in children and adults with Asperger's syndrome.

Problems with attention

Hans Asperger noted that 'We regularly find a disturbance of active attention in autistic children' (Asperger [1944] 1991, p.76), and subsequent studies have suggested that at least 75 per cent of children with Asperger's syndrome also have a profile of learning abilities indicative of an additional diagnosis of Attention Deficit Disorder (Fein *et al.* 2005; Goldstein and Schwebach 2004; Holtmann, Bolte and Poustka 2005; Nyden *et al.* 1999; Schatz, Weimer and Trauner 2002; Sturm, Fernell and Gillberg 2004; Yoshida and Uchiyama 2004).

Psychologists divide attention into four components: the ability to sustain attention, to pay attention to relevant information, to shift attention when needed, and to encode attention – that is, to remember what was attended to. Children with Asperger's syndrome appear to have problems with all four aspects of attention (Nyden *et al.* 1999). The duration of attention to school work can be an obvious problem but the degree of attention can vary according to the level of motivation. If the child is attending to an activity associated with his or her special interest, the level of attention can be excessive. The child appears to be almost in a trance and oblivious of external cues that it is time to move on to another activity or to pay attention to the comments, requests and instructions of a teacher or parent. It appears nothing short of an earthquake would break the level of concentration. The amount of sustained attention can also depend on whether the child wants to give the attention to what an adult wants him or her to do. The child with Asperger's syndrome may have his or her own agenda for what to attend to.

Even when appearing to be attentive to the task set by the teacher, the child may not be attending to what is relevant in the material in front of him or her. Typical children can more easily identify and selectively attend to what is relevant to the context or problem. Children with Asperger's syndrome are often distracted and confused by irrelevant detail and they don't automatically know what to look at. They may need specific instruction as to exactly what to look at on the page.

Some academic activities require the ability to shift attention during the activity and focus on new information. Unfortunately, children with Asperger's syndrome can have difficulty 'changing track' while engaged in a 'train of thought'. There can also be problems with memory processes such that the learned information is not stored or encoded as well as one would expect. Such children may not remember what to attend to when they encounter the same problem again. This characteristic can affect social situations. Children and adults with Asperger's syndrome process social information using intellect rather than intuition and can have problems remembering what the relevant social cues are and changing their mental 'track' when interacting with more than one person.

One of the features of impaired executive function is a difficulty switching attention from one task to another. The person with Asperger's syndrome usually has considerable problems switching thoughts to a new activity until there has been closure, i.e. the activity has been successfully completed. Other children appear to have the capacity to pause a thought or activity and to move easily to the next activity. In the classroom, children with Asperger's syndrome can resist changing activities until they have completed the previous activity, knowing that their thinking cannot cope as easily with transitions without closure. A teacher or parent may need to provide multiple verbal warnings when an activity is going to change, perhaps counting down and, if possible, allowing the child with Asperger's syndrome extra time to finish the task.

Remedial programs for children with Asperger's syndrome who have problems with attention will be very similar to those designed for children with Attention Deficit Disorder. For example:

- relevant information should be highlighted

- assignments should be broken down into smaller units, in keeping with the child's attention span

- the teacher should regularly monitor and give feedback to maintain attention

- the amount of environmental distractions should be reduced

- a quiet, isolated work space should be provided

- consideration should be given to the possible value of medication if there is an additional diagnosis of Attention Deficit Disorder.

We are now developing strategies to maintain and improve attention that can be used at school and at home specifically for children with a mix of Asperger's syndrome and Attention Deficit Disorder (Kutscher 2005; Wilkinson 2005).

Executive function

The psychological term *executive function* includes:

- organizational and planning abilities
- working memory
- inhibition and impulse control
- self-reflection and self-monitoring
- time management and prioritizing
- understanding complex or abstract concepts
- using new strategies.

We now have considerable research evidence to confirm that some children, but more especially adolescents and adults, with Asperger's syndrome have impaired executive function (Goldberg *et al.* 2005; Goldstein, Johnson and Minshew 2001; Hughes, Russell and Robbins 1994; Joseph, McGrath and Tager-Flusberg 2005; Kleinhans, Akshoomoff and Delis 2005; Landa and Goldberg 2005; Ozonoff *et al.* 2004; Ozonoff, South and Provencal 2005b; Prior and Hoffmann 1990; Rumsey and Hamburger 1990; Shu *et al.* 2001; Szatmari *et al.* 1990).

In the early school years, the main signs of impaired executive function are difficulties with inhibiting a response (i.e. being impulsive), working memory and using new strategies. The child with Asperger's syndrome can be notorious for being impulsive in school work and in social situations, appearing to respond without thinking of the context, consequences and previous experience. By the age of eight years, a typical child is able to 'switch on' and use his or her frontal lobe to inhibit a response and think before deciding what to do or say. The child with Asperger's syndrome can be capable of thoughtful deliberation before responding, but under conditions of stress, or if feeling overwhelmed or confused, can be impulsive. It is important to encourage the child to relax and consider other options before responding and to recognize that being impulsive can be a sign of confusion and stress.

Working memory is the ability to maintain or hold information 'on line' when solving a problem. The child with Asperger's syndrome may have an exceptional long-term memory, and is perhaps able to recite the credits or dialogue of his or her favourite film, but has difficulty with the mental recall and manipulation of information relevant to an academic task. The child's working memory capacity may be less than that of his or her peers. Other children have a 'bucket' capacity for remembering and using relevant information, but the child with Asperger's syndrome has a memory 'cup' which affects the amount of information he or she can retrieve from the memory 'well'.

Another problem with working memory is a tendency to forget a thought quickly. One of the reasons children with Asperger's syndrome are notorious for interrupting others was explained by one child who said he had to say what was on his mind because if he waited he would forget what he was going to say.

Impaired executive function can include a difficulty considering alternative problem-solving strategies. Harold Stone, a man with Asperger's syndrome, explained to me that the thinking of children and adults with Asperger's syndrome can be represented by a train on a singular track. If it is the right track, the child will quickly arrive at the destination, the solution to the problem. However, I have observed that children with Asperger's syndrome can be the last to know if they are on the wrong track, or to recognize that there may be other tracks to the destination. Thus, there may be a problem with flexible thinking, one of the characteristics of impaired executive function. Typical children and adults are able to react quickly to feedback and are prepared to change strategies or direction. Their vehicle of thought is not a train but a four-wheel-drive vehicle that easily changes direction and is able to go 'off road'.

Research has indicated that children with Asperger's syndrome tend to continue using incorrect strategies and are less likely to learn from their mistakes, even when they know their strategy isn't working (Shu *et al.* 2001). An adult with Asperger's syndrome explained to me that, when solving a problem, he assumed that his solution was correct and did not need to be changed. His thoughts were 'This is the right way to solve the problem, why isn't it working?', which caused considerable frustration. This also explains the frequent comment from parents and teachers that the child with Asperger's syndrome does not appear to learn from his or her mistakes. We now recognize this characteristic as an example of impaired executive function that is due to a problem of neurology (the functioning of the frontal lobes), rather than being the child's choice.

In the middle school years, problems with executive function can become apparent as the school curriculum changes to become more complex and self-directed, and teachers and parents have age-appropriate expectations based on the maturing cognitive abilities of age peers. In the primary or elementary school years, success in subjects such as history can be measured by the ability to recall facts such as dates. By the middle school years, assessment in history has changed, and requires that the child shows ability in writing essays that have a clear organizational structure, and that he or she can recognize, compare and evaluate different perspectives and interpretations. Adolescents with impaired executive function have problems with the organizing and planning aspects of class work, assignments and homework. Jerry Newport, an adult with Asperger's syndrome, said that, as regards planning, 'I don't see the pot holes down the road' (personal communication).

Stephen Shore has also provided a personal insight into problems with organizational abilities in his description: 'Without appropriate support, the child with Asperger's syndrome may feel he is drowning in a million different sub-tasks. Many of us have trouble prioritizing and organizing tasks' (personal communication). Teachers may complain that the adolescent with Asperger's syndrome can't seem to 'get his act together', and are critical of the person for being disorganized. This is another sign of impaired executive function and not necessarily due to the child's laziness or lack of commitment to school work. The person with Asperger's syndrome may also become distressed in situations at school that do not provide an opportunity for mental rehearsal or preparation for change. A spontaneous change in the method of class assessment or tests can create considerable confusion and anxiety.

Some adolescents with Asperger's syndrome can also have difficulty with abstract reasoning, prioritizing which task to concentrate on first, and time management, especially how long to spend on a designated activity. This can be exasperating for parents and teachers, who know that the child has the intellectual capacity to complete the work to a high standard, but impaired executive function will contribute to a delay in the submission of the work and therefore incur penalties.

There can also be problems with self-reflection and self-monitoring. By the middle school years, typical children have developed the capacity to have a mental 'conversation' to solve a problem (Russell 1997). The internal thinking process can include a dialogue, discussing the merits of various options and solutions. This process may not be as efficient in the thinking of a child or adolescent with Asperger's syndrome as it is in typical peers. Many people with Asperger's syndrome 'think in pictures' and are less likely to use an inner voice or conversation to facilitate problem solving (Grandin 1995). The adolescent with Asperger's syndrome may need the teacher or adult's voice to guide his or her thoughts.

Some children and adolescents with Asperger's syndrome facilitate problem solving by having an external (rather than internal) conversation and, as they are thinking and problem solving, find that it helps to talk to themselves. This adaptive way of problem solving and learning has both advantages and disadvantages: while peers may be distracted by the self-talk, and consider the child to be weird, teachers can listen in to the child's reasoning and correct any errors in knowledge and logic.

One strategy to reduce the problems associated with impaired executive functioning is to have someone act as an 'executive secretary'. The child's parent may have realized that he or she has already become an executive secretary, providing guidance with organizing and planning, especially with regards to completing homework assignments. The executive secretary (a parent or teacher) may also need to be assertive in dictating a time schedule, proofreading draft reports, colour coding subject books, encouraging alternative strategies and 'to do' checklists, and establishing a clear schedule of activities. Such close monitoring and guidance may appear to be excessive for an adolescent or young adult with recognized intellectual ability.

A parent who provides the support as an executive secretary may be labelled as over-protective by school agencies and family members, but that parent has learned that, without such support, the person with Asperger's syndrome would not achieve the grades that reflect his or her actual abilities. I encourage a parent or teacher to take on this very important role of executive secretary. We hope that this will be a temporary appointment as the person with Asperger's syndrome achieves greater independence with organizational skills. However, the executive secretary mother may not be able to resign until her role is replaced with an executive secretary wife.

PROBLEM SOLVING

The child with Asperger's syndrome may prefer to use his or her own idiosyncratic approach to problem solving, which I describe as the 'Frank Sinatra Syndrome' or 'My Way'. Adults with Asperger's syndrome may be famous (or notorious) for being an icon-oclast and rejecting popular beliefs and conventional wisdom. The child does not consider the recommendations of the teacher or the approaches being used by other children. This can have the potential advantage of producing an original response, not considered by other children, but unfortunately the majority of school work is based on the development of problem solving in typical children, and 'my way' can lead to the teacher becoming exasperated trying to encourage the child to consider conventional strategies first.

It is important to encourage flexibility in thinking and this can start at an early age. When playing with very young children with Asperger's syndrome, an adult can play the game of 'What else could it be?' For typical children, an aspect of imaginative social play is the flexible thinking that allows an object to represent something else, or to have several functions. Many children with Asperger's syndrome, however, have fixed ideas as to the function of objects. When playing with a young child with Asperger's syndrome, I may hold a straight section of train track from the Thomas the Tank Engine train set and ask the child what it is, then what else it could be. Suggestions are made, such as the wings of an aeroplane (enacting the flight of an aircraft, using the track to represent wings), a ladder to climb to a tree house (with two fingers enacting climbing up the 'ladder'), or a ruler to draw a straight line (enacting the track being a ruler). Another activity is the game of 'How many uses can you think of for…?' (e.g., a brick, clothes peg, etc.). These games can be great fun, and will encourage flexible and creative thinking and facilitate social play with peers.

When an adult is playing with a young child with Asperger's syndrome, it is impor-tant that the adult occasionally uses, or deliberately creates, a real situation where a solution to a problem is required. The adult can vocalize his or her thoughts so that the child with Asperger's syndrome can listen to the various approaches the adult is consid-ering to solve the problem. However, when a solution is found, the adult can encourage continued concentration, and determine whether another approach would have also been successful. This is an example of 'We can do this but we could also do this,' which encourages the recognition that there may be more than one way to solve a problem. As the adult vocalizes his or her thoughts, the vocalizations need to include comments such as 'If I stay calm, I'll find the solution more quickly' and 'The smart and friendly thing to do is to ask for help.'

In the school years, teachers will need to use the same strategy of vocalizing their thoughts when giving guidance for an academic problem faced by the child. It is also important to remember that the student with Asperger's syndrome is more mentally flexible when relaxed. If he or she is becoming agitated because the solution is elusive, the first priority is to encourage a calm attitude or temporary diversion to a calming activity so that he or she is better able to listen, focus and consider alternative strategies.

Some unconventional problem-solving strategies used by people with Asperger's syndrome can be interpreted as disrespectful. Mick explained, 'I look at an inanimate object, it helps me to think. I can concentrate more if I look at a blank wall, but people think I am ignoring them.' Other people need to recognize that such behaviour is a constructive action to facilitate thinking, while the person with Asperger's syndrome may need to explain this action to avoid being misunderstood.

Coping with mistakes

The learning profile of children and adults with Asperger's syndrome can include a tendency to focus on errors, a need to fix an irregularity and a desire to be a perfectionist. This can lead to a fear of making a mistake and the child's refusal to commence an activity unless he or she can complete it perfectly. The avoidance of errors can mean that children with Asperger's syndrome prefer accuracy rather than speed, which can affect performance in timed tests and lead to their thinking being described as pedantic. Creative adults with Asperger's syndrome, such as composers, engineers and architects, often cannot cope with any deviation from their original design.

Children with Asperger's syndrome may perceive themselves more as adults than children and expect of themselves an adult level of competence in an activity. Young children and adolescents with Asperger's syndrome may fear feeling or appearing stupid and dread ridicule by peers for not knowing what to do. There can also be a limited acceptance that they are wrong, which may be perceived by others as an expression of arrogance. Any advice may be perceived and reacted to as personal criticism, potentially antagonizing teachers and friends.

It is important to change the child's perception of errors and mistakes. People with Asperger's syndrome often value intellectual abilities in themselves and others, and young children can be encouraged to recognize that the development of cognitive 'strength' is similar to that of physical strength, in that the brain needs exercise on difficult or strenuous mental activity to improve intellectual ability. If all mental tasks were easy, we would not improve our intellect. Intellectual effort makes the brain smarter.

Social Stories™ can be used to explain that we learn more from our mistakes than our successes; mistakes can lead to interesting discoveries, and an error is an opportunity, not a disaster. Adults will need to model how to respond to a mistake and have a constructive response to the child's errors, with comments such as 'This is a difficult problem designed to make you think and learn, and together we can find a solution.' It must also be remembered that while there can be a fear of making a mistake, there can be an enormous delight in getting something right, and success and perfection may be a more important motivator than pleasing an adult or impressing peers.

I have noted that children, and sometimes adults, with Asperger's syndrome have a tendency to point out the errors of other people, being unaware that such a comment breaks the social conventions, and can be embarrassing or offensive. Your status does not matter; the child with Asperger's syndrome will point out your mistake and think that you should be grateful to them for doing this. Teachers in particular do not like their mistakes being loudly announced to the class. Social Stories™ and Comic Strip Conversations can be used to enable the child with Asperger's syndrome to understand how someone's errors can be identified without causing offence.

School achievement in reading and mathematics

Research has indicated that overall the school achievements of children with Asperger's syndrome in reading and mathematics are consistent with their peers (Dickerson, Mayes and Calhoun 2003; Griswold *et al.* 2002; Reitzel and Szatmari 2003; Smith-Myles *et al.* 2002). However, in statistical terms, the standard variations are large, with more children with Asperger's syndrome at the extremes of school achievement in reading and numeracy that one would expect. A review of 74 of Asperger's clinical cases found that 23 per cent were outstanding at mathematics, 12 per cent had an outstanding artistic talent, but 17 per cent had significant problems with reading and writing (Hippler and Klicpera 2004). We recognize that hyperlexia (an advanced ability in word recognition with relatively poor comprehension of the words or storyline) is more common than we would expect in children with Asperger's syndrome (Grigorenko *et al.* 2002; Tirosh and Canby 1993). But a recent study of academic achievement suggests that one in five children with Asperger's syndrome have significant problems with reading and almost half of children with Asperger's syndrome have problems with mathematics (Reitzel and Szatmari 2003). Thus, an individual child with Asperger's syndrome is more likely than his or her peers to have signs of school achievement in reading and mathematics or a lack of achievement in these areas.

We are not sure why individual children with Asperger's syndrome achieve high scores on reading tests, but we do know that such children subsequently tend to achieve high grades in tests of school achievement, due to a relatively advanced ability to learn from written material (Grigorenko *et al.* 2002). It is obviously an advantage to be a good reader at school. We are also not sure why some children with Asperger's syndrome have specific problems with reading. We do know that such children can have specific perceptual and language problems that will affect reading ability. For example, a child with Asperger's syndrome described to me how he could learn to read a specific word, but when the word was printed in a different font, he perceived it as a completely new word. Perceptual, cognitive and language-processing problems and family history could suggest some of the characteristics associated with dyslexia.

From my clinical experience, conventional remedial reading programs have not been as effective with children with Asperger's syndrome as one would expect. The child may need a thorough assessment by a specialist neuropsychologist or reading expert to determine exactly why he or she is having difficulty learning to read. We may also need to discover new strategies for such children and to be aware of the effect on a child's self-esteem if he or she continues to have reading difficulties in the upper school grades. One interesting aspect of Asperger's syndrome is that some children who have been assessed as having a significant delay in learning to read can, over a few days, acquire the ability to read at an age-appropriate level. Luke Jackson, a teenager with Asperger's syndrome, has written a guide for fellow teenagers with Asperger's syndrome, and he describes how 'The school gave me all sorts of extra help with reading and I couldn't even remember one letter from the other. However much anyone taught me, it just would not sink in.' Then almost overnight, at the age of seven years, he acquired the ability to read. In his guide book, he writes, 'I hope this encourages parents never to give up on a child who seems unable to learn to read. I told mum and school that someone had "switched a light on in my head"' (L. Jackson 2002, p.117).

There are children with Asperger's syndrome who appear to have mastered the general ability to read but have specific problems with silent reading and independent reading, i.e. the reading level at which an individual child can read comfortably to him- or herself (Smith Myles *et al.* 2002). It is interesting to note that in the Smith Myles *et al.* study, children with Asperger's syndrome who were delayed in their silent reading ability achieved a higher level of reading comprehension when reading aloud. Actually saying what you are reading can facilitate comprehension, but as children mature they are expected to read silently. For some children with Asperger's syndrome, vocalizing thoughts and reading aloud can encourage greater comprehension and problem solving.

The special interest and ability in mathematics that some children with Asperger's syndrome can develop may be explained by the cognitive profile associated with Asperger's syndrome. Great mathematicians have tended to develop mathematical concepts using visual images, where numbers are conceived as shapes, not quantity; and visual reasoning and imagery can be relatively advanced in some children with Asperger's syndrome. We also recognize that the personalities of some of the great mathematicians included many of the characteristics of Asperger's syndrome (Harpur, Lawlor and Fitzgerald 2004; James 2006). Marc Fleisher has Asperger's syndrome and a natural talent with mathematics. He has a postgraduate degree in mathematics and describes his enjoyment:

> Mathematics is filled with tiny details and fascinations that just cry out to be discovered. It is the very nature of the subject that can appeal to many with an eye for detail, including autistic individuals. (Fleisher 2006, p.182)

The difficulty for children with Asperger's syndrome who are able to solve complex mathematical problems can be explaining in words how they achieved the answer. Hans

Asperger described how one of the children he diagnosed said, 'I can't do this orally, only headily' (1991, p.71). The child can provide the correct answer to a mathematical problem but not easily translate into speech the mental processes used to solve the problem. This can mystify teachers and lead to problems with tests when the person with Asperger's syndrome is unable to explain his or her methods on the test or exam paper.

One of the learning-profile characteristics associated with Asperger's syndrome is a strong drive to seek certainty, and the child or adult appears uncomfortable with any situation in which there is more than one right answer. At school, they tend to prefer subjects that provide certainty such as mathematics, and avoid subjects that involve value judgements such as English literature. Thus, a tendency to visualize numbers and to seek certainty could be two of the factors that explain a propensity to develop mathematical talent.

Some children with Asperger's syndrome have considerable difficulty understanding even basic mathematical concepts and we use the term *dyscalculia* to describe such difficulties. As with possible signs of dyslexia, which affects reading abilities, the child with signs of dyscalculia will need a thorough assessment of the cognitive abilities required to develop mathematical skills. The problem may not be the completion of simple arithmetic problems or remembering the times tables, but applying mathematical knowledge in everyday situations (Jordan 2003). We have yet to determine why this should be, and what we can do, other than offer patient remedial tuition in the development and especially the application of mathematical concepts.

Weak central coherence

Uta Frith and Francesca Happé have examined the learning profile and information processing of children with autism and Asperger's syndrome and noticed some intriguing phenomena (Frith and Happé 1994). Such children can be remarkably good at attending to detail but appear to have considerable difficulty perceiving and understanding the overall picture, or gist. A useful metaphor to understand this aspect of weak central coherence is to imagine rolling a piece of paper into a tube and closing one eye, placing the tube against the open eye like a telescope, and looking at the world through the tube: details are visible, but the context is not perceived.

Typical peers will have a broader cognitive perspective than the child with Asperger's syndrome. When learning in the classroom, the problem may not be attention, but focus. Some activities are difficult to complete on time because the child with Asperger's syndrome has become preoccupied with the detail, focusing on parts rather than wholes. A teacher or parent will sometimes need to explain to the child where to look.

A more recent term is monotropism (Murray, Lesser and Lawson 2005). A person with Asperger's syndrome has unusual strategies for the allocation of attention, and large areas of potential information are not being cognitively registered. This leads to a very fragmented view of the world. The person may learn isolated facts but have difficulty with an overall analysis. As an amateur photographer, I conceptualize the problem as perceiving the world through a telephoto lens rather than a wide-angle lens.

When having to process complex information, typical children are able to organize simultaneous events into a coherent framework and to process information at a deeper level. A central coherent theme is soon identified. Children and adults with Asperger's syndrome appear to have a problem determining what is relevant and what is redundant, and deciphering the overall pattern or meaning to create a mental framework. Psychologists use the term *weak central coherence* to describe this style of information processing.

Weak central coherence explains some of the talents and difficulties people with Asperger's syndrome have in cognitive, linguistic and social abilities. In cognitive terms, the person can sometimes identify details and notice connections that are not perceived by others who have a different mental framework. Identifying new connections and representation can contribute to being a successful scientist or artist, while an attention to detail is an advantage to a contract lawyer, accountant or copy editor proofreading a manuscript. One of the disadvantages is that it takes more time, and requires repetition and consistency to decipher the pattern in those school activities where the simultaneous processing of information from many different sources is needed.

In language, typical children can remember the gist of the message, the key parts, which makes the information easier to remember. In conversation, having weak central coherence means the person may remember the details but not the overall story; they may be notorious for giving irrelevant information, and have difficulty summarizing and saying just the important points.

Having strong as opposed to weak central coherence means a person can easily identify what is relevant or redundant in a situation. When a typical person walks into a large room that has many people and activities, the brain could be overwhelmed with the amount of new information, but copes with the situation by identifying what is important to attend to. We have a priority system, and the usual priority is to notice the people and conversations, not the pattern on the carpet or the light fittings. People with Asperger's syndrome are less able to determine what to notice and what is irrelevant. After the event, typical people will tend to remember the people, their emotions and conversations, and the other information is quickly forgotten. In contrast, the person with Asperger's syndrome may not remember who was there but does remember what other people would consider as trivial or irrelevant details.

Perhaps the most complex information for the child with Asperger's syndrome to process is social and emotional. Once the child has deciphered the social rules, he or she can become extremely agitated when the social rules are violated, showing extreme intolerance of made-up rules and cheating. The child also becomes a class policeman, observant of any social rule violations and resolutely administering consequences. As many typical teenagers are determined to test and violate the social rules or conventions, the teenager with Asperger's syndrome appears to be their constant critic, obviously not a popular characteristic with typical adolescents.

The DSM-IV diagnostic criteria for Asperger's syndrome include that the child develops an 'apparently inflexible adherence to specific, non-functional routines or rituals' (American Psychiatric Association 2000, p.84). The development of routines and rituals can be a sign of anxiety and we know that children with Asperger's syndrome have a propensity to be anxious (see Chapter 6), but another reason for the development of routines can be weak central coherence, i.e. difficulty determining the patterns or coherence in everyday life. We recognize that young children with Asperger's syndrome have a propensity to establish and enforce routines. Once a pattern has emerged it must be maintained. Unfortunately, the components of the anticipated sequence may increase over time. For example, the bedtime routine may have started with lining up only three toys, but becomes an elaborate ritual where dozens of toys have to be placed according to strict rules of order and symmetry. When a journey to a destination has followed the same route several times, there is the expectation that this must be the only route and no deviation is tolerated. The following quotation illustrates why there is a determination to create order and certainty:

> Reality to an autistic person is a confusing, interacting mass of events, people, places, sounds and sights. There seem to be no clear boundaries, order or meaning to anything. A large part of my life is spent just trying to work out the pattern behind everything. Set routines, times, particular routes and rituals all help to get order into an unbearably chaotic life. (Jolliffe *et al.* 1992, p.16)

Donna Williams describes how:

> I loved to copy, create and order things. I loved our set of encyclopaedias. They had letters and numbers on the side, and I was always checking to make sure they were in order or putting them that way. I was making order out of chaos. Searching for categories did not stop with the encyclopaedias. I would read the telephone directory, counting the number of Browns listed, or counting the number of variations on a particular name, or the rarity of others. I was exploring the concept of consistency. It may have seemed that my world was upside down, but I was looking to get a grip on consistency. The constant change of most things never seemed to give me any chance to prepare myself for them. Because of this I found pleasure and comfort in doing the same things over and over again. (Williams 1998, p.42)

We can understand why a child with Asperger's syndrome, who has weak central coherence, imposes routines and rituals in his or her daily life to help determine the elusive pattern or coherence. Routine appears to be established to make life predictable and impose order, as novelty, chaos or uncertainty cause confusion and frustration. The establishment of a routine ensures there is no opportunity for change or the need to create a new coherence or framework to understand what is happening and what is expected of you.

Early childhood memories

Weak central coherence may explain an intriguing aspect of Asperger's syndrome, namely the ability to remember events in very early childhood (Lyons and Fitzgerald 2005). Typical adults can recall autobiographical events from when they were about three to six years old, having great difficulty remembering earlier events in their childhood. Parents of a child or adult with Asperger's syndrome often remark on their son or daughter's ability to give vivid and accurate descriptions of events that occurred during infancy. For example, Albert's parents commented how 'he can remember things when he was so small, like just one incident would happen and nothing would be mentioned about it and a couple of years later he would bring this incident up and remember every detail' (Cesaroni and Garber 1991, p.308). Albert relates:

> I remember when I was one year old I went to Nashville, the air sometimes smelled like firewood. I remember hearing music, it bugged me a lot. I knew I was in a different place, I woke up and smelled the air; it was like a whole bunch of old buildings. (Cesaroni and Garber 1991, p.307)

Early autobiographical memories can be predominantly visual and of experiences of importance to the person; for example, Candy explained that her 'memories consist of objects rather than people or personal stuff' (personal communication).

We are not precisely sure why a person with Asperger's syndrome can have exemplary long-term memory for details and facts and an ability to recall events in infancy. A plausible explanation is that people with Asperger's syndrome have a different pattern of brain wiring from birth and weak central coherence affects the perception, cognitive processing and storing and retrieval of memories. The result is an ability to recall events in infancy that others cannot retrieve.

The ability for the accurate recall of scenes can extend to remembering whole pages of a book. This eidetic or photographic memory can be extremely helpful in examinations, although I have known of university students with Asperger's syndrome who have been falsely accused of cheating because their examination answers have included perfect and lengthy reproductions of the principal texts for the course. I have also known of boys, but rarely girls, with Asperger's syndrome who have a remarkable memory for directions and places they have been. The young child may give accurate directions of how to get to my clinic from the back seat of the family car, to the great relief of his mother who wants to arrive on time for the appointment.

CLASSROOM STRATEGIES TO ENCOURAGE COGNITIVE DEVELOPMENT

Experience has indicated that children with Asperger's syndrome appear to make the greatest advances in cognitive and academic abilities in a quiet, well-structured classroom. In her biography of her son, Lisa Pyles refers to the psychologist's description of her young son at school: 'John just seems like a puppy learning to stay. Every ounce of concentration is wrapped up in just being in the classroom, in staying put when his instincts are telling him to run away. There is nothing left in him for academics' (Pyles 2002, p.23).

Thus, there will need to be an acute awareness of perceptual overload and subsequent stress, and careful consideration of where the child sits to reduce distractions and interruptions and to see and hear the teacher clearly. Social engineering may be necessary by placing the child near benevolent peers who can provide guidance when the teacher is busy. There should be minimal changes in routines and staff, a visible daily schedule of activities and preparation for transitions. If the class teacher at primary school has to be away and a relief teacher is called in, the school may need to contact the child's parents and warn them of the imminent change. In some cases it may be wise to keep the child at home that day for the sake of the child and probably the relief teacher.

The teacher will have to monitor the child's progress regularly to ensure he or she is 'on track' and knows what to do next. Sometimes the establishment of a work station will encourage concentration. Older children will benefit from comprehensive class notes and study guides, as adolescents with Asperger's syndrome are not usually as proficient as their peers in note taking and copying information from the board. The teacher will be aware of problems with executive function and provide assistance with organizational and planning skills, using a 'to do' list and sometimes allowing additional time for completing an activity or assignment.

When children have an overall IQ within the normal range, school authorities tend to assume such children do not qualify for in-class support for learning problems. However, many children with Asperger's syndrome have an overall IQ within the normal range but an extremely uneven profile of intellectual or cognitive skills. Despite an average or above-average IQ, children with Asperger's syndrome have a different way of thinking and learning, and some children have specific learning problems that standardized tests of intelligence are not designed to detect. The class teacher may genuinely need, and should then request and receive, in-class assistance to encourage cognitive and academic development for a child who is not intellectually disabled but has an unconventional profile of cognitive abilities.

Access to a special education support teacher or learning support unit at the school can provide additional and sometimes individual instruction and guidance in preparing and completing assignments and homework. The child with Asperger's syndrome may have difficulty understanding a particular concept in the noisy, distracting, social and linguistic environment of the classroom, but understand the concept more easily if the material is presented as part of a computer-based curriculum. Many school subjects, from kindergarten to grade 12, are available on CD-Rom.

There are children with Asperger's syndrome whose school attainments are significantly above their age peers but whose social maturity is considerably below their peers. At the end of the school year, there may be some discussion between representatives of the school and the child's parents as to whether the child should repeat the current grade so that the social maturity differences are less conspicuous, or advance to the next grade or jump ahead a grade to be with intellectual peers.

Children with Asperger's syndrome can become very agitated if the school work is too easy, and often prefer to relate to their intellectual peers when learning in the class-room. There may be many other factors relevant to the decision to delay or accelerate the child through the grades, but I usually advocate for the child with Asperger's syndrome to be in a class of his or her intellectual peers, with an interesting and thereby motivating curriculum. Obviously programs will need to be provided to encourage social maturity to close the gap between intellectual and social development.

THE KNOWLEDGE AND PERSONALITY OF THE TEACHER

Over 60 years ago, Hans Asperger stated that:

> These children often show a surprising sensitivity to the personality of the teacher. However difficult they are, even under optimal conditions, they can be guided and taught, but only by those who give them understanding and genuine affection, people who show kindness towards them and yes, humour. The teacher's underlying emotional attitude influences, involuntarily and unconsciously, the mood and behaviour of the child. Of course, the management and guidance of such children essentially requires a proper knowledge of their peculiarities as well as genuine pedagogic talent and experience. Mere teaching efficiency is not enough. (Asperger [1944] 1991, p.48)

The class teacher needs to create an 'Asperger-friendly' environment based on the social, linguistic and cognitive abilities of the child. To create such an environment, it is essential that the class teacher should have access to information and expertise on Asperger's syndrome and attend relevant training courses. The school will need to maintain a library of resources on Asperger's syndrome, and the education services should consider the in-class support of a teacher assistant to help teach the social curriculum, assist with emotion management, facilitate social inclusion and provide remedial guidance for some academic activities.

There are personality attributes associated with being a successful teacher of a child with Asperger's syndrome. I have observed many children with Asperger's syndrome being taught well, in a range of school settings, and noted that the greatest cognitive and academic progress has been achieved by teachers who show an empathic understanding of the child. Such teachers are flexible in their teaching strategies, assessments and expectations. They invariably like and admire the child, respect his or her abilities and know the child's motivators and learning profile. Carol Gray has suggested that successful teachers must have an understanding of the child's delayed Theory of Mind abilities (that is, a delay in their understanding of what someone may be thinking or feeling); but the teacher must also have a 'Theory of Asperger Mind' (that is, an understanding of how the child may be thinking or feeling) (personal communication).

An example is provided by Nita Jackson who describes one of her teachers:

> Mr Osbourne was always bubbly and ready to make a light-hearted joke out of anything. He rarely got angry or raised his voice like most of my other teachers did. He let me hide in the music department's store cupboard at break time, without even blinking an eye, it was as though he understood and accepted why I needed to go to ridiculous measures to separate myself from society. I respected him for not probing for answers like everyone else did. Occasionally he would tap on the door, say 'boo!' and offer me a biscuit (which I never declined). On the last day of term, I bought him a tin of biscuits in return for the amount of biscuity yumminess he had allowed me. (N. Jackson 2002, p.34)

It is also important to remember that no two children with Asperger's syndrome have exactly the same profile of abilities, experiences and personality. Teaching practices that have been used successfully with one or two children with Asperger's syndrome may not be appropriate for subsequent children enrolled in the teacher's class; sometimes, new strategies need to be developed for each child.

Another requirement when teaching a child with Asperger's syndrome is to not be offended by comments that may superficially appear to be rude or insolent. When the teacher asks the child 'Would you like to put away your free play activities?' and the reply is a simple 'No', the child is being honest rather than impolite. It is also important to avoid sarcasm, as the child is likely to make a literal interpretation of what is said.

The teacher also needs to be aware that conventional motivators may not be as effective in comparison to other children in the class. Hans Asperger was very interested in educational strategies for the children he saw, and wrote:

> While demonstrations of love, affection and flattery are pleasing to normal children and often induce in them desired behaviour, such approaches only succeed in irritating Fritz, as well as all other similar children. (Asperger [1944] 1991, p.47)

More successful motivators include appealing to intellectual self-esteem by commenting on how smart the child is, incorporating aspects of the special interest in the activity, and reducing the potential for risk or errors.

Hans Asperger went on to state that:

> All educational transactions have to be done with the affect 'turned off'. The teacher must never become angry nor should he aim to become loved. The teacher must, at all costs, be calm and collected and must remain in control. (Asperger [1944] 1991, p.47)

These are sound words of advice. Being annoyed or affectionate when they are trying to concentrate can cause greater confusion or irritation for children with Asperger's syndrome. There are times when quiet assertion is needed, and the child's increasing agitation not allowed to create a reciprocal reaction in the adult.

Hans Asperger also suggested that 'another pedagogic trick is to announce any educational measures not as personal requests, but as objective impersonal law' (Asperger [1944] 1991, p.48). Sometimes the teacher or school principal has to show the child a copy of the relevant school rules to confirm that the teacher is enforcing an accepted rule and not being mean or vindictive.

Homework

A major cause of anguish for children and teenagers with Asperger's syndrome, their families and teachers is the satisfactory completion of homework. Why should this group of children have such an emotional reaction to the mere thought of having to start their homework, and such difficulty completing assigned tasks? There may be two explanations. The first is based on their degree of stress and mental exhaustion during their day at school, and the second is due to their profile of cognitive skills.

As with their classroom peers, children with Asperger's syndrome have to learn the traditional educational curriculum but they encounter many more stressful experiences than do other children in their class. They have to deal with an additional, parallel curriculum, namely the social curriculum. They have to use their intellectual reasoning to determine the social rules of the classroom and the playground. Other children do not have to learn social integration skills consciously, but these children have to decipher the social cues and codes and cognitively determine what to do and say in social situations. Often their primary feedback is criticism for an error, with little recognition from others when they make the correct response. Unfortunately, learning only from your mistakes is not the most constructive way to learn. Thus, these children have to concentrate on an extra curriculum that leaves them intellectually and emotionally exhausted at the end of the school day. They also have difficulty reading and responding to the emotional signals of the teacher and other children, and coping with the complex socializing, noise and chaos of the playground, the unexpected changes in the school routine and the intense sensory experiences of a noisy classroom. Throughout the school day they rarely have an opportunity to relax.

When I talk to children with Asperger's syndrome who are having difficulty learning the social curriculum and coping with the stress of school, they often explain that they want a clear division between home and school. Their comment is 'School is for learning; home is for fun or relaxation.' Thus, the prospect of interrupting their much-needed and deserved fun and relaxation with homework is more than they can cope with. Sean Barron explained that 'I didn't have a clue about why some *school*work had to be done at *home*. What we did at school was supposed to stay there, period' (Grandin and Barron 2005, p.94).

Children with Asperger's syndrome have an unusual profile of cognitive skills that must be recognized and accommodated when they are undertaking academic work at school and especially at home. Due to impaired executive function they have difficulty planning, organizing and prioritizing, a tendency to be impulsive and inflexible when problem solving, and a limited working memory. Other features include a difficulty generating new ideas, and determining what is relevant or redundant; poor time perception and time management; and a need for supervision and guidance. There is also the likelihood of specific learning problems such as a reading difficulty.

The following strategies are designed to minimize the effects of impaired executive function at home and help the child complete his or her homework assignments with less stress for the child and family.

Create a conducive learning environment

The area where the child works must be conducive to concentration and learning. A useful model is the child's classroom with appropriate seating and lighting, and removal of any distractions. Distractions can be visual, such as the presence of toys or television, which are a constant reminder of what the child would rather be doing; or auditory, such as the noise from electrical appliances and the chatter of siblings. Ensure the working surface only has equipment relevant to the task. The working environment must also be safe from curious younger brothers and sisters.

It is extremely helpful if parents create a daily homework timetable for the child and exchange a diary or log book between home and school. The diary or log book should include the teacher's expectations regarding the duration and content of each homework activity or assignment. Sometimes the homework can take hours when the teacher intended only several minutes on a specified task. The teacher can also provide parents with a list of all the necessary equipment and resources needed at home to complete a homework assignment.

The homework diary and planner can help the child remember which books to take home and the specific homework for each evening. An executive diary from a stationery store may make this strategy more appealing to the child. The techniques are explained as being appropriate for adult executives rather than for children with learning problems.

A timer can be used to remind the child how much time is remaining to complete each section of homework. It is also important to ensure that time scheduled for homework does not coincide with the child's favourite television programme. If it does, he or she may have priority use of the video recorder and can watch the programme once the homework is complete.

If regular breaks are necessary to promote concentration, the work can be divided into segments to indicate how much work the child has to complete before he or she can take a momentary break. The usual mistake is to expect too much prolonged concentration, especially after an intellectually exhausting day at school.

Teacher's preparation of homework

The teacher can highlight key aspects of the homework sheet, provide written explanations and ask questions to ensure the child knows which aspects of the homework material are relevant to his or her preparation of the assignment. The teacher can ask the child to formulate a plan before commencing the assignment to ensure the work is coherent and logical, especially if the homework is an essay. If the assignment takes several days to complete, it is important that the teacher regularly reviews the child's rough drafts and progress, which also increases the likelihood that the homework assignment will be completed on time.

Memory problems

If the child has difficulty remembering exactly what was set for homework and remembering relevant information during homework (a characteristic of impaired executive function), a solution is to buy an executive toy. A small digital cassette recorder used for dictation can provide a record of the teacher's spoken instructions, and the child can add his or her own comments or personal memo to the recording as a reminder of key information. The child and his or her parent will then know exactly what was said and what is relevant to the task. Another strategy is to have the telephone number of another child in the class, to ask the classmate for the relevant information.

Supervision

Parents and teachers soon become aware that a significant amount of supervision is going to be required. For a parent with other family commitments at the time that the child is doing his or her homework, this can be a major problem.

The child may have difficulty getting started and knowing what to do first. Procrastination can be an issue, and a parent may have to supervise the start of the homework. But once the child has started, this is not the end of the supervision. A parent will also need to be available if the child requires assistance should confusion arise, and to ensure that he or she has chosen the appropriate strategy. There can be a tendency for such children to have a closed mind to alternative strategies and a determination to pursue a particular approach, when other children would have recognized that it would be wise to consider an alternative approach. A technique to show that there is more than one line of thought is to provide the child with a list of alternative strategies to solve the particular problem: the child may need to know there is a 'plan B'.

Supervision is also necessary to help the child prioritize and plan, assist with word retrieval problems and maintain motivation. Motivation can be enhanced by specific rewards for concentration and effort.

Cognitive style

Special consideration should be given to the child's cognitive strengths and weaknesses. If the child's relative strength is in visual reasoning, then flow diagrams, graphic organizers and mind maps and demonstrations will enhance his or her understanding (Hubbard 2005). If the child's strength is in verbal skills then written instructions and discussion using metaphors (especially metaphors associated with the special interest) will help. Additional strategies include the use of a computer and keyboard, especially for those children who have problems with handwriting. Sometimes a parent acts as an 'executive secretary', types the material for the child and proofreads the answers. Homework is often a collaborative rather than solitary activity. Parents know from many years of experience that without their involvement, the work would not be completed on time or to the standard required.

Children with Asperger's syndrome often enjoy having access to a computer and may be more able to understand an educational concept if it is presented on a computer screen. Material presented by a person adds a social and linguistic dimension to the situation, which can increase the child's confusion. Teachers should therefore consider adapting the homework so that a considerable proportion of the work is conducted using a computer. Word processing facilities, especially graphics, grammar and spell check programs, are invaluable in improving the legibility and quality of the finished product.

If the parent is unable to help the child solve a particular problem, a solution is to come to an arrangement with the teacher whereby the teacher may be contacted by telephone without concern as to the time of day or night, such that he or she can talk directly to the child. Regular use of this approach can lead to a significant change in the type and amount of homework.

Finally, teaching a child with Asperger's syndrome requires special skills, and a parent is not expected to have those teaching skills. As a parent, one is also more emotionally involved than a class teacher and it can be difficult to be objective and emotionally detached. One option is to hire a homework tutor to provide the skilled guidance and supervision. However, this may be beyond the financial resources of most families.

Reducing the amount of work required at home

If homework is associated with such anguish, what can be done to reduce the despair of the child who is exhausted from a full day at school, the parents who try to motivate their child, and the teacher who recognizes that homework is not the most effective means of education for such children? If the standard amount of homework is demanded of the child, then everyone must recognize the considerable degree of time and commitment that is necessary from all parties to ensure it is completed satisfactorily and on time.

One option is to enable the child to complete the 'homework' at school. It can be undertaken at lunchtime and before or after classes in the child's home class or the school library. However, he or she would still require supervision and guidance from a teacher or assistant. In high school, some children have been able to graduate taking fewer subjects, and the extra time available in the school day has been dedicated to homework.

If all these strategies are unsuccessful, what is the alternative? I have yet to read a research paper that has clearly established a correlation between the hours of homework in childhood and adult success in terms of employment and quality of life. People may argue that homework encourages self-directed learning, but children with Asperger's syndrome often excel at self-directed learning when interested in the activity: their problem is learning in the social context of the classroom.

My opinion is that the child with Asperger's syndrome should be exempt from punishment for not completing homework assignments on time, and that there should be a maximum duration of homework of 30 minutes, unless the child or adolescent wants to spend more time on his or her homework. After that time, the parent signs the assignment and homework log to indicate that this was the amount of work completed in the time available, and the grade for homework should be based on the work completed. This recommendation can provide a great relief from stress for the child with Asperger's syndrome, his or her family and probably the teacher.

VISUAL THINKING

People with Asperger's syndrome have a different way of thinking, sometimes thinking in pictures rather than words. In a fascinating study, a group of adults with Asperger's syndrome spent several days wearing a small device that produced a beep at random intervals (Hurlburt, Happé and Frith 1994). They were asked to 'freeze' the content of their thinking when they heard the beep and record the nature of their thoughts. When this procedure is used with typical people, they describe a range of inner thoughts involving speech, feelings, bodily sensations and visual images.

However, the adults with Asperger's syndrome reported their thoughts primarily or solely in the form of images. Some people with Asperger's syndrome appear to have a predominantly visual style of thinking. This can have several advantages, as outlined by Temple Grandin:

> My mind is completely visual and spatial work such as drawing is easy. I taught myself drafting in six months. I have designed big steel and concrete cattle facilities, but remembering a phone number or adding up numbers in my head is still difficult. I have to write them down. Every piece of information I have memorized

is visual. If I have to remember an abstract concept I 'see' the page of the book or my notes in my mind and 'read' information from it. Melodies are the only things I can memorize without a visual image. I remember very little that I hear unless it is emotionally arousing or I can form a visual image. In class I take careful notes, because I would forget the auditory material. When I think about abstract concepts such as human relationships, I use visual similes. For example, relationships between people are like a glass sliding door. The door must be opened gently, if it is kicked it may shatter. If I had to learn a foreign language, I would have to do it by reading, and make it visual. (Grandin 1984, p.145)

Temple has written a book that explores her visual thinking and how this has affected her life and enabled her to develop quite remarkable design skills (Grandin 1995).

The disadvantage of this way of thinking is that school work is primarily presented for a verbal way of thinking. A teacher often uses speech and a lecture style to explain an educational concept rather than provide a practical demonstration. A strategy to help 'visualizers' is to make greater use of diagrams, models and active participation. For example, in maths lessons the child can have an abacus on his or her desk. The child can also learn to imagine the principles or events as real scenes. Adults with Asperger's syndrome have explained to me how they learned history or science by visualizing events – for example, running a mental video recording of changing molecular structures.

There are considerable advantages with this type of thinking. A person with Asperger's syndrome who is a visual thinker may have a natural talent for chess and snooker, and the greatest scientist of the twentieth century, Albert Einstein, was a visual thinker. He failed his school language tests but relied on visual methods of study. His theory of relativity is based on visual imagery of moving boxcars and riding on light beams. It is interesting that his personality and family history have elements indicative of Asperger's syndrome (Grandin 1984).

COGNITIVE TALENTS

There are children and adults with Asperger's syndrome who have cognitive abilities that are significantly above average, i.e. an IQ of over 130, and are sometimes described as gifted and talented (Lovecky 2004). This can provide both several advantages and disadvantages to the child. The advantages include a greater capacity to process and learn social cues and conventions intellectually. Advanced intellectual maturity may be admired by a teacher, and winning competitions can lead to greater status for the child and school. Academic success can raise the self-esteem of both young people and adults; often their social naïvety and eccentricity can be accepted, even appreciated, as part of the 'absent-minded professor' image. Cognitive talents could lead to a lucrative career developing technology or an illustrious career conducting research. However, there are many disadvantages.

Children with Asperger's syndrome are more socially and emotionally immature than their peers, which contributes towards their being socially isolated, ridiculed and tormented. Having considerably advanced intellectual maturity in comparison to one's peers can further increase social isolation and alienation. The child may have no peer group in his or her classroom, socially or intellectually. Having an impressive vocabulary and knowledge can lead adults to expect an equivalent maturity in social reasoning, emotion management and behaviour; they may be unjustly critical of the child who is unable to express these abilities as maturely as his or her age peers.

Having advanced intellectual maturity can be associated with a relatively high level of moral development and ideals. The young child with Asperger's syndrome then becomes extremely distressed in situations of injustice, such as cruelty to animals, and expresses concern about the effects of natural disasters on people. There can also be high ideals regarding fairness, affecting interactions and games with peers, who have a more flexible and egocentric view of the rules.

As with typical children who are intellectually gifted, the child has a conceptual capacity beyond what he or she can manage emotionally. The child may worry about concepts that would be beyond the thoughts of other children of that age. The gifted and talented child with Asperger's syndrome has fewer coping mechanisms than typical peers for managing the increased anxiety associated with advanced intellectual ability.

The profile of cognitive abilities associated with Asperger's syndrome can also affect the expression of cognitive talents. The person's conceptualization or solution may be extraordinary but the practical aspects of organizing the ideas into a coherent framework, and communicating thinking using speech, can be a significant problem. The child or adult knows the idea or solution is perfect but no one seems to be able to understand it.

We know that children and adults with Asperger's syndrome have a tendency to focus on the individual components of a problem. A detailed focus on components may identify aspects overlooked by others (Hermelin 2001), but presents the disadvantage of over-responding emotionally to relatively less significant problems. People with Asperger's syndrome are often perfectionists with high self-imposed standards of achievement, and tend to abandon a project quickly if there is little initial success. The child may have advanced intellectual abilities but have high self-imposed standards that can lead to considerable frustration. Children with Asperger's syndrome are notorious for their inability to cope with frustration.

When young children with Asperger's syndrome have considerably more mature intellectual reasoning than their peers, there can be an ability to create imaginary stories that are fascinating to other children (Lovecky 2004). The child can become the leader of a group of young children, eager to enact the stories. Later in childhood, creativity and talent in the arts may be a form of self-expression and personal satisfaction that is not primarily intended for an audience or admiration from peers (Hermelin 2001).

Deirdre Lovecky (2004) has studied children with Asperger's syndrome who are gifted and talented and noted that, at school, such children are rarely given work matching their cognitive ability. It is important that the class teacher recognizes the intellectual potential of such children and arranges an advanced curriculum. The child will also benefit from being enrolled in programs for gifted children, not just to extend knowledge and cognitive development, but also to provide an opportunity to meet a potential friend. The friendship may be based on exchanging information and intellectual discussions, but where else can the child find an intellectual peer of the same age to become a genuine friend?

We now recognize that significant advances in science and the arts have been attributable to individuals who had a different way of thinking and possessed many of the cognitive characteristics associated with Asperger's syndrome (James 2006). Typical people have a social/linguistic way of thinking, but there can be advantages in having an alternative perception and profile of cognitive abilities that can lead to valued talents. Liliana, a woman with Asperger's syndrome and considerable intellectual ability, said to me that 'language is a cage for thought', and many advances in science and philosophy have been achieved by alternative conceptualizations that have not been based on linguistic thought.

Lee, a student at Oxford University, explains that:

> I think that Asperger Syndrome is another perspective on the world. It's certainly helped me with the mathematical side of things. I find it very easy to think in highly abstract terms. I can solve a Rubik's Cube in two minutes. (Molloy and Vasil 2004, p.40)

And Rachel considers that:

> One of the reasons I joined Mensa was that I wanted to use it as a hallmark of my intelligence and say 'I have this amount of intelligence and can prove it because I'm in Mensa!' On the whole I do think most people with Asperger's tend to be fairly intelligent. If I could change myself and get rid of the Asperger's, I honestly don't think I would because I'm sure I'd lose part of my intelligence. (Molloy and Vasil 2004, p.43)

We need people with Asperger's syndrome to bring a new perspective on the problems of tomorrow.

KEY POINTS AND STRATEGIES

- Some young children with Asperger's syndrome start school with academic abilities above their grade level.

- There seem to be more children with Asperger's syndrome than one might expect at the extremes of cognitive ability.

- Profile of learning abilities at school:
    - Teachers soon recognize that the child has a distinctive learning style, being talented in understanding the logical and physical world, noticing details and remembering and arranging facts in a systematic fashion.
    - Children with Asperger's syndrome can be easily distracted, especially in the classroom. When problem solving, they appear to have a 'one-track mind' and a fear of failure.
    - As the child progresses through the school grades, teachers identify problems with organizational abilities, especially with regard to homework assignments and essays.
    - If the child with Asperger's syndrome is not successful socially at school, then academic success becomes more important as the primary motivation to attend school and for the development of self-esteem.
    - The profile or pattern of intellectual abilities is more important than the overall or Full Scale IQ.
    - At least 75 per cent of children with Asperger's syndrome also have a profile of learning abilities indicative of an additional diagnosis of Attention Deficit Disorder.
    - Psychologists divide attention into four components: the ability to sustain attention, to pay attention to relevant information, to shift attention when needed, and to encode attention – that is, to remember what was attended to. Children with Asperger's syndrome appear to have problems with all four aspects of attention.

- Executive function:
    - We now have considerable research evidence to confirm that some children, but more especially adolescents and adults, with Asperger's syndrome have impaired executive function.

        The psychological term *executive function* includes:
        - organizational and planning abilities
        - working memory
        - inhibition and impulse control
        - self-reflection and self-monitoring
        - time management and prioritizing

- understanding complex or abstract concepts
- using new strategies.
  - One strategy to reduce the problems associated with impaired executive functioning is to have someone act as an 'executive secretary'.
- Problem solving:
  - Research has indicated that children with Asperger's syndrome tend to continue using incorrect strategies and are less likely to learn from their mistakes, even when they know their strategy isn't working.
  - The child with Asperger's syndrome may prefer to use his or her own idiosyncratic approach to problem solving.
  - It is important to encourage flexibility in thinking and this can start at an early age. When playing with very young children with Asperger's syndrome, an adult can play the game of 'What else could it be?'
  - An adult can vocalize his or her thoughts when problem solving so that the child with Asperger's syndrome can listen to the various approaches the adult is considering in order to solve the problem.
- Coping with mistakes:
  - The learning profile of children and adults with Asperger's syndrome can include a tendency to focus on errors, a need to fix an irregularity and a desire to be a perfectionist.
  - It is important to change the child's perception of errors and mistakes.
  - Social Stories™ can be used to explain that we learn more from our mistakes than our successes; mistakes can lead to interesting discoveries, and an error is an opportunity, not a disaster.
- School achievement in reading and mathematics:
  - There are more children with Asperger's syndrome at the extremes of school achievement in reading and numeracy that one would expect.
  - From my clinical experience, conventional remedial reading programs have not been as effective with children with Asperger's syndrome as one would expect.
  - The difficulty for children with Asperger's syndrome who are able to solve complex mathematical problems can be explaining in words how they achieved the answer.
- Weak central coherence:
  - Children with Asperger's syndrome can be remarkably good at attending to detail but appear to have considerable difficulty perceiving and understanding the overall picture or gist.
  - Parents of a child or adult with Asperger's syndrome often remark on their son or daughter's ability to give vivid and accurate descriptions of events that occurred during infancy.

- Classroom strategies to encourage cognitive development:
  - Children with Asperger's syndrome appear to make the greatest advances in cognitive and academic abilities in a quiet, well-structured classroom.
  - The class teacher needs to create an 'Asperger friendly' environment based on the social, linguistic and cognitive abilities of the child. To create such an environment, it is essential that the class teacher should have access to information and expertise on Asperger's syndrome and attend relevant training courses.
  - The greatest cognitive and academic progress has been achieved by teachers who show an empathic understanding of the child. Such teachers are flexible in their teaching strategies, assessments and expectations. They invariably like and admire the child, respect his or her abilities and know the child's motivators and learning profile.

- Homework:
  - A major cause of anguish for children and teenagers with Asperger's syndrome, their families and teachers is the satisfactory completion of homework.
  - The area where the child works at home must be conducive to concentration and learning.
  - It is extremely helpful if parents create a daily homework timetable for the child and exchange a diary or log book between home and school.
  - The teacher can highlight key aspects of the homework sheet, provide written explanations and ask questions to ensure the child knows which aspects of the homework material are relevant to his or her preparation of the assignment.
  - My opinion is that the child with Asperger's syndrome should be exempt from punishment for not completing homework assignments on time, and that there should be a maximum duration of homework of 30 minutes, unless the child or adolescent wants to spend more time on his or her homework.

- We now recognize that significant advances in science and the arts have been attributable to individuals who had a different way of thinking and possessed many of the cognitive characteristics associated with Asperger's syndrome.

CHAPTER 10

Movement and Coordination

The clumsiness was particularly well demonstrated during PE
lessons. He was never able to swing with the rhythm of the group.
His movements never unfolded naturally and spontaneously – and
therefore pleasingly – from the proper coordination of the motor
system.

– Hans Asperger ([1944] 1991)

As much as people with Asperger's syndrome have a different way of thinking, they can
also have a different way of moving. When walking or running, the child's coordination
can be immature, and adults with Asperger's syndrome may have a strange, sometimes
idiosyncratic gait that lacks fluency and efficiency. On careful observation, there can be
a lack of synchrony in the movement of the arms and legs, especially when the person is
running (Gillberg 1989; Hallett *et al.* 1993). Parents often report that the child was
delayed by a month or two in learning to walk (Eisenmajer *et al.* 1996; Manjiviona and
Prior 1995), and needed considerable guidance in learning activities that required
manual dexterity such as tying shoelaces, dressing and using eating utensils (Szatmari,
Bartolucci and Bremner 1989a). Teachers may notice problems with fine motor skills,
such as the ability to write and use scissors. Activities that require coordination and
balance can also be affected, such as learning to ride a bicycle, skate or use a scooter.
Children and sometimes adults with Asperger's syndrome can have difficulty knowing
where their body is in space, which may often cause them to trip, bump into objects and
spill drinks. The overall appearance can be of someone who is clumsy.

The movement and coordination problems can be obvious to the physical education
(PE) teacher and other children during PE classes and sports, and in playground games
that require ball skills. The child with Asperger's syndrome can be immature in the
development of the ability to catch, throw and kick a ball (Tantam 1991). When
catching a ball with two hands, the arm movements are often poorly coordinated and

affected by problems with timing; i.e. the hands close in the correct position, but a fraction of a second too late. The child has taken too long to think about what to do. When throwing a ball, children with Asperger's syndrome will often not look in the direction of the target before throwing, which will affect their accuracy (Manjiviona and Prior 1995). One of the consequences of not being successful or popular at ball games is the exclusion of the child from some of the social games in the playground. Such children may choose to actively avoid these activities, knowing they are not as able as their peers. However, when they bravely attempt to join in the activity, they can be deliberately excluded by other children due to being perceived as a liability, not an asset, to the team. Thus, children with Asperger's syndrome are less able to improve ball skills by practising with their peers.

From an early age, parents need to provide tuition and practice in ball skills, not in order that their child becomes an exceptional sportsperson, but to ensure that he or she has the basic competence to be included in the popular ball games of peers. However, it is interesting that some children with Asperger's syndrome have a greater coordination and fluency of movement when swimming, develop remarkable agility when using the trampoline, acquire coordination through practice in solitary sports, such as golf, that can become a special interest, and enjoy recreational activities such as riding. This can be to a level in advance of peers.

Movement skills can be assessed by observation and a range of standardized tests that measure specific movement abilities. For the naïve observer, there is an impression of clumsiness in the majority of children with Asperger's syndrome, but several studies using specialized assessment procedures have indicated that specific expressions of movement disturbance occur in almost all children with Asperger's syndrome (Ghaziuddin et al. 1994; Gillberg 1989; Gowen and Miall 2005; Green et al. 2002; Hippler and Klicpera 2004; Klin et al. 1995; Manjiviona and Prior 1995; Miyahara et al. 1997).

Thus Christopher Gillberg has included motor clumsiness as one of his six diagnostic criteria (Gillberg and Gillberg 1989). In contrast, the criteria of Peter Szatmari and colleagues, the DSM-IV criteria of the American Psychiatric Association, and the ICD-10 criteria of the World Health Organization make no direct reference to movement abilities. However, the DSM-IV has a list of features associated with Asperger's syndrome that includes the presence of motor clumsiness and awkwardness that is relatively mild but may contribute to peer rejection and social isolation. At present, clumsiness is considered as a characteristic associated with Asperger's syndrome, but not a defining feature in three of the four diagnostic criteria.

PROFILE OF MOVEMENT ABILITIES

The profile of movement abilities can include impaired manual dexterity (Gunter, Ghaziuddin and Ellis 2002; Manjiviona and Prior 1995; Miyahara et al. 1997), impaired coordination, balance, grasp and tone (Nass and Gutman 1997), and slower speed on manual tasks (Nass and Gutman 1997; Szatmari *et al.* 1989a). There can be a problem with balance, as tested by examining the ability to stand on one leg with eyes closed, and tandem walking, i.e. the task of walking a straight line as though it were a tightrope (Iwanaga, Kawasaki and Tsuchida 2000; Manjiviona and Prior 1995; Tantam 1991). Temple Grandin describes how she is 'unable to balance when I place one foot in front of the other (tandem walking)' (Grandin 1984). Nita Jackson describes her difficulties with walking:

> But learning to walk was the worst. Never thinking of using my arms to help me, my upper body always remained stiff, as if my arms were sewn to my sides. I found tandem walking (placing one foot in front of the other as though I were treading a tightrope) impossible, so I developed this odd gait – waddling like a duck or a human with severe bladder problems. This was only one of the many reasons my peers found for bullying me. (N. Jackson 2002, p.87)

These characteristics will affect the child's ability to use adventure playground equipment, and his or her competence in some activities in the gymnasium. They will also increase the child's vulnerability to being teased.

Hans Asperger noted that some of the children he saw had unusual facial expressions. For one child, he described how 'His facial expressions were sparse and rigid' (Asperger [1944] 1991, p.57). There can be a lack of variation in facial movements to express thoughts and feelings. A 'flat' facial expression that lacks tone and subtle movements can also make the person appear sad. Clumsy or gauche body language is included in the diagnostic criteria of Christopher Gillberg (Gillberg and Gillberg 1989). I have also observed that the body language may not be a synchronized 'dance' with the conversation partner.

While we have considerable research and clinical knowledge regarding the social, emotional, linguistic and cognitive abilities of people with Asperger's syndrome, we know relatively little about movement abilities (Smith 2000). In the next decade, there must be an increase in research regarding this particular aspect of Asperger's syndrome and more remedial strategies developed and evaluated to improve movement and coordination.

EARLY DETECTION OF MOVEMENT DISTURBANCE

Recent research has indicated that abnormal movement patterns can be detected in infants who later develop the clinical signs of Asperger's syndrome. Osnat Teitelbaum and colleagues analysed the home video recordings of the early years of 16 children with Asperger's syndrome (Teitelbaum *et al.* 2004). The movement patterns and reflexes of the children were examined in considerable detail and the study identified primitive reflexes that persisted too long, and reflexes that did not appear at the expected age. The authors noted that some of the infants who later developed Asperger's syndrome had an unusual mouth shape, described as a *moebius mouth*: that is, a tented upper lip and flat lower lip. There were indications of unusual asymmetry when the children were lying on their backs and reaching for and manipulating toys – for example, only using one hand – and a different movement or rotation from supine to prone, i.e. where they changed position from lying on their backs to their tummies. The development of sitting can be delayed by a few months, and the crawling movement may not have the basic diagonally opposing limb patterns. Analysis of the infants' attempts to walk identified problems with falling, such as a tendency to fall to one side and a failure to use protective reflexes.

Another reflex that was late in developing was that of turning the head to maintain a vertical position when the body is rotated. Between six and eight months old, typical infants can be held in the air at the waist and their body slowly tilted about 45 degrees to one side then back to the vertical position and then tilted to the other side and they will be expected to have a compensatory movement of the head to maintain a vertical head position. This is known as the 'Tilting Test', and a delay in achieving this ability could be another indicator of the delayed reflexes observed in infants who later develop signs of Asperger's syndrome.

Further research is needed to confirm and describe in more detail the unusual movement patterns and delay in reflexes during infancy that could be associated with Asperger's syndrome. Parents will be interested in assessment procedures that could indicate whether a new addition to the family is developing signs of Asperger's syndrome, and paediatricians may consider using such assessments as an early screening system to identify an infant whose development will require careful monitoring for other signs of the syndrome.

THE MENTAL PLANNING AND COORDINATION OF MOVEMENT

A person is described as having *apraxia* when there are problems with the conceptualization and planning of movement, so that the action is less proficient and coordinated than one would expect. Studies have indicated that children with Asperger's syndrome have problems with the mental preparation and planning of movement with relatively intact motor pathways (Minshew, Goldstein and Siegel 1997; Rinehart *et al.* 2001; Rogers *et al.* 1996; Smith and Bryson 1998; Weimer *et al.* 2001). Poorly planned movement and a slow mental preparation time may be a more precise description than simply being clumsy.

Ben describes the experience of having a delay or feeling of disengagement between thought and action:

> I have always felt a disconnection between my body and my brain. Sometimes it's as if I don't have a body. My body has failed me. I fall down when I try to turn. I have problems seeing. I can't focus. I can't make my hands move the way I want them to. (LaSalle 2003, p.47)

There may also be problems with proprioception – that is, the integration of information about the position and movement of the body in space (Weimer *et al.* 2001) and the ability to maintain posture and balance (Gepner and Mestre 2002; Molloy, Dietrich, and Bhattacharya 2003). These are skills that are often used in the climbing and adventure games of children. There can be a tendency to fall off climbing apparatus and a risk of falling and injury when climbing a tree. The child with Asperger's syndrome may again be reluctant to participate in such activities with peers and friends. I have also known several children with Asperger's syndrome who really enjoy being upside down for long periods of time. These children, while watching television, adopt a position whereby their feet are at the top of the chair and their head rests just above the floor.

When examining general movement abilities of children with Asperger's syndrome, there can be signs of *ataxia*; that is, less orderly muscular coordination and an abnormal pattern of movement. This can include movements being performed with abnormal force, rhythm and accuracy, and an unsteady gait. Observations of walking and running, climbing stairs, jumping, and touching a target (the finger to nose test) of children with Asperger's syndrome indicate signs of ataxia (Ahsgren *et al.* 2005). Occupational therapists, physiotherapists and medical specialists in developmental movement disorders will need to consider screening new referrals for the possibility of an additional diagnosis of Asperger's syndrome (Ahsgren *et al.* 2005).

One of the movement disturbances associated with Asperger's syndrome is lax joints (Tantam, Evered and Hersov 1990). We do not know if this is a structural abnormality or due to low muscle tone, but the autobiography of David Miedzianik describes how:

> At infant school I can seem to remember playing a lot of games and them learning us to write. They used to tell me off a lot for holding my pen wrong at infant and primary school. I still don't hold my pen very good to this day, so my handwriting has never been good. I think a lot of the reason why I hold my pen badly is that the joints of my finger tips are double jointed and I can bend my fingers right back. (Miedzianik 1986, p.4)

Should problems occur from lax joints or immature or unusual grasp, then the child may be referred to an occupational therapist or physiotherapist for assessment and remedial activities. This should be a priority with a young child, since so much school work requires the use of a pencil or pen.

When Asperger originally defined the features of the syndrome, he described problems copying various rhythms. This characteristic has been described in one of Temple Grandin's autobiographical essays:

> Both as a child and as an adult I have difficulty keeping in time with a rhythm. At a concert where people are clapping in time with the music, I have to follow another person sitting beside me. I can keep a rhythm moderately well by myself, but it is extremely difficult to synchronize my rhythmic motions with other people or with musical accompaniment. (Grandin 1984, p.165)

This explains a feature that is quite conspicuous when walking next to a person with Asperger's syndrome. As two people walk side by side they tend to synchronize the movements of their limbs, much as occurs when soldiers are on parade: their movements have the same rhythm. The person with Asperger's syndrome appears to walk to the beat of a different drum.

HANDWRITING

Hans Asperger was the first to describe the problems some children have with handwriting. His original published study was based on the careful observations of four children, and for one child, Fritz, he observed that 'in his tense fist the pencil could not run smoothly', and with another, Ernst, 'The pen did not obey him, it stuck and it spluttered' (Asperger [1944] 1991, p.63). Teachers and parents can become quite concerned about difficulties with handwriting. The individual letters can be poorly formed and larger than would be expected, for children and adults (Beversdorf *et al.* 2001). The technical term is *macrographia*. The child can take too long to complete each letter, causing delay in completing written tasks. While the rest of the class have written several sentences, the child with Asperger's syndrome is still deliberating over the first sentence, trying to write legibly, and becoming increasingly frustrated or embarrassed about his or her inability to write neatly and consistently.

Sometimes the word, written in pencil, has been frequently rubbed out as the child considers the letters are not perfect, an exact copy of the printed text in the book. An activity in class may be refused because of an aversion to the requirement to write, not necessarily an aversion to the topic. Teachers may become frustrated by the illegibility of the handwriting, but need to remember that this is an expression of a movement disorder, not necessarily a lack of commitment to the work.

Some children with Asperger's syndrome become fascinated by handwriting and develop a special interest in calligraphy. The problem here is that the child takes too long to complete a written assignment in class. Each letter may be perfect but the child has become more absorbed in the formation of the letters than the content of the sentence.

When a child with Asperger's syndrome has a problem with handwriting, there are several options. Remedial exercises to improve motor coordination – basically, lots of practice – can improve the fine motor skills needed to write legibly, but such activities can be extremely boring and resisted by the child. An occupational therapist can suggest modifications to improve handwriting skills, such as a slightly slanted writing surface and a pen that is easier to grasp. A scribe can be used in class to write for the child. However, I suggest to teachers and parents that handwriting is becoming an obsolete skill in the twenty-first century: modern technology can come to the rescue in terms of typing, not handwriting.

The young child with Asperger's syndrome should be encouraged to learn to type and use a keyboard, computer and printer in the classroom. While basic writing skills are still needed, as the current generation of children become adults, they will be able to talk to a word-processing device which will record and print speech. Few people today write someone a handwritten letter; communication is predominantly by typed e-mail. High school and university exams for adolescents and young adults with Asperger's syndrome can be completed by typing answers to questions, which is a more efficient means of expressing knowledge and more easily read by examiners. Thus, teachers and parents should not be overly concerned about poor handwriting skills; rather, ensure that the child learns to type. When this option is not available, some children may need to be allowed extra time to complete tasks and exams.

ACTIVITIES AND STRATEGIES TO IMPROVE MOVEMENT AND COORDINATION

When there is recognition of problems with the development and coordination of movement, an assessment by an occupational therapist or physiotherapist can determine the degree of delay and the profile of movement abilities. This provides a baseline against which progress can be measured and remedial activities designed, implemented and evaluated. The assessment can indicate adjustments that need to be made both in the person's daily life and in the expectations of others, to accommodate specific movement disturbance. It is also important to assess how impaired movement abilities may be affecting the child's daily life, especially in terms of self-care skills, self-esteem, inclusion or exclusion by peers, and the potential for the child to be ridiculed. Being described as clumsy has significant practical and psychological implications for a child.

A therapist can suggest activities to be done at home that will improve movement abilities, and may include the child in a movement therapy program. It is important that the remedial activities at home, in therapy and at school are enjoyable. The child with Asperger's syndrome will be acutely aware of being less able than his or her peers and reluctant to participate unless the activity is intrinsically enjoyable and there is clear progress, encouragement and success.

The physical education teacher needs to be aware of the nature of Asperger's syndrome and how to adapt PE activities (Groft and Block 2003). The adaptations should include an emphasis on physical fitness rather than competitive team sports. When requiring the child to participate in ball games, the teacher should discourage other children from laughing if the child fumbles with the ball, and should not have team leaders select team members, which so often results both in the child with Asperger's syndrome being chosen last, and in groans from the other children that they must have such a clumsy child as a member of their team.

It is also important that the PE teacher realizes that the gymnasium is an aversive environment for children with Asperger's syndrome. The noise levels can be high, with the shouts of children reverberating from the walls; the fast-moving action hectic and bewildering for a child with motor planning problems; and close physical contact with other children inevitable. The teacher will need to be able to handle the degree of distress or over-reaction when the child makes an error, or his or her team loses.

There are advantages in providing a mentor who can support and protect the child with Asperger's syndrome from ridicule. The PE teacher can be inventive with regard to some team games. For example, the child's ability to identify errors and knowledge of the rules would make him or her an ideal referee's assistant, while an ability with numbers might make the child the ideal person to keep score and be responsible for the school league tables.

When treating specific movement problems, it will help if the teacher or therapist demonstrates what to do from beside, rather than facing, the person with Asperger's syndrome. Video recordings may be used to enable the child to see his or her movements, and to document how the program has improved specific abilities (Manjiviona and Prior 1995). Sometimes, hands-on-hands teaching will provide guidance in the movements required. Finally, while a daily fitness program can improve movement and coordination abilities, the release of physical energy can also be an emotional restorative for children with Asperger's syndrome, who have a problem with emotion expression and management.

INVOLUNTARY MOVEMENTS OR TICS

Clinical experience and observation of children and adults with Asperger's syndrome has indicated that there can be occasional involuntary movements or tics. Research has indicated that between 20 and 60 per cent of children with Asperger's syndrome develop tics (Gadow and DeVincent 2005; Hippler and Klicpera 2004; Kerbeshian and Burd 1986, 1996; Marriage *et al.* 1993; Nass and Gutman 1997; Sverd 1991). The tics can range from momentary 'twitches' to complex movements. Sometimes the vocal muscles produce an involuntary sound or phrase. Table 10.1 gives some examples of simple and complex motor and vocal tics.

The involuntary movement or sound is unexpected and purposeless. If a child with Asperger's syndrome develops tics, the first signs are usually recognized in early childhood, and over time the frequency and complexity of the tics gradually increases, with a relative peak in involuntary movements between the ages of 10 and 12 years. In late adolescence, the frequency of tics tends to diminish, with 40 per cent of children who develop tics being tic-free by age 18 (Burd *et al.* 2001).

The child's 'vocabulary' of tics can change over time, as different types of tic come and go, and there can be months when the child is relatively tic-free. Tics can disappear when the child is concentrating on an activity and become more noticeable during specific activities, such as answering open-ended questions (Nass and Gutman 1997). Involuntary movements can occur when the child is relaxed, for example when sitting and watching the television; and while stress does not directly cause the tic, the frequency of tics can be greater when experiencing stress.

Table 10.1 **Simple and complex motor tics**

Simple motor tics	Complex motor tics
Eye blinking	Hopping
Facial grimacing	Twirling
Nose twitching	Touching objects
Lip pouting	Biting lip
Shoulder shrugging	Facial gestures
Arm jerking	Licking
Head nodding	Pinching (self and others)
Tongue protrusion	Waving both arms, bent at the elbow, like bird
Throat clearing	wings
Sniffing	Muttering under the breath
Grunting	Animal noises
Whistling	Repetition of word or phrase just uttered
Coughing	Complex breathing patterns
Snorting	
Barking	
Sucking sound	

The tics may not just be involuntary movements and sounds. I have known adolescents who have Asperger's syndrome and a tic disorder make comments such as 'irrational thoughts pop up into my brain'. I call these thought and emotion tics. The thought and subsequent action or feeling may not be related to the context. Sometimes the thought can be to do something inappropriate and potentially embarrassing or the emotion tic can be a sudden feeling of intense sadness, anger or anxiety. These feelings last only a few seconds but can be of concern if they occur frequently throughout the day.

We know that tics are due to a disorder in the planning loop between the cortex and the movement centres of the brain, and the activity of the neurotransmitters dopamine and norepinephrine (Kutscher 2005). Medical treatment to reduce the frequency of tics is based on lowering dopamine levels. Parents need to be aware that some medications, such as the stimulant medication to treat ADHD, increase dopamine levels and can increase the frequency of tics.

As the movement is involuntary, the child does not consciously know when the tic is going to occur and thus has difficulty inhibiting the movement or sound. Unfortunately, actions such as intermittent sniffing can be infuriating for family members and lead to teasing and ridicule by peers at school. It is important that family members, teachers and peers do not criticize or ridicule the child for his or her involuntary movements or sounds. Sometimes it is best simply to ignore the tics and for a parent to offer sympathy and emotional support if the child is distressed by the response of others to his or her involuntary movements and sounds. The tics can interfere with activities in the class-room, with the child taking longer to complete work due to the frequency of involun-tary actions that disrupt his or her attention, and sometimes distract other children. The teacher can be a role model for the acceptance of the tics, if necessary providing extra time for the child to complete an activity, and encouraging the other children to try to ignore the movements or sounds.

Clinical psychologists and psychiatrists are concerned about the development of tics, as clinical experience and recent research has indicated that some children with Asperger's syndrome can develop signs of a further three distinct developmental disor-ders. Tourette's syndrome is diagnosed in a child when there is a combination of at least two motor tics and at least one vocal tic, and the tics have lasted at least a year. Children with a combination of Asperger's syndrome and Tourette's syndrome are also at greater risk of having signs of ADHD, and of developing an anxiety disorder such as Obsessive Compulsive Disorder (Epstein and Saltzman-Benaiah 2005; Gadow and DeVincent 2005). Thus, although the development of tics is considered as relatively benign, when identifying tics during a diagnostic assessment, clinicians should also screen for signs of ADHD, and be aware of the possibility that the child could also develop signs of OCD. Clinicians also need to be aware of how this particular combination of disorders will affect the child's daily life, and be familiar with any treatment and education modifications that may be required.

DETERIORATION IN MOVEMENT ABILITIES

There have been reported cases in the research literature of adolescents with Asperger's syndrome developing a slow and steady deterioration in movement abilities (Dhossche 1998; Ghaziuddin, Quinlan and Ghaziuddin 2005; Hare and Malone 2004; Realmuto and August 1991; Wing and Attwood 1987; Wing and Shah 2000). Such cases are extremely unusual. The pattern of deterioration is of an increased slowness affecting movements and spoken responses. The person has difficulty starting and completing movements and becomes increasingly reliant on physical guidance and verbal prompt-ing during activities such as making a bed or getting dressed. Sometimes the person may momentarily 'freeze' during an activity, and at times may demonstrate a resting tremor, a slow shuffling gait, muscle rigidity and a flat, almost mask-like face. These characteris-tics resemble the movement patterns associated with catatonia and Parkinson's disease.

The deterioration in movement tends to occur between the ages of 10 and 19 years, and is more likely in an adolescent with autism rather than Asperger's syndrome: i.e. the person has a significant learning and language disability. However, there have been rare cases of such deterioration in teenagers with Asperger's syndrome. The pattern of deteri-oration only resembles, but cannot be directly comparable with, our conceptualization of catatonia and Parkinson's disease, and we should consider using a new term: autistic catatonia (Hare and Malone 2004). We are not sure if the deterioration in movement abilities is due to a specific neurological condition, an unusual expression of the psycho-motor retardation and lack of motivation associated with a clinical depression, or a significant deterioration in the cognitive ability to plan a movement and execute a response, i.e. for the thought to be converted into action.

Fortunately, we are exploring a range of treatment options (Dhossche 1998; Ghaziuddin *et al.* 2005; Hare and Malone 2004). Should the person develop signs of autistic catatonia, it is important that he or she is referred to a neurologist or neuropsychiatrist for a thorough examination of movement skills. Medication and other therapeutic techniques can significantly reduce the expression of this rare movement disorder. There are also simple techniques that parents can use to help initiate or re-start the movement. For example, another person touching the limb or hand that needs to move can be of considerable help, or working alongside the person with a duplicate set of equipment can be enough to start the required movement. Listening to music can maintain movement fluency. Physiotherapists have also developed activities for people with Parkinson's disease that could be applied to an adolescent with Asperger's syndrome and autistic catatonia.

EXCELLENCE IN MOVEMENT ABILITIES

While we know that Asperger's syndrome can be associated with impaired movement abilities, I have known of many children and adults with Asperger's syndrome who have achieved abilities in movement skills that have been exceptional and contributed towards winning national and international championships. The movement disturbance does not appear to affect some sporting activities such as swimming, using the trampoline, playing golf and horse riding. These are also activities that can be practised in solitude. Because of relative success in these activities, the child with Asperger's syndrome can develop a special interest in the activity and, with extensive practice and single-minded determination, achieve a level of proficiency that reaches a very high standard.

There can be ability with endurance sports such as marathon running. Once the running movement has become efficient, the person with Asperger's syndrome can be remarkably tolerant of discomfort and able to just keep running. Some sports such as fencing can be enjoyed by children with Asperger's syndrome. The participant has to wear a mask (no problems with eye contact with the opponent) and there are set movements and responses to learn. Martial arts can also be appealing, especially if there is a slow-motion approach to initially learning defensive and offensive actions. The history and culture of martial arts can also be an intellectual interest for the child with Asperger's syndrome. The indoor games of pool and snooker are not sports associated with agility, but adolescents with Asperger's syndrome can have a natural understanding of the geometry of the moving balls. Although Jerry Newport, a man with Asperger's syndrome, said to me, 'I never had a sense of natural grace,' children with Asperger's syndrome do have the potential to participate in and enjoy a variety of sports and sometimes even to excel at specific sports.

KEY POINTS AND STRATEGIES

- There is an impression of clumsiness in at least 60 per cent of children with Asperger's syndrome, but several studies using specialized assessment procedures have indicated that specific expressions of movement disturbance occur in almost all children with Asperger's syndrome.

- When walking or running, the child's coordination can be immature, and adults with Asperger's syndrome may have a strange, sometimes idiosyncratic gait that lacks fluency and efficiency.

- Teachers may notice problems with fine motor skills, such as the ability to write and use scissors.

- Some children with Asperger's syndrome can be immature in the development of the ability to catch, throw and kick a ball.

- From an early age, parents need to provide tuition and practice in ball skills, not in order that their child becomes an exceptional sportsperson, but to ensure that he or she has the basic competence to be included in the popular ball games of peers.

- Recent research has indicated that abnormal movement patterns can be detected in infants who later develop the clinical signs of Asperger's syndrome.

- Poorly planned movement and slower mental preparation time may be a more precise description than simply being clumsy.

- Teachers and parents can become quite concerned about difficulties with handwriting.

- I suggest to teachers and parents that handwriting is becoming an obsolete skill in the twenty-first century: modern technology can come to the rescue in terms of typing rather than handwriting.

- The physical education teacher needs to be aware of the nature of Asperger's syndrome and how to adapt PE activities.

- Clinical experience and observation of children and adults with Asperger's syndrome has indicated that there can be occasional involuntary movements or tics.

- The movement disturbance does not appear to affect some sporting activities such as swimming, using the trampoline, playing golf and horse riding.

CHAPTER 11

Sensory Sensitivity

In the sense of taste we find almost invariably very pronounced likes and dislikes. It is no different with the sense of touch. Many children have an abnormally strong dislike of particular tactile sensations. They cannot tolerate the roughness of new shirts, or of mended socks. Washing water too can often be a source of unpleasant sensations and, hence, of unpleasant scenes. There is hypersensitivity too against noise. Yet the same children who are often distinctly hypersensitive to noise in particular situations, in other situations may appear to be hyposensitive.

– Hans Asperger ([1944] 1991)

Clinicians and academics define Asperger's syndrome primarily by the person's profile of abilities in the areas of social reasoning, empathy, language and cognitive abilities, but one of the attributes of Asperger's syndrome, clearly identified in autobiographies and parents' description of their child, is a hyper- and hyposensitivity to specific sensory experiences. Recent research studies and review papers have confirmed an unusual pattern of sensory perception and reaction (Dunn, Smith Myles and Orr 2002; Harrison and Hare 2004; Hippler and Klicpera 2004; Jones, Quigney and Huws 2003; O'Neill and Jones 1997; Rogers and Ozonoff 2005). Some adults with Asperger's syndrome consider their sensory sensitivity has a greater impact on their daily lives than problems with making friends, managing emotions and finding appropriate employment. Unfortunately, clinicians and academics have tended to ignore this aspect of Asperger's syndrome and we do not have a satisfactory explanation of why the person has an unusual sensory sensitivity, or a range of effective strategies to modify sensory sensitivity.

The most common sensitivity is to very specific sounds but there can also be sensitivity to tactile experiences, light intensity, the taste and texture of food and specific aromas. There can be an under- or over-reaction to the experience of pain and discomfort, and the sense of balance, movement perception and body orientation can be unusual. One or several sensory systems can be affected such that everyday sensations are perceived as unbearably intense or apparently not perceived at all. Parents are often bewildered as to why these sensations are intolerable or not noticed, while the person with Asperger's syndrome is equally bewildered as to why other people do not have the same level of sensitivity.

Parents often report that the child may genuinely notice sounds that are too faint for others to hear, is overly startled by sudden noises, or perceives sounds of a particular pitch (such as the sound of a hand-dryer or vacuum cleaner) as unbearable. The child has to cover his or her ears to block out the sound or is desperate to get away from the specific noise. The child may dislike gentle gestures of affection such as a hug or kiss, as the sensory (not necessarily the emotional) experience is unpleasant. Bright sunlight can be almost 'blinding', specific colours are avoided as being too intense, and the child may notice and become transfixed by visual details, such as dust floating in a shaft of sunlight. A young child with Asperger's syndrome may have a self-imposed restricted diet that excludes food of a specific texture, taste, smell or temperature. Aromas such as perfumes or cleaning products can be avidly avoided because they cause the child to feel nauseous. There can also be problems with the sense of balance and the child may fear having his or her feet leave the ground and hate being upside down.

In contrast, there can be a lack of sensitivity to some sensory experiences, such as not responding to particular sounds, a failure to express pain when injured, or an apparent lack of need for warm clothing in an extremely cold winter. The sensory system can at one moment be hypersensitive and, in another moment, hyposensitive. However, some sensory experiences evoke intense pleasure, such as the sound and tactile sensation of a washing machine vibrating or the range of colours emitted by a street light.

SENSORY OVERLOAD

Children and adults with Asperger's syndrome often describe feeling a sensation of sensory overload. Clare Sainsbury has Asperger's syndrome and she explains the effects of sensory problems at school:

> The corridors and halls of almost any mainstream school are a constant tumult of noises echoing, fluorescent lights (a particular source of visual and auditory stress for people on the autistic spectrum), bells ringing, people bumping into each other, the smells of cleaning products and so on. For anyone with the sensory hyper-sensitivities and processing problems typical of an autistic spectrum condition, the result is that we often spend most of our day perilously close to sensory overload. (Sainsbury 2000, p.101)

The intense sensory experiences, described by Nita Jackson as 'dynamic sensory surges' (N. Jackson 2002, p.53), result in the person with Asperger's syndrome being extremely stressed, anxious and almost 'shell shocked' in situations that are not perceived as aversive but enjoyable for other children. The child with sensory sensitivity becomes hypervigilant, tense and distractible in sensory stimulating environments such as the classroom, unsure when the next painful sensory experience will occur. The child actively avoids specific situations such as school corridors, playgrounds, busy shopping malls and supermarkets which are known to be too intense a sensory experience. The fearful anticipation can become so severe, an anxiety disorder can develop, such as a phobia of dogs because they might suddenly bark, or agoraphobia (fear of public places), as home is a relatively safe and controlled sensory experience. Some social situations such as attending a birthday party may be avoided, not only because of uncertainty regarding the expected social conventions, but also because of the noise levels of exuberant children and the risk of balloons popping.

THE DIAGNOSTIC ASSESSMENT AND DIAGNOSTIC CRITERIA

We know that sensory sensitivity can be identified in infants who later develop the other signs of autism or Asperger's syndrome (Dawson *et al.* 2000; Gillberg *et al.* 1990), and specific aspects of sensory sensitivity could be included in a prospective screening assessment for very young children at risk for subsequently developing other signs of Asperger's syndrome. We also know that the signs are more conspicuous in early childhood and gradually diminish during adolescence, but can remain a life-long characteristic for some adults with Asperger's syndrome (Baranek, Foster and Berkson 1997; Church *et al.* 2000).

Screening instruments are designed to identify a child who may have signs of Asperger's syndrome and needs a comprehensive diagnostic assessment by an experienced clinician. The current screening instruments (see Chapter 1) include questions on sensory sensitivity, as clinicians recognize that an unusual pattern of sensory sensitivity differentiates children with Asperger's syndrome from typical children (Rogers and Ozonoff 2005). Sensory sensitivity is recognized as a feature of severe autism, and the primary diagnostic assessment instrument for autism, the Autism Diagnostic Interview – Revised or ADI-R (Rutter, Le Couteur and Lord 2003), includes a series of questions for parents that examine whether the child has ever been oversensitive to noise or had an unusual reaction to tastes, aromas or tactile experiences. At present, there is no equivalent to the ADI-R for Asperger's syndrome, but I and other clinicians include the compilation of information on sensory sensitivity during the diagnostic assessment, and a history of unusual sensory perception is considered as a confirmatory sign of Asperger's syndrome. However, unusual sensory perception is not included in any of the four diagnostic criteria for Asperger's syndrome. Future revisions of the diagnostic criteria should include reference to an unusual sensory perception, especially as the consequences can have a significant effect on the person's quality of life.

A conceptual framework

Clinicians and academics need a conceptual and descriptive framework to examine the sensory experiences of children and adults with Asperger's syndrome, and Bogdashina (2003) and Harrison and Hare (2004) have suggested that a person with Asperger's syndrome can have:

- both hyper- and hyposensitivity to sensory experiences
- sensory distortions
- sensory 'tune outs'
- sensory overload
- unusual sensory processing
- difficulty identifying the source channel of sensory information.

Some sensory and perceptual experiences cause great discomfort and the person often develops a range of adaptive coping and compensatory strategies. However, some sensory experiences such as listening to a clock ticking and chiming can be extremely enjoyable and the person is eager to gain access to those experiences that are enjoyable (Jones *et al.* 2003). Whether it causes pleasure or discomfort, the sensory world is certainly perceived differently by people with Asperger's syndrome.

Assessment instruments

We now have a choice of several assessment instruments that are designed to measure sensory sensitivity in all sensory modalities. The Sensory Behaviour Schedule (SBS) is a 17-item screening questionnaire designed to provide a brief description of sensory perception and associated behaviours (Harrison and Hare 2004). The Sensory Profile is a 125-item questionnaire that measures the degree to which children from the ages of 5 to 11 years exhibit problems in sensory processing, sensory modulation, behavioural and emotional responses to sensory experiences and hyper- and hypo-responsiveness (Dunn 1999b). For greater convenience there is also the Short Sensory Profile that only takes about ten minutes for parents to complete (Dunn 1999a).

The Sensory Profile Checklist Revised, or SPCR, is an extremely comprehensive assessment instrument for children with autism and Asperger's syndrome. The checklist has 232 questions for parents to complete that identify sensory strengths and weaknesses, and is designed to identify appropriate remedial activities (Bogdashina 2003).

Clinicians can develop their own assessment instruments, including a checklist of known sensory experiences that may be factors that contribute to anxious or agitated behaviour. An assessment of the child's circumstances at school can include examining sensory experiences such as the sounds of marker pens on a whiteboard, the flickering light and noise from fluorescent lighting, creaking chairs and floors, the room temperature, amount of background noise and aromas of deodorants, art equipment and cleaning products. When I observe a child with Asperger's syndrome who is in circumstances associated with challenging behaviour I close my eyes and listen, take a deep breath and identify any aromas and try to 'look through the eyes' and sensory system of a child with Asperger's syndrome.

SOUND SENSITIVITY

Between 70 and 85 per cent of children with Asperger's syndrome have an extreme sensitivity to specific sounds (Bromley *et al.* 2004; Smith Myles *et al.* 2000). Clinical observation and personal accounts of people with Asperger's syndrome suggest that there are three types of noise that are perceived as extremely unpleasant. The first category is sudden, unexpected noises, that one adult with Asperger's syndrome described as 'sharp', such as a dog barking, telephone ringing, someone coughing, a school fire alarm, the clicking of a pen top, or crackling sounds. The second category is high-pitched, continuous sounds, particularly the sound of small electric motors used in domestic electrical equipment such as food processors or vacuum cleaners or the high-pitched sound of a toilet flushing. The third category is confusing, complex or multiple sounds such as occur in shopping centres or noisy social gatherings.

As a parent or teacher, it may be difficult to empathize with the person, as these sounds are not perceived by typical people as unduly unpleasant. However, a suitable analogy for the experience is the discomfort many people have to specific sounds, such as the noise of fingernails scraping down a school blackboard. The mere thought of this sound can make some people shiver with revulsion.

The following quotations by people with Asperger's syndrome illustrate the intensity of the sensory experience and associated pain or discomfort. The first is by Temple Grandin:

> Loud, sudden noises still startle me. My reaction to them is more intense than other people's. I still hate balloons, because I never know when one will pop and make me jump. Sustained high-pitched motor noises, such as hair dryers and bathroom vent fans, still bother me, lower frequency motor noises do not. (Grandin 1988, p.3)

Darren White described how:

> I was also frightened of the vacuum cleaner, the food mixer and the liquidiser because they sounded about five times as loud as they actually were.
>
> The bus engine started with a clap of thunder, the engine sounding almost four times as loud as normal and I had my hands in my ears for most of the journey. (White and White 1987, pp.224–5)

Therese Jolliffe described her auditory sensitivity:

> The following are just some of the noises that still upset me enough to cover up my ears to avoid them; shouting, noisy crowded places, polystyrene being touched, balloons and aeroplanes, noisy vehicles on building sites, hammering and banging, electric tools being used, the sound of the sea, the sound of felt-tip or marker pens being used to colour in and fireworks. Despite this I can read music and play it and there are certain types of music I love. In fact when I am feeling angry and despairing of everything, music is the only way of making me feel calmer inside. (Jolliffe *et al.* 1992, p.15)

Liane Holliday Willey has identified specific sounds that are extremely distressing for her:

> High frequency and brassy, tin sounds clawed my nerves. Whistles, party noise makers, flutes and trumpets and any close relative of those sounds disarmed my calm and made my world very uninviting. (Willey 1999, p.22)

Will Hadcroft explains how the anticipation of an unpleasant auditory experience can make the person extremely anxious:

> I was perpetually nervous, frightened of everything. I hated trains going over railway bridges whilst I was underneath, I was frightened of balloons bursting, the suddenness of party poppers and the crack made by Christmas crackers. I was very cautious of anything that might make an unexpected loud noise. It goes without saying that I was terrified of thunder; even later, when I knew that it was lightning which was the dangerous part, I always feared the thunder more. Guy Fawkes Night also made me tense, although I loved watching the fireworks. (Hadcroft 2005, p.22)

It is possible to use acute auditory sensitivity as an advantage; for example, Albert knew when a train was due to arrive at the station several minutes before his parents could hear it. He said, 'I can always hear it, mommy and dad can't, it felt noisy in my ears and body' (Cesaroni and Garber 1991, p.306). A child at my clinical practice had a special interest in buses and recognized the unique engine sound of every bus that had been near his home. With his secondary interest in vehicle number plates, he could identify the number plate of the imminent but invisible bus. He was also reluctant to play in the garden at home. When asked why, he replied that he hated the 'clack-clack' noise of the wings of flying insects, such as butterflies.

There can be auditory distortion and 'tune outs'. The fluctuating distortion is described by Darren:

> Another trick which my ears played was to change the volume of sounds around me. Sometimes when other kids spoke to me I could scarcely hear them and sometimes they sounded like bullets. (White and White 1987, p.224)

Donna Williams explained that:

Sometimes people would have to repeat a particular sentence several times for me as I would hear it in bits and the way in which my mind segmented their sentence into words left me with a strange and sometimes unintelligible message. It was a bit like when someone plays around with the volume switch on the TV. (Williams 1998, p.64)

We are not sure whether a sensory 'tune out' is due to being so intensely preoccupied with an activity that the auditory signals do not interrupt the intense concentration, or whether there is a genuine temporary and fluctuating loss of the perception and processing of auditory information. However, this characteristic can lead to parents considering that their young son or daughter with Asperger's syndrome may also be deaf. Donna Williams described that:

My mother and father thought I was deaf. Standing behind me, they'd take it in turns to make loud noises without so much as a blink in response. I was taken to have my hearing tested. The test showed I wasn't deaf, and that was that. Years later, I had my hearing tested again. At the time, it was found that my hearing was better than average, and I was able to hear some frequencies that only animals normally hear. The problem with my hearing was obviously one of a fluctuation in the awareness of sound. (Williams 1998, p.44)

How does the person with Asperger's syndrome cope with such auditory sensitivity? Some learn to switch off or tune out certain sounds, as described by Temple Grandin:

When I was confronted with loud or confusing noise I could not modulate it. I either had to shut it all out and withdraw, or let it all in like a freight train. To avoid its onslaught, I would often withdraw and shut the world out. As an adult I still have problems modulating auditory input. When I use telephones at the airport I am unable to screen out the background noise without screening out the voice on the phone. Other people can use telephones in a noisy environment, but I cannot, even though my hearing is normal. (Grandin 1988, p.3)

Other techniques include humming to block out the noise, or focusing intently on a particular activity – a form of intense absorption, being 'mesmerized' – to prevent the intrusion of unpleasant sensory experiences.

Strategies to reduce sound sensitivity

It is important to first identify which auditory experiences are perceived as painfully intense, with the child communicating distress by covering his or her ears, flinching or blinking in response to sudden noises, or simply telling an adult which sounds are hurting. Some of these sounds can then be avoided. For example, if the noise of the vacuum cleaner is too intense, the vacuuming can be done when the child has gone to school. There are simple, practical solutions. A very young girl with Asperger's syndrome could not tolerate the scraping noise of chairs being moved in her classroom by other children and the teacher. This sound was eliminated when the legs of each chair were provided with a felt cover, and at last she could concentrate on her school work.

A barrier to reduce the level of auditory stimulation can be used, such as silicone ear plugs, kept in the person's pocket, ready to be inserted when the noise becomes intolerable. These are particularly useful in situations known to be noisy, such as the school cafeteria. In her quotation in a previous paragraph, Therese Jolliffe suggests another strategy, namely '…when I am feeling angry and despairing of everything, music is the only way of making me feel calmer inside' (Jolliffe et al. 1992, p.15). We are starting to recognize that listening to music using headphones can camouflage the noise that is perceived as too intense and enable the person to walk calmly round the shopping centre or concentrate on work in a noisy classroom.

It will also help if the cause and duration of the sound that is perceived as unbearable is explained. Social Stories™ developed by Carol Gray (see Chapter 3) are extremely versatile and can be adapted to focus on auditory sensitivity. A Social Story™ for a child who was sensitive to the noise of hand-dryers in public toilets included a description of the function and design of the machine, and assurance that it would automatically switch off after a set time. This reassuring knowledge can reduce anxiety and increase tolerance.

Clearly it is important that parents and teachers are aware of a child's auditory sensitivity and try to minimize the level of sudden noises, reduce the background sounds and conversation, and avoid specific auditory experiences known to be perceived as unbearably intense. This will reduce the person's level of anxiety and encourage concentration and socialization.

There are two therapies that have been used to reduce auditory sensitivity in children with autism and Asperger's syndrome. Sensory Integration Therapy (Ayers 1972) has been developed by occupational therapists and is based on the pioneering work of Jean Ayers. The therapy uses a range of specialized play equipment to improve the processing, modulation, organization and integration of sensory information. Controlled and enjoyable sensory experiences are used in a treatment plan conducted by an occupational therapist for several hours a week, usually over a number of months. Despite the popularity of this treatment, there is remarkably little empirical evidence of the efficacy of Sensory Integration Therapy (Baranek 2002; Dawson and Watling 2000). However, as Grace Baranek stated in her review of the research literature, a lack of empirical data regarding Sensory Integration Therapy does not imply that the treatment is ineffective, but rather that efficacy has not yet been objectively demonstrated.

Auditory Integration Therapy, or AIT, was originally developed by Guy Berard in France (Berard 1993). The therapy requires the person to listen to ten hours of electronically modified music through headphones during two half-hour daily sessions over ten days. An initial assessment is conducted using an audiogram to identify the frequencies to which the person is hypersensitive. Then a special electronic modulating and filtering device is used to randomly modulate high and low frequencies and filter out selected frequencies based on information obtained from the results of the audiogram assessment. The treatment is expensive, and while there are anecdotal reports of some success in reducing auditory sensitivity, overall there is a lack of empirical support for AIT (Baranek 2002; Dawson and Watling 2000).

While some sounds are perceived as extremely unpleasant, it is important to remember that some sounds are extremely pleasurable: for example, a young child being fascinated by specific theme tunes, or the sound of a ticking clock. Donna Williams explained that:

> One sound, however, which I loved to hear was the sound of anything metal. Unfortunately for my mother, our doorbell fell into this category, and I spent ages obsessively ringing it. (Williams 1998, p.45)

> My mother had recently rented a piano, and I loved the sound of anything that tinkled and had since I was very small. I would string safety-pins together and, when I wasn't chewing on them, would tinkle them in my ear. Similarly, I loved the sound of metal striking metal, and my two most favourite objects were a piece of cut crystal and a tuning fork which I carried with me for years. (Williams 1998, p.68)

TACTILE SENSITIVITY

Sensitivity to specific types of touch or tactile experiences occurs in over 50 per cent of children with a diagnosis of Asperger's syndrome (Bromley *et al.* 2004; Smith Myles *et al.* 2000). There can be an extreme sensitivity to a particular type of touch, the degree of pressure or the touching of particular parts of the body. Temple Grandin describes her acute tactile sensitivity when she was a young child:

> As a baby I resisted being touched and when I became a little older I can remember stiffening, flinching, and pulling away from relatives when they hugged me. (Grandin 1984, p.155)

> As a child I wanted to feel the comfort of being held, but then I would shrink away for fear of losing control and being engulfed when people hugged me. (Grandin 1984, p.151)

For Temple, the forms of touch used in social greetings or gestures of affection were perceived as too intense or overwhelming, a 'tidal wave' of sensation. Here, the avoidance of some social interactions was due to a physiological reaction to touch.

The child with Asperger's syndrome may fear the close proximity of other children due to the risk of accidental or unexpected touch, and meeting relatives because of the probability of gestures of affection, such as a hug or kiss, which are perceived as being too intense a sensation.

Liane Holliday Willey explained that in her childhood:

> I often found it impossible even to touch some objects. I hated stiff things, satiny things, scratchy things, things that fit me too tightly. Thinking about them, imagining them, visualising them…any time my thoughts found them, goose bumps and chills and a general sense of unease would follow. I routinely stripped off everything I had on even if we were in a public place. (Willey 1999, pp.21–2)

As far as I am aware, as an adult, Liane no longer continues the latter activity. However, in a recent e-mail to me she commented on her continuing tactile sensitivity and explained that sometimes she has to stop at a clothing store to buy something new if she is too far from her house and can't bear what she is wearing. I understand this is not an excuse prepared for her husband to justify buying more clothes.

As a child, Temple Grandin also had an aversion to the tactile sensations of specific types of clothing:

> Some episodes of bad behaviour were directly caused by sensory difficulties. I often misbehaved in church and screamed because my Sunday clothes felt different. During cold weather when I had to walk outside in a skirt my legs hurt. Scratchy petticoats drove me crazy; a feeling that would be insignificant to most people may feel like sandpaper rubbing the skin raw to an autistic child. Certain types of stimulation are greatly over amplified by a damaged nervous system. The problem could have been solved by finding Sunday clothes that felt the same as everyday clothes. As an adult, I am often extremely uncomfortable if I have to wear a new type of underwear. Most people habituate to different types of clothes, but I keep feeling them for hours. Today I buy everyday clothes and good clothes that feel the same. (Grandin 1988, pp.4–5)

The child may insist on having a limited wardrobe to ensure consistency of tactile experience. The problem for parents is having to wash these items, and their durability. Once a particular garment is tolerated, parents may need to buy several of increasing size, to cope with washing, wear and tear and the child's growth.

Particular areas of the body appear to be more sensitive, namely the child's head, upper arms and palms. The child may become extremely distressed when having his or her hair washed, combed or cut. Stephen Shore described his reaction to having to have a haircut as a child:

> Haircuts were always a major event. They hurt! To try to calm me, my parents would say that hair is dead and has no feeling. It was impossible for me to communicate that the pulling on the scalp was causing the discomfort. Having someone else wash my hair was also a problem. Now that I am older and my nervous system has matured, a haircut is no longer an issue. (Shore 2001, p.19)

The experience of having a haircut can also be affected by auditory sensitivity, namely an aversion to the 'sharp' sound of scissors cutting hair and the vibration of electric clippers. There can also be a reaction to the tactile sensation of cut hair falling on the child's face or shoulders, and for very young children, the unpleasant feeling of instability from not having one's feet on the ground when sitting in a barber's chair designed for an adult.

Asperger noted that some of the children he saw hated the sensation of water on their face. Leah wrote to me and explained that:

> I hated having showers as a child, and preferred baths. The sensation of water splashing my face was unbearable. I still hate it. I would go for weeks at a time without bathing and was amazed when I found out that kids had a regular shower, every day even!

This characteristic will obviously have an effect on matters such as personal hygiene and the degree of welcome when initiating an interaction with peers.

The tactile sensitivity can affect the tolerance of certain activities in the classroom. The child with Asperger's syndrome may have an aversion to glue on his or her hands, finger painting, using playdough and participating in dressing-up activities due to an intense dislike of the tactile sensations of the costumes. There can also be an over-reaction to being tickled and an excessive reaction to unexpected touch on specific areas of the body, such as being touched at the base of the back. Once this has been dis-covered by adolescents, there can be the temptation to tease and torment the teenager with Asperger's syndrome by poking a finger in his or her back and enjoying the obvious startle reaction and discomfort.

Tactile sensitivity can also affect the sensual and sexual relationship between an adult with Asperger's syndrome and his or her partner (Aston 2003; Hénault 2005). Everyday gestures of affection, for example a reassuring touch on the forearm or an expression of affection and love by an embracing hug, may not be perceived as a pleasant sensation by the person with Asperger's syndrome. The typical partner may resent the obvious lack of enjoyment in response to affectionate touch and the rarity of such gestures initiated by the partner with Asperger's syndrome. When engaged in more intimate touch that should provide mutual sensual pleasure, the person with Asperger's syndrome may have extreme tactile sensitivity and find such experiences unpleasant and difficult even to tolerate, let alone enjoy. The aversion to physical touch during moments of sexual intimacy may be due to a problem with sensory perception rather than a lack of love and commitment to the relationship.

Strategies to reduce tactile sensitivity

What can be done to reduce tactile sensitivity? Family members, teachers and friends need to be aware of difficulties with the perception and reaction to some tactile experi-ences, and not force the person to endure the experience if it can be avoided. The young child with Asperger's syndrome can play with toys and engage in educational activities that do not cause distress due to the child's being tactile defensive (the technical term for being sensitive to specific tactile experiences). Sensory Integration Therapy can reduce tactile defensiveness but, as described in the section on auditory sensitivity, there is a lack of empirical evidence of the effectiveness of Sensory Integration Therapy.

Family members can reduce the frequency and duration of gestures of affection used in greetings and let the person with Asperger's syndrome know when and how he or she will be touched, so that the sensation is not a total surprise and likely to elicit a startle reaction. Parents can remove tags from clothing and encourage the child to tolerate hair washing and cutting. Sometimes a head massage, or slowly but firmly rubbing the child's head and shoulders with a towel prior to using the scissors or electric cutters, can reduce the hypersensitivity of the child's scalp. Sometimes the problem is the intensity of the touch, where there is a greater sensitivity to light touch, while more intense physical pressure is acceptable or even enjoyed. Temple Grandin found deep pressure or squeezing was enjoyable and calming:

> I would pull away and stiffen when hugged, but I craved back rubs. Rubbing skin has a calming effect. I craved deep-pressure stimulation. I used to get under the sofa cushions and have my sister sit on them. Pressure had a very calming and relaxing effect. As a child, I loved crawling into small, snug spaces. I felt secure, relaxed, and safe. (Grandin 1988, p.4)

She designed a 'squeeze machine', lined with foam rubber, which enclosed almost her whole body and provided firm pressure. She found the machine created a soothing and relaxing experience that gradually desensitized her.

Liane Holliday Willey has considerable tactile pleasure from being underwater. In her autobiography she described how:

> I found solace underwater. I loved the sensation that came from floating with the water. I was liquid, tranquil, smooth; I was hushed. The water was solid and strong. It held me safe in its black, awesome darkness and it offered me quiet – pure and effortless quiet. Entire mornings would pass me by while I swam under-water for great periods of time, pushing my lungs to hold on to the quiet and dark until they forced me to find air. (Willey 1999, p.22)

Thus, there are some solitary tactile experiences that are enjoyable; but having tactile defensiveness not only affects the person's mental state, it also affects interpersonal relationships, as typical people often touch each other. The request to 'keep in touch' may not be an invitation readily accepted by the person with Asperger's syndrome.

SENSITIVITY TO TASTE AND SMELL

Parents often report that their young child with Asperger's syndrome has a remarkable ability to detect odours that others do not notice, and can be extremely fussy in his or her choice of food. Over 50 per cent of children with Asperger's syndrome have olfactory and taste sensitivity (Bromley *et al.* 2004; Smith Myles *et al.* 2000).

Sean Barron has explained his perception of the taste and texture of food:

I had a big problem with food. I liked to eat things that were bland and uncompli-cated. My favourite foods were cereal – dry, with no milk – bread, pancakes, macaroni and spaghetti, potatoes, potatoes and milk. Because these were the foods I ate early in life, I found them comforting and soothing. I didn't want to try anything new.

I was supersensitive to the texture of food, and I had to touch everything with my fingers to see how it felt before I could put it in my mouth. I really hated it when food had things mixed with it like noodles with vegetables or bread with fillings to make sandwiches. I could never, never put any of it into my mouth. I knew if I did I would get violently sick. (Barron and Barron 1992, p.96)

Stephen Shore endured similar sensory experiences:

Canned asparagus was intolerable due to its slimy texture, and I didn't eat tomatoes for a year after a cherry tomato had burst in my mouth while I was eating it. The sensory stimulation of having that small piece of fruit explode in my mouth was too much to bear and I was not going to take any chances of that happening again.

Carrots in a green salad and celery in a tuna fish salad are still intolerable to me because the contrast in texture between carrots or celery and salad or tuna fish is too great. However, I enjoy eating celery and baby carrots by themselves. Often as a child, less now, I would eat things serially, finishing one item on the plate before going on to the next. (Shore 2001, p.44)

The young child may insist on a plain or restricted diet, such as only having boiled rice or sausages and chips for every evening meal for several years. Unfortunately, the sensi-tivity and subsequent avoidance of food that has a specific fibrous or 'wet' texture, and the combination of certain foods, can be the source of agitation for the whole family at meal times. Mothers in particular can be in a state of despair that the child will not con-template any new or more nutritious food. Fortunately, most children with Asperger's syndrome who have this type of sensitivity have been able to widen their diet as they mature, and for many children, this characteristic has almost disappeared by early adolescence.

There can also be an element of tactile defensiveness when eating some foods. We recognize the reaction of retching when a person places a finger down his or her throat. This reaction is an automatic reflex to avoid a solid object in the throat, and the sensation is extremely unpleasant. However, a child with Asperger's syndrome may have the same reaction to fibrous food in his or her mouth, not just the throat.

Sometimes the resistance to eating a particular fruit or vegetable is due to a height-ened sensitivity to specific aromas. The aroma is perceived as delicious to a typical child or adult, but the child with Asperger's syndrome may have a greater olfactory sensitivity and range of perception, and detect certain aromas as overly pungent. When I ask children with Asperger's syndrome who have this characteristic to describe the range of aromas they experience when eating a ripe peach, for example, they may respond with descriptions such as 'it smells like urine' or 'it smells as if it is rotten.'

Olfactory sensitivity can result in the person becoming nauseous when detecting someone's perfume or deodorant. An adult said to me that he perceived perfumes as having a similar smell to insecticides. A child with olfactory sensitivity may avoid the aromas of paints and art supplies at school, the school cafeteria or rooms where a cleaner has used a particular detergent or cleaning agent.

The heightened sense of smell can have some advantages. I know of several adults with Asperger's syndrome who have combined an acute sense of smell with a special interest in wines to become celebrated wine experts and connoisseurs. As Liane Holliday Willey walked to her table at a restaurant, her acute sense of smell enabled her to warn a diner at another table that her sea food was off and would make her very ill. She also uses the ability to smell sickness in her daughters by smelling their breath (personal communication).

Strategies to increase dietary diversity

It is important to avoid programs of force feeding or starvation to encourage a more varied diet. The child has an increased sensitivity to certain types of food: it is not a simple behaviour problem where the child is being deliberately defiant. Nevertheless, parents will have to ensure that the child eats an appropriate range of food, and a dietician may provide guidance on what is nutritious but tolerable to the child in terms of texture, aroma or taste. Gradually the sensitivity diminishes, but the fear and consequent avoidance may continue. When this occurs, a program of systematic desensitization can be introduced by a clinical psychologist. The child can first be encouraged to describe the sensory experience and identify foods that are rated as some of the least unpleasant and more likely to be tolerated with encouragement. When introducing a low preference food, the child initially only has to lick and taste, rather than chew or swallow, the food. When trying specific food sensations, the child should be encouraged to be relaxed, with a supportive adult present, and achieve congratulations and perhaps an appropriate reward for being brave. A program of Sensory Integration Therapy may also be beneficial. Nevertheless, some adults with Asperger's syndrome continue to have a very restricted diet consisting of the same essential ingredients, cooked and presented in the same way, throughout their lives. At least the preparation may be very efficient through considerable practice.

VISUAL SENSITIVITY

Sensitivity to particular levels of illumination or colours, or a distortion of visual perception occurs in about one in five children with Asperger's syndrome (Smith Myles *et al.* 2000). Such children and adults report being 'blinded by brightness' and avoid intense levels of illumination. For example, Darren referred to how on 'bright days my sight blurred'. Occasionally there may be a sensitivity to a particular colour, for example:

I also remember one Christmas when I got a new bike for a present. It was yellow. I would not look at it. Extra red was added to the colour making it look orange, and it blurred upwards making it look like it was on fire.

I also couldn't see blue clearly, it looked too light and it looked like ice. (White and White 1987, p.224)

There can also be an intense fascination with visual detail, noticing specks on a carpet or blemishes on someone's skin. When the child with Asperger's syndrome has a natural talent at drawing, and this is combined with the special interest and considerable drawing practice, the result can be works of art that achieve an effect of photographic realism. For example, a young child who has an interest in trains can be precocious in learning to draw railway scenes in perspective, including almost every detail of the loco-motive. In contrast, the people in the scene may be drawn at an age-appropriate level of representation.

There are reports of visual distortion, as described by Darren:

I used to hate small shops because my eyesight used to make them look as if they were even smaller than they actually were. (White and White 1987, p.224)

This can lead to fear or anxiety as a response to certain types of visual experience, as explained by Therese Jolliffe:

It may be because things that I see do not always make the right impression that I am frightened of so many things that can be seen; people, particularly their faces, very bright lights, crowds, things moving suddenly, large machines and buildings that are unfamiliar, unfamiliar places, my own shadow, the dark, bridges, rivers, canals, streams and the sea. (Jolliffe et al. 1992, p.15)

Certain visual experiences can be confusing, for example light reflecting on the class-room whiteboard effectively making the text illegible and creating a disturbing distrac-tion. Liane Holliday Willey described that:

Bright lights, mid-day sun, reflected lights, flickering lights, fluorescent lights; each seemed to sear my eyes. Together, the sharp sounds and the bright lights were more than enough to overload my senses. My head would feel tight, my stomach would churn, and my pulse would run my heart ragged until I found a safety zone. (Willey 1999, p.22)

In an e-mail to me, Carolyn explained that:

With fluorescent lights it's not only the glare that gets me, it's the flicker as well. It produces 'shadows' in my vision (which were very scary when I was young) and long exposure can lead to confusion and dizziness often resulting in migraine.

There have been descriptions of not being able to see something that is clearly visible and that the person is searching for (Smith Myles et al. 2000). The person with Asperger's syndrome may have more examples than one would expect of the natural phenomenon of not seeing something 'right before your eyes'. The child may be asked to find a particular book in his or her desk or cupboard, and despite the book being easy for others to see, the child does not recognize the book he or she is looking for. This can be infuriating for the child and the teacher.

But not all visual experiences are disturbing. For the person with Asperger's syndrome, there can be intense pleasure in examples of visual symmetry. For young children this can be the parallel lines and sleepers or ties of a railway track, a picket fence or electricity pylons in a rural landscape. Adults with Asperger's syndrome may extend the interest in symmetry to an appreciation of architecture. Liane Holliday Willey has a remarkable knowledge and appreciation of architecture:

> To this day, architectural design remains one of my most favored subjects and now that I am older I indulge my interest, giving in to the joy it brings me. In many ways it is the perfect elixir for whatever ails me. When I feel tangled and tense, I get out my history of architecture and design books and set my eyes on the kinds of spaces and arenas that make sense to me; the linear, the straight lined and the level buildings that paint pictures of strong balance. (Willey 1999, p.48)

Several famous architects may have had some of the personality characteristics associated with Asperger's syndrome. However, an appreciation of the symmetry of buildings can be a disadvantage. Liane has explained to me that if she sees buildings that are asymmetrical or, as she says, 'jagged' in their design, she feels nauseous and very anxious.

Strategies to reduce visual sensitivity

Parents and teachers can avoid placing the child in circumstances associated with intense or disturbing visual sensations: for example, not seating the child at the side of the car that receives the full glare of the sun, or at the school desk illuminated by strong sunlight. Another approach is to use sunglasses and visors indoors to avoid intense light or glare, or to have a workstation to screen out excessive visual stimulation. The child may have a natural screen, by growing long hair that acts as a curtain and barrier to visual (and social) experiences. Concern regarding the perceived intensity of colours can lead to a preference for wearing only black clothes, which is not necessarily a fashion statement.

There are remedial programs that might have an effect on reducing a child's visual sensitivity. Helen Irlen has developed the use of tinted glasses to improve visual perception and reduce perceptual overload and visual disturbance. Tinted non-optical lenses (*Irlen filters*) are designed to filter out those frequencies of the light spectrum to which the person is sensitive. There is an initial screening process using a special questionnaire and a testing procedure to determine the appropriate colour prescription. There are currently no empirical studies that have confirmed the value of the lenses for people with Asperger's syndrome, but I know of several children and adults who have reported a considerable reduction in visual sensitivity and sensory overload when wearing Irlen lenses.

Vision therapy has been developed by behavioural optometrists to 'retrain' the eyes and the structures in the brain that process visual information. An assessment is made of potential visual dysfunction and any compensatory mechanisms that are being used, such as tilting or turning the head, using peripheral vision and preferring to use one eye. The remedial therapy program is conducted using weekly therapy sessions and assignments at home. To date, there is no empirical evidence to support vision therapy with people with Asperger's syndrome.

It is also important to remember that when a person with Asperger's syndrome is extremely distressed or agitated, he or she will benefit from having an area or room to retreat into and calm down, away from other people. The area needs to have sensory aspects that are calming and soothing. This can include the symmetry of furnishings, the colour of the walls and the carpet and no sounds, aromas or tactile experiences that are perceived as unpleasant.

THE SENSE OF BALANCE AND MOVEMENT

Some children with Asperger's syndrome have problems with the vestibular system that affects their sense of balance, perception of movement and coordination (Smith Myles *et al.* 2000). An appealing description is that the child is 'gravitationally insecure', becoming anxious if his or her feet leave the ground, and feeling disorientated when having to change body position rapidly, as required in ball games such as soccer. The sense of balance can also be affected in that the person experiences an extremely uncomfortable feeling when upside down.

Liane Holliday Willey explained that:

> Motion is not my friend. My stomach tips and spills when I look at a merry-go-round, or drive my car over a hill or around a corner too quickly. When my first baby was born, I soon learned my troubles with vestibular motion went beyond amusement parks and car rides. I could not rock my girls. I could sway, though, and this I did even in my rocking chair. (Willey 1999, p.76)

In contrast, I have known children with Asperger's syndrome who have experienced extreme pleasure when on a roller-coaster ride, to such an extent that roller coasters have become a special interest. They are great to listen to and watch.

We are only just beginning to explore the problems children and adults with Asperger's syndrome may have with the vestibular system, but if a child does have problems with the sense of balance and movement, Sensory Integration Therapy would be recommended.

THE PERCEPTION OF PAIN AND TEMPERATURE

The child or adult with Asperger's syndrome may appear very stoic, and not flinch or show distress in response to levels of pain that others would consider unbearable. The child's attention can be drawn to a bruise or cut but the child can't remember how it happened. Splinters may be removed without concern, hot drinks consumed without distress. On hot days warm clothing may be worn, or on freezing winter days the person may insist on continuing to wear summer clothes. It is as if he or she has an idiosyncratic internal thermostat.

There can be a hypo- and hypersensitivity to pain (Bromley *et al.* 2004). The low threshold for some types of pain and discomfort can be a frequent source of distress for the child whose reaction can be judged by peers as being a 'cry baby'. However, children with Asperger's syndrome are more likely to be hypo- than hypersensitive to pain. A high pain threshold was described to me by the father of a teenager with Asperger's syndrome:

> Two years ago my son came home with a badly scraped leg, heavily bruised with numerous cuts. I ran to get the first aid kit. When I came back and told him to sit down, that I wanted to treat his injuries, he couldn't understand it. He said 'there is nothing wrong, it doesn't hurt' and 'it happens all the time' and proceeded to go to his bedroom. This was a common occurrence over the 18 years. He also does not feel cold like others. In the winter he rarely wears a jacket and wears short sleeve shirts to school and feels very comfortable.

By chance, I met a young American man with Asperger's syndrome while on vacation in the desert centre of Australia during winter. We were part of a group of tourists enjoying an evening meal that had been prepared outdoors so that we could see the brilliant desert stars and listen to an after-dinner lecture by an astronomer. However, the temperatures were below freezing and everyone, except the young man with Asperger's syndrome, was complaining how cold they were feeling and wearing many layers of warm clothing. The young man was only wearing a T-shirt and refused the offers of warm clothing from his companions. He explained he was quite comfortable, but his lack of clothing for the freezing desert night made everyone else feel uncomfortable.

Another example was described in an e-mail to me by Carolyn. She explained that:

> My response to pain and temperature seems to be similar to my response to trivial or traumatic events. At low levels of stimulation the response is exaggerated, but at higher levels the senses seem to shut down and I can function better than normal in most instances. A trivial event can quite dramatically hamper my ability to function, but when faced with trauma, I can think logically and act calmly and efficiently when others would panic under the same situation.

Asperger noted that one in four of the children he saw were late in being toilet trained (Hippler and Klicpera 2004). It is possible that such children were less able to perceive the internal signals of bladder and bowel discomfort to prevent toileting 'accidents'.

The lack of reaction to discomfort, pain and extremes of temperature can also prevent the very young child with Asperger's syndrome from learning to avoid certain dangerous actions, resulting in frequent trips to the local casualty department. Medical staff may be surprised at the audacity of the child or consider the parents negligent.

One of the most worrying aspects for parents is how to detect when the child is in chronic pain and needs medical help. Ear infections or appendicitis may progress to a dangerous level before being detected. The side effects of medication may not be reported. Dental and menstrual pain and discomfort can occur but not be mentioned. The parents of one child noted he did not seem his usual self for a few days, but was not indicating he was experiencing significant pain. They eventually took him to a doctor who diagnosed a twisted testicle which had to be removed. If the child shows minimal response to pain, it is essential that parents are vigilant for any signs of discomfort, check for physical signs of illness such as high body temperature or swelling, and use the strategies developed for expressing feelings in Chapter 6, such as an emotion thermometer, to enable the child to communicate the intensity of pain. It is also important to write a Social Story™ to explain to the child why reporting pain to an adult is vital to help the child feel well again, and avoid more serious consequences.

UNUSUAL SENSORY PROCESSING

There is a rare form of sensory perception, *synaesthesia*, where the person experiences a sensation in one sensory system, yet perceives the sensation in another modality. The most common expression is for the person to see colours every time he or she hears a particular sound (coloured hearing), or perceives a specific aroma. This is not a characteristic unique to Asperger's syndrome, but several adults with Asperger's syndrome have described this unusual phenomenon. For example, Jim described how 'Sometimes the channels get confused, as when sounds come through as colour' (Cesaroni and Garber 1991, p.305). He explained that specific sounds are often accompanied by vague sensations of colour, shape, texture, movement, scent or flavour. Liane explained that 'I would search long and hard to find words that tickled, words that had smooth textures, and words that warmed when I spoke them' (Willey 1999, p.31).

Jim also noticed that auditory stimuli interfered with other sensory processes; for example, he had to 'turn off kitchen appliances so that I could taste something' (Cesaroni and Garber 1991, p.305). Unusual sensory processing can include a difficulty identifying the source channel of sensory information. Jim explained that 'Sometimes I know that something is coming in somewhere, but I can't tell right away what sense it's coming through' (Cesaroni and Garber 1991, p.305). The experience must be quite bewildering; unfortunately, we have only just begun to explore this area of sensory perception (Bogdashina 2003).

The final words of this chapter on sensory sensitivity are by Liane Holliday Willey, who has come to accept her sensory perception and living in 'surround sound', and describes how:

> I think my girls have learned to accept the public me without too much pain and embarrassment. Sure, they remind me not to talk to myself in public, not to use a loud voice around others, not to bring up the subject of my dogs to every living soul, not to ramble on in my conversations, not to cover my ears at the park and yell '*Who in their right mind can stand all this noise?*' and not to cover my nose and scream '*My God that stinks!*' But that is just fine with me, for all along the way, they never, ever forget to tell me that despite all of my quirks and batty nuances, they love me no matter what. (Willey 1999, pp.93–4)

KEY POINTS AND STRATEGIES

- Some adults with Asperger's syndrome consider their sensory sensitivity has a greater impact on their daily lives than problems with making friends, managing emotions and finding appropriate employment.

- The most common sensitivity is to very specific sounds but there can also be sensitivity to tactile experiences, light intensity, the taste and texture of food and specific aromas. There can be an under- or over-reaction to the experience of pain and discomfort, and the sense of balance, movement perception and body orientation can be unusual.

- The child with sensory sensitivity becomes hypervigilant, tense and distractible in sensory stimulating environments such as the classroom, unsure when the next painful sensory experience will occur.

- We know that the signs are more conspicuous in early childhood and gradually diminish during adolescence, but can remain a life-long characteristic for some adults with Asperger's syndrome.

- Sound sensitivity:
  - There are three types of noise that are perceived as extremely unpleasant. The first category is sudden, unexpected noises, the second category is high-pitched, continuous sounds and the third category is confusing, complex or multiple sounds.
  - Some of these sounds can be avoided. Silicone ear plugs can become a barrier to reduce the level of auditory stimulation. For young children, it will also help if the cause and duration of the sound that is perceived as unbearable is explained using a Social Story™.
  - There are two therapies that have been used to reduce auditory sensitivity in children with Asperger's syndrome: Sensory Integration

Therapy and Auditory Integration Therapy. The efficacy of these two treatments has not yet been objectively demonstrated.

- There can be an extreme sensitivity to a particular type of touch, the degree of pressure or the touching of particular parts of the body.
- Olfactory and dietary sensitivity:
  - Parents often report that their young child with Asperger's syndrome has a remarkable ability to detect odours that others do not notice, and can be extremely fussy in his or her choice of food.
  - Gradually the sensitivity diminishes, but the fear and consequent avoidance may continue. When this occurs, a program of systematic desensitization can be introduced by a clinical psychologist.
- Visual sensitivity:
  - Sensitivity to particular levels of illumination or colours, or a distortion of visual perception occurs in about one in five children with Asperger's syndrome.
  - Parents and teachers can avoid placing the child in circumstances associated with intense or disturbing visual sensations: for example, not seating the child at the side of the car that receives the full glare of the sun, or at the school desk illuminated by strong sunlight.
- Some children are 'gravitationally insecure', becoming anxious if their feet leave the ground, and feeling disorientated when having to change body position rapidly.
- Perception of pain:
  - The child or adult with Asperger's syndrome may appear very stoic and not flinch or show distress in response to levels of pain that others would consider unbearable.
  - One of the most worrying aspects for parents is how to detect when the child is in chronic pain and needs medical help.
  - It is important to write a Social Story™ to explain to the child why reporting pain to an adult is vital to help the child feel well again, and avoid more serious consequences.

CHAPTER 12

Life After School: College and Career

We can see in the autistic person, far more clearly than with any normal child, a predestination for a particular profession from earliest youth. A particular line of work often grows naturally out of their special abilities.

– Hans Asperger ([1944] 1991)

Over the last decade there has been an extraordinary increase in the number of children who have been diagnosed as having Asperger's syndrome. Those children are growing up and many are enrolling at college or university. In the past, some promising undergraduates with Asperger's syndrome have not been able to cope with the transition from school to college, the need for greater independence skills, and the academic and social demands of being a student at university. The stress and lack of support can contribute to the development of an anxiety disorder or depression, and the possibility of withdrawal from the course. Fortunately, we now have greater knowledge of the support needed by university students with Asperger's syndrome (Fleisher 2003; Harpur *et al.* 2004; Palmer 2006).

There may be several colleges, universities and courses that would be suitable for a person with Asperger's syndrome, and it will help in the decision process if the student, parents and school staff discuss the advantages and disadvantages of each option. Information can be obtained from downloading course details from the relevant web sites and visiting the campus and academic departments. Current and graduate students can provide a consumer's opinion of courses and academic staff. Parents will be interested in the support services for students with Asperger's syndrome. When the student has registered for a specific course, a member of the teaching or support staff at the student's high school could liaise with the university to provide information on the support the student will need as an undergraduate.

Some high-school students with Asperger's syndrome are reluctant to inform the university of their diagnosis, wanting a 'fresh start' and not to be considered as different from the other students. There may need to be discussion on the advantages and disadvantages of self-disclosure, and a decision on whether to inform the university of the person's diagnosis so that the staff can provide any necessary support. I usually encourage students to inform the college or university. The issue may not be whether to inform but how to inform.

The student with Asperger's syndrome will have to prepare for a very different lifestyle, and before enrolment there will need to be decisions made regarding accommodation, finances and practical and emotional support. There are advantages in students with Asperger's syndrome remaining at home, at least during the first college year, so that a parent can provide support in the areas of budgeting, self-care (such as laundry, meal preparation and reminders regarding personal hygiene) and the organizational aspects required to complete course assignments on time, and monitor the student's level of stress. If the student has to leave home then the support services for undergraduates will need to know of the extra support and supervision that will probably be needed.

The student will need to decide on the number of course units to be undertaken each semester, and it may be wise to start with less than the maximum number of units. Students with Asperger's syndrome will need more 'free' time to adjust to the new lifestyle, learning environment and academic requirements. They will also need guidance regarding the new social conventions and protocol at lectures and tutorials, when working on assignments in a group, and sending e-mail messages to staff. An appointed student 'buddy' or mentor can provide friendly advice regarding social protocols and expectations.

The student will have a new daily and weekly routine, and will benefit from a study plan and initial support organizing and managing the new academic commitments. Students with Asperger's syndrome will probably need to meet their academic tutors more frequently than other students to ensure they are 'on the right track', and acquiring the 'mindset' needed for the course. There are advantages in having an academic mentor who becomes knowledgeable on Asperger's syndrome to act as the student's advocate during academic staff discussions of students.

The cognitive, social, motor and sensory profiles of students with Asperger's syndrome need to be considered when deciding course assignments and setting exams. Students may have difficulty translating thought and solutions into speech, handwriting is sometimes indecipherable, there will be problems with the interpersonal skills required to contribute to a group project, and they may well be overly sensitive to criticism and failure. There can be concerns regarding self-esteem, anxiety and sensitivity to sensory experiences that may affect specific courses. There are practical solutions such as typing rather than talking to explain a concept or solution, using a keyboard during an exam to avoid problems with handwriting, and considering solitary rather than group assignments. The academic staff will need to understand the nature of Asperger's syndrome and to modify explanations and expectations accordingly, and not be confused, offended or annoyed by some of the characteristics of Asperger's syndrome expressed by a particular student.

Student life is not all academic study and the person with Asperger's syndrome will probably want to make friends and participate in student social activities. There are the usual student societies and clubs that can provide recreational and social opportunities. Some universities have a support group specifically for students with Asperger's syndrome. The group provides advice on many concerns, from feelings of social isolation to strategies to improve study skills. Older students with Asperger's syndrome can provide empathy and emotional support for the 'freshmen'.

The student with Asperger's syndrome will also benefit from friendships with typical students to provide academic support, such as sharing resources and proofreading essays, as well as guidance when the person with Asperger's syndrome is socially naïve and vulnerable to teasing and ridicule. There will also be issues regarding relationship experiences and sexuality, and the availability of alcohol and drugs. Thus, the student with Asperger's syndrome will need support from both academic staff and fellow students.

Student life can be stressful, and the person with Asperger's syndrome should be encouraged to communicate feelings of anxiety, anger or sadness with a student counsellor. The Cognitive Behaviour Therapy and emotion management strategies described in Chapter 6 can be extremely beneficial for students with Asperger's syndrome. I have found that the reasons for a student with Asperger's syndrome failing or withdrawing from a course are more likely to be related to issues with stress management than a lack of intellectual ability or commitment to the course.

I suspect that some colleges and universities will gradually develop experience and expertise in supporting students with Asperger's syndrome due to having academic and support staff who understand and welcome such students. There will be an unofficial 'good university guide for students with Asperger's syndrome' and these universities will become the first choice of future students and their parents. Some universities such as Oxford and Cambridge already have a reputation of supporting eccentric and talented students and academic staff. An interesting outcome will be graduates with Asperger's syndrome pursuing research into Asperger's syndrome.

When the person with Asperger's syndrome does graduate from university, it is a time for a greater celebration than for other students, as the person has had to adapt to a new lifestyle, become more self-reliant and become part of a new social hierarchy. After graduation, there will be decisions with regard to what to do next. Some adults with Asperger's syndrome adapt so well to academic life that academia and research become their life-long career. Others will need to decide how to apply their academic qualifications in their new career.

SUITABLE CAREERS FOR PEOPLE WITH ASPERGER'S SYNDROME

There is no career that would be impossible for a person with Asperger's syndrome. I have met several thousand adults with Asperger's syndrome who have had a very wide range of careers, from a part-time postman to the owner and chief executive of a successful international company. The list of professions includes teaching, politics, aviation, engineering and psychology, and trades such as electrician, mechanic and wildlife ranger. People with Asperger's syndrome have particular qualities, but there are also specific difficulties, and we are starting to determine why some people with Asperger's syndrome may not achieve employment appropriate to their abilities and qualifications. We are also beginning to devise strategies to help them find and keep enjoyable and productive employment.

Employment qualities

A performance appraisal of an employee with Asperger's syndrome would most likely conclude that he or she is:

- reliable
- persistent
- a perfectionist
- easily able to identify errors
- technically able
- in possession of a sense of social justice and integrity
- likely to question protocols
- accurate
- attentive to detail
- logical
- conscientious
- knowledgeable
- original in problem solving
- honest
- likely to thrive on routine and clear expectations.

However, there will also be difficulties. He or she may have problems with:

- teamwork skills

- being a line manager

- conventional methods

- sensory perception

- time keeping and work routines

- managing and communicating stress and anxiety

- realistic career expectations

- matching the job to his or her qualifications – tendency to be over-qualified

- misinterpretation of instructions

- coping with change

- accepting advice (may be perceived as criticism)

- personal grooming and hygiene

- fitting in with the group – may be gullible and vulnerable to being teased and tormented

- asking for help

- organizing and planning

- conflict resolution – liable to blame others

- interpersonal skills.

The general experience of people with Asperger's syndrome is that finding and keeping an appropriate job or career is not as easy as it is for typical people with the same qualifications. However, there are strategies, services and resources that facilitate successful employment.

STRATEGIES FOR SUCCESSFUL EMPLOYMENT

The first stage is to conduct a thorough assessment of the person's vocational abilities and experiences. This will include cognitive abilities, personality, motivation, interests and interpersonal skills. There is an employment workbook specifically designed for adolescents and adults with Asperger's syndrome, which determines the person's employment strengths and weaknesses and helps resolve issues identified from previous work experience (Myer 2001). A vocational abilities assessment should be conducted some time before the person graduates from school, college or university to provide an opportunity to improve specific abilities before seeking employment. This can include improving cooperative skills needed in teamwork, the art of conversation and interaction during work breaks, and how to cope with changing job expectations.

There will need to be careful consideration with regard to choosing a particular career path. The person may have had a specific career ambition for some time and need guidance as to whether the ambition is realistic, and advice as to the necessary qualifications and experience. The person's special interest can become a career path. People with Asperger's syndrome are renowned for their expertise and this can lead to a successful career as an academic conducting research in the area of the special interest, for example. Other people may accept the person's eccentric personality when he or she has a valued knowledge, for example in identifying and valuing antiques, or solving a problem with a computer. Advanced visual reasoning abilities and a decade of playing with construction toys and engines can lead to a successful career as an engineer or mechanic. The ability to draw, sing, play an instrument, compose music and write fantasy novels can indicate a career in the arts. A sense of social justice and being a naturally kind and considerate person can lead to a career in the caring and justice professions, especially teaching, the police force, medicine and related disciplines, and caring for animals. An interest in languages, the law and mathematics can be the basis of a career as a translator, lawyer or accountant. An interest in maps can lead to employment as a taxi or truck driver, or postman.

Some adolescents and young adults with Asperger's syndrome may have very little idea what type of employment would be suitable for their abilities and personality. Parents may suggest a variety of work experience while the teenager is still attending school, in order to identify potential careers. The intention is not necessarily to increase the teenager's income, as some of the work experience may be in a voluntary capacity, but to increase work-related skills and knowledge to make informed career choices. The school, college or university career service will need to be aware of the employment issues for people with Asperger's syndrome and allocate appropriate support and training before graduation. For some trades and professions, there may be greater success in learning specific vocational skills using the traditional master and apprentice training rather than classroom-based learning.

The next stage is to prepare a CV (curriculum vitae) that includes a portfolio of relevant work experience and achievements, interests and abilities, and may include photographs or a digital record of previous work accomplishments and testimonials. The person with Asperger's syndrome is probably not as proficient as other job candidates at the interpersonal skills and confidence needed during a job interview to 'sell' his or her abilities to an employer, but a well-constructed and informative CV can help an employer identify greater abilities than the person's performance during the interview. The person with Asperger's syndrome will also need guidance in constructing the CV and completing job applications.

One of the issues faced by adults with Asperger's syndrome when completing a job application, and during a job interview, is whether to disclose information about the diagnosis and how much information to disclose. This is very much a personal decision, based on many factors, and there are two recent publications that can provide guidance regarding disclosure (Murray 2006; Shore 2004). In general, it is better to be honest with an employer.

Some people with Asperger's syndrome are able to achieve successful employment with very little support and encouragement, but for those who have difficulties finding the right job, there are several books that provide advice for the individual, families, employment agencies and employers (Fast 2004; Grandin and Duffy 2004; Hawkins 2004; National Autistic Society 2005). The person may need to rehearse having a job interview and discuss with someone who knows him or her well whether to accept a particular offer of employment. It is not a case of accepting just any offer of employment; the job must be suitable for the person with Asperger's syndrome. If the job is not successful, this can have a detrimental effect on the person's self-esteem and likelihood of subsequent employment. The person's ability to cope with stress must be considered, and sometimes it is wise to start with part-time employment until the person has greater experience and achieved the self-confidence needed to cope with full-time employment.

Once employed, there are specific issues that will need to be addressed. The person with Asperger's syndrome may need initial and continuing support and guidance from his or her employer regarding job expectations (especially if there are any unexpected changes), the interpersonal skills necessary to work effectively and cooperatively in a team, and the organizational skills required, especially work priorities and time management. However, I have found that problems with personal hygiene have been the quickest reason for a person with Asperger's syndrome to lose a job. The line manager may need to supplement spoken instructions with written instructions to avoid problems with auditory memory, and remember not to explain the next task until the last one is completed, to avoid confusion. The employee with Asperger's syndrome will also need regular feedback confirming success, areas of ability to improve and how to achieve improvement.

Knowledge from the relevant literature, a positive attitude on behalf of the employer and employee, and time to adjust to each other may be all that is needed to help an adult with Asperger's syndrome achieve successful long-term employment. However, there are adults with Asperger's syndrome who cannot easily find and maintain employment. Governments have realized that an unemployed adult with Asperger's syndrome is likely to be receiving welfare benefits, and practical, financial and emotional support from his or her family, and may well become depressed and have low self-esteem if unemployed. Equally, the community is not able to benefit from the talents of people with Asperger's syndrome if they remain unemployed. To address this problem, a supported employment service has been developed and evaluated in the United Kingdom.

The Prospects employment service

Prospects is a joint project between the British government and the National Autistic Society, initially based in London but now also in Glasgow, Sheffield and Manchester. The employment service has achieved a remarkable 70 per cent employment rate for 130 adults with Asperger's syndrome and High Functioning Autism (Howlin, Alcock and Burkin 2005). The service provides employment consultants to help the person with Asperger's syndrome find and maintain employment over several years. The recent evaluation of the first eight years of the project found that the main characteristics of Asperger's syndrome that affected employment were organizational skills (especially time keeping, concentration and coping with more than one task at a time), communication difficulties, immature social skills, anxiety and coping with change.

The majority of employment was in the areas of office work and technical and computer industries, with employment primarily in large private companies but also in the government and public sector, small enterprises and charitable organizations. The cost of the scheme was several thousand pounds for each person employed, but once employed, the benefits to the government were a reduction in welfare payments and an increase in tax revenue from the person employed. The benefits to the person with Asperger's syndrome were an increase in disposable income, greater self-esteem, the development of a new social network and the ability to demonstrate specific talents and abilities. The evaluation study of Prospects found agreement between the employers and employees that both parties could not have managed without the services of a specialist employment consultant (Howlin *et al.* 2005).

The employment consultant has many roles: teacher, social worker and psychologist, as well as being an advocate and translator between two 'cultures' with different languages and expectations. The consultant has to know the client's employment strengths and weaknesses, identify a suitable job vacancy, prepare the person for the interview, liaise between employer, client and the client's family, educate the employer and, if necessary, educate fellow employees and identify someone who can become a mentor. The consultant also has to provide emotional and practical support and monitor the ongoing work situation as a 'trouble shooter', in order to resolve any areas of potential conflict or disappointment. The individual support for a client is initially intensive, up to 50 hours a month, but this gradually reduces to only a few hours each month. Being an employment consultant for clients with Asperger's syndrome is a difficult task, but one that can also be very satisfying, especially when the quality of life of the person with Asperger's syndrome improves considerably due to having an enjoyable and productive job.

An interesting employment initiative has been developed in Aarhus, Denmark. In 2004 a company was established with all employees having a diagnosis of Asperger's syndrome or autism. The company, *Specialisterne* (the Specialists), tests electronic equipment such as new telephones and computer programs. The owner of the company (the father of a child with autism) specifically wanted employees with Asperger's syndrome because of their eye for detail and enjoyment of repetitive testing procedures. Each person with Asperger's syndrome has his or her own office, and working hours are flexible. There is also a member of staff to provide support for personal and interpersonal problems. This may in fact not be a unique venture, as I have noted that some international companies in the information technology area already have a considerably high percentage of specialist staff with undiagnosed Asperger's syndrome, or at least a very similar personality profile. Personnel or Human Resources departments of large companies are becoming more knowledgeable regarding Asperger's syndrome and how the company can benefit from and develop the abilities of employees with Asperger's syndrome. This can include avoiding transferring the person to work situations that could cause considerable stress.

Promotion to management

After the employment abilities of the person with Asperger's syndrome are proven, there may be a review of his or her progress and consideration of promotion to line manager. I recently saw a man with Asperger's syndrome who was employed by a large company to repair office machinery. He had acquired a legendary expertise in the mechanics and electronics of copying and fax machines, and was renowned for his ability to quickly identify the cause of the problem, repair the fault and move on to the next assignment. His employer used him as an example of excellent work practice to new employees. In gratitude for his excellent work, the company decided to promote him to become a line manager for the repair staff, and to be based at head office.

Although he had a natural talent with machines, he did not have a natural talent with minds. He could not understand or cope with the office politics, egos, corporate policy and paper work. He started to flounder and, as can be typical of adults with Asperger's syndrome, did not disclose his difficulties to his line manager or his wife. Eventually the stress became too much for him and he attempted suicide. A review of his developmental history by a psychiatrist indicated a diagnosis of Asperger's syndrome. The treatment of his depression was relatively straightforward – a return to a position of responsibility and productivity he could cope with, and in which he could be successful.

A recent publication has addressed the issues faced by adults with Asperger's syndrome who work in management positions, and provides valuable advice (Johnson 2005). Other strategies include having an executive secretary who can compensate for difficulties with organizational and interpersonal problems, an understanding workforce that recognizes and adapts to the person's potentially abrasive manner, and senior management who do not transfer the person with Asperger's syndrome to a position that will cause intolerable stress for all members of the workforce.

There are other strategies to consider during the person's employment lifetime. Eventually the person may have the ability to become self-employed, perhaps working from home, and developing an expertise in an area that does not require being part of a team or organizational hierarchy. For example, many people with Asperger's syndrome are often natural inventors, experts and craftsmen. However, the person may benefit from the help of family members who can provide advice in situations where the person with Asperger's syndrome may not be a good judge of character, and may be vulnerable to financial exploitation; or where the person needs a colleague who has the interpersonal skills needed to deal with the public, or prospective purchasers of equipment designed and made by the person with Asperger's syndrome.

THE PSYCHOLOGICAL VALUE OF EMPLOYMENT

Unemployment has been associated with clinical depression for typical people and this is certainly the case for people with Asperger's syndrome. Depression can also occur when the person is under-employed – that is, he or she is over-qualified for the job. For example, the person may have postgraduate qualifications in information technology, but has only been able to achieve work as a manual labourer or filling supermarket shelves. Thus, having a job that is fulfilling and valued can be a preventative measure for a clinical depression.

Finally, I have noted that some careers and professions are particularly appropriate for people with Asperger's syndrome. Universities are renowned for their tolerance of unusual characters, especially if they show originality and dedication to their research. I have often made the comment that not only are universities a 'cathedral' for the worship of knowledge, they are also 'sheltered workshops' for the socially challenged.

There are several other careers, not yet mentioned in this section, that may be appropriate for a person with Asperger's syndrome. One is that of a librarian, with a library being a quiet work environment. Another is a career in the military, with the person with Asperger's syndrome being relatively calm when under fire and not letting emotionality or discomfort obstruct the military objective. And, last, careers such as a tour guide or telemarketer, where there is a well-practised script and one-way communication, can be ideal for the person with Asperger's syndrome.

Unemployment not only means no income, it also means there is a lack of purpose and structure to the day, a lack of self-worth and, especially for people with Asperger's syndrome, a lack of self-identity. A career or vocation well matched to the abilities and character of the person with Asperger's syndrome can provide this much-needed self-worth and self-identity, along with a real reason to keep going. When I ask adults with Asperger's syndrome to describe themselves, the descriptions are usually what they do, their job or special interest, rather than their family or social network. As Temple Grandin said to me: 'I am what I do.'

KEY POINTS AND STRATEGIES

- College and university:
  - When the student has registered for a specific college course, a member of the teaching or support staff at the student's high school should liaise with the university to provide information on the support the student will need as an undergraduate.
  - There are advantages in students with Asperger's syndrome remaining at home, at least during the first college year, so that a parent can provide support in the areas of budgeting, self-care and the organizational aspects required to complete course assignments on time, and monitor the student's level of stress.
  - The student will need to decide on the number of course units to be undertaken each semester, and it may be wise to start with less than the maximum number of units.
  - The student will need guidance regarding the new social conventions and protocol at lectures and tutorials, when working on assignments in a group, and sending e-mail messages to staff. An appointed student 'buddy' or mentor can provide friendly advice regarding social protocols and expectations.
  - Students with Asperger's syndrome will probably need to meet their academic tutors more frequently than other students to ensure they are 'on the right track', and acquiring the 'mindset' needed for the course.
  - The cognitive, social, motor and sensory profiles of students with Asperger's syndrome need to be considered when deciding course assignments and setting exams.
  - There are practical solutions such as typing rather than talking to explain a concept or solution, using a keyboard during an exam to avoid problems with handwriting, and considering solitary rather than group assignments.
  - Some universities have a support group specifically for students with Asperger's syndrome.
  - Students are more likely to fail or withdraw from a course because of issues with stress management than a lack of intellectual ability or commitment to the course.
- Careers:
  - The general experience of people with Asperger's syndrome is that finding and keeping an appropriate job or career is not as easy as it is for typical people with the same qualifications.
  - For some trades and professions, there may be greater success in learning specific vocational skills using the traditional master and apprentice training rather than classroom-based learning.

- The person with Asperger's syndrome needs to prepare a CV that includes a portfolio of relevant work experience and achievements, interests and abilities, and may include photographs or a digital record of previous work accomplishments and testimonials.

- The person may need to rehearse having a job interview and discuss with someone who knows him or her well whether to accept a particular offer of employment. It is not a case of accepting just any offer of employment.

- The person with Asperger's syndrome may need initial and continuing support and guidance from his or her employer regarding job expectations, the interpersonal skills necessary to work effectively and cooperatively in a team, and the organizational skills required, especially work priorities and time management.

- The benefits to the person with Asperger's syndrome of successful employment are an increase in disposable income, greater self-esteem, the development of a new social network and the ability to demonstrate specific talents and abilities.

CHAPTER 13

Long-term Relationships

Many of those who do marry show tensions and problems in their marriage.

— Hans Asperger ([1944] 1991)

A man or a woman with Asperger's syndrome can develop intimate personal relationships and become a life-long partner. For such a relationship to begin, both parties would have initially found the other person to be attractive. What are the characteristics that someone would find attractive in a person with Asperger's syndrome?

CHOICE OF PARTNER

From my clinical experience, and the research of Maxine Aston (2003), men with Asperger's syndrome have several positive attributes for a prospective partner. The first meeting may be through a shared interest such as the care of animals, similar religious beliefs or studying the same course. Many women describe their first impression of their partner, who at this stage may not have had a diagnosis, as someone who is kind, attentive and slightly immature: the highly desirable 'handsome and silent stranger'. Children with Asperger's syndrome are often perceived as having angelic faces, and as adults may have symmetrical facial features that are aesthetically appealing. The person may be more handsome than previous partners and considered a good 'catch' in terms of looks, especially if the woman has doubts regarding her own self-esteem and physical attractiveness. The lack of social and conversational skills can lead to his being perceived as the 'silent stranger', whose social abilities will be unlocked and transformed by a partner who is an expert on empathy and socializing. There can be a strong maternal compassion for the person's limited social abilities, with a belief that his social confusion and lack of social confidence were due to his circumstances as a child, and can be repaired over time. Love will change everything.

The attractiveness of a man with Asperger's syndrome as a partner can be enhanced by his intellectual abilities, career prospects and degree of attention to his partner during courtship. The devotion can be very flattering, though others might perceive the adulation as bordering on obsessive. The hobby or special interest can initially be perceived as endearing and 'typical of boys and men'. The person with Asperger's syndrome may have an appealing 'Peter Pan' quality.

Men with Asperger's syndrome can also be admired for speaking their mind, having a sense of social justice and strong moral convictions. They are often described as having 'old-world' values, and being less motivated than other men for physically intimate activities, or for spending time with male friends. The man with Asperger's syndrome appears to have a 'feminine', rather than 'macho' quality – the ideal partner for the modern woman.

The man with Asperger's syndrome is usually a late developer in terms of emotional and relationship maturity, and this could be his first serious relationship, while his same-age peers have had several long-term relationships already. There is therefore the advantage of no previous relationship 'baggage'.

Many women have described to me how their partner with Asperger's syndrome resembled their father. Having a parent with Asperger's syndrome may contribute towards determining the type of person you choose to become your partner.

When men with Asperger's syndrome are asked what was initially appealing about their partner, they often describe one physical quality, such as hair, or specific personality characteristics, especially being maternal in looking after (or already having) children, or caring for injured animals. Men with Asperger's syndrome are often less concerned about their partner's physique than other men, and also less concerned about age or cultural differences.

Sometimes the person with Asperger's syndrome appears to have created a mental 'job description' for a prospective partner, searching for a suitable 'applicant' that can compensate for recognized difficulties in life. Once a candidate has been found, that person is pursued with determination that can be hard to resist. One of the 'job requirements' is having advanced social and maternal abilities. Thus, an attractive partner will be someone who is at the opposite end of the empathy and social understanding continuum. People with Asperger's syndrome may also know they need a partner who can act as an executive secretary to help with organizational problems, and continue many of the emotional support functions provided by their mother when they were living at home. Men with Asperger's syndrome often elicit strong maternal feelings in women, and know that is what they need in a partner. They also usually seek someone who has strong moral values, who, once married, is likely to be dedicated to making the relationship succeed.

What is it that typical men find attractive in a woman with Asperger's syndrome? The characteristics can be similar to the characteristics women find appealing in a man with Asperger's syndrome. The woman's social immaturity and naïvety can be appealing to men who have natural paternal and compassionate qualities. There can be the obvious physical attractiveness and admirable talents and abilities. The sometimes emotionally aloof personality may be reminiscent of the man's mother; and there can be the shared enjoyment of common interests and appreciation of the initial degree of adulation.

While men with Asperger's syndrome tend to seek a partner who can compensate for their difficulties in daily life – that is, someone from the other end of the continuum of social and emotional abilities – women with Asperger's syndrome often seek a partner with a personality similar to themselves. They feel more comfortable with someone who does not have a great social life and does not seek frequent physical intimacy. As both partners have similar characteristics and expectations, the relationship can be successful and enduring.

Unfortunately, people with Asperger's syndrome may not be very good at identifying the 'predators' in life, and some women with Asperger's syndrome have not been wise in their choice of partner. They have become the victim of relationship predators and suffered various forms of abuse. The woman with Asperger's syndrome may initially feel sorry for the man, much as she would for a stray dog, but is unable to extricate herself from a history of being attractive to and attracted by disreputable characters. Having low self-esteem can also affect the choice of partner for a woman with Asperger's syndrome. Deborah explained in an e-mail to me: 'I set my expectations very low and as a result gravitated toward abusive people. I cannot stress the importance of recognizing how important self esteem is to an autistic adult.'

PROBLEMS IN THE RELATIONSHIP

The courtship may not provide an indication of the problems that can develop later in the relationship. The person with Asperger's syndrome may have developed a superficial expertise in romance and dating from careful observation, and by mimicking actors and using the script from television programmes and films. Some partners have explained that they never saw the real person before they were married, and after their wedding day, the person abandoned the persona that was previously so attractive. As one woman said, 'He had won the prize and didn't have to pretend any more.'

There are many potential problems in the relationship. Often, what was endearing at the start later becomes a problem. The initial optimism that the partner with Asperger's syndrome will gradually change and become more emotionally mature and socially skilled can dissolve into despair that social skills are static due to limited motivation to be more sociable. This can be due to the intellectual effort needed to socialize, subsequent exhaustion, and a fear of making a social mistake. Joint social contact with friends can slowly diminish. The partner with Asperger's syndrome does not want or need the same degree of social contact they enjoyed as a couple when they were courting. The non-Asperger syndrome partner may reluctantly agree to reduce the frequency and duration of social contact with family, friends and colleagues for the sake of the relationship. They gradually absorb the characteristics of Asperger's syndrome into their own personality.

The most common problem for the non-Asperger's syndrome partner is feeling lonely. The partner with Asperger's syndrome can be content with his or her own company for long periods of time. Although the couple are living together, conversations may be few, and primarily involve the exchange of information rather than an enjoyment of each other's company, experiences and shared opinions. As a man with Asperger's syndrome said, 'My pleasure doesn't come from an emotional or interpersonal exchange.'

In a typical relationship, there is the expectation of regular expressions of love and affection. Chris, a married man with Asperger's syndrome, explained that:

> I have an enormous difficulty with the verbal expression of affection. It is not just a case of feeling embarrassed or self-conscious with it. I understand that this may be difficult for anyone else to understand, but it takes a great deal of effort of will to tell my wife how I feel about her. (Slater-Walker and Slater-Walker 2002, p.89)

His wife added her comments to her husband's infrequent words and gestures that communicate feelings of love:

> Chris told me once that he loved me. I have since discovered that it is not necessary for the person with AS to repeat these small intimacies that are frequently part of a relationship; the fact has been stated once, and that is enough. (Slater-Walker and Slater-Walker 2002, p.99)

For the person with Asperger's syndrome, the frequent reiteration of the obvious or known facts is illogical.

The non-Asperger's syndrome partner suffers affection deprivation which can be a contributory factor to low self-esteem and depression. The typical partner is metaphorically a rose trying to blossom in an affection desert (Long 2003). The partner with Asperger's syndrome wants to be a friend and a lover but has little idea of how to do either (Jacobs 2006).

A recent survey of women who have a partner with Asperger's syndrome included the question 'Does your partner love you?' and 50 per cent replied, 'I don't know' (Jacobs 2006). What was missing in the relationship were daily words and gestures of affection, tangible expressions of love. People with Asperger's syndrome have difficulties with the communication of emotions, and this includes love (see Chapter 6). When a partner said to her husband with Asperger's syndrome, 'You never show you care,' he replied, 'Well, I fixed the fence, didn't I?' The person with Asperger's syndrome may express his or her love in more practical terms; or, to change a quotation from *Star Trek* (Spock, examining an extra-terrestrial: 'It's life, Jim, but not as we know it') in Asperger's syndrome, it is love, but not as we know it.

A metaphor for the need and capacity for affection can be that typical people have a bucket that needs to be filled, whereas people with Asperger's syndrome have a cup that is quickly filled to capacity. The person with Asperger's syndrome may not express sufficient affection to meet the needs of his or her partner. However, I have known of relationships where the partner with Asperger's syndrome expresses affection too frequently, though this may be more as an aspect of severe anxiety and need for maternal reassurance. As a man with Asperger's syndrome said: 'We feel and show affection but not enough and at the wrong intensity.' The person with Asperger's syndrome can be overly detached or attached.

During times of personal distress, when empathy and words and gestures of affection would be expected as an emotional restorative, the typical partner may be left alone to 'get over it'. I have noted that this is not a callous act; the partner with Asperger's syndrome is probably very kind, but in his or her mind, the most effective emotional restorative is solitude. They often describe how a hug is perceived as an uncomfortable squeeze and does not automatically make them feel better. Indeed, the comment from the typical partner can be that hugging a partner with Asperger's syndrome is like 'hugging a piece of wood'. The person does not relax and enjoy such close proximity and touch.

Being alone is often the main emotional recovery mechanism for people with Asperger's syndrome, and they may assume that is also the case for their partner. They may also not know how to respond, or fear making the situation worse. I observed a situation where a husband with Asperger's syndrome was sitting next to his wife, who was in tears. He remained still and did not offer any words or gestures of affection. Later, when I discussed this situation with him, and asked if he noticed that his wife was crying, he replied, 'Yes, but I didn't want to do the wrong thing.'

There may be issues associated with sexual intimacy. The person with Asperger's syndrome may not by nature be a romantic person who understands the value in a relationship of an amorous atmosphere, foreplay and close physical contact. Ron, a man with Asperger's syndrome, said, 'Intimacy means for me being invaded or overwhelmed. I experienced none of the proverbial sexual chemistry with anyone.' There can also be sensory experiences during moments of sexual intimacy that are perceived as unpleasant by the person with Asperger's syndrome, affecting the enjoyment of both partners.

Knowledge on sexuality may also be limited, or the source material of concern. Men with Asperger's syndrome may consider pornography as an authoritative guide book for sexual activities, and women with Asperger's syndrome may have used television 'soap operas' as a guide to the script and actions in intimate relationships. Non-Asperger's syndrome partners may also have difficulty having a romantic and passionate relationship with someone they often have to 'mother', and who may have the emotional maturity of an adolescent.

Sexuality can become a special interest in terms of acquiring information and an interest in sexual diversity and activities. The desire for sexual activities and sexual intimacy can be excessive, almost compulsive. However, the partner of a man or woman with Asperger's syndrome is more likely to be concerned about the lack of sexual desire rather than an excess. The partner with Asperger's syndrome may become asexual once he or she has children or once the couple have formally committed themselves to the relationship. In a relationship counselling session, the partner of a man with Asperger's syndrome was visibly distressed when announcing to me that she and her husband had not had sex for over a year. Her husband, who has Asperger's syndrome, appeared to be confused and said to her, 'Why would you want sex when we have enough children?'

There are other problems. In modern western society we have tended to replace the word husband or wife with the word partner. This is a reflection of changing attitudes towards relationships. Women today are justifiably no longer content with their partner just being the provider of the income for the family. They expect their partner to share the work load at home, for domestic chores and caring for the children, and to be their best friend in terms of conversation, sharing experiences and emotional support. Sharing, and being a best friend, are not attributes that are easy for the person with Asperger's syndrome to achieve.

There can be problems with the ability of the person with Asperger's syndrome to manage anxiety, and this can affect the relationship. The partner can become very controlling, and life for the whole family is based around rigid routines. Partners with Asperger's syndrome can impose their pronouncements without consultation with their typical partner, who resents being excluded from major decisions, such as relocation or a change of career. For those adults with Asperger's syndrome who continue to have problems with executive function (see Chapter 9), the typical partner often has to take the responsibility for the family finances, budgeting and resolving the organizational and interpersonal problems that have developed in the partner's work situation. This adds to the stress and responsibility of the typical partner.

In any relationship, there will inevitably be areas of disagreement and conflict. Unfortunately, people with Asperger's syndrome can have a history of limited ability to manage conflict successfully. They may have a limited range of options and may not be skilled in the art of negotiation, accepting alternative perspectives or agreeing to compromise. There can be an inability to accept even partial responsibility. Partners complain, 'it is never his fault', 'I always get the blame' and 'I'm always criticized, I'm never encouraged'. There can be concerns about verbal abuse, especially as a response to perceived criticism, with an apparent inability to show remorse and to forgive and forget. This can be due to a difficulty with understanding the thoughts, feelings and perspectives of others, a central characteristic of Asperger's syndrome. The person with Asperger's syndrome may also have problems with anger management that further complicate the relationship.

A recent survey of the mental and physical health of couples where the male partner has Asperger's syndrome, a diagnosis not shared by the female partner, indicated that the relationship has very different health effects for each partner (Aston 2003). Most men with Asperger's syndrome felt that their mental and physical health had significantly improved due to the relationship. They stated that they felt less stressed and would much prefer to be in the relationship than alone. They had achieved an inner satisfaction with the relationship. In contrast, the overwhelming majority of non-Asperger's syndrome partners stated that their mental health had significantly deteriorated due to the relationship. They felt emotionally exhausted and neglected, and many reported signs of a clinical depression. A majority of respondents in the survey also stated that the relationship had contributed to deterioration in physical health. Thus, the relationship was considered as contributing to improved mental and physical health by the majority of partners with Asperger's syndrome, but the reverse for the non-Asperger's syndrome partner. This explains the perception of many partners with Asperger's syndrome that the relationship is just fine, and they cannot understand why their relationship skills are criticized. The relationship is just fine for their needs, while their partner feels more like a housekeeper, accountant and mother figure.

STRATEGIES TO STRENGTHEN THE RELATIONSHIP

I have provided relationship counselling to couples where one partner has a diagnosis of Asperger's syndrome, and I have great respect for the ability of the non-Asperger's syndrome partners to commit themselves to the relationship. Among their many attributes are belief in their partner, remaining faithful to the relationship, intuition that he or she 'can't' rather than 'won't', and an ability to imagine and have compassion for what it must be like to have Asperger's syndrome.

Clinical and counselling experience suggests that there are three requisites for a successful relationship (Aston 2003). The first is that both partners acknowledge the diagnosis. The non-Asperger's syndrome partners may be the first of the two to accomplish this and no longer feel self-blame or insane. Their circumstances are finally validated and eventually understood by family and friends. They also tend to feel better able to cope on a day-to-day basis. However, acknowledging the diagnosis can be the end of hope that their partner will naturally improve his or her relationship skills.

The acceptance of the diagnosis for those with Asperger's syndrome is important in enabling them to recognize their relationship strengths and weaknesses. There can be the dawn of realization of how their behaviour and attitudes affect their partners, and a greater sense of cooperation between the partners in identifying changes to improve the relationship and mutual understanding.

The second requisite is motivation for both partners to change and learn. There is usually more motivation for change from the non-Asperger's syndrome partner, who may already have a more flexible attitude to change and a foundation of considerable relationship skills. The third requisite is access to relationship counselling, modified to accommodate the profile of abilities of the partner with Asperger's syndrome, and a willingness to implement suggestions from specialists in Asperger's syndrome, the relevant literature and support groups.

Many couples who attend conventional relationship counselling have found that the standard relationship therapy is less likely to be successful when one of the partners has Asperger's syndrome. The relationship counsellor needs to be knowledgeable in Asperger's syndrome and to modify counselling techniques to accommodate the specific problems people with Asperger's syndrome have with empathy, self-insight and self-disclosure, the communication of emotions and previous relationship experiences.

We now have self-help literature on relationships written by couples with one partner who has Asperger's syndrome, and by specialists in Asperger's syndrome (Aston 2003; Edmonds and Worton 2005; Jacobs 2006; Lawson 2005; Rodman 2003; Slater-Walker and Slater-Walker 2002; Stanford 2003).

It is important to remember that my descriptions of relationship difficulties and support strategies are based on my experience of relationship counselling of adults who did not benefit from a diagnosis in early childhood and subsequent guidance through-out childhood in the development of friendship and relationship abilities. Such individuals have spent a lifetime knowing they are different, and developing camouflaging and compensatory mechanisms that may contribute to some social success at a superficial level but can be detrimental to an intimate relationship with a partner. I suspect that the new generation of children and adolescents who have the advantage of a diagnosis and greater understanding of Asperger's syndrome by themselves, relatives and friends are more likely to have a successful long-term relationship that is mutually satisfying.

While the partner with Asperger's syndrome will benefit from guidance and encouragement in improving relationship skills, there are strategies to assist the non-Asperger's syndrome partner. Once the diagnosis has been accepted by the family, there can be greater emotional support from close family members and friends. It is important that the person develops a network of friends to reduce the sense of isolation, and learns to re-experience the enjoyment of social occasions, perhaps without the presence of the partner with Asperger's syndrome. It is important that he or she does not feel guilty that the partner is not there. There are considerable relationship advantages in the non-Asperger's syndrome partner having a special friend who has an intuitive ability to repair emotions, and can become a soul mate to provide empathy. An occasional escape or holiday with friends can also provide an opportunity to regain confidence in social abilities and rapport. A positive attitude is also of paramount importance. As one partner said, 'When life gives you a lemon, make lemonade.'

HAVING A PARENT WITH ASPERGER'S SYNDROME

When the relationship evolves into being parents, the partner and now parent with Asperger's syndrome probably has little understanding of the needs and behaviour of typical children and adolescents. The non-Asperger's syndrome partner may feel as if she or he is effectively a solo parent. The family often have to accommodate the imposition of inflexible routines and expectations in behaviour, the intolerance of noise, mess and any intrusion into the parent's solitary activities, perceived 'invasion' of the home by the children's friends, and a black and white analysis of people. The person with Asperger's syndrome usually needs reassurance but may rarely reassure family members, has little interest in events of emotional significance to others, and can often criticize but rarely compliment. The emotional atmosphere can be affected by negativism, causing tension and dampening the enthusiasm of others. The family are all too aware of quick mood changes, especially sudden rage, and try not to antagonize the person due to fear of the intense emotional reaction.

A mild expression of such behaviour and attitudes can be excused by family members and society as typical of some men, but society has different expectations of mothers. A mother is expected to have an instinctive ability to nurture and meet the emotional needs of children. This instinct may not be as reliable with a mother who has Asperger's syndrome. Sometimes a woman with Asperger's syndrome who is single and pregnant may acknowledge her limited maternal instinct and, for the benefit of the newborn child, the baby becomes available for adoption. It is important to recognize that although parenting instinct may be less reliable, a mother or father with Asperger's syndrome can learn how to become a good parent. I have known many mothers and fathers with Asperger's syndrome who have acquired, through reading and guidance, the ability to understand the development and needs of their children, and have become exemplary parents. There are certain prerequisites: the first is recognition by the parent with Asperger's syndrome of the need for guidance, and the second is access to advice. The non-Asperger's syndrome partner is usually naturally gifted in the intuitive ability to raise children and needs to be perceived as the resident expert.

What are the reactions of the typical children in the family to having a parent with Asperger's syndrome? Each child will have his or her own way of coping. The typical child can sometimes feel that he or she is 'invisible' or a nuisance to the parent with Asperger's syndrome, and may feel deprived of the acceptance, reassurance, encouragement and love that he or she expects and needs. A daughter said she never felt loved by her father with Asperger's syndrome. When affection is given, the feeling is that it is 'cold' and may not actually be comforting. The child only feels valued for his or her achievements, not for him- or herself. Conversations with the parent with Asperger's syndrome can be a prolonged monologue of the adult's own problems, with only a brief and superficial interest in the child's problems. The child learns not to express emotions such as distress or to expect compassion. There can also be embarrassment with regard to how the parent affects the development of friendships. The daughter of a woman with Asperger's syndrome sent me the following example that illustrates many aspects of having a parent with Asperger's syndrome:

> I almost had an Australian pen friend when I was 6 years old. I was very excited to receive a letter from the other side of the world, long before the Internet existed. I could hardly contain my excitement and couldn't wait to write to this new friend and exchange my news. I had read the letter and wanted to answer her questions,

but my mother had other ideas. 'There are spelling mistakes in this letter, first you must correct her spelling mistakes and send the corrected letter back to her. This is how she will learn to spell'. I don't know whether this little girl learned to spell because I never heard from her again.

There are several coping mechanisms. The lack of affection and encouragement, and high expectations can result in the child becoming an adult who is a high achiever, as an attempt to eventually experience the parental adulation that was missing throughout childhood. Another mechanism is to escape the situation, spending time with the families of friends, and leaving home as soon as possible, preferably some distance away, to avoid family reunions. One of the reactions can be an intense hatred of the parent with Asperger's syndrome for not being the parent the child needs. The child may encourage the non-Asperger's syndrome parent to seek a divorce, but separation is not easy, since it is clear that the partner with Asperger's syndrome probably could not cope, practically or emotionally, alone.

When children become adults and recognize later in life that one of their parents had Asperger's syndrome, they can finally understand the personality, abilities and motives of their mother or father. A daughter explained that, 'I never felt loved by my father. The diagnosis has enabled me to love and accept my family and remove their ability to hurt me emotionally.'

There can be a natural bond, or antagonism, between a parent and child who both have Asperger's syndrome. Liane Holliday Willey has a very close and supportive relationship with her father. He recognized that his daughter would need to acquire the knowledge he had learned about people, socializing and conversations. He became her social mentor, with daily advice on what to do and say in social situations. Father and daughter understood and respected each other's perspective and experiences. This is not always the case. The enforced proximity of two inflexible and dominating characters with Asperger's syndrome can lead to animosity and arguments. The non-Asperger's syndrome partner and parent becomes an experienced diplomat, trying to 'keep the peace' and facing problems of conflicting loyalties. Having two people with Asperger's syndrome in the same family can be like having two magnets – they either attract or repel each other.

In Liane Holliday Willey's family, Asperger's syndrome has occurred in some family members in each generation. She has a daughter with Asperger's syndrome and her father has some of the associated characteristics. Liane's family have a very positive attitude towards Asperger's syndrome and she explained that:

> In our family, we always encourage our aspie to realize she is filled to the brim with admirable traits and powerful abilities, yet we are equally as faithful in trying to get her to be aware of her social, emotional and cognitive inefficiencies. Keeping the balance of the power such that we help her to work from her strengths, we present her with academic and affective strategies geared to help her

turn her inefficiencies into firm proficiencies. Our goal is to help our daughter do what my father and I were able to do, join the world on its terms without losing sight of who we are and what we need. (Willey 2001, p.149)

KEY POINTS AND STRATEGIES

- The male partner with Asperger's syndrome:
    - Many women describe their first impression of their partner, who at this stage may not have had a diagnosis, as someone who is kind, attentive and slightly immature: the highly desirable 'handsome and silent stranger'.
    - There can be a strong maternal compassion for the person's limited social abilities.
    - The attractiveness of a man with Asperger's syndrome as a partner can be enhanced by his intellectual abilities, career prospects and degree of attention to his partner during courtship.
    - The partner with Asperger's syndrome is usually a late developer in terms of emotional and relationship maturity.
    - Many women have described how their partner with Asperger's syndrome resembled their father.
    - Men with Asperger's syndrome are often less concerned about their partner's physique than other men, and also less concerned about age or cultural differences.

- While men with Asperger's syndrome tend to seek a partner who can compensate for their difficulties in daily life – that is, someone from the other end of the continuum of social and emotional abilities – women with Asperger's syndrome often seek a partner with a personality similar to themselves.

- Problems in the relationship:
    - The courtship may not provide an indication of the problems that can develop later in the relationship.
    - The initial optimism that the partner with Asperger's syndrome will gradually change and become more emotionally mature and socially skilled can dissolve into despair that social skills are static due to limited motivation to be more sociable.
    - The most common problem for the non-Asperger's syndrome partner is feeling lonely.
    - The non-Asperger's syndrome partner often suffers affection deprivation which can be a contributory factor to low self-esteem and depression.

- The person with Asperger's syndrome may express his or her love in more practical terms than through gestures of affection.
- A metaphor for the need and capacity for affection is that typical people have a bucket that needs to be filled, whereas people with Asperger's syndrome have a cup that is quickly filled to capacity.

- Successful strategies to overcome difficulties:
  - Clinical and counselling experience suggests that there are three requisites for a successful relationship. The first is that both partners acknowledge the diagnosis. The second requisite is motivation for both partners to change and learn. The third is access to relationship counselling modified to accommodate the profile of abilities and experiences of the partner with Asperger's syndrome.
  - There are strategies to assist the non-Asperger's syndrome partner, namely to develop a network of friends to reduce the sense of isolation and re-experience the enjoyment of social occasions.

- The parent with Asperger's syndrome:
  - When the relationship evolves into being parents, the partner and now parent with Asperger's syndrome probably has little understanding of the needs and behaviour of typical children and adolescents.
  - A mother or father with Asperger's syndrome can learn how to become a good parent.
  - When children become adults and recognize later in life that one of their parents had Asperger's syndrome, they can finally understand the personality, abilities and motives of their mother or father.
  - There can be a natural bond, or antagonism, between a parent and child who both have Asperger's syndrome.

CHAPTER 14

Psychotherapy

They are strangely impenetrable and difficult to fathom. Their emotional life remains a closed book.

– Hans Asperger ([1944] 1991)

There are many different types of psychotherapy that have been used with children and adults with Asperger's syndrome, but very few published case studies. In my opinion, traditional psychoanalytical psychotherapy has very little to offer a child or adult with Asperger's syndrome, an opinion shared by some psychotherapists (Jacobsen 2003, 2004). However there are published case studies that have used traditional and modified psychoanalytical psychotherapy (Adamo 2004; Alvarez and Reid 1999; Pozzi 2003; Rhode and Klauber 2004; Youell 1999). The detailed psychoanalysis of the mother and infant relationship can be irrelevant to understanding the mind of a child with Asperger's syndrome, and lead to the mother developing considerable guilt and the child being very confused. Asperger's syndrome is not caused by an inability of a child's mother to love and relate to her son or daughter. This may seem obvious, but unfortunately, in some countries, such as France, the traditional psychoanalytical concept of autism and Asperger's syndrome is the dominant theoretical model and the basis of treatment.

The methods of analysis used in traditional psychoanalytical therapy are based on a conceptualization of the development of typical children, but children with Asperger's syndrome perceive and relate to a very different world. In psychoanalytical therapies, the pretend play of the child is analysed to explore his or her inner thoughts. The natural pretend play of young children with Asperger's syndrome is often an accurate re-enactment or 'echo' of a scene from the child's favourite story, and is not necessarily a metaphor for his or her life or to be attributed with projected meanings. When using projective testing, the child with Asperger's syndrome is more likely to provide factual information than projections of the self. The child is simply describing what he or she sees.

The Rorschach profile of children with Asperger's syndrome is consistent with the diagnostic criteria (Holaday, Moak and Shipley 2001). There is an under-reporting of human content, human movement and cooperative movement, and indications of 'impoverished or unrewarding social relationships' and 'social ineptness'. The responses are also significantly different from normative data regarding the display or experience of emotion and the ability to establish and maintain intimacy and closeness. The test is sensitive to some of the characteristics of Asperger's syndrome.

The Minnesota Multiphasic Personality Inventory (second edition) has been administered to adults with Asperger's syndrome, and their profile on the MMPI reflects personality characteristics of social isolation, interpersonal difficulties, depressed mood and coping deficits (Ozonoff *et al.* 2005a). The personality profile is consistent with the clinical descriptions and also included discomfort in social situations, social reservation and introversion, shyness and social anxiety. The study also identified limitations in insight and self- (and other) awareness which would be consistent with our psychological models of Asperger's syndrome, especially delayed Theory of Mind abilities.

Psychotherapy can be of considerable value to parents in helping understand the psychological reactions to having a son, daughter or partner with Asperger's syndrome, and the frustration of saying, 'I shouldn't have to tell you' (Jacobsen 2003). This comment, often said in exasperation, would probably have been said many times to a person with Asperger's syndrome and is usually due to not understanding the nature of Asperger's syndrome.

A parent or partner may need insight into the mind of the person with Asperger's syndrome from a psychotherapist to facilitate coming to terms with someone who does not relate to family members in conventional ways, and provide insight into the associated emotions and necessary adjustments. We know that having someone explain the nature of Asperger's syndrome and the child's perspective can enrich the relationship between child and parent (Pakenham, Sofronoff and Samios 2004), and improve the quality of the relationship when a partner has Asperger's syndrome (Aston 2003).

Children and adults with Asperger's syndrome can benefit from psychotherapy, but the therapy needs to be based on a thorough understanding of the nature of Asperger's syndrome, especially the ability of the person to understand and communicate thoughts and feelings, and the concept of self in terms of self-image, self-esteem and self-acceptance, based on the life experiences of someone with Asperger's syndrome. This will require the psychotherapist to know the latest cognitive psychology research on Asperger's syndrome, especially the studies on Theory of Mind, executive function and weak central coherence; to have read the experiences described in the autobiographies; and to be prepared to make appropriate modifications to conventional psychotherapies. Eventually we may see the development of a completely new theoretical perspective and psychotherapy based not on the abilities, experiences and thoughts of typical children, but on the different profile of abilities, experiences and thoughts of a child with Asperger's syndrome.

The development of a rapport between client and psychotherapist is essential, but clients with Asperger's syndrome can either instantly, and permanently, like or dislike other people, especially professionals. There will need to be some careful consideration with regard to identifying a psychotherapist who is likely to be accepted by the person with Asperger's syndrome. The psychotherapist will need an understanding of the linguistic profile associated with Asperger's syndrome, including difficulties with the pragmatic aspects of language, especially conversational turn-taking and knowing when and how to interrupt, and a tendency to make literal interpretations and to be pedantic. The client with Asperger's syndrome will require more time to cognitively process explanations, and will benefit from a clear, structured and systematic approach with shorter but more frequent therapy sessions. It will also help to have the main points from each session typed and made available to the client and to review those points at the start of the next session. The psychotherapist will need to explain the nature and boundaries of a therapeutic relationship, such as when is an appropriate time to contact the psychotherapist by telephone, knowing what the therapist needs to know, and recognizing that he or she is helping in a professional capacity, not as a personal friend (Hare and Paine 1997).

Although psychotherapy can be extremely valuable in helping a person with Asperger's syndrome, there are difficulties in finding a psychotherapist with extensive experience with clients who have Asperger's syndrome, and meeting the cost of lengthy therapy. Some families will have the financial resources for weekly therapy sessions that may last from several months to several years but this will be beyond the financial resources of most families and not likely to be available from government support services or private health insurance.

Learning about each other's mind

One of the components of psychotherapy is for the psychotherapist to learn about the client's inner thoughts. The understanding and expression of inner thoughts, of themselves and others, can be a considerable problem for people with Asperger's syndrome. Liane Holliday Willey explains that 'Self-analysis does not come easy to the aspie, particularly the male aspie. Some of us never get to the point where we can look inward and explain outward' (Willey 2001, p.87).

We use the term Theory of Mind, first used by cognitive psychologists, to explain this characteristic, but the concept can also be understood within the psychoanalytical framework (Mayes, Cohen and Klin 1993). The psychotherapist will need to incorporate the strategies described in Chapter 5 to enable the person with Asperger's syndrome to develop a greater maturity and insight into the thoughts, feelings and intentions of others, and to help develop the person's vocabulary to precisely describe emotions as described in Chapter 6.

Conventional psychotherapy relies on a conversation between client and psychotherapist in a face-to-face interaction. We know that the client with Asperger's syndrome will have a limited ability to express inner thoughts and emotions eloquently using speech, and greater difficulties, in comparison to typical clients, in processing the psychotherapist's speech and intentions and deciphering subtle social and emotional cues. This will make the psychotherapeutic interaction more confusing and stressful in comparison to other clients. I have found that the client can be more relaxed and able to provide greater insight into inner thoughts and experiences by asking him or her to engage in a therapeutic 'conversation' using two connected computers or exchanging e-mails. People with Asperger's syndrome have considerable difficulty with the social and conversational aspects of life, and when these are minimized, the person is better able to explain and learn.

Another approach is to use art as a means of expression, such as drawing an event, and using speech and thought bubbles as occurs when making a 'Comic Strip Conversation' (see Chapter 6). The client may prefer to choose music that accurately expresses the thought or emotion or, in the case of children, re-enact a scene from a favourite movie or story that resembles the event or emotions. These indirect strategies can give a remarkable insight into the inner world of the person with Asperger's syndrome.

Past incidents of injustice, to themselves or others, are difficult for people with Asperger's syndrome to understand and resolve. Memories of being bullied, misunderstood, blamed or betrayed can intrude on their thoughts as an everyday experience, many years after the event occurred. The scene can be mentally replayed as an attempt to understand the motives of the participants and determine who is to blame, to achieve understanding and resolution. The psychotherapist can use Comic Strip Conversations to first establish the client's perception and interpretation of the thoughts and feelings of each participant, and can then provide greater insight into the minds and motivations of the participants to achieve closure. When there is a lack of intuitive insight, the psychotherapist can provide explanations and information. The ghosts of the past can be laid to rest by knowledge and understanding of thoughts and intentions that were previously elusive.

The psychotherapist may not be able to use transference constructively as with other clients, but can become a mentor, someone who understands and provides education, enabling the person with Asperger's syndrome to articulate his or her perspective and intentions better. The client with Asperger's syndrome can also become more aware of how his or her words and actions affect the thoughts of others.

Thus, long-term psychotherapy can help the person with Asperger's syndrome understand key events in his or her life, and cope in a world that does not always understand the perspective and intentions of someone with Asperger's syndrome. The process of determining 'where I come from', a combination of understanding the nature of

Asperger's syndrome, previous experiences and how the characteristics have affected the individual, will help in another component of psychotherapy, understanding 'who I am now' – the concept of self.

The concept of self

At some stage in childhood, the person with Asperger's syndrome recognizes that he or she is different to other children. In Chapter 1 there was a description of the four psychological reactions to that realization, namely depression, escape into imagination, arrogance, and survival by imitation. Psychotherapy can help children or adults with Asperger's syndrome achieve a realistic appreciation of who they are and to recognize their strengths more than their weaknesses.

The person with Asperger's syndrome can be very self-critical, one of the contributory factors to a clinical depression. Caroline, a teenager with Asperger's syndrome, said to me that 'The worst thing about disappointing yourself is that you never forgive yourself fully.' Psychotherapy can help reduce the self-doubt and self-criticism. The negative self-image can be reduced by the Attributes Activity described in Chapter 15 to help the person identify his or her qualities, and perceive him- or herself as someone who is different, not necessarily defective. Collaboration between family and key people in the person's life can encourage an increase in successful and pleasurable activities, facilitating greater social success and the encouragement of self-esteem.

The psychological reaction of escape into imagination can become a concern when the fantasy world begins to intrude into reality. Escape into an imaginary world can be an understandable reaction to feeling alienated from the real world, but under extreme stress could lead to the development of delusions and loss of contact with reality: a psychosis. The child with Asperger's syndrome may try to cope with life by imagining being a super-hero to achieve power and value. Psychotherapy can help the child develop a concept of self that is grounded and realistic, again based on an appreciation of personality qualities rather than dwelling on difficulties with social integration and comparison with socially able peers. Due to a previous history of being a victim of teasing, the adolescent with Asperger's syndrome could develop a paranoid delusion that other people's intentions are invariably malicious. Psychotherapy and guidance in Theory of Mind abilities can help the person understand the intentions of others and to be more objective. Psychotherapy can also encourage self-talk to provide a more objective perception and interpretation of the intentions of others.

A person with Asperger's syndrome could develop a compensatory self-concept of him- or herself as someone who is superior, and this causes others to perceive the person as arrogant. Again, psychotherapy can help the person achieve a realistic appreciation of his or her abilities and the attributes of others. Therapy will need to include insight into how such an attitude affects relationships and the ability to make and keep friends, as well as the value of admitting making a mistake, and avoiding feelings of anger towards people who do not meet high expectations.

When the reaction to Asperger's syndrome is to achieve social acceptance by acting, using a pre-determined script and designated role, people with Asperger's syndrome may camouflage their social difficulties but not be true to their real selves or understand who they really are. Their personality is determined by the role they take in a particular situation and imitating those who are successful in a particular situation. An adult with Asperger's syndrome who is a retired professional actor, said to me that, 'It was only in my adult years I developed my identity.' During his childhood through to his young adult years he did not know who he was, other than a repertoire of roles. Psychotherapy can help the person in the search for self-identity, awareness and acceptance.

Therapy activities for self-identity

The first stage in self-identity is for the person to understand the nature of Asperger's syndrome and which characteristics associated with the syndrome are expressed in his or her profile of abilities and personality. The second stage is to use semi-projective sentence completion activities, such as: 'I am…; I sometimes…; I feel …when…', etc., to enable the psychotherapist to have a greater understanding of the person's self-representation. I have found that descriptions of self-identity often include low self-esteem with regard to physical and social abilities, but a high opinion of intellectual abilities.

When children and adults with Asperger's syndrome are asked to describe themselves, they tend to define their personality in terms of what they like to do or collect, but not their social network of family and friends (Lee and Hobson 1998). When I asked Danny, an adolescent with Asperger's syndrome, to describe his own personality, and the personalities of people he knew, he replied, 'I don't know what the names of personalities are.'

When talking to children with Asperger's syndrome about their special interest, the listener can be amazed at the depth of knowledge but also the ability of the children to understand or develop their own classification or cataloguing system for the interest. However, this is in stark contrast to their immaturity in the natural cataloguing system of people based on descriptions of character or personality. The child or adult with Asperger's syndrome may be able to categorize objects and facts according to a logical framework but have considerable difficulty developing a framework for people.

The problem appears to be one of immaturity in the concept of characterization. Very young typical children first divide people into one of only two groups or character dimensions, nice and not nice. The next stage is to accept that someone can have several characteristics. The typical child can describe his or her teacher as 'She can be kind but then she can be mean sometimes.' A person can be perceived as having more than one personality attribute. Typical children start to understand who of their peers are good guys and bad guys, who to approach and who to avoid. They also learn to adapt their behaviour according to the personality or character of the person they are with. As children develop, they increase their vocabulary to describe different personality attributes and broaden their concept of personality. Eventually friendship is not based on proximity, possessions or physical abilities but aspects of personality such as being funny, caring and trustworthy. The child has matured beyond using visible characteristics to describe people to an appreciation of someone's mind, and an ability to describe and appreciate that mind.

The third stage is to develop a vocabulary and understanding of characterization and personalities. This can help the person with Asperger's syndrome understand the personalities of others and eventually his or her own personality or character. I ask young children to think of someone they know well, and what animal could represent that person. For example, their mother could be represented by a busy beaver; someone who teases them as a predatory tiger or a shark. When I ask the children what animal would represent me, the general opinion is that I would be represented by a dog, happy to see them and someone who accepts them! When asked to decide on which animal would represent their own character, the suggestions can range from a timid mouse to a wise owl. This activity can be used to determine which characters are to be avoided, being recognized as 'dangerous animals'; the concept of trust and duplicity – 'a wolf in sheep's clothing'; and which animals or characters are compatible with their own character representation. The characterization activity can also use cars, buildings, rooms or furniture, to represent particular people; for example, a teacher might be represented by a library, or an unpleasant person by a smelly toilet. I have found that humour is a valuable component of psychotherapy (and education) of people with Asperger's syndrome.

The child's special interest can also be used to develop characterization abilities. A child with Asperger's syndrome had a special interest in Russian military aircraft. I asked him, 'If your mother were a Russian military aircraft, what aircraft would she be?' He replied that she would be an old and heavy Illushin transport plane, because she walks slowly and carries so many things in her handbag. When asked what aircraft he would be, he replied that he would be the latest MiG fighter, and be very fast. His characterization was very perceptive, as he also had signs of ADHD.

The popular children's books *Mr Men* and *Little Miss* by Roger Hargreaves include characters such as Mr Grumpy, Mr Silly, Mr Nosey, Little Miss Helpful and Little Miss Dotty that can develop the young child's vocabulary and conceptualization of personalities. The psychotherapist can ask whether the child knows anyone who may be a little bit like one of the story characters; for example, the school principal can sometimes be like Mr Nosey (though it may be wise not to tell him who he resembles). The psychotherapist can create a new character, Mr or Little Miss Asperger's Syndrome, to illustrate the characteristics of Asperger's syndrome and how the other characters in the stories would react to that person. An extension of story writing is to work with the child on an imaginary story where he or she is the hero because of their Asperger qualities. We also have fiction for children that includes characters and heroes with Asperger's syndrome (see the Resources section towards the end of the book).

Adolescents can use computer games such as 'The Sims' to explore different character types and create a character with their personality and abilities. Drama activities, especially when recorded and watched on video, can be used to increase the understanding of characterization, and explore the experience of being someone else and observing someone portraying *their* character. The clients are then more able to perceive themselves as others perceive them.

Liane Holliday Willey described to me how, as a teenager and young adult, she had difficulty identifying bad characters, which could place her in vulnerable situations. She knew that her typical friends were very good at character judgements and when she met someone who could potentially move from acquaintance to friend, she asked her friends to meet that person and to give her advice on whether she should move to the next stage of friendship with him or her.

Psychotherapy can be used to develop an insight that can be invaluable when creating social opportunities and making decisions about friendships or close relationships. One of the values of the program on characterization is its potential to define the person's character and determine the type of person that matches or complements that character type. The metaphor of a puzzle with two pieces can be used: the person's 'puzzle shape' (character and profile of abilities) is unusual, and the development of insight into one's character or personality may help him or her to find and connect to a matching 'shape' (a person with complementary characteristics) who may become a genuine friend or prospective partner.

Adults with Asperger's syndrome can benefit from reading autobiographies of women and men with Asperger's syndrome to identify with similar experiences and emotions. One option in long-term psychotherapy is for the client to type his or her autobiography and review past events with the psychotherapist in the new light created by a greater understanding of Asperger's syndrome and the thoughts and intentions of others.

A recent study of the temperament and character of adults with Asperger's syndrome identified a tendency to have an anxious and 'obsessional' personality, and be passive, dependent and explosive (Soderstrom, Rastam and Gillberg 2002). The study also identified a tendency to have an immature character and problems with self-directedness, such as having an externalised locus of control – that is, assuming their personal feelings of pleasure or discomfort are not due to the consequences of their own efforts but due to the actions and intentions of others.

The theory of personal constructs, originally developed by George Kelly in the 1950s, has a scientific and logical theoretical framework and practical therapy that is well suited to the mindset of people with Asperger's syndrome (Hare, Jones and Paine 1999). Personal Construct Psychology (PCP) is based on the principle that people develop their own unique models of reality (Fransella 2005). This approach is especially applicable to someone with Asperger's syndrome. The repertory grid technique of PCP uses a measuring system and mathematical formula that provides a visual and succinct representation of self-characterization, the way the person construes his or her world and relates to others and directions for change in self-understanding and personal qualities.

The procedure is to construct a simple repertory grid of *elements* and *constructs*. The elements are people and the client is asked to write on a set of blank cards the names of the important people in his or her life, with one name on each card, and two additional cards with the words 'how I would like to be' and 'how I am now'. The elements (people) are then used to identify the constructs or dimensions that the person uses to identify similarities and differences between people. The person takes two or three cards at random and is asked in what ways the elements, or people, are similar and in what ways they are different. The answer then becomes a construct enabling discussion of the words which describe the two extremes of the construct, for example helpful versus unhelpful. The two extremes of the construct are written at the ends of a large piece of paper. The person is then shown all the cards and asked 'Who is the most...?' and he or she places the cards in rank order between the two extremes. A record is made by the clinician of the rank order of the elements. The cards are re-sorted and the person takes another two or three elements, identifies another construct, and the procedure is repeated until several (or sufficient) constructs are identified. The arrangement of elements and constructs and their inter-correlations can be analysed visually and by a computer program. In my opinion, the psychotherapies of first choice with children and adults with Asperger's syndrome are Cognitive Behaviour Therapy (see Chapter 6) and Personal Construct Psychology.

I have noted that adults with Asperger's syndrome tend to have immature constructs, and some constructs are more likely with this population. For example, one of the likely constructs for adults with Asperger's syndrome is intellectual ability, which has a high personal value. Thus, being called stupid is considered a particularly hurtful insult as the person with Asperger's syndrome clearly admires people with high intellect. There can also be the development of an intellectual arrogance as part of the personality profile. This discovery has been valuable information for me and I have changed my method of commendation for children with Asperger's syndrome. For a typical child, to be told that something he or she has done has made someone happy or proud is a powerful reward or motivator. The altruistic desire to please people can be less of a motivation for children with Asperger's syndrome. I usually prefer to appeal to the intellectual vanity of such children, and commend the child for his or her intelligence, how smart he or she is, rather than commenting on how pleased I am.

Two of the ultimate goals in life and psychotherapy are to understand and accept who you are. Some children and adults with Asperger's syndrome appear to have achieved this without formal therapy. Warwick, a 12-year-old boy with Asperger's syndrome, wrote an e-mail to me, stating, 'I would like to see ASD children accepted with our funny ways. I find tiring and stressful and annoying spending so much time watching what you do. Sometimes I just want to be me and I'm glad to be me.' An adult with Asperger's syndrome said to me, 'I no longer wish normal. I embrace my aspieness, I want to share my joy at being me.' Rebecca sent me an e-mail and wrote:

> I am what you might call one of the idiosyncratic members of society. I am one of the unforgiven. I have been referred to as a space cadet and a freak. Or, depending on your generation, a nerd, a geek, a spaz or a dweeb. But what's in a name? I am an Aspie. Of all the names I have been called in my lifetime, I like Aspie the best because it means that I am in good company.

Liane Holliday Willey's father said that 'If people with Asperger's syndrome had a better press agent, we'd be in charge and not the neurotypicals' (personal communication).

In her autobiography, Donna Williams explained that 'It seemed that other people's "normality" was the road to my insanity' (Williams 1998, p.54). The best psychotherapy may be provided by people who have personal experience of Asperger's syndrome and have achieved self-acceptance. Nita Jackson, a young woman with Asperger's syndrome, advises people with Asperger's syndrome that:

> You've got to accept yourself for who you are – however tough this may be. Being in denial will only hinder you. Acknowledge your syndrome, research it, and remember that anyone who is unkind to you because of your difference isn't worth it in the first place. This is easier said than done I know – I'm not completely there yet! Accepting yourself, therefore, is the key to personal success... And, most importantly, be true to yourself, because ultimately, you only have yourself to depend on. (N. Jackson 2002, pp.16–17)

KEY POINTS AND STRATEGIES

- Traditional psychoanalytical psychotherapy has very little to offer a child or adult with Asperger's syndrome.

- Asperger's syndrome is not caused by an inability of a child's mother to love and relate to her son or daughter.

- When using projective testing, the child with Asperger's syndrome is more likely to provide factual information than projections of the self.

- Children and adults with Asperger's syndrome can benefit from psychotherapy, but the therapy needs to be based on a thorough understanding of the nature of Asperger's syndrome, especially the ability of the person to understand and communicate thoughts and feelings, and the concept of self in terms of self-image, self-esteem and self-acceptance, based on the life experiences of someone with Asperger's syndrome.

- The psychotherapist will need to know the latest cognitive psychology research on Asperger's syndrome, especially the studies on Theory of Mind, executive function and weak central coherence; to have read the experiences described in the autobiographies; and to be prepared to make appropriate modifications to conventional psychotherapies.

- The client with Asperger's syndrome can be more relaxed and able to provide greater insight into inner thoughts and experiences by being asked to engage in a therapeutic 'conversation' using two connected computers, exchanging e-mails or drawing events as a Comic Strip Conversation.

- The psychotherapist may not be able to use transference constructively as with other clients, but can become a mentor, someone who understands and provides education, enabling the person with Asperger's syndrome to articulate his or her perspective and intentions better.

- Long-term psychotherapy can help the person with Asperger's syndrome understand key events in his or her life, and cope in a world that does not always understand the perspective and intentions of someone with Asperger's syndrome.

- Psychotherapy can help children or adults with Asperger's syndrome achieve a realistic appreciation of who they are and to recognize their strengths more than their weaknesses.

  ○ The first stage in self-identity is for the person to understand the nature of Asperger's syndrome and which characteristics associated with the syndrome are expressed in his or her profile of abilities and personality.

  ○ The second stage is to use semi-projective sentence completion activities to enable the psychotherapist to have a greater understanding of the person's self-representation.

  ○ The third stage is to develop a vocabulary and understanding of characterization and personalities.

- The theory of personal constructs, originally developed by George Kelly in the 1950s, has a scientific and logical theoretical framework and practical therapy that is well suited to the mindset of people with Asperger's syndrome.

- Two of the ultimate goals in life and psychotherapy are to understand who you are and accept who you are. Some children and adults with Asperger's syndrome appear to have achieved this without formal therapy.

CHAPTER 15

Frequently Asked Questions

This final chapter attempts to answer some of those questions frequently asked by parents, professionals and people with Asperger's syndrome that have not been answered in previous chapters. For over 20 years clinicians and academics have been studying why people with Asperger's syndrome are different, and have an increasing knowledge base that can provide provisional answers. The question that is most often asked, especially when a person has been given a diagnosis of Asperger's syndrome, is 'What causes Asperger's syndrome?'

1. WHAT CAUSES ASPERGER'S SYNDROME?

First of all, we know that Asperger's syndrome is not caused by inadequate parenting or psychological or physical trauma. Unfortunately, parents often think the behaviour and profile of abilities are somehow caused by a defect in their own character or parenting skills, perhaps not providing enough love for the child; or some traumatic event such as witnessing an accident, or falling from a tree. Parents should abandon feelings of personal guilt. The research studies have clearly established that Asperger's syndrome is due to a dysfunction of specific structures and systems in the brain. In short, the brain is 'wired' differently, not necessarily defectively, and this was not caused by what a parent did or did not do during the child's development.

We are now able to conduct brain imaging studies of typical people that can identify the structures and systems that operate together to form the 'social brain', and examine whether any of these structures function differently for people with Asperger's syndrome. Research studies that have used brain imaging technology and neuropsychological tests have confirmed that Asperger's syndrome is associated with a dysfunction of the 'social brain', which comprises components of the frontal and temporal regions of the cortex – to be more precise, the medial prefrontal and orbitofrontal areas of the frontal lobes, the superior temporal sulcus, inferior basal temporal cortex, and temporal poles of the temporal lobes. There is also evidence of dysfunction of the amygdala, the basal ganglia and cerebellum (Frith 2004; Gowen and Miall 2005; Toal,

Murphy and Murphy 2005). The latest research suggests that there is weak connectivity between these components (Welchew *et al.* 2005). There is also evidence to suggest right hemisphere cortical dysfunction (Gunter *et al.* 2002) and an abnormality of the dopamine system (Nieminen-von Wendt *et al.* 2004). The neurological research examining brain function is consistent with the psychological profile of abilities in social reasoning, empathy, communication and cognition that are characteristics of Asperger's syndrome. Thus, we now know which structures in the brain are functioning or 'wired' differently.

But why did those areas of the brain develop differently? Probably for the majority of people with Asperger's syndrome, the reason is due to genetic factors. Asperger originally noticed a ghosting or shadow of the syndrome in the parents (particularly fathers) of the children he saw, and proposed the condition could be inherited. Subsequent research has confirmed that for some families there are strikingly similar characteristics in family members. Research has indicated that, using strict diagnostic criteria for Asperger's syndrome, about 20 per cent of fathers and 5 per cent of mothers of a child with Asperger's syndrome have the syndrome themselves (Volkmar *et al.* 1998). While this information may not be a total surprise for their partner, they have usually not had a formal diagnosis. If one uses a broader description of Asperger's syndrome, almost 50 per cent of first-degree relatives of a child with Asperger's syndrome have similar characteristics (Bailey *et al.* 1998; Volkmar *et al.* 1998). When considering second- and third-degree relatives, more than two thirds of children with Asperger's syndrome have a relative with a similar pattern of abilities (Cederlund and Gillberg 2004). There is something in the genes.

In Chapter 1, I use the metaphor of completing a 100-piece jigsaw puzzle to describe the diagnostic assessment for Asperger's syndrome. Some pieces or aspects of Asperger's syndrome have a detrimental effect on the person's quality of life while others can be beneficial. Family members who have more of the characteristics of Asperger's syndrome than would be expected in a typical person may have inherited beneficial characteristics that contribute towards their success in careers such as engineering, accountancy and the arts. We know that there is a greater than expected number of engineers among the parents and grandparents of children with Asperger's syndrome (Baron-Cohen *et al.* 2001b). The children of such individuals may then be at greater risk of having even more characteristics associated with Asperger's syndrome, such that there are sufficient for a diagnosis. The siblings of such a child will probably want to know the likely recurrence rate for Asperger's syndrome when they have their own children. At present, we have not identified the precise means of transmission or susceptibility genes but in the not-too-distant future, we may be able to identify the genetic transmission for a particular family.

A question often asked by the mother of a child with Asperger's syndrome is whether a difficult pregnancy or birth could have been the cause of the characteristics of Asperger's syndrome, or at least a contributory factor to the degree of expression. In

Lorna Wing's (1981) original paper that first used the diagnostic term Asperger's syndrome, she noted that some of her cases had a history of pre-, peri- and post-natal conditions that could have caused cerebral (i.e. brain) dysfunction. Her original observation has been confirmed by subsequent studies. Pregnancy complications have been identified in 31 per cent of children with Asperger's syndrome, and peri-natal or birth complications in about 60 per cent (Cederlund and Gillberg 2004). However, no single complication during pregnancy or birth has been consistently identified as being associated with the later development of the signs of Asperger's syndrome. We also do not know if it was an already existing impairment in foetal development that subsequently affected obstetric events, with a difficult birth then increasing the degree of expression.

There does appear to be a greater incidence of babies who are small for gestational age, and marginally older mothers when the child was born (Cederlund and Gillberg 2004; Ghaziuddin, Shakal and Tsai 1995). There also appear to be more children with Asperger's syndrome than we would expect who were born either pre-term (36 weeks or less) or post-maturely (42 weeks or more) (Cederlund and Gillberg 2004). It is possible that factors that affect brain development during pregnancy and birth could affect the 'social brain' and contribute to the development of Asperger's syndrome.

Recent studies have indicated that for at least one in four children with Asperger's syndrome, their brain and head circumference grew at a faster rate than would be expected in the first few months after being born. The children developed macrocephalus or an unusually large head and brain (Cederlund and Gillberg 2004; Gillberg and de Souza 2002; Palmen *et al.* 2005). There may be two subgroups of children with Asperger's syndrome who have macrocephalus, one which includes children who had a large head at birth, and one which includes children who showed a rapid increase in brain size during early infancy. The initial acceleration eventually slows, so that in later childhood typical children have 'caught up', such that the differences in head circumference may not be so conspicuous when the child is about five years old. At the moment we do not have a satisfactory and proven explanation as to why this occurs. We know that brain enlargement can occur in young children with Asperger's syndrome and autism. There is also preliminary information to suggest that the frontal, temporal and parietal, but not the occipital, areas of the brain are enlarged (Carper *et al.* 2002), and there is an increase in grey matter but not white matter (Palmen *et al.* 2005). Sometimes having a rapidly growing and relatively big brain, or at least parts of it, is not an advantage.

We recognize that Asperger's syndrome is part of the autism spectrum, and research on the aetiology or causes of autism may provide information on the causes of Asperger's syndrome. Thus, future research may indicate whether Asperger's syndrome could be caused by infections during pregnancy and in the child's early infancy, inborn errors of metabolism such that the digestion of specific foods produces toxins that affect brain development, or other biological factors that could affect brain development.

At present we cannot state with any certainty the specific cause of Asperger's syndrome in any child or adult, but at least we have some idea as to the possible causes, and know that parents can rest assured that it is not due to faulty parenting.

2. SHOULD YOU EXPLAIN THE DIAGNOSIS TO THE CHILD?

The immediate answer is yes. Clinical experience indicates that it is extremely important that the diagnosis is explained as soon as possible and preferably before inappropriate compensatory reactions are developed. The child is then more likely to achieve self-acceptance, without unfair comparisons with other children, and be less likely to develop signs of an anxiety disorder, depression or conduct disorder. The child can then be a knowledgeable participant in the design of programs, knowing his or her strengths and weaknesses, and why he or she regularly has to see a particular specialist while siblings and peers do not. The child can experience a huge sense of relief to know that he or she is not 'weird', just 'wired' differently.

3. WHEN AND HOW DO YOU EXPLAIN THE DIAGNOSIS?

At what age do you explain the diagnosis? Children who are younger than about eight years may not consider themselves as particularly different to their peers, and have difficulty understanding the concept of a developmental disorder as complex as Asperger's syndrome. The explanation for young children will need to be age appropriate and provide information that is relevant from the child's perspective. The main themes will be the benefits of programs to help the child make friends and enjoy playing with other children, and to help in learning and achieving success with school work. There can be a discussion and activities to explain the concept of individual differences, for example those children in the class who find it easy to learn to read, and others who find it more difficult. The clinician or parents can then explain that there is another form of reading, namely 'reading' people and social situations, and that we have programs to help children who have this particular reading difficulty. At present, parents rather than a specialist in Asperger's syndrome are most likely to explain the diagnosis and its implications to a child. There are many books that can help explain the diagnosis and I have provided a list of recommended books on explaining the diagnosis in the Resources section towards the end of the book. Parents can supplement an explanation of Asperger's syndrome by encouraging the child to read story books with the person with Asperger's syndrome being the hero. In particular, Kathy Hoopmann has written several excellent adventure stories that children and adolescents with Asperger's syndrome find fascinating and they identify with the experiences and abilities of the hero of the story.

The Attributes Activity

For children over the age of about eight years, I have developed the Attributes Activity to explain the diagnosis to the child and family, including siblings and grandparents. I arrange a gathering of family members, including the child or adolescent who has recently been diagnosed as having Asperger's syndrome. The first activity is to have temporarily attached to the wall of the room large sheets of paper, or to have the use of a large whiteboard with coloured pens. Each sheet is divided into two columns, one column headed 'Qualities' and the other 'Difficulties'. I suggest the child's mother or father as the first person to complete the activity, which involves identifying and listing both personal qualities and difficulties (these can include practical abilities, knowledge, personality and passions). After the first focus person has made his or her suggestions, which the clinician writes on the paper/board, the family add their own suggestions. I ensure that this is a positive activity, commenting on the various attributes and ensuring that there are more qualities than difficulties. Another member of the family is then nominated or volunteers to suggest his or her qualities and difficulties. The child or adolescent with Asperger's syndrome is able to observe and participate, and understands what is expected when it is time for his or her turn.

Table 15.1 **Representation of the Attributes Activity for a Child with Asperger's Syndrome**

Qualities	Difficulties
Honest	Accepting mistakes
Determined	Making friends
An expert on insects and the *Titanic*	Taking advice
Aware of sounds that others cannot hear	Managing my anger
Kind	Handwriting
Forthright	Knowing what someone is thinking
A loner (and happy to be so)	Avoiding being teased
A perfectionist	Showing as much affection as other family members expect
A reliable friend	
Good at drawing	Coping with sudden noises
Observant of details that others do not see	Explaining thoughts using speech
Exceptional at remembering things that other people have forgotten	
Humorous in a unique way	
Advanced in the knowledge of mathematics	
Liked by adults	

Sometimes the person with Asperger's syndrome is reluctant to suggest, or may not consider him- or herself to have, many qualities or attributes. The family are encouraged to make suggestions and the clinician can nominate a few suggestions from knowledge of the person. There will need to be some care when nominating difficulties so that the person does not feel victimized. Table 15.1 is a representation of the Attributes Activity for a child with Asperger's syndrome.

The clinician comments on each quality and difficulty nominated by the child with Asperger's syndrome and then explains that scientists are often looking for patterns; when they find a consistent pattern, they like to give it a name. Reference is then made to Dr Hans Asperger who, over 60 years ago, saw at his clinic in Vienna many children whose characteristics he observed to be similar. He published the first clinical description that has become known as Asperger's syndrome.

I usually say to the child, 'Congratulations, you have Asperger's syndrome,' and explain that this means he or she is not mad, bad or defective, but has a different way of thinking. The discussion continues with an explanation of how some of the child's talents or qualities are due to having Asperger's syndrome, such as his or her extensive knowledge about spark plugs, ability to draw with photographic realism, attention to detail and being naturally talented in mathematics. This is to introduce the benefits of having the characteristics of Asperger's syndrome. The Attributes Activity can be conducted by parents of young children without the presence of a specialist in Asperger's syndrome but I have found that adolescents are more likely to accept the explanation of qualities and difficulties from a clinician rather than parents.

The next stage is to discuss the difficulties and the strategies needed to improve specific abilities at home and at school. This can include the advantages of programs to improve social understanding, Cognitive Behaviour Therapy and/or medication that can help with emotion management, and ideas and encouragement to improve friendships. The clinician provides a summary of the person's qualities and difficulties that are due to having Asperger's syndrome, and mentions successful people in the areas of science, information technology, politics and the arts who benefited from the signs of Asperger's syndrome in their own profile of abilities (Fitzgerald 2005; James 2006; Ledgin 2002; Paradiz 2002).

Hans Asperger wrote that:

> It seems that for success in science or art, a dash of autism is essential. For success, the necessary ingredient may be an ability to turn away from the everyday world, from the simply practical, an ability to re-think a subject with originality so as to create in new untrodden ways, with all abilities canalised into the one speciality. (Asperger 1979, p.49)

As Temple Grandin, a woman who has Asperger's syndrome who has become a successful engineer, author and academic, said, 'If the world was left to you socialites, we would still be in caves talking to each other' (Personal communication).

The Attributes Activity can also be used with adults and family members or a partner. When using the activity with a couple where one partner has Asperger's syndrome, I ask the typical partner to explain his or her love for the partner with Asperger's syndrome, and what the appeal was when they first met. I have noted that the attributes of the partner with Asperger's syndrome can include being physically attractive (the silent handsome stranger) and loyal, having a remarkable intellect and original ideas, being a man with a feminine side, being a challenge to get to know and, during the time of dating, being very attentive. As with all relationships, over time other attributes become more noticeable and some diminish, but a few of the relationship attributes can be explained as being associated with the characteristics of Asperger's syndrome in an adult.

When explaining the development of the profile of abilities associated with Asperger's syndrome to an adolescent or adult, I sometimes use the metaphor of a clearing in a forest. The 'clearing' represents the development of the brain, and the emergence of plants and saplings in the clearing represents the development of different brain functions. In the clearing, one sapling grows very rapidly and creates a canopy above the other plants and a root structure that restrict access to sunshine and nutrients, thus inhibiting the growth of competing plants. The dominant sapling, which soon becomes a tree, represents the parts of the brain dedicated to social reasoning. If that 'social reasoning' sapling does not develop quickly and become dominant, then other trees, or abilities, may become stronger. These plants represent abilities in mechanical reasoning, music, art, mathematics and science, and the perception of sensory experiences. The person may then see Asperger's syndrome as an explanation of his or her talents as well as difficulties.

The Attributes Activity closes with explanation of some of the clinician's thoughts on Asperger's syndrome. Such individuals have different priorities, perception of the world and way of thinking. The brain is wired differently, not defectively. The person prioritizes the pursuit of knowledge, perfection, truth, and the understanding of the physical world above feelings and interpersonal experiences. This can lead to valued talents but also vulnerabilities in the social world, and will affect self-esteem. The person will perceive the diagnosis according to how the clinician explains it.

I usually record the descriptions of the person with Asperger's syndrome and the explanation of the syndrome on an audio tape for the family to listen to, so that they can refresh their memories of key points. The person's qualities and difficulties are also included in a report for the family or as a Social Story™ for a child. Another option is for the specialist and parents to write the child a letter outlining the nature of Asperger's syndrome, the advantages and disadvantages of having Asperger's syndrome and information tailored to the child (Yoshida *et al.* 2005).

I prefer to use the term Asperger's syndrome rather than Asperger's disorder when explaining the diagnosis, as the child can be confused regarding the concept of a disorder. This point is illustrated by Thomas in the biography written by his mother:

> While riding along in the back seat of our car, my eleven-year-old son, Thomas, reads a book on Asperger's syndrome and asks, 'Mom, in this book, they talk about Asperger's disorder. Why do they refer to Asperger's as a disorder?'
>
> 'Not sure, but it's a good question,' I tell him.
>
> He continues, 'I'm going to write the author of this book and tell her she used an incorrect term. Actually, I'm not in disorder. I am definitely in-order.'
>
> 'Great idea,' I reply. (Barber 2006, p.3)

After explaining the diagnosis to the child or adult, it is important to discuss who else needs to know. Children may be concerned about how their peers will respond to the news and any potential negative reaction. Adults will want to know if it is wise to tell friends, prospective employers and colleagues. The clinician will examine and discuss the issues surrounding disclosure for the client, based on his or her circumstances, the advantages and disadvantages of certain people knowing, and how much information to disclose.

The child's opinion is respected regarding the question of whether or not peers should be told. If the child does want the other children to know, there needs to be an agreement as to how widely the information will be disseminated, who will provide the explanation, how it will be done, and whether the child with Asperger's syndrome should be present. Carol Gray has developed a program, *The Sixth Sense*, to explain Asperger's syndrome to a class of children in an elementary or primary school (Gray 2002b). She has designed a range of classroom activities based on learning about the five senses that is extended to include a sixth sense, the perception of social cues. Children can then discover what it would be like to have difficulty perceiving the social cues and thoughts and feelings of others, and what they can do to help someone develop the sixth sense. We now have other published resources to help explain Asperger's syndrome to peers and siblings (see the Resources section towards the end of the book).

An adult who has recently been diagnosed will also need to discuss who to tell and how to explain Asperger's syndrome to the family, social network and work associates. Some adults have a more reserved personality and are very cautious regarding disclosure, deciding to limit the news to carefully selected individuals. Other adults are more open and brazen in their disclosure. Liane Holliday Willey chose to have a 'coming out party', while others have had a special T-shirt created with a message such as 'Asperger's and Proud' or 'Asperger's – a different way of thinking'. The diagnosis is then very conspicuous.

4. ARE PEOPLE WITH ASPERGER'S SYNDROME MORE LIKELY TO BE INVOLVED IN CRIMINAL ACTIVITIES?

There are published case studies of adults with Asperger's syndrome who have committed serious criminal offences (Baron-Cohen 1988; Barry Walsh and Mullen 2004; Cooper, Mohamed and Collacott 1993; Everall and Le Couteur 1990; Howlin 2004;

Mawson, Grounds and Tantam 1985; Murrie *et al.* 2002). The popular press has sometimes referred to a convicted offender's diagnosis of Asperger's syndrome when reporting notorious crimes. This could lead to the assumption that people with Asperger's syndrome are more likely to commit a serious criminal act. However, research has clearly established that the rate of convictions for adults with Asperger's syndrome is actually the same as for the general population and that the incidence of violent offences is remarkably low (Ghaziuddin, Tsai and Ghaziuddin 1991; Isager *et al.* 2005). Having Asperger's syndrome does not mean a person is more likely to be involved in criminal activities or commit a serious offence.

The overwhelming majority of people with Asperger's syndrome are law-abiding citizens, often with very clear and conventional opinions as to what is morally and legally right and wrong. But for those adults with Asperger's syndrome who commit an offence, there are types of crimes that are relatively more common due to the nature of Asperger's syndrome.

Although children and adolescents are not usually convicted of a criminal offence, some children and teenagers with Asperger's syndrome can engage in behaviour that can lead to being suspended from school or receiving a caution from the police.

Chapter 4, on teasing and bullying, describes how a child with Asperger's syndrome can retaliate with actions that contravene school and criminal law. The child, and sometimes the adult, with Asperger's syndrome may ruminate for many years over past slights and injustices and seek resolution and revenge by means that are illegal (Tantam 2000a). The social naïvety and immaturity of adolescents with Asperger's syndrome can also make them vulnerable to being 'set up' by peers, who encourage them to commit an offence. Adults may then misinterpret intentions and statements made 'in the heat of the moment', which can lead to the consideration of criminal charges. The child or adolescent with Asperger's syndrome may achieve a notoriety that is not justified.

A malicious subgroup

Some of the children Asperger diagnosed as having autistic personality were originally referred for behaviours that today would be indicative of conduct disorder (Hippler and Klicpera 2004). Within this group, he identified a very small minority of children who act maliciously with deliberate intention and sometimes satisfaction. He used the term 'autistic malice' (Asperger [1944] 1991, p.77).

From my clinical experience of children and adolescents with Asperger's syndrome who commit malicious acts, there are several factors that lead to such behaviour. When the child with Asperger's syndrome feels alienated from peers, due to a lack of social competence and acceptance, and perhaps further alienated because of learning difficulties or superior intellectual abilities, he or she can achieve authority in a social situation by intimidation. The child becomes a 'little dictator', using threats of violence (more likely to be used by males with Asperger's syndrome) and emotional blackmail (more likely to be used by females with Asperger's syndrome), to gain power and control over peers and family. Experience indicates that such behaviour is not modelled on a parent. Indeed, the parents are often very meek and easily intimidated. By surrendering to the child's authoritarian and egocentric demands they have unwittingly reinforced such behaviour. I have known rare cases of adolescents with the 'little dictator' characteristics who regularly and maliciously physically assault a parent to the extent that eventually the police are called and the adolescent charged with a serious offence.

Some adolescents with Asperger's syndrome realize they have difficulties with empathy and understanding the emotions of other people, and develop a special interest in creating situations and making statements as a 'psychological experiment' to be able to predict someone's emotional reaction. The statements can be extremely disturbing for the subject in the experiment: for example, an adolescent informing his aunt, in a way that is credible, that her much-loved pet has just been killed by running in front of a passing car. The act or 'experiment' is malicious and intended to explore or enjoy the emotional reaction of distress or fear in someone. The subject of the experiment is unlikely to have done anything to justify an act of retaliation. The only link may be that the subject is a happy person who is successful in the areas of ability that are elusive for the person with Asperger's syndrome. The morbid intellectual curiosity or desire to make someone suffer, as he or she has suffered, can be of great concern to the person's family and could come to the attention of the police, depending on who the person chooses as a subject of his or her experiment. At present we have limited knowledge regarding what to do to change the behaviour and thinking of adolescents and adults in the malicious subgroup. Prison is unlikely to be a deterrent. We hope that long-term psychotherapy to understand the person's thinking and self-image may achieve a readjustment in behaviour and interpersonal skills.

Types of offences

I have known people with Asperger's syndrome who have committed offences ranging from being a public nuisance to homicide. The charge of public nuisance has tended to occur when the person with Asperger's syndrome has pursued a perceived sense of injustice in an interpersonal dispute as a matter of principle to the point where the disagreement has become absurd, or ended in confrontation and offensive behaviour. The person's strong moral code can lead to a confrontation and argument with people who are perceived as 'immoral', because they are wearing provocative clothing, for example dressing in the style of a particular sub-culture. A complaint is made to the police regarding the person with Asperger's syndrome, and the police decide on appropriate charges.

Problems with access to a special interest can lead to charges of stealing to obtain money to buy items to add to the collection, or stealing the item of special interest itself. The item stolen can be unusual, such as a rare lamppost or tractor, which may have no practical use to the person and cannot be sold for financial gain. The likely culprit is often quickly identified, and incriminating evidence easily found by the police. The compulsive nature of the special interest could make some adults with Asperger's syndrome, who are usually very honest, tempted to commit an offence.

We do recognize that problems with sexual expression and experiences can lead to a person with Asperger's syndrome being charged with a sexual offence. The charges tend to be for sexually inappropriate behaviour rather than sexually abusive or sexually violent behaviour (Ray, Marks and Bray-Garretson 2004). The person may have difficulty distinguishing between kindness and attraction, and assume a friendly act was an indication of romantic or sexual attraction. This can lead to a crush or infatuation with the person. Due to problems with Theory of Mind abilities and reading social cues, the person with Asperger's syndrome assumes that the degree of adulation is reciprocal, and signs of rejection or annoyance are not recognized. The person may be charged with offences related to stalking.

The focus or expression of sexual pleasure can also be of concern. For example, the person with Asperger's syndrome may not have had the usual social, sensual and sexual experiences of typical adolescents, and may develop sexually arousing fantasies involving objects, clothing, children or animals. The technical term is paraphilia. Acting out some paraphilias is illegal. The person with Asperger's syndrome may have been sexually abused and subsequently repeat the offence with others, assuming such sexual behaviour is acceptable, or as an attempt to understand why someone would engage in, and appear to enjoy, such behaviour.

A curiosity and confusion regarding sexuality can lead to the desire for more information and the development of a solitary and clandestine special interest in pornography. There can then be the assumption that the sexual behaviour seen in films and described in magazines is a script for a first date. When certain suggestions are made, the person can be labelled a pervert or sexual deviant, and face the possibility of charges of sexual assault. There has been the suggestion that having Asperger's syndrome could be a factor in at least one case of sexual serial homicide (Silva, Ferrari and Leong 2002). Thus, I strongly advocate guidance in sexuality for adolescents and adults with Asperger's syndrome, using the programs designed by specialists in Asperger's syndrome (Hénault 2005), and appropriate modifications for treatment programs for sexual offenders (Ray et al. 2004).

Many years ago, I remember someone mentioning that Hans Asperger had said that adults with autistic personality disorder could become talented in code breaking, and their abilities in mathematics and codes valued by military intelligence. In his paper published in 1938 he advocated against the newly introduced Nazi law for 'the prevention of offspring suffering from hereditary diseases'. It seems he felt by pointing out the skills of those with autistic personality disorder, he was emphasizing their potential advantage to the military, thus preventing such children from being taken from their parents and killed. He was certainly a brave man to challenge Nazi doctrine.

When I met his daughter, Maria, in Zurich several years ago, I asked her if it is true that he made those comments on code breaking and she replied with an emphatic yes.

She also explained that he was considered as a person of suspicion by the Nazi authorities. I explained to Maria that his comments were remarkably astute and that during the second world war, British military intelligence had benefited from the characteristics of Asperger's syndrome among the mathematicians who had contributed to cracking the German Enigma code. Their contribution to the ending of the war was invaluable.

Today, codes and electronics can become a special interest of young adults with Asperger's syndrome that can lead to criminal charges of hacking. The person with Asperger's syndrome may break into a computer data system as an intellectual exercise and not necessarily to steal money or information as a form of industrial espionage. There may be no personal gain, other than the prestige of being smarter than the designers of the computer program. Sometimes the motivation is to seek retribution for creating a program that is faulty or becomes a virtual monopoly that offends the sense of social justice of the person with Asperger's syndrome. However, such factors are not likely to be viewed as mitigating circumstances by a court. If these abilities were used constructively, for example working for an Internet security company or military intelligence, then the person can pursue the interest as a valued and lucrative career.

A child or adolescent with Asperger's syndrome may develop a fascination with the flickering light and colours of flames, and the subsequent setting of fires may lead to a charge of arson (Everall and Le Couteur 1990; Isager *et al.* 2005). This is considered a very serious criminal offence. I have also known adults with Asperger's syndrome who have been charged with homicide or attempted homicide. Murder can be the consequence of an argument that became unexpectedly violent, where the mental state and sense of reality of the person with Asperger's syndrome deteriorates into a 'blind rage' with fatal consequences. The homicide can be premeditated as a form of self-defence, or may be for personal gain, for example taking a weapon to school to prevent further bullying and initiating the assault that was intended to be fatal. There are also case studies of murder clearly and simply for personal advantage (Murrie *et al.* 2002). However, the reader must recognize that homicide by a person with Asperger's syndrome is extremely rare, and we have no research evidence to suggest the rate of homicide is any greater than in the general population, or whether having Asperger's syndrome was a relevant factor.

The criminal justice system

A police interview with someone with Asperger's syndrome will inevitably be different to one with a typical person, or with someone who has a history of previous convictions. During a police interview, people with Asperger's syndrome are not more likely to be suggestible, but can be noticeably compliant and courteous to requests from the police (North, Russell and Gudjonsson 2005). The person may not have an obvious psychiatric disorder or learning disability requiring special consideration during the interview. The police officers will probably not know how to identify the signs of Asperger's syndrome in a suspect or witness, or the characteristics that could affect the ability to provide information relevant to the crime. Experience has indicated that people with Asperger's syndrome who have committed an offence have often been quick to confess and justify their actions. They cannot understand what all the fuss is about; their actions were logical, justified and appropriate and described without any associated emotions or remorse.

When a diagnosis of Asperger's syndrome is recognized by the criminal justice system, it is wise to refer the person to a forensic clinician who has experience of people with Asperger's syndrome in order to determine the degree to which the diagnosis could be relevant in relation to the alleged offence and, if convicted, the subsequent sentencing. All components of the justice system can benefit by involving specialists in the forensic psychological and psychiatric assessment of people with Asperger's syndrome. At present we know that between 3 and 11 per cent of referrals to forensic psychiatric clinics are for young offenders with Asperger's syndrome (Person and Branden 2005; Siponmaa et al. 2001). There are also advantages in having a designated national forensic assessment unit specifically for people with Asperger's syndrome (Ekkehart, Staufenberg and Kells 2005).

The assessment will include an expert opinion on the fitness to plead, especially the ability to comprehend relevant legal concepts and court procedures. The court should accept that Asperger's syndrome is a mental disorder, but there is likely to be some disagreement regarding whether insanity could be used as a defence. Deficient empathy and a different subjective reality, and the nature of the crime, could suggest an altered state of mind (Barry Walsh and Mullen 2004). However, the result of being found to be of unsound mind will have implications for sentencing that must be considered. We know that there are more patients with Asperger's syndrome in secure mental health units than we would expect (Scragg and Shah 1994). A custodial sentence may have been avoided, but there may be doubt as to whether confinement to a secure psychiatric unit for mentally abnormal offenders for an indeterminate time is an appropriate alternative to prison.

A lack of expected empathy and remorse could suggest the person has signs of being a psychopath. A psychopath usually has a superficial charm and a previous history of ingenious and intuitive ways of exploiting and manipulating others. They are the ultimate human predators. The person with Asperger's syndrome is socially naïve and immature, and usually at the opposite end of the predator–prey spectrum (Murrie et al. 2002). Both have problems with empathy, but for different reasons.

When the court, and especially a jury, learn about the characteristics of the defendant with Asperger's syndrome, there can be the possibility of sympathy, compassion and leniency, but a defendant's genuine lack of remorse or appreciation of the effect of his or her actions on other people could lead to an antipathy that affects judgements and sentencing. A judge may also be concerned about the likelihood of re-offending, and will feel obliged to protect society. In my opinion, a defendant's diagnosis of Asperger's syndrome is usually more relevant to sentencing than judgements of fitness to plead.

Each country and state will have different legislation and criminal codes that would be relevant to a defendant with a diagnosis of Asperger's syndrome. At present there is limited case law to set a recognized precedent and to guide the criminal justice system. From my own experience of the forensic aspects of Asperger's syndrome, courts are often reluctant to impose a custodial sentence, especially for relatively minor crimes. This is a wise decision. I have seen prisoners with Asperger's syndrome who have been victimized and severely abused by other inmates. A recent example was a young man with Asperger's syndrome who had committed robbery to gain money to purchase new acquisitions for his special interest. While in prison he was subjected to almost daily sexual assault. He reported the offences to the prison authorities, but the assaults continued. He was desperate to avoid further assaults and realized that he had few options. He recognized that one option was for him to be sent to solitary confinement. He started a small fire in the industrial workshop in the hope that he would be punished by a period in solitary confinement. Unfortunately, the fire spread at a rate he could not control and the workshop was burned down. He was then charged with another serious offence, arson, and faced the prospect of even more years in prison. However, in this case, there was a happy ending. When the charge of arson was presented to a judge and the circumstances of the prisoner with Asperger's syndrome explained by his defence council, the charges were dismissed.

When sentencing a person with Asperger's syndrome it is important to consider the reasons for the offences, and to have available appropriate programs to reduce the likelihood of re-offending. The programs can include those to improve social skills and encourage friendships with peers who do not engage in or encourage criminal acts; anger management training; treatment of an underlying anxiety disorder to reduce the compulsive nature of the special interest; resolution of past injustices; and guidance in relationships and sexuality. Part of the sentencing requirements can be participation in these programs and therapies. However, this is assuming such services are available and are provided by someone who is experienced in treating or supporting a person with Asperger's syndrome.

When a custodial sentence is imposed, prison and probation authorities must consider how the diagnosis will affect the person, and ensure there are appropriate safeguards and support while in prison and on probation. For those who could be detained under a mental health act, there is an alternative to a secure forensic psychiatry hospital. In the United Kingdom, the National Autistic Society runs a secure unit for 12 people with Asperger's syndrome or autism. The Hayes Unit, near Bristol, comprises two houses with staff trained in supporting people with Asperger's syndrome. The unit has programs in life skills and emotion management and access to relevant expertise. By experiencing an 'Asperger-friendly' environment, having the opportunity to improve specific abilities, and receiving follow-up support, the person is less likely to re-offend when released from the unit.

5. CAN ASPERGER'S SYNDROME BE CONFUSED WITH SCHIZOPHRENIA?

Hans Asperger was keen to differentiate autistic personality disorder from schizophrenia, and noted that, 'While the schizophrenic patient seems to show progressive loss of contact, the children we are discussing lack contact from the start' (Asperger [1944] 1991, p.39). However, in the past and still today, some young adults with Asperger's syndrome are referred for a psychiatric assessment for schizophrenia.

A person with Asperger's syndrome may develop what appear to be signs of paranoia, but this may be an understandable response to very real social experiences. Children with Asperger's syndrome encounter a greater degree of deliberate and provocative teasing than their peers. Once another child has deliberately teased the child with Asperger's syndrome, any subsequent confusing interaction with that child can cause the child with Asperger's syndrome to make the assumption that the interaction was intentionally hostile. This can eventually lead to long-term feelings of persecution and the expectation that people will have malicious intent.

One of the concerns of clinicians is differentiating between the anticipated consequences of an impaired or delayed Theory of Mind, and the paranoia and persecutory delusions associated with schizophrenia. A recent study examined the potential link between impaired or delayed Theory of Mind and paranoia in young adults with Asperger's syndrome (Blackshaw *et al.* 2001). An incident such as being ignored by a friend could be conceptualized in terms of the situation (he did not see you, was in a hurry, etc.) which uses the circumstances as an explanation; or it could be conceptualized in terms of his mental intentions (he didn't want to talk to you, or he wanted to make you feel embarrassed or ignored). The study used a series of tests and questionnaires to measure the degree of impaired Theory of Mind and paranoia. The individuals with Asperger's syndrome scored lower on tests of Theory of Mind and higher on measures of paranoia than normal controls, but an analysis of the results of the study found that the paranoia was due to impaired Theory of Mind abilities, and was qualitatively different to the characteristics of paranoia observed in people with a diagnosis of schizophrenia. The paranoia was not a defence strategy, as occurs in schizophrenia, but due to confusion in understanding the subtleties of social interaction and social rules.

A subsequent study of persecutory beliefs and Theory of Mind abilities compared people with Asperger's syndrome with patients with paranoid delusions, and found that the low-level paranoid signs observed in some people with Asperger's syndrome are due to different mechanisms than those involved in psychotic delusion (Craig *et al.* 2004). A person with Asperger's syndrome can develop feelings of persecution and paranoia but there is a qualitative difference between these and the feelings of paranoia that are a sign of schizophrenia.

One of the compensatory mechanisms for a person with Asperger's syndrome, who may achieve limited social success and understanding, is to create a fantasy life that can include imaginary friends and imaginary worlds in which he or she is understood and socially successful. The contrast between the real and imaginary world can become quite acute during adolescence, and under extreme stress the adolescent with Asperger's syndrome may create a fantasy world that becomes not simply a mental sanctuary and source of enjoyment, but a cause of concern to others, that the distinction between the fantasy world and reality is becoming blurred. A tendency to escape into imagination as a compensatory mechanism can then become interpreted as a delusional state of mind (LaSalle 2003).

I have also noted that some children and adults with Asperger's syndrome tend to vocalize their thoughts, apparently unaware of how confusing or annoying this can be to other people. The thought vocalization can occur as a means of problem solving, with some adolescents stating that they can improve their thinking by talking to themselves, or the person has difficulty 'disengaging mind from mouth'. When listening to speech that occurs out of a social context, the content is often a replay of the conversations of the day, in an attempt to understand the various levels of meaning, or as a rehearsal of what to say for some future occasion. When lonely, the adolescent can talk aloud to an imaginary person or friend, and is not necessarily engaged in a dialogue in response to an auditory hallucination.

Problems with the pragmatic aspects of language can also explain a tendency to switch topics that can be confusing to the other person, and could be interpreted as evidence of the thought disorder associated with schizophrenia. If in doubt as to what to say, the person with Asperger's syndrome may change the topic to something that he or she knows about and would prefer to talk about. Another problem with the pragmatic and semantic aspects of language that occurs with people with Asperger's syndrome is their making a literal interpretation of a question. A psychiatrist may ask a question such as 'Do you hear voices?' to which Wendy Lawson, who has Asperger's syndrome, replied, 'Yes' – the correct answer based on a literal interpretation of the question (Lawson 1998). After all, she heard voices of people talking around her every day. Her answer contributed to the psychiatrist's opinion that she had schizophrenia.

We know that many children with Asperger's syndrome think in pictures (Chapter 9) and when I enquire whether such children also have an inner voice, to help them manage an emotion or situation, they are often bewildered and state that they do not have an inner voice or conversation when thinking. This characteristic is probably due to a delay in the self-reflection aspects of Theory of Mind, and probably associated with an immature development of the frontal lobes. Typical children achieve this ability when they are about five years old. However, during adolescence, this attribute can 'switch on' for the first time for a teenager with Asperger's syndrome, who then reports having voices and conversations in his or her head which could be interpreted as a sign of schizophrenia. It is important to distinguish between an inner voice as a natural aspect of thought and problem solving, and the auditory hallucinations of schizophrenia.

Clinicians recognize that severe depression and other mood disorders such as bipolar disorder and anxiety disorders can sometimes lead to psychotic features and mood congruent delusions (Ghaziuddin 2005b). In particular, a person with severe depression may develop auditory hallucinations that are related to the depression, for example voices telling the person to kill himself, but there can be a qualitative difference from the voices associated with schizophrenia. In psychotic depression the voices often talk to the person directly, whereas in schizophrenia the voices usually talk about the person (Ghaziuddin 2005b).

The superficial similarities between some of the signs and consequences of Asperger's syndrome and schizophrenia do not imply that someone with Asperger's syndrome is 'immune' from schizophrenia. There are people with Asperger's syndrome who develop the unequivocal signs of schizophrenia (Ghaziuddin 2005b; Stahlberg *et al.* 2004). However, Asperger noted that only one of his 200 cases developed clear signs of schizophrenia (Wolff 1995). We have yet to establish the actual co-morbidity of Asperger's syndrome and schizophrenia, but at present there is no evidence in the research literature that schizophrenia is any more common in people with Asperger's syndrome than it is in the general population (Tantam 2000a).

There are families that have a child with Asperger's syndrome and a relative diagnosed with schizophrenia (Ghaziuddin 2005a). However, sometimes we cannot be sure if the relative had schizophrenia or the characteristics of Asperger's syndrome that resembled some of the features of schizophrenia. In the past, people with Asperger's syndrome who were referred to an adult psychiatrist who would not have known about Asperger's syndrome, may well have received a diagnosis of atypical schizophrenia (Perlman 2000). I obtained my clinical qualifications during the last days of the large mental hospitals around London that accommodated hundreds of chronic psychiatric patients. With hindsight, I now recognize that some of the patients in the old institutions with a diagnosis of atypical schizophrenia would today be diagnosed as having Asperger's syndrome. If such individuals are now resident in community psychiatric services, they may benefit from a re-assessment of their original diagnosis. The family of a person with Asperger's syndrome who has a relative diagnosed with schizophrenia may consider whether the characteristics of Asperger's syndrome are a more accurate description of the person, and whether the original diagnosis should be re-examined by a specialist in adults with Asperger's syndrome.

6. WHAT ARE THE LONG-TERM OUTCOMES?

Over several decades I have been able to observe and contribute to the increasing maturity, abilities and self-acceptance of several thousand children and adults with Asperger's syndrome. The pre-school children I saw when I started my clinic for people with Asperger's syndrome in 1992 are now young adults. I have also diagnosed and continue to support adults with Asperger's syndrome in their search for a sense of identity, relationship with their partner and children and success in their career. For those who have had a successful outcome, I have identified several important factors that have contributed to the success. The important factors are:

- The diagnosis occurs in early childhood to reduce the secondary psychological problems such as depression and denial.

- The person and his or her family accept the diagnosis.

- The person has a mentor – that is, a teacher, relative, professional or person with Asperger's syndrome who understands Asperger's syndrome and provides guidance and inspiration.

- The person acquires knowledge about Asperger's syndrome through reading autobiographies and self-help books written for children or adults with Asperger's syndrome.

- A parent, partner or friend is there to provide emotional and practical support, camouflage any difficulties and provide a life-long commitment to the person.

- The person achieves success at work or in the special interest which offsets the challenges in his or her social life. Social success eventually becomes less important in the person's life, and a sense of identity and self-worth is not measured by companionship but by achievement. This point is illustrated by Temple Grandin:

  > I know that things are missing in my life, but I have an exciting career that occupies my every waking hour. Keeping myself busy keeps my mind off what I may be missing. Sometimes parents and professionals worry too much about the social life of an adult with autism. I make social contacts via my work. If a person develops her talents, she will have contacts with people who share her interests. (Grandin 1995, p.139)

- The person is eventually able to accept his or her strengths and deficits and no longer has a desire to become someone that he or she cannot be: there is a realization that he or she has qualities others admire.

- There may be a natural recovery. As much as there are late walkers or talkers, there can be late socializers, although 'late' can be by several decades. Eventually the person is able to achieve his or her life goals.

Professionals and service agencies tend to see children and adults with Asperger's syndrome who are having problems that are conspicuous and difficult to treat or resolve, and this may lead to an overly pessimistic view of the long-term outcome. Asperger's syndrome is a developmental disorder and eventually the person does learn to improve his or her ability to socialize, converse and understand the thoughts and feelings of others, and the accurate and subtle expression of his or her feelings. I use the analogy of completing a jigsaw puzzle of several thousand pieces without a picture on the box.

Over time, small, isolated sections of the puzzle are completed, but the overall 'picture' is not apparent. Eventually there are sufficient 'islands' of parts of the puzzle to allow one to recognize the full picture, and all the pieces fall into place. The puzzle of social understanding and self-acceptance is solved. I have met many adults with Asperger's syndrome who have described how, in their mature years, they eventually managed to intellectually grasp the mechanisms of social relatedness. From then on the only people who know how fluent social integration has been achieved are the person's family and close friends.

From my extensive clinical experience of people with Asperger's syndrome of all ages, and from knowing specific children and adults with Asperger's syndrome over several decades, I have observed that, for some adults, the conspicuous signs of Asperger's syndrome can decrease over time. We recognize the continuum of expression of autism from the silent and aloof child to the person with Asperger's syndrome. We have only just begun to explore the area of the autism continuum between Asperger's syndrome and the normal range. I have known some adolescents and adults with Asperger's syndrome who have progressed to a point on the continuum where only subtle differences and difficulties remain. The person has progressed to a description of personality rather than a diagnostic category used by psychologists and psychiatrists to justify access to psychological or psychiatric treatment. Digby Tantam has used the term 'lifelong eccentricity' to describe the long-term outcome of individuals with Asperger's syndrome (Tantam 1988b). The term eccentricity is not used in a derogatory sense. There is always a logical explanation of the apparently eccentric behaviour of people with Asperger's syndrome. I have valued friends and relatives with Asperger's syndrome. I see people with Asperger's syndrome as a bright thread in the rich tapestry of life. Our civilization would be extremely dull and sterile if we did not have and treasure people with Asperger's syndrome.

Sean Barron describes the outcome that is possible for many people with Asperger's syndrome:

> Thankfully, the social connections I so desperately wanted growing up have been made. My relationship with my family is extraordinary. I have a network of wonderful friends, a job as a newspaper reporter that satisfies me at an intellectual level and a woman whom I've been dating since 2003. All the people in my life affect me in positive ways. (Grandin and Barron 2005, p.82)

7. WHAT HAPPENED TO JACK?

My guide to Asperger's syndrome began with a fictitious description of a child with Asperger's syndrome, Jack, going to the birthday party of his school friend Alicia. Parents may ask: what could be the future for Jack? I would like to end with a plausible description of Jack as an adult, based on my extensive experience of several thousand children and adults with Asperger's syndrome and my being able to observe the long-term development of children I originally saw several decades ago.

There was a loud knock on the office door. The new Human Resources Manager knew this must be Dr Jack Johnstone announcing his arrival for his annual performance review. He had listened to his colleagues talking about Jack and was eager to finally meet him. The company manufactured energy storage systems and Jack was working on a new energy storage system for vehicles to replace petrol-based engines. The research and development section usually employed a team of scientists to design new products, but Jack worked on his own.

The security staff knew him well. He would often be working in the research department until long after midnight. Jack had explained to his line manager that he worked more efficiently when the building was quiet and there was no one around to interrupt him with superficial conversations about the local football team's home game or what he thought of the new secretary's legs.

The Human Resources Manager had Jack's file on his desk. It was by far the largest file he had seen on a member of staff. There was the basic information on his academic qualifications, reference to his Ph.D. in electrical engineering, and testimonials from previous employers referring to his honesty, integrity and determination. However, there were notes in his file made by the previous Human Resources Manager that were written to assist his line manager and the company. There was a brief explanation of a condition called Asperger's syndrome and how this explained Jack's abilities and personality. The original diagnosis had been made in 2005 when he was nine years old and he had benefited from support at school to develop interpersonal skills, and extension classes to develop his talent for engineering. It was now 2028 and he had moved from academia to industry only two years ago.

There was a detailed description of his qualities in terms of knowledge, alternative ways of thinking and problem solving, and his high standard of work, but there was also advice regarding his difficulties in working in a team, tendency to be very forthright and his inability to cope emotionally with sudden changes in job specifications. His ideas had contributed to the recent improvement in the company's profits as he had designed a new long-life battery for hand-held games consoles. He was considered to be eccentric, but a very valuable member of staff.

There was some office gossip about Jack. He was in his early thirties, lived at home with his parents, and had a close friend he sometimes talked about, Alicia, whom he had met when he was at primary school. He had a relatively small circle of friends at work but apparently had never had a long-term relationship. He had dedicated himself to his research and seemed uncomfortable at social occasions such as the Christmas party, last year staying for only 20 minutes. He explained that he had to return home as he had a hobby breeding rare marsupials and needed to ensure his koalas had a fresh supply of eucalyptus leaves. But just over six months ago, a new personal assistant was appointed for the company accountant. She was a single mother with two teenage children and was very popular for her ability to make people feel relaxed in her company, and amazed everyone with how efficiently she organized the accountant's diary. She met Jack when he handed her his monthly expenses sheet, and from that day both their lives were transformed. They were planning to get married next month.

The Human Resources Manager said, 'Come in', and Jack entered the room. He was not sure what to expect but the person before him was certainly memorable. He had untidy hair, hadn't shaved for a few days and in his shirt pocket there were at least four pencils, two pens and an old-style calculator. One of the pens had recently leaked black ink onto his shirt. There were no formal pleasantries as Jack sat down and proceeded to give a monologue on his work performance over the last year and his projects for the next year. He seemed to be relieved when he had given the required information.

It was now the turn of the Human Resources Manager to give feedback to Jack regarding his work over the last year. His ideas had been highly original, although sometimes difficult to understand when he verbally explained the principles, but his computer model using 3D graphics was very clear. He was liked by his colleagues, although he did tend to keep repeating the same jokes. Jack had been the winner of the inter-departmental Trivial Pursuit championship and he was perceived as a kind, shy and dedicated colleague.

Jack was thoughtful for a moment and he agreed with the appraisal. He politely asked how the Human Resources Manager was coping with his new position, whether he had found a school for his children and what he thought of the new CEO (chief executive officer). As Jack left the room, he remembered his early childhood: how when he was young he felt that he was not understood or appreciated by the other children at his school, and during his adolescence he had suffered from low self-esteem and longed to be popular. Other children in his class tormented him that he was a failure, but if only those children could see him now! He was not a failure, he was a success. This thought comforted him as he opened the door of his new 7 Series BMW, and realized he was late for the meeting to go through the final preparations for his wedding.

Glossary

alexithymia	Impaired ability to identify and describe feeling states.
amygdala	A part of the brain associated with the recognition and regulation of emotions.
apraxia	Problems with the conceptualization and planning of movement, so that the action is less proficient and coordinated than one would expect.
Asperger's syndrome	An expression of autism located at the milder end of the spectrum of autistic disorders.
ataxia	Less orderly muscular coordination and an abnormal pattern of movement.
Attention Deficit Hyperactivity Disorder (ADHD)	Problems with sustained attention, impulsivity and hyperactivity.
autistic personality disorder	The original term used by Hans Asperger for what subsequently became know as Asperger's syndrome.
Cognitive Behaviour Therapy (CBT)	An effective treatment to change the way a person thinks about and responds to emotions such as anxiety, sadness and anger. CBT focuses on the maturity, complexity, subtlety and vocabulary of emotions, and dysfunctional or illogical thinking and incorrect assumptions.
Comic Strip Conversations	Simple drawings such as 'stick figures', thought and speech bubbles, and text in different colours to illustrate the sequence of actions, emotions and thoughts in a specific social situation. Originally developed by Carol Gray.
DSM-IV	*Diagnostic and Statistical Manual of Mental Disorders, 4th Edition.*
dyscalculia	Difficulty understanding even basic mathematical concepts.
faux pas	An indiscreet remark or action.

High Functioning Autism (HFA)	The term has been used to describe children who had the classic signs of autism in early childhood but who, as they developed, were shown in formal testing of cognitive skills to have a greater degree of intellectual ability, with greater social and adaptive behaviour skills and communication skills than is usual with children with autism.
hyperlexia	An advanced ability in word recognition with relatively poor comprehension of the words or storyline.
ICD-10	*International Classification of Diseases, 10th Edition.*
incidence	The actual number of people with a confirmed diagnosis.
IQ	Intelligence Quotient.
Irlen filters	Tinted non-optical lenses that are designed to filter out those frequencies of the light spectrum to which a person is sensitive.
macrocephalus	An unusually large head and brain.
macrographia	Difficulties with handwriting.
moebius mouth	A tented upper lip and flat lower lip.
monotropism	Difficulty perceiving and understanding the overall picture or gist, focusing on parts rather than wholes.
Non-verbal Learning Disability (NLD)	The main characteristics of NLD are deficits in the following: visual-perceptual-organizational abilities; complex psychomotor skills and tactile perception; adapting to novel situations; time perception; mechanical arithmetic; and social perception and social interaction skills. There are relative assets in auditory perception, word recognition, rote verbal learning and spelling.
Obsessive Compulsive Disorder (OCD)	In OCD the person has intrusive thoughts about things that he or she does not want to think about: the thoughts are described as *egodystonic*, i.e. distressing and unpleasant. In typical people the intrusive thoughts are often about cleanliness, aggression, religion and sex. The obsessive thoughts of children and adults with Asperger's syndrome are much more likely to be about cleanliness, bullying, teasing, making a mistake and being criticized.
olfactory	Sense of smell.
paraphilia	Sexually arousing fantasies involving objects, clothing, children or animals. Acting out some paraphilias is illegal.
Pathological Demand Avoidance	Passive avoidance of cooperation and social inclusion at school and at home.

Pervasive Developmental Disorder	A severe impairment in reciprocal social interaction skills and communication skills, and the presence of repetitive behavior, interests and activities.
Post Traumatic Stress Disorder (PTSD)	PTSD can be the consequence of experiencing a traumatic event or series of events. The clinical signs of PTSD include attempts to avoid the incident or memories of the incident, and signs of anxiety, depression, anger and even hallucinations associated with the precipitating event.
pragmatic aspects of language	The modification and use of language in a social context.
prevalence	How many people have the condition in the general population.
proprioception	The integration of information about the position and movement of the body in space.
prosopagnosia	Face blindness.
selective mutism	Avoidance of speech.
Semantic Pragmatic Language Disorder (SPLD)	Relatively good language skills in the areas of syntax, vocabulary and phonology but poor use of language in a social context, i.e. the art of conversation or the pragmatic aspects of language.
Social Story™	A Social Story™ describes a situation, skill or concept in terms of relevant social cues, perspectives and common responses in a specifically defined style and format. Originally developed by Carol Gray.
synaesthesia	A rare form of sensory perception, where the person experiences a sensation in one sensory system, yet perceives the sensation in another modality.
tactile defensiveness	Being sensitive to specific tactile experiences.
Theory of Mind	The ability to recognize and understand thoughts, beliefs, desires and intentions of other people in order to make sense of their behaviour and predict what they are going to do next.
tics	Occasional involuntary movements or sounds.
Tourette's disorder	Multiple motor tics and one or more vocal tics.
weak central coherence	Difficulty perceiving and understanding the overall picture or gist, focusing on parts rather than wholes.
working memory	The ability to maintain or hold information 'on line' when solving a problem.

Resources

EXPLAINING THE DIAGNOSIS
To the child...

Over the last few years, there have been several guide books using varying styles that have been written to explain the diagnosis of Asperger's syndrome to children of different ages. Parents, especially mothers, who have recognized the importance of their own child's understanding of the diagnosis, have written several of the guides. The choice of which guide book would be most suitable for a particular child is a decision for his or her parents based on their knowledge of their son's or daughter's interests, reading age and sense of humour.

Faherty, C. (2000) *What Does It Mean to Me? A Workbook Explaining Self-awareness and Life Lessons to the Child or Youth with High Functioning Autism or Aspergers.* Arlington, TX: Future Horizons.

Gagnon, E. and Smith-Myles, B. (1999) *This is Asperger Syndrome.* Kansas: Autism Asperger Publishing Company.

Gerland, G. (2000) *Finding Out About Asperger Syndrome, High Functioning Autism and PDD.* London: Jessica Kingsley Publishers.

Ives, M. (1999) *What is Asperger Syndrome and How Will It Affect Me?* London: The National Autistic Society.

Schnurr, R. (1999) *Asperger's Huh? A Child's Perspective.* Gloucester, Ontario: Anisor Publishing.

Vermeulen, P. (2000) *I Am Special: Introducing Children and Young People to Their Autistic Spectrum Disorder.* London: Jessica Kingsley Publishers.

To other people...

There is a series of books that explain the diagnosis to the child, siblings, other family members and teachers written by Josie Santomauro. I am sure that the books will soon be published and available to readers throughout the world. In the meantime, more information about Josie's books is available using the following website: www.users.tpg .com.au/jsanto/asperger.htm

Gretchen, M. (2005) *Help for the Child with Asperger's Syndrome: A Parent's Guide to Negotiating the Social Service Maze.* London: Jessica Kingsley Publishers. The advice is mainly for families living in the United States.

Tullemans, A. (2004) *Talking to Family and Friends about the Diagnosis.* Redcliffe, QLD, Australia: DJ Publishers.

FICTION

We also have fiction and adventure stories written for children and adolescents, where the central hero of the story has Asperger's syndrome. These stories, as well as augmenting children's knowledge of Asperger's syndrome, encourage them to identify with the experiences of the central character. The reader will also recognize how some of the characteristics and abilities associated with Asperger's syndrome can create a hero. The following is a list of current fiction where the central character has Asperger's syndrome:

Hadcroft, W. (2005) *Anne Droyd and Century Lodge.* London: Jessica Kingsley Publishers.
Haddon, M. (2003) *The Curious Incident of the Dog in the Night-Time.* Oxford: David Fickling Books.
Hoopmann, K. (2001a) *Blue Bottle Mystery: An Asperger Adventure.* London: Jessica Kingsley Publishers.
Hoopmann, K. (2001b) *Of Mice and Aliens: An Asperger Adventure.* London: Jessica Kingsley Publishers.
Hoopmann, K. (2002) *Lisa and the Lacemaker.* London: Jessica Kingsley Publishers.
Hoopmann, K. (2003) *Haze.* London: Jessica Kingsley Publishers.
Ogaz, N. (2002) *Buster and the Amazing Daisy.* London: Jessica Kingsley Publishers.
Welton, J. (2005) *Adam's Alternative Sports Day: An Asperger Story.* London: Jessica Kingsley Publishers.

AUTOBIOGRAPHIES

Another resource that can help explain the nature of Asperger's syndrome from a personal perspective is the autobiographies written by children, adolescents and adults who have Asperger's syndrome. Each author has a life story to tell, with experiences that the reader with Asperger's syndrome can identify with, and parents can read to understand their son or daughter's experiences. The following is a list of autobiographies:

Children

Hall, K. (2001) *Asperger Syndrome, the Universe and Everything.* London: Jessica Kingsley Publishers.

Adolescents

Jackson, L. (2002) *Freaks, Geeks and Asperger Syndrome: A User Guide to Adolescence.* London: Jessica Kingsley Publishers.
Jackson, N. (2002) *Standing Down Falling Up: Asperger's Syndrome from the Inside Out.* Bristol: Lucky Duck Publishing.
Peers, J. (2003) *Asparagus Dreams.* London: Jessica Kingsley Publishers.

Adults

Attwood, T. and Willey, L.H. (2000) *Crossing the Bridge* (Video). Higganum, CT: Starfish Speciality Press.
Birch, J. (2003) *Congratulations! It's Asperger Syndrome.* London: Jessica Kingsley Publishers.
Fleisher, M. (2003) *Making Sense of the Unfeasible: My Life Journey with Asperger Syndrome.* London: Jessica Kingsley Publishers.
Gerland, G. (1997) *A Real Person: Life on the Outside.* London: Souvenir Press.
Grandin, T. (1995) *Thinking in Pictures and Other Reports from My Life with Autism.* New York: Doubleday.

Hadcroft, W. (2005) *The Feeling's Unmutual: Growing up with Asperger Syndrome (Undiagnosed)*. London: Jessica Kingsley Publishers.

Kearns Miller, J. (2003) *Women From Another Planet? Our Lives in the Universe of Autism*. Private publication.

Lawson, W. (1998) *Life Behind Glass: A Personal Account of Autism Spectrum Disorder*. London: Jessica Kingsley Publishers.

Sanders, R. (2002) *Overcoming Asperger's: Personal Experience and Insight*. Murfreesboro, TN: Armstrong Valley Publishing Company.

Schneider, E. (1999) *Discovering My Autism*. London: Jessica Kingsley Publishers.

Shore, S. (2001) *Beyond the Wall: Personal Experiences with Autism and Asperger Syndrome*. Kansas: Autism Asperger Publishing Company.

Willey, L.H. (1999) *Pretending to be Normal: Living with Asperger's Syndrome*. London: Jessica Kingsley Publishers.

Williams, D. (1998) *Nobody Nowhere: The Remarkable Autobiography of an Autistic Girl*. London: Jessica Kingsley Publishers.

BIOGRAPHIES

The following biographies are also part-autobiography and were primarily written by a parent, usually a mother, or family member of someone with Asperger's syndrome. They provide a family perspective of the development of someone with Asperger's syndrome and the search for a diagnosis and services.

Barnhill, G. (2002) *Right Address...Wrong Planet*. Kansas: Autism Asperger Publishing Company.

Fling, E. (2000) *Eating an Artichoke: A Mother's Perspective on Asperger Syndrome*. London: Jessica Kingsley Publishers.

LaSalle, B. (2003) *Finding Ben: A Mother's Journey Through the Maze of Asperger's*. New York: Contemporary Books.

Paradiz, V. (2002) *Elijah's Cup: A Family's Journey into the Community and Culture of High Functioning Autism and Asperger's Syndrome*. New York: The Free Press.

BOOKS FOR SIBLINGS, FRIENDS AND FAMILY

Bleach, F. (2001) *Everybody is Different: A Book for Young People Who Have Brothers and Sisters with Autism*. London: The National Autistic Society.

Davies, J. (1994) *Able Autistic Children – Children with Asperger's Syndrome: A Booklet for brothers and sisters*. Nottingham: The Early Years Diagnosis Centre.

Welton, J. (2004) *Can I Tell You About Asperger Syndrome?* London: Jessica Kingsley Publishers.

POSITIVE DIAGNOSTIC CRITERIA

Carol Gray and I were concerned that when an adult with Asperger's syndrome reads the diagnostic criteria, the characteristics are almost exclusively those that are qualitatively different in terms of being less able than the person's peers, with a very distinct value judgement on what is acceptable and clinically significant. We noticed that children and adults with Asperger's syndrome have specific qualities that can be superior to their peers. To provide a counter-argument, we wrote diagnostic criteria that describe positive and affirmative characteristics of Asperger's syndrome in adults, in a paper entitled *The Discovery of 'Aspie' Criteria* which can be downloaded from my website, www.tonyattwood.com.au.

DVD

I have presented seminars for professionals and parents on the diagnosis of Asperger's syndrome in children and adults. The seminars include the presentation of a recording of my diagnostic assessment of a ten-year-old boy, and a review of the diagnostic criteria and explanation of assessment strategies for clinicians. One of the seminars has been recorded as a DVD entitled *Asperger's Diagnostic Assessment* and is available from www.futurehorizons-autism.com.

BOOKS TO HELP WITH FRIENDSHIP SKILLS
Stage one of friendship

Berry, J. (1996) *Let's Talk About: Being Helpful.* New York: Scholastic Inc.
Rogers, F. (1987) *Mr Rogers' Neighborhood: Making Friends.* New York: The Putnam and Grosset Group.

The *Mr Men* books, by Roger Hargreaves, can encourage the development of characterization skills and are published in America by Price Stern Sloan and in the United Kingdom and Australia by Ladybird and Penguin Books.

Stage two of friendship

Brandenberg, A. (1995) *Communication: is Telling and Listening.* London: Mammoth.
Brown, L.K. and Brown, M. (1998) *How to Be a Friend: A Guide to Making Friends and Keeping Them.* Boston: Little, Brown and Company.
Buehner, C. (1998) *I Did It, I'm Sorry.* New York: Puffin Books.
Howlin, P., Baron-Cohen, S. and Hadwin, J. (1999) *Teaching Children with Autism to Mind-Read: A Practical Guide.* Chichester: John Wiley and Sons.
Leedy, L. (1996) *How Humans Make Friends.* New York: Holiday House.
McGrath, H. (1997) *Dirty Tricks: Classroom Games for Teaching Social Skills.* Melbourne: Adison Wesley Longman.
McGrath, H. and Francey, S. (1991) *Friendly Kids Friendly Classrooms: Teaching Social Skills and Confidence in the Classroom.* Melbourne: Addison Wesley Longman.
Roffey, S., Tarrant, T. and Majors, K. (1994) *Young Friends: Schools and Friendship.* London: Cassell Publishers.
Schroeder, A. (2003) *The Socially Speaking Game.* Wisbech: LDA: a division of McGraw-Hill children's publishing. More information at www.LDAlearning.com.
Wilson, C. (1993) *Room 14: A Social Language Program.* East Moline, IL: Linguisystems.

Stage three of friendship

American Girl Library (1996) *The Care and Keeping of Friends.* Middleton, WI: Pleasant Company Publications.
Schmidt, J. (1997) *Making and Keeping Friends: Ready-to-use Lessons, Stories and Activities for Building Relationships (Grades 4–8).* Greenville, NC: Brookcliff Publishers.

Sheindlin, Judge Judy (2001) *You Can't Judge a Book by its Cover: Cool Rules for School*. New York: Cliff Street Books: an imprint of HarperCollins Publishers.

Sheindlin, Judge Judy (2002) *Win or Lose by How You Choose*. New York: Cliff Street Books: an imprint of HarperCollins Publishers.

Stage four of friendship

Beck, T.A. (1994) *Building Healthy Friendships: Teaching Friendship Skills to Young People*. Saratoga, CA: R and E Publishers.

Canfield, J., Hanson, M.V. and Kirberger, K. (1998) *Chicken Soup: Teenage Soul Journal*. Deerfield Beach, FL: Health Communications Inc.

Cornelius, H. and Faire, S. (1998) *Everyone Can Win: How to Resolve Conflict*. Roseville, NSW, Australia: Simon and Schuster.

Decker, B. (1996) *The Art of Communicating: Achieving Interpersonal Impact in Business*, revised edition. Menlo Park, CA: Crisp Publications Inc.

Gabor, D. (2001) *How to Start a Conversation and Make Friends*. Revised and updated. New York: Simon and Schuster.

Matthews, A. (1990) *Making Friends: A Guide to Getting Along with People*. Singapore: Media Masters.

McGrath, H. and Edwards, H. (1997) *Friends: A Practical Guide to Understanding Relationships*. Marrickville, NSW, Australia: CHOICE Books.

Pease, A. (1995) *Body Language: How to Read Others' Thought by Their Gestures*. Mona Vale, NSW, Australia: Camel Publishing Company.

SOCIAL UNDERSTANDING
Literature on relationship abilities and Asperger's syndrome

Aston, M. (2003) *Aspergers in Love: Couple Relationships and Family Affairs*. London: Jessica Kingsley Publishers.

Edmonds, G. and Worton, D. (2005) *The Asperger Love Guide: A Practical Guide for Adults with Asperger's Syndrome to Seeking, Establishing and Maintaining Successful Relationships*. London: Paul Chapman Publishing.

Jacobs, B. (2004) *Loving Mr Spock: The Story of a Different Kind of Love*. Arlington, TX: Future Horizons.

Jacobs, B. (2006) *Loving Mr Spock: Understanding an Aloof Lover – Could it be Asperger's Syndrome?* London: Jessica Kingsley Publishers.

Lawson, W. (2005) *Sex, Sexuality and the Autism Spectrum*. London: Jessica Kingsley Publishers.

Rodman, K. (2003) *Asperger's Syndrome and Adults...Is Anyone Listening? Essays and Poems by Partners, Parents and Family Members of Adults with Asperger's Syndrome*. London: Jessica Kingsley Publishers.

Slater-Walker, G. and Slater-Walker, C. (2002) *An Asperger Marriage*. London: Jessica Kingsley Publishers.

Stanford, A. (2003) *Asperger Syndrome and Long-term Relationships*. London: Jessica Kingsley Publishers.

Computer programs – Theory of Mind

Mind Reading: The Interactive Guide to Emotions. Distributed by Jessica Kingsley Publishers, London. The program uses an interactive DVD and can be used with children from age six to adults. More information available from www.jkp.com.

Social Stories™

More information on Social Stories™ and the work of Carol Gray can be obtained from the web site www.thegraycenter.org.

SOCIAL SKILLS PROGRAMS DESIGNED FOR CHILDREN AND ADULTS WITH ASPERGER'S SYNDROME

Bereket, R. *Playing It Right: Social Skills Activities for Parents and Teachers of Young Children with Aspergers, Autism and PDD: Age 3+.* Not yet published.

Carter, M. and Santomauro, J. (2004) *Space Travellers: An Interactive Program for Developing Social Understanding, Social Competence and Social Skills for Students with Asperger Syndrome, Autism and Other Social Cognitive Challenges.* Kansas: Autism Asperger Publishing Company. More information at www.asperger.net.

Garcia Winner, M. (2000) *Inside Out: What Makes a Person with Social Cognitive Deficits Tick?* San Jose, CA: Michelle Garcia Winner. More information at www.socialthinking.com.

Garcia Winner, M. (2002) *Thinking About YOU Thinking About ME: Philosophy and Strategies to Further Develop Perspective Taking and Communication Abilities for Persons with Social Cognitive Deficits.* San Jose, CA: Michelle Garcia Winner. More information available at www.socialthinking.com.

Gutstein, S. and Steely, R. (2002a) *Relationship Development Intervention with Older Children, Adolescents and Adults: Social and Emotional Development Activities for Asperger Syndrome, Autism, PDD and NLD.* London: Jessica Kingsley Publishers.

Gutstein, S. and Steely, R. (2002b) *Relationship Development Intervention with Young Children: Social and Emotional Development Activities for Asperger Syndrome, Autism, PDD and NLD.* London: Jessica Kingsley Publishers.

McAfee, J. (2002) *Navigating the Social World: A Curriculum for Individuals with Asperger's Syndrome, High Functioning Autism and Related Disorders.* Arlington, TX: Future Horizons.

Moyes, R. (2001) *Incorporating Social Goals in the Classroom: A Guide for Teachers and Parents of Children with High-functioning Autism and Asperger Syndrome.* London: Jessica Kingsley Publishers.

RESOURCES FOR EMOTION EDUCATION AND MANAGEMENT

Books

Akin, T., Cowan, D., Palomares, S. and Schuster, S. (1993) *Feelings Are Facts: Helping Kids Understand, Manage and Learn from Their Feelings.* Torrance, CA: Innerchoice Publishing.

Cardon, T. (2004) *Let's Talk Emotions: Helping Children with Social Cognitive Deficits, Including AS, HFA, and NVLD, Learn to Understand and Express Empathy and Emotions.* Kansas: Autism Asperger Publishing Company.

Dunn Buron, K. and Curtis, M. (2003) *The Incredible 5-Point Scale: Assisting Students with Autism Spectrum Disorders in Understanding Social Interactions and Controlling Their Emotional Responses.* Kansas: Autism Asperger Publishing Company.

Freyman, S. and Elffers, J. (1999) *How Are You Peeling? Foods with Moods.* New York: Arthur A. Levine Books.

Green, J. (2004) *How Do I Feel? An Interactive Reading Book of Emotions.* Santa Clarita, CA: Greenhouse Publications.

Kipfer, B. (1994) *1400 Things for Kids to be Happy About.* New York: Workman Publishing.

Matthews, A. (1988) *Being Happy: A Handbook to Greater Confidence and Security.* Singapore: Media Masters.

Sunderland, M. and Engelheart, P. (1993) *Draw On Your Emotions.* Bicester, UK: Winslow Press.

Resource material

Attwood, T., Moller Nielsen, A. and Callesen, K. (2004) *The CAT-kit: Cognitive Affective Training.* www.cat-kit.com.

Feeling and Faces Games (1994) Carson, CA: Lakeshore Learning Materials. www.lakeshorelearning.com

My Feelings Kit (2002) Oceans of Emotions. www.oceansofemotions.com.

Computer software

Maines, B. (2003) *Reading Faces and Learning About Human Emotions.* Bristol: Lucky Duck Publishing.

Mind Reading: The Interactive Guide to Emotions distributed by Jessica Kingsley Publishers. This program uses an interactive DVD-ROM and can be used with children from age six to asults. Also available on CD-ROM. More information available from www.jkp.com/mindreading.

Cognitive Behaviour Therapy programs

Attwood, T. (2004a) *Exploring Feelings: Cognitive Behaviour Therapy to Manage Anger.* Arlington, TX: Future Horizons.

Attwood, T. (2004b) *Exploring Feelings: Cognitive Behaviour Therapy to Manage Anxiety.* Arlington, TX: Future Horizons.

Barrett, P., Webster, H. and Turner, C. (2000) *Friends: Prevention of Anxiety and Depression for Children and Youth.* Bowen Hills, Australia: Australian Academic Press.

Dynes, R. (2001) *Anxiety Management in 10 Group-work Sessions.* Bicester, UK: Speechmark Publishing.

Greenberger, D. and Padesky, C. (1995) *Mind Over Mood: Change How You Feel by Changing the Way You Think.* New York: The Guilford Press.

Practical guides for emotion management

Anger

Faupel, A., Herrick, E. and Sharp, P. (1998) *Anger Management: A Practical Guide.* London: David Fulton Publishers.

Greene, R. (1998) *The Explosive Child.* New York: HarperCollins Publishers.

Smith Myles, B. and Southwick, J. (1999) *Asperger Syndrome and Difficult Moments: Practical Solutions for Tantrums, Rage and Meltdowns.* Kansas: Autism Asperger Publishing Co.

Anxiety

Phillips, N. (1996) *The Panic Book.* Concord West, NSW, Australia: Shrink-Rap Press.

Wever, C. (1994) *The Secret Problem.* Concord West, NSW, Australia: Shrink-Rap Press.

Depression

Phillips, N. (1999) *Too Blue: A Book About Depression.* Concord West, NSW, Australia: Shrink-Rap Press.

WEB SITES

There are now hundreds of web pages that provide information on Asperger's syndrome. Many of the web pages have links to other sites that can become a web of connections. The following web pages are a starting point and are in my 'favourites' list on my computer.

- For information on my studies of children and adults with Asperger's syndrome and other publications go to www.tonyattwood.com.au. This web address will also provide a list of seminars and workshops that I will be presenting. I may be coming to your local area and you can listen to my latest thoughts on Asperger's syndrome. The web address of the clinic for children and adults run by my friend and colleague Michelle Garnett in Brisbane, Australia, is www.mindsandhearts.net.

- For parents, I strongly recommend the OASIS web page www.udel.edu/bkirby/asperger, especially the message boards to post questions and access the wisdom and experiences of parents of children and adults with Asperger's syndrome throughout the world. I also recommend the web page of the National Autistic Society (NAS) in the United Kingdom for information for parents. The NAS web address is www.nas.org.uk. The web address for the Asperger's syndrome support group in Brisbane, Australia, is www.asperger.asn.au. My own web page will have a list of web pages for support groups in Australia, America and Europe.

- For people with Asperger's syndrome I recommend the following:
  - www.lukejackson.info
  - http://oddsandfriends.typepad.com/askanaspie
  - www.aspergeradults.ca/aspergrrrlz.html. This site is for girls and women with Asperger's syndrome.

- For information on the ideas and strategies developed by Carol Gray go to www.thegraycenter.org.

- The primary publisher of books on Asperger's syndrome is Jessica Kingsley Publishers and you can read about the latest publications at www.jkp.com.

- Another publisher of books on Asperger's syndrome and organizer of conferences and workshops in the USA is www.futurehorizons-autism.com.

References

Abele, E. and Grenier, D. (2005) 'The language of social communication: running pragmatic groups in schools and clinical settings.' In L. Baker and L. Welkowitz (eds) *Asperger's Syndrome: Intervening in Schools, Clinics, and Communities.* Mahwah, NJ: Lawrence Erlbaum Associates.

Adamo, S. (2004) 'An adolescent and his imaginary companions: from quasi-delusional constructs to creative imagination.' *Journal of Child Psychotherapy 30,* 275–295.

Adams, C., Green, J., Gilchrist, A. and Cox, A. (2002) 'Conversational behaviour of children with Asperger syndrome and conduct disorder.' *Journal of Child Psychology and Psychiatry 43,* 679–690.

Adolphs, R., Sears, L. and Piven, J. (2001) 'Abnormal processing of social information from faces in autism.' *Journal of Cognitive Neuroscience 13,* 232–240.

Ahearn, W., Castine, T., Nault, K. and Green, G. (2001) 'An assessment of food acceptance in children with autism or pervasive developmental disorder not otherwise specified.' *Journal of Autism and Developmental Disorders 31,* 505–511.

Ahsgren, I., Baldwin, I., Goetzinger-Falk, C., Arikson, A., Flodmark, O. and Gillberg, C. (2005) 'Ataxia, autism and the cerebellum: a clinical study of 32 individuals with congenital ataxia.' *Developmental Medicine and Child Neurology 47,* 193–198.

Alcantara, J., Weisblatt, E., Moore, B. and Bolton, P. (2004) 'Speech-in-noise perception in high-functioning individuals with autism or Asperger's syndrome.' *Journal of Child Psychology and Psychiatry 45,* 1107–1114.

Alexander, R., Michael, D. and Gangadharan, S. (2004) 'The use of risperidone in adults with Asperger Syndrome.' *British Journal of Developmental Disabilities 50,* 109–115.

Alvarez, A. and Reid, S. (eds) (1999) *Autism and Personality: Findings from the Tavistock Autism Workshop.* London: Routledge.

American Psychiatric Association (APA) (1994) *Diagnostic and Statistical Manual of Mental Disorders,* 4th Edition. Washington, DC: American Psychiatric Association.

American Psychiatric Association (APA) (2000) *Diagnostic and Statistical Manual of Mental Disorders,* 4th Edition (Text Revision). Washington, DC: American Psychiatric Association.

Andron, L. and Weber, E.G. (1998) *From Solitary Perseveration to Social Relatedness: Facilitating Social Interaction for Children, Adolescents and Adults with Autism – A Family-centred Group Approach.* Unpublished manuscript. Los Angeles: University of California.

Apple, A., Billingsley, F. and Schwartz, I. (2005) 'Effects of video modelling alone and with self-management on compliment-giving behaviours of children with High-Functioning ASD.' *Journal of Positive Behaviour Interventions 7,* 33–46.

Asperger, H. (1938) 'Das psychisch abnorme Kind.' *Wiener klinische Wochenschrift 49,* 1–12. ('The mentally abnormal child.' *Viennese Clinical Weekly 49.*)

Asperger, H. (1944) 'Die autistischen Psychopathen im Kindesalter.' *Archiv fur Psychiatrie und Nervenkrankheiten 177,* 76–137.

Asperger, H. (1952) *Heilpädagogik. Einführung in die Psychopathologie des Kindes für Ärzte, Lehrer, Psychologen und Fürsorgerinnen.* Wien: Springer.

Asperger, H. (1979) 'Problems of infantile autism.' *Communication: Journal of the National Autistic Society, London 13,* 45–52.

Asperger, H. (1991) [1944] 'Autistic psychopathy in childhood.' In U. Frith (ed) *Autism and Asperger Syndrome.* Cambridge: Cambridge University Press.

Aston, M. (2003) *Aspergers in Love: Couple Relationships and Family Affairs.* London: Jessica Kingsley Publishers.

Attwood, T. (1998) *Asperger's Syndrome: A Guide for Parents and Professionals.* London: Jessica Kingsley Publishers.

Attwood, T. (2000) 'Strategies for improving the social integration of children with Asperger syndrome.' *Autism 4,* 85–100.

Attwood, T. (2003a) 'Frameworks for behavioural interventions.' *Child and Adolescent Psychiatric Clinics 12,* 65–86.

Attwood, T. (2003b) 'Understanding and managing circumscribed interests.' In M. Prior (ed) *Learning and Behavior Problems in Asperger Syndrome.* New York: The Guilford Press.

Attwood, T. (2004a) *Exploring Feelings: Cognitive Behaviour Therapy to Manage Anger.* Arlington, TX: Future Horizons.

Attwood, T. (2004b) *Exploring Feelings: Cognitive Behaviour Therapy to Manage Anxiety.* Arlington, TX: Future Horizons.

Attwood, T. (2004c) 'Strategies to reduce the bullying of young children with Asperger Syndrome.' *Australian Journal of Early Childhood 29,* 15–23.

Attwood, T. (2004d) 'Theory of Mind and Asperger syndrome.' In L.J. Baker and L.A. Welkowitz (eds) *Asperger Syndrome: Intervening in Schools, Clinics and Communities.* Hillsdale, NJ: Lawrence Erlbaum Associates.

Attwood, T., Frith, U. and Hermelin, B. (1988) 'The understanding and use of interpersonal gestures by autistic Down's Syndrome children.' *Journal of Autism and Developmental Disorders 18,* 214–257.

Attwood, T. and Willey, L.H. (2000) *Crossing the Bridge* (Video). Higganum, CT: Starfish Speciality Press.

Ayers, A. (1972) *Sensory Integration and Learning Disabilities.* Los Angeles, CA: Western Psychological Services.

Bailey, A., Palferman, S., Heavey, L. and LeCouteur, A. (1998) 'Autism: the phenotype in relatives.' *Journal of Autism and Developmental Disorders 28,* 369–392.

Baird, G., Charman, T., Baron-Cohen, S., Cox, A., Sweetenham, J., Wheelwright, S. and Drew, A. (2000) 'A screening instrument for autism at 18 months of age: a 6-year follow-up study.' *Journal of the American Academy of Child and Adolescent Psychiatry 39,* 694–702.

Baranek, G. (2002) 'Efficacy of sensory and motor interventions for children with autism.' *Journal of Autism and Developmental Disorders 32,* 397–422.

Baranek, G., Foster, L. and Berkson, G. (1997) 'Sensory defensiveness in persons with developmental disabilities.' *Occupational Therapy Journal of Research 17,* 173–185.

Barber, K. (2006) *Living Your Best Life with Asperger's Syndrome.* London: SAGE Publications.

Barnhill, G., Hagiwara, T., Smith Myles, B. and Simpson, R. (2000) 'Asperger Syndrome: a study of the cognitive profiles of 37 children and adolescents.' *Focus on Autism and Other Developmental Disabilities 15,* 146–160.

Barnhill, G. and Smith Myles, B. (2001) 'Attributional style and depression in adolescents with Asperger syndrome.' *Journal of Positive Behavior Interventions 3,* 175–182.

Barnhill, G., Tapscott Cook, K., Tebbenkamp, K. and Smith Myles, B. (2002) 'The effectiveness of social skills intervention targeting nonverbal communication for adolescents with Asperger syndrome and related pervasive developmental delays.' *Focus on Autism and Other Developmental Disabilities 17*, 112–118.

Baron-Cohen, S. (1988) 'An assessment of violence in a young man with Asperger's Syndrome.' *Journal of Child Psychology and Psychiatry 29*, 351–360.

Baron-Cohen, S. (1990) 'Do autistic children have obsessions and compulsions?' *British Journal of Clinical Psychology 28*, 193–200.

Baron-Cohen, S. (1995) *Mind Blindness: An Essay on Autism and Theory of Mind.* Cambridge, MA: MIT Press.

Baron-Cohen, S. (2003) *The Essential Difference: Men, Women and the Extreme Male Brain.* London: The Penguin Press.

Baron-Cohen, S. and Jolliffe, T. (1997) 'Another advanced test of theory of mind: evidence from very high functioning adults with autism or Asperger's Syndrome.' *Journal of Child Psychology and Psychiatry 38*, 813–822.

Baron-Cohen, S., O'Riordan, M., Stone, V., Jones, R. and Plaisted, K. (1999a) 'Recognition of Faux Pas by normally developing children and children with Asperger syndrome or High-Functioning Autism.' *Journal of Autism and Developmental Disorders 29*, 407–418.

Baron-Cohen, S., Ring, H.A., Wheelwright, S., Bullmore, E.T., Brammer, M.J., Simmons, A. and William, S.C.R. (1999b) 'Social intelligence in the normal autistic brain: an FMRI study.' *European Journal of Neuroscience 11*, 1891–1898.

Baron-Cohen, S. and Staunton, R. (1994) 'Do children with autism acquire the phonology of their peers? An examination of group identification through the window of bilingualism.' *First Language 14*, 241–248.

Baron-Cohen, S. and Wheelwright, S. (1999) '"Obsessions" in children with autism or Asperger Syndrome: content analysis in terms of core domains of cognition.' *British Journal of Psychiatry 175*, 484–490.

Baron-Cohen, S. and Wheelwright, S. (2003) 'The Friendship Questionnaire: an investigation of adults with Asperger Syndrome or High Functioning Autism, and normal sex differences.' *Journal of Autism and Developmental Disorders 33*, 509–518.

Baron-Cohen, S. and Wheelwright, S. (2004) 'The Empathy Quotient: an investigation of adults with Asperger syndrome or High Functioning Autism and normal sex differences.' *Journal of Autism and Developmental Disorders 34*, 163–175.

Baron-Cohen, S., Wheelwright, S., Hill, J., Raste, Y. and Plumb, I. (2001a) 'The "Reading the Mind in the Eyes" Test, revised version: a study with normal adults with Asperger Syndrome or high-functioning autism.' *Journal of Child Psychology and Psychiatry 42*, 241–251.

Baron-Cohen, S., Wheelwright, S., Robinson, J. and Woodbury Smith, M. (2005) 'The Adult Asperger Assessment (AAA): a diagnostic method.' *Journal of Autism and Developmental Disorders 35*, 807–819.

Baron-Cohen, S., Wheelwright, S., Skinner, R., Martin, J. and Clubley, E. (2001b) 'The Autism Spectrum Quotient (AQ): evidence from Asperger syndrome/high-functioning autism, males and females, scientists and mathematicians.' *Journal of Autism and Developmental Disorders 31*, 5–17.

Barron, J. and Barron, S. (1992) *There's a Boy in Here.* New York: Simon and Schuster.

Barry, T., Klinger, L., Lee, J.M. and Palardy, N. (2003) 'Examining the effectiveness of an outpatient clinic-based social skills group for high-functioning children with autism.' *Journal of Autism and Developmental Disorders 33*, 685–699.

Barry Walsh, J. and Mullen, P. (2004) 'Forensic aspects of Asperger's syndrome.' *Journal of Forensic Psychiatry and Psychology 15*, 96–107.

Barton, J., Cherkasova, M., Hefter, R., Cox, T., O'Connor, M. and Manoach, D. (2004) 'Are patients with social developmental disorders prosopagnosic? Perceptual heterogeneity in the Asperger and socio-emotional processing disorders.' *Brain 127*, 1706–1716.

Bashe, P. and Kirby, B.L. (2001) *The Oasis Guide to Asperger Syndrome*. New York: Crown Publishers.

Bauminger, N. (2002) 'The facilitation of social-emotional understanding and social interaction in high-functioning children with autism: intervention outcomes.' *Journal of Autism and Developmental Disorders 31*, 461–469.

Bauminger, N. and Kasari, C. (1999) 'Brief report: theory of mind in high-functioning children with autism.' *Journal of Autism and Developmental Disorders 29*, 81–86.

Bauminger, N. and Kasari, C. (2000) 'Loneliness and friendship in high functioning children with autism.' *Child Development 71*, 447–456.

Bauminger, N. and Shulman, C. (2003) 'The development and maintenance of friendship in high-functioning children with autism.' *Autism 7*, 81–97.

Bauminger, N., Shulman, C. and Agam, G. (2003) 'Peer interaction and loneliness in high-functioning children with autism.' *Journal of Autism and Developmental Disorders 33*, 489–506.

Bejerot, S., Nylander, L. and Lindstrom, E. (2001) 'Autistic traits in obsessive-compulsive disorder.' *Nordic Journal of Psychiatry 55*, 169–176.

Berard, G. (1993) *Hearing Equals Behaviour*. New Canaan, CT: Keats Publishing.

Berthier, M.L. (1995) 'Hypomania following bereavement in Asperger's Syndrome: a case study.' *Neuropsychiatry, Neuropsychology and Behavioural Neurology 8*, 222–228.

Berthoz, S. and Hill, E. (2005) 'The validity of using self-reports to assess emotion regulation abilities in adults with autism spectrum disorder.' *European Psychiatry 20*, 291–298.

Beversdorf, D., Anderson, J., Manning, S., Anderson, S., Nordgren, R., Felopulos, G. and Bauman, M. (2001) 'Brief report: macrographia in high-functioning adults with Autism Spectrum Disorder.' *Journal of Autism and Developmental Disorders 31*, 97–101.

Bishop, D. (2000) 'What's so special about Asperger syndrome? The need for further exploration of the borderlands of autism.' In A. Klin, F. Volkmar and S. Sparrow (eds) *Asperger Syndrome*. New York: Guilford Press.

Bishop, D. and Baird, G. (2001) 'Parent and teacher report of pragmatic aspects of communication: use of the Children's Communication Checklist in a clinical setting.' *Developmental Medicine and Child Neurology 4*, 809–818.

Bishop, D. and Frazier Norbury, C. (2005) 'Executive functions in children with communication impairments, in relation to autistic symptomatology.' *Autism 9*, 7–27.

Blackshaw, A.J., Kinderman, P., Hare, D.J. and Hatton, C. (2001) 'Theory of mind, causal attribution and paranoia in Asperger syndrome.' *Autism 5*, 147–163.

Bogdashina, O. (2003) *Sensory Perceptual Issues in Autism and Asperger Syndrome: Different Sensory Experiences, Different Perceptual Worlds*. London: Jessica Kingsley Publishers.

Bolte, S., Ozkara, N. and Poustka, F. (2002) 'Autism spectrum disorders and low body weight: is there really a systematic association?' *International Journal of Eating Disorders 32*, 349–351.

Bolton, P., Pickles, A., Murphy, M. and Rutter, M. (1998) 'Autism, affective and other psychiatric disorders: patterns of familial aggregation.' *Psychological Medicine 28*, 385–395.

Botroff, V., Bartak, L., Langford, P., Page, M. and Tong, B. (1995) 'Social cognitive skills and implications for social skills training in adolescents with autism.' Paper presented at the 1995 Australian Autism Conference, Flinders University, Adelaide, Australia.

Broderick, C., Caswell, R., Gregory, S., Marzolini, S. and Wilson, O. (2002) 'Can I join the club? A social integration scheme for adolescents with Asperger's syndrome.' *Autism 6*, 427–431.

Bromley, J., Hare, D., Davison, K. and Emerson, E. (2004) 'Mothers supporting a child with autistic spectrum disorders: social support, mental health status and satisfaction with services.' *Autism 8*, 419–433.

Brown Rubinstein, M. (2005) *Raising NLD Superstars*. London: Jessica Kingsley Publishers.

Buehner, C. (1998) *I Did It, I'm Sorry*. New York: Puffin Books.

Burd, L., Kerbeshian, P., Barth, A., Klug, M., Avery, P. and Benz, B. (2001) 'Long term follow-up of an epidemiologically defined cohort of patients with Tourette syndrome.' *Journal of Child Neurology 16*, 431–437.

Campbell, J. (2005) 'Diagnostic assessment of Asperger's disorder: a review of five third-party rating scales.' *Journal of Autism and Developmental Disorders 35*, 25–35.

Capps, L., Kehres, J. and Sigman, M. (1998) 'Conversational abilities among children with autism and children with developmental delays.' *Autism 2*, 325–344.

Carper, R., Moses, P., Tigue, Z. and Courschesne, E. (2002) 'Cerebral lobes in autism: early hyperplasia and abnormal age effects.' *NeuroImage 16*, 1038–1051.

Carrington, S. and Forder, T. (1999) 'An affective skills programme using multimedia for a child with Asperger's syndrome.' *Australian Journal of Learning Disabilities 4*, 5–9.

Carrington, S. and Graham, L. (2001) 'Perceptions of school by two teenage boys with Asperger syndrome and their mothers: a qualitative study.' *Autism 5*, 37–48.

Castelli, F., Frith, C., Happé, F. and Frith, U. (2002) 'Autism, Asperger syndrome and brain mechanisms for the attribution of mental states to animated shapes.' *Brain 125*, 1839–1849.

Cederlund, M. and Gillberg, C. (2004) 'One hundred males with Asperger syndrome: a clinical study of background and associated factors.' *Developmental Medicine and Child Neurology 46*, 652–661.

Cesaroni, L. and Garber, M. (1991) 'Exploring the experience of autism through first hand accounts.' *Journal of Autism and Developmental Disorders 21*, 303–313.

Chakrabarti, S. and Fombonne, E. (2001) 'Pervasive developmental disorders in pre-school children.' *Journal of the American Medical Association 285*, 3093–3099.

Chen, P., Chen, S., Yang, Y., Yeh, T., Chen, C. and Lo, H. (2003) 'Asperger's disorder: a case report of repeated stealing and the collecting behaviours of an adolescent patient.' *Acta Psychiatrica Scandinavica 107*, 73–76.

Chin, H.Y. and Bernard-Opitz, V. (2000) 'Teaching conversation skills to children with autism: effect on the development of a Theory of Mind.' *Journal of Autism and Developmental Disorders 30*, 569–583.

Church, C., Alisanski, S. and Amanullah, S. (2000) 'The social, behavioural and academic experiences of children with Asperger disorder.' *Focus on Autism and Other Developmental Disabilities 15*, 12–20.

Clarke, D., Baxter, M., Perry, D. and Prasher, V. (1999) 'Affective and psychotic disorders in adults with autism: seven case reports.' *Autism 3*, 149–164.

Cooper, S.A., Mohamed, W.N. and Collacott, R.A. (1993) 'Possible Asperger's Syndrome in a mentally handicapped transvestite offender.' *Journal of Intellectual Disability Research 37*, 189–194.

Craig, J., Hatton, C., Craig, F. and Bentall, R. (2004) 'Persecutory beliefs, attributions and theory of mind: comparison of patients with paranoid delusions, Asperger's syndrome and healthy controls.' *Schizophrenia Research 69*, 29–33.

Critchley, H.D., Daly, E.M., Bullmore, E.T., Williams, S.C.R., Van Amelsvoort, T., Robertson, D.M., Rowe, A., Phillips, M., McAlonan, G., Howlin, P. and Murphy, D. (2000) 'The functional neuroanatomy of social behaviour.' *Brain 123*, 2203–2212.

Darlington, J. (2001) 'Humor, imagination and empathy in autism.' In L. Andron (ed) *Our Journey Through High Functioning Autism and Asperger Syndrome: A Roadmap*. London: Jessica Kingsley Publishers.

Dawson, G., Osterling, J., Melzoff, A. and Kuhl, P. (2000) 'Case study of the development of an infant with autism from birth to 2 years of age.' *Journal of Applied Developmental Psychology 21*, 299–313.

Dawson, G. and Watling, R. (2000) 'Interventions to facilitate auditory, visual, and motor integration in autism: a review of the evidence.' *Journal of Autism and Developmental Disorders 30*, 415–421.

DeLong, G. (1994) 'Children with autistic spectrum disorder and a family history of affective disorder.' *Developmental Medicine and Child Neurology 36*, 647–688.

DeLong, G. and Dwyer, J. (1988) 'Correlation of family history with specific autistic subgroups: Asperger's syndrome and bipolar affective disease.' *Journal of Autism and Developmental Disorders 18,* 593–600.

DeMyer, M., Hingtgen, J. and Jackson, R. (1981) 'Infantile autism reviewed: a decade of research.' *Schizophrenic Bulletin 7,* 388–451.

Dewey, M. (1991) 'Living with Asperger's Syndrome.' In U. Frith (ed) *Autism and Asperger's Syndrome.* Cambridge: Cambridge University Press.

Dhossche, D. (1998) 'Brief report: catatonia in autistic disorders.' *Journal of Autism and Developmental Disorders 28,* 329–331.

Dickerson Mayes, S. and Calhoun, S. (2003) 'Ability profiles in children with autism: influence of age and IQ.' *Autism 7,* 65–80.

Dickerson Mayes, S., Calhoun, S. and Crites, D. (2001) 'Does DSM-IV Asperger's disorder exist?' *Journal of Abnormal Child Psychology 29,* 263–272.

Dissanayake, C. (2004) 'Change in behavioural symptoms in children with High Functioning Autism and Asperger syndrome: evidence for one disorder?' *Australian Journal of Early Childhood 29,* 48–57.

Donnelly, J. and Bovee, J.-P. (2003) 'Reflections on play: recollections from a mother and her son with Asperger Syndrome.' *Autism 7,* 471–476.

Duchaine, B., Nieminen-von Wendt, T., New, J. and Kulomaki, T. (2003) 'Dissociations of visual recognition in a genetic prosopagnosic: evidence for separate developmental processes.' *Neurocase 9,* 380–389.

Dunn, W. (1999a) 'Development and validation of the Short Sensory Profile.' In W. Dunn (ed) *The Sensory Profile Examiners' Manual.* San Antonio, TX: Psychological Corporation.

Dunn, W. (1999b) *Sensory Profile.* San Antonio, TX: Psychological Corporation.

Dunn, W., Smith Myles, B. and Orr, S. (2002) 'Sensory processing issues associated with Asperger syndrome: a preliminary investigation.' *American Journal of Occupational Therapy 56,* 97–102.

Edmonds, G. and Worton, D. (2005) *The Asperger Love Guide: A Practical Guide for Adults with Asperger's Syndrome to Seeking, Establishing and Maintaining Successful Relationships.* London: Sage Publications.

Ehlers, S. and Gillberg, C. (1993) 'The epidemiology of Asperger's Syndrome - a total population study.' *Journal of Child Psychology and Psychiatry 34,* 1327–1350.

Ehlers, S., Gillberg, C. and Wing, L. (1999) 'A screening questionnaire for Asperger syndrome and other high-functioning autism spectrum disorders in school age children.' *Journal of Autism and Developmental Disorders 29,* 129–141.

Ehlers, S., Nyden, A., Gillberg, C., Dahlgren-Sandberg, A., Dahlgren, S.O., Hjelmquist, E. and Oden, A. (1997) 'Asperger syndrome, autism and attention disorders: a comparative study of the cognitive profiles of 120 children.' *Journal of Child Psychology and Psychiatry 38,* 207–217.

Eisenmajer, R., Prior, M., Leekham, S., Wing, L., Gould, J., Welham, M. and Ong, B. (1996) 'Comparison of clinical symptoms in autism and Asperger's disorder.' *Journal of the American Academy of Child and Adolescent Psychiatry 35,* 1523–1531.

Eisenmajer, R., Prior, M., Leekham, S., Wing, L., Ong, B., Gould, J. and Welham, M. (1998) 'Delayed language onset as a predictor of clinical symptoms in Pervasive Developmental Disorders.' *Journal of Autism and Developmental Disorders 28,* 527–533.

Ekkehart, F., Staufenberg, A. and Kells, M. (2005) 'High risk or offending conduct in Asperger's syndrome: a forensic neuropsychiatric AS outpatient clinic cohort.' Paper presented at the 1st International Symposium on Autism Spectrum Disorder in a Forensic Context, September, Copenhagen, Denmark.

Ekman, P. (2003) *Emotions Revealed: Recognizing Faces and Feelings to Improve Communication and Emotional Life.* New York: Times Books.

Epstein, T. and Saltzman-Benaiah, J. (2005) 'Tourette syndrome and Asperger syndrome: overlapping symptoms and treatment implications.' In K. Stoddart (ed) *Children, Youth and Adults with Asperger Syndrome: Integrating Multiple Perspectives*. London: Jessica Kingsley Publishers.

Everall, I.P. and Le Couteur, A. (1990) 'Firesetting in an adolescent boy with Asperger's Syndrome.' *British Journal of Psychiatry 157*, 284–287.

Fast, Y. (2004) *Employment for Individuals with Asperger Syndrome or Non-Verbal Learning Disability: Stories and Strategies*. London: Jessica Kingsley Publishers.

Fein, D., Dixon, P., Paul, J. and Levin, H. (2005) 'Brief report: pervasive developmental disorder can evolve into ADHD: case illustrations.' *Journal of Autism and Developmental Disorders 35*, 525–534.

Fine, C., Lumsden, J. and Blair, R.J.R. (2001) 'Dissociation between theory of mind and executive functions in a patient with early left amygdala damage.' *Brain Journal of Neurology 124*, 287–298.

Fine, J., Bartolucci, G., Ginsberg, G. and Szatmari, P. (1991) 'The use of intonation to communicate in Pervasive Developmental Disorders.' *Journal of Child Psychology and Psychiatry 32*, 777–782.

Fine, J., Bartolucci, G., Szatmari, P. and Ginsberg, G. (1994) 'Cohesive discourse in Pervasive Developmental Disorders.' *Journal of Autism and Developmental Disorders 24*, 315–329.

Fitzgerald, M. (2005) *The Genesis of Artistic Creativity: Asperger's Syndrome and the Arts*. London: Jessica Kingsley Publishers.

Fitzpatrick, E. (2004) 'The use of cognitive behavioural strategies in the management of anger in a child with an autistic disorder: an evaluation.' *Good Autism Practice 5*, 3–17.

Fleisher, M. (2003) *Making Sense of the Unfeasible: My Life Journey with Asperger Syndrome*. London: Jessica Kingsley Publishers.

Fleisher, M. (2006) *Survival Strategies for People on the Autism Spectrum*. London: Jessica Kingsley Publishers.

Fransella, F. (ed) (2005) *The Essential Practitioner's Handbook of Personal Construct Psychology*. Chichester: John Wiley and Sons.

Frazier, J., Doyle, R., Chiu, S. and Coyle, J. (2002) 'Treating a child with Asperger's disorder and comorbid bipolar disorder.' *American Journal of Psychiatry 159*, 13–21.

Frith, U. (1989) *Autism: Explaining the Enigma*. Oxford: Basil Blackwell Ltd.

Frith, U. (2004) 'Emanuel Miller lecture: Confusions and controversies about Asperger syndrome.' *Journal of Child Psychology and Psychiatry 45*, 672–686.

Frith, U. and Happé, F. (1994) 'Autism: beyond "theory of mind".' *Cognition 50*, 115–132.

Frith, U. and Happé, F. (1999) 'Self-consciousness and autism. What is it like to be autistic?' *Mind and Language 14*, 1–22.

Gabor, D. (2001) *How to Start a Conversation and Make Friends*. New York: Simon and Schuster.

Gadow, K. and DeVincent, C. (2005) 'Clinical significance of tics and Attention-Deficit Hyperactivity Disorder (ADHD) in children with Pervasive Developmental Disorder.' *Journal of Child Neurology 20*, 481–488.

Gagnon, E. (2001) *Power Cards. Using Special Interests to Motivate Children and Youth with Asperger Syndrome and Autism*. Kansas: Autism Asperger Publishing Company.

Gallucci, G., Hackerman, F. and Schmidt, C. (2005) 'Gender identity disorder in an adult male with Asperger's syndrome.' *Sexuality and Disability 23*, 35–40.

Garnett, M. and Attwood, T. (1998) 'The Australian Scale for Asperger's Syndrome.' In T. Attwood (ed) *Asperger's Syndrome: A Guide for Parents and Professionals*. London: Jessica Kingsley Publishers.

Gepner, B. and Mestre, D. (2002) 'Brief report: Postural reactivity to fast visual motion differentiates autistic from children with Asperger syndrome.' *Journal of Autism and Developmental Disorders 32*, 231–238.

Ghaziuddin, M. (2005a) 'A family history study of Asperger syndrome.' *Journal of Autism and Developmental Disorders 35*, 177–182.

Ghaziuddin, M. (2005b) *Mental Health Aspects of Autism and Asperger Syndrome*. London: Jessica Kingsley Publishers.

Ghaziuddin, M., Butler, E., Tsai, L. and Ghaziuddin, N. (1994) 'Is clumsiness a marker for Asperger syndrome?' *Journal of Intellectual Disability Research 38*, 519–527.

Ghaziuddin, M. and Gerstein, L. (1996) 'Pedantic speaking style differentiates Asperger's syndrome from high-functioning autism.' *Journal of Autism and Developmental Disorders 26*, 585–595.

Ghaziuddin, M. and Greden, J. (1998) 'Depression in children with autism/pervasive developmental disorders: a case-control family history study.' *Journal of Autism and Developmental Disorders 28*, 111–115.

Ghaziuddin, M. and Mountain Kimchi, K. (2004) 'Defining the intellectual profile of Asperger syndrome: comparison with High-Functioning Autism.' *Journal of Autism and Developmental Disorders 34*, 279–284.

Ghaziuddin, M., Quinlan, P. and Ghaziuddin, N. (2005) 'Catatonia in autism: a distinct subtype?' *Journal of Intellectual Disability Research 49*, 102–105.

Ghaziuddin, M., Shakal, J. and Tsai, L. (1995) 'Obstetric factors in Asperger syndrome: comparison with high functioning autism.' *Journal of Intellectual Disability Research 39*, 538–543.

Ghaziuddin, M., Thomas, P., Napier, E., Kearney, G., Tsai, L., Welch, K. and Fraser, W. (2000) 'Brief report: brief syntactic analysis in Asperger syndrome: a preliminary study.' *Journal of Autism and Developmental Disorders 30*, 67–70.

Ghaziuddin, M., Tsai, L. and Ghaziuddin, N. (1991) 'Brief report: Violence in Asperger Syndrome – a critique.' *Journal of Autism and Developmental Disorders 21*, 349–354.

Ghaziuddin, M., Tsai, L. and Ghaziuddin, N. (1992) 'Brief report: A comparison of the diagnostic criteria for Asperger syndrome.' *Journal of Autism and Developmental Disorders 22*, 643–649.

Ghaziuddin, M., Wieder-Mikhail, W. and Ghaziuddin, N. (1998) 'Comorbidity of Asperger Syndrome: a preliminary report.' *Journal of Intellectual Disability Research 42*, 279–283.

Gillberg, C. (1989) 'Asperger's Syndrome in 23 Swedish children.' *Developmental Medicine and Child Neurology 31*, 520–531.

Gillberg, C. (1991) 'Clinical and neurobiological aspects of Asperger syndrome in six family studies.' In U. Frith (ed) *Autism and Asperger Syndrome*. Cambridge: Cambridge University Press.

Gillberg, C. (1998) 'Asperger syndrome and High Functioning Autism.' *British Journal of Psychiatry 171*, 200–209.

Gillberg, C. (2002) *A Guide to Asperger Syndrome*. Cambridge: Cambridge University Press.

Gillberg, C. and Billstedt, E. (2000) 'Autism and Asperger syndrome: coexistence with other clinical disorders.' *Acta Psychiatrica Scandinavica 102*, 321–330.

Gillberg, C. and de Souza, L. (2002) 'Head circumference in autism, Asperger syndrome, and ADHD: a comparative study.' *Developmental Medicine and Child Neurology 44*, 296–300.

Gillberg, C., Ehlers, S., Schaumann, H., Jacobsson, G., Dahlgren, S., Lindblom, R., Bagenholm, A., Tjuus, T. and Blinder, E. (1990) 'Autism under age 3 years: a clinical study of 28 cases referred for autistic symptoms in infancy.' *Journal of Child Psychology and Psychiatry 31*, 921–934.

Gillberg, C., Gillberg, C., Rastam, M. and Wentz, E. (2001) 'The Asperger Syndrome (and high-functioning autism) Diagnostic Interview (ASDI): a preliminary study of a new structured clinical interview.' *Autism 5*, 57–66.

Gillberg, C. and Gillberg, I.C. (1989) 'Asperger Syndrome – some epidemiological considerations: a research note.' *Journal of Child Psychology and Psychiatry 30*, 631–638.

Gillberg, C. and Rastam, M. (1992) 'Do some cases of anorexia nervosa reflect underlying autistic-like conditions?' *Behavioural Neurology 5*, 27–32.

Gillberg, I.C., Gillberg, C., Rastam, M. and Johansson, M. (1996) 'The cognitive profile of anorexia nervosa: a comparative study including a community based sample.' *Comprehensive Psychiatry 37*, 23–30.

Gilliam, J. (2002) *GADS Examiner's Manual.* Austin, TX: PRO-ED.

Gillot, A., Furniss, F. and Walter, A. (2001) 'Anxiety in high-functioning children with autism.' *Autism* 5, 277–286.

Goldberg, M., Mostofsky, S., Cutting, L., Mahone, E., Astor, B., Denckla, M. and Landa, R. (2005) 'Subtle executive impairment in children with autism and children with ADHD.' *Journal of Autism and Developmental Disorders 35,* 279–293.

Goldstein, G., Johnson, C. and Minshew, N. (2001) 'Attentional processes in autism.' *Journal of Autism and Developmental Disorders 31,* 433–440.

Goldstein, S. and Schwebach, A. (2004) 'The comorbidity of pervasive developmental disorder and attention deficit hyper-activity disorder: results of a retrospective chart review.' *Journal of Autism and Developmental Disorders 34,* 329–339.

Gowen, E. and Miall, C. (2005) 'Behavioural aspects of cerebellar function in adults with Asperger syndrome.' *The Cerebellum 4,* 279–289.

Graham, P. (1998) *Cognitive Behaviour Therapy for Children and Families.* Cambridge: Cambridge University Press.

Grandin, T. (1984) 'My experiences as an autistic child and review of selected literature.' *Journal of Orthomolecular Psychiatry 13,* 144–174.

Grandin, T. (1988) 'Teaching tips from a recovered autistic.' *Focus on Autistic Behaviour 3,* 1–8.

Grandin, T. (1990) 'Sensory problems in autism.' Paper presented at the Annual Conference of the Autism Society of America, Buena Park, California.

Grandin, T. (1995) *Thinking in Pictures and Other Reports From My Life with Autism.* New York: Doubleday.

Grandin, T. and Barron, S. (2005) *Unwritten Rules of Social Relationships: Decoding Social Mysteries Through the Unique Perspectives of Autism.* Arlington, TX: Future Horizons.

Grandin, T. and Duffy, K. (2004) *Developing Talents: Careers for Individuals with Asperger Syndrome and High-Functioning Autism.* Kansas: Autism Asperger Publishing Company.

Grave, J. and Blissett, J. (2004) 'Is cognitive behavior therapy developmentally appropriate for young children? Review of the evidence.' *Clinical Psychology Review 24,* 399–420.

Gray, C. (1994) *Comic Strip Conversations.* Arlington: Future Education.

Gray, C. (1998) 'Social Stories™ and Comic Strip Conversations with students with Asperger Syndrome and High-Functioning Autism.' In E. Schopler, G. Mesibov and L.J. Kunce (eds) *Asperger's Syndrome or High-Functioning Autism?* New York: Plenum Press.

Gray, C. (1999) 'Gray's guide to compliments.' Supplement in *The Morning News 11.*

Gray, C. (2002a) *My Social Stories Book.* London: Jessica Kingsley Publishers.

Gray, C. (2002b) *The Sixth Sense II.* Arlington, TX: Future Horizons.

Gray, C. (2004a) 'Gray's guide to bullying parts I–III.' *The Morning News 16,* 1–60.

Gray, C. (2004b) 'Social Stories 10.0.' *Jenison Autism Journal 15,* 2–21.

Green, D., Baird, G., Barnett, A., Henderson, L., Huber, J. and Henderson, S. (2002) 'The severity and nature of motor impairment in Asperger's syndrome: a comparison with specific developmental disorder of motor function.' *Journal of Child Psychology and Psychiatry 43,* 655–668.

Green, J., Gilchrist, A., Burton, D. and Cox, A. (2000) 'Social and psychiatric functioning in adolescents with Asperger Syndrome compared with conduct disorder.' *Journal of Autism and Developmental Disorders 30,* 279–293.

Gresley, L. (2000) 'Cognitive adaptation to the diagnosis of Asperger syndrome and the relationship with depression and adjustment.' Doctoral dissertation, University of Exeter.

Grigorenko, E., Klin, A., Pauls, D., Senft, R., Hooper, C. and Volkmar, F. (2002) 'A descriptive study of hyperlexia in a clinically referred sample of children with developmental delays.' *Journal of Autism and Developmental Disorders 32,* 3–12.

Griswold, D., Barnhill, G., Smith Myles, B., Hagiwara, T. and Simpson, R. (2002) 'Asperger Syndrome and academic achievement.' *Focus on Autism and Other Developmental Disabilities 17*, 94–102.

Groden, J., Diller, A., Bausman, M., Velicer, W., Norman, G. and Cautella, J. (2001) 'The development of a stress survey schedule for persons with autism and other developmental disabilities.' *Journal of Autism and Developmental Disorders 31*, 207–217.

Groft, M. and Block, M. (2003) 'Children with Asperger syndrome: implications for general physical education and youth sports.' *Journal of Physical Education, Recreation and Dance 74*, 38–46.

Gunter, H., Ghaziuddin, M. and Ellis, H. (2002) 'Asperger syndrome: tests of right hemisphere functioning and interhemispheric communication.' *Journal of Autism and Developmental Disorders 32*, 263–281.

Hadcroft, W. (2005) *The Feeling's Unmutual: Growing Up with Asperger Syndrome (Undiagnosed)*. London: Jessica Kingsley Publishers.

Hadwin, J., Baron-Cohen, S., Howlin, P. and Hill, K. (1996) 'Can we teach children with autism to understand emotions, belief, or pretence?' *Development and Psychopathology 8*, 345–365.

Hagiwara, T. and Myles, B.S. (1999) 'A multimedia social story intervention: teaching skills to children with autism.' *Focus on Autism and Other Developmental Disabilities 14*, 82–95.

Hallett, M., Lebieclausko, M., Thomas, S., Stanhope, S., Dondela, M. and Rumsey, J. (1993) 'Locomotion of autistic adults.' *Archives of Neurology 50*, 1304–1308.

Happé, F. (1994) 'An advanced test of theory of mind: understanding of story characters' thoughts and feelings by able autistic, mentally handicapped, and normal children and adults.' *Journal of Autism and Developmental Disorders 24*, 129–154.

Hare, D.J. (1997) 'The use of Cognitive-Behavioural Therapy with people with Asperger Syndrome: a case study.' *Autism 1*, 215–225.

Hare, D.J., Jones, J. and Paine, C. (1999) 'Approaching reality: the use of personal construct assessment in working with people with Asperger syndrome.' *Autism 3*, 165–176.

Hare, D.J. and Malone, C. (2004) 'Catatonia and autistic spectrum disorders.' *Autism 8*, 183–195.

Hare, D.J. and Paine, C. (1997) 'Developing cognitive behavioural treatments for people with Asperger's syndrome.' *Clinical Psychology Forum 110*, 5–8.

Harpur, J., Lawlor, M. and Fitzgerald, M. (2004) *Succeeding in College with Asperger Syndrome: A Student Guide*. London: Jessica Kingsley Publishers.

Harrison, J. and Hare, D. (2004) 'Brief report: Assessment of sensory abnormalities in people with autistic spectrum disorders.' *Journal of Autism and Developmental Disorders 34*, 727–730.

Hawkins, G. (2004) *How to Find Work That Works for People with Asperger Syndrome*. London: Jessica Kingsley Publishers.

Hay, D., Payne, A. and Chadwick, A. (2004) 'Peer relations in childhood.' *Journal of Child Psychology and Psychiatry 45*, 84–108.

Hebebrand, J., Henninghausen, K., Nau, S., Himmelmann, G., Schulz, E., Schafer, H. and Remschmidt, H. (1997) 'Low body weight in male children and adolescents with schizoid personality disorder or Asperger's disorder.' *Acta Psychiatrica Scandinavica 96*, 64–67.

Heider, F. and Simmel, M. (1944) 'An experimental study of apparent behaviour.' *American Journal of Psychology 57*, 243–259.

Heinrichs, R. (2003) *Perfect Targets: Asperger Syndrome and Bullying: Practical Solutions for Surviving the Social World*. Kansas: Autism Asperger Publishing Company.

Hénault, I. (2005) *Asperger's Syndrome and Sexuality: From Adolescence Through Adulthood*. London: Jessica Kingsley Publishers.

Hermelin, B. (2001) *Bright Splinters of the Mind*. London: Jessica Kingsley Publishers.

Hill, E., Berthoz, S. and Frith, U. (2004) 'Cognitive processing of own emotions in individuals with autistic spectrum disorder and in their relatives.' *Journal of Autism and Developmental Disorders 34,* 229–235.

Hillier, A. and Allinson, L. (2002) 'Beyond expectations: autism, understanding embarrassment, and the relationship with theory of mind.' *Autism 6,* 299–314.

Hinton, M. and Kern, L. (1999) 'Increasing homework completion by incorporating student interests.' *Journal of Positive Behaviour Interventions 1,* 231–234, 241.

Hippler, K. and Klicpera, C. (2004) 'A retrospective analysis of the clinical case records of "autistic psychopaths" diagnosed by Hans Asperger and his team at the University Children's Hospital, Vienna.' In U. Frith and E. Hill (eds) *Autism: Mind and Brain.* Oxford: Oxford University Press.

Hodges, E., Malone, J. and Perry, D. (1997) 'Individual risk and social risk as interacting determinants of victimization in the peer group.' *Developmental Psychology 32,* 1033–1039.

Holaday, M., Moak, J. and Shipley, M. (2001) 'Rorschach protocols from children and adolescents with Asperger's disorder.' *Journal of Personality Assessment 76,* 482–495.

Holtmann, M., Bolte, S. and Poustka, F. (2005) 'Letters to the editor: ADHD, Asperger syndrome and High Functioning Autism.' *Journal of the American Academy of Child and Adolescent Psychiatry 44,* 1101.

Howlin, P. (2000) 'Assessment instruments for Asperger syndrome.' *Child Psychology and Psychiatry Review 5,* 120–129.

Howlin, P. (2003) 'Outcome in high-functioning adults with autism with and without early language delays: implications for the differentiation between autism and Asperger syndrome.' *Journal of Autism and Developmental Disorders 33,* 3–13.

Howlin, P. (2004) *Autism and Asperger Syndrome: Preparing for Adulthood,* 2nd edition. London: Routledge.

Howlin, P., Alcock, J. and Burkin, C. (2005) 'An eight year follow-up of a specialist supported employment service for high ability adults with autism or Asperger syndrome.' *Autism 9,* 533–549.

Howlin, P. and Asgharian, A. (1999) 'The diagnosis of autism and Asperger syndrome: findings from a survey of 770 families.' *Developmental Medicine and Child Neurology 41,* 834–839.

Howlin, P., Baron-Cohen, S. and Hadwin, J. (1999) *Teaching Children with Autism to Mind-Read: A Practical Guide.* Chichester: John Wiley and Sons.

Howlin, P. and Yates, P. (1999) 'The potential effectiveness of social skills groups for adults with autism.' *Autism 3,* 299–307.

Hubbard, A. (2005) 'Academic modifications.' In B. Smith Myles (ed) *Children and Youth with Asperger Syndrome: Strategies for Success in Inclusive Settings.* Thousand Oaks, CA: Corwin Press.

Hughes, C., Russell, J. and Robbins, T. (1994) 'Evidence for executive dysfunction in autism.' *Neuropsychologia 32,* 477–492.

Hurlburt, R., Happé, F. and Frith, U. (1994) 'Sampling the form of inner experience in three adults with Asperger's Syndrome.' *Psychological Medicine 24,* 385–395.

Isager, T., Mouridsen, S., Rich, B. and Nedergaard, N. (2005) 'Autism spectrum disorders and criminal behaviour: a case control study.' Paper presented at the 1st International Symposium on Autism Spectrum Disorder in a Forensic Context, September, Copenhagen, Denmark.

Ivey, M., Heflin, L. and Alberto, P. (2004) 'The use of Social Stories to promote independent behaviours in novel events for children with PDD-NOS.' *Focus on Autism and Other Developmental Disabilities 19,* 164–176.

Iwanaga, R., Kawasaki, C. and Tsuchida, R. (2000) 'Brief report: Comparison of sensory-motor and cognitive function between autism and Asperger syndrome in preschool children.' *Journal of Autism and Developmental Disorders 30,* 169–174.

Jackson, L. (2002) *Freaks, Geeks and Asperger Syndrome: A User Guide to Adolescence.* London: Jessica Kingsley Publishers.

Jackson, N. (2002) *Standing Down Falling Up: Asperger's Syndrome from the Inside Out.* Bristol: Lucky Duck Publishing.

Jacobs, B. (2006) *Loving Mr Spock: Understanding an Aloof Lover – Could it be Asperger Sundrome?* London: Jessica Kingsley Publishers.

Jacobsen, P. (2003) *Asperger Syndrome and Psychotherapy: Understanding Asperger Perspectives.* London: Jessica Kingsley Publishers.

Jacobsen, P. (2004) 'A brief overview of the principles of psychotherapy with Asperger's syndrome.' *Clinical Child Psychology and Psychiatry 9*, 567–578.

James, I. (2006) *Asperger's Syndrome and High Achievement: Some Very Remarkable People.* London: Jessica Kingsley Publishers.

Jansson Verkasalo, E., Kujala, T., Jussila, K., Matilla, L., Moilanen, I., Naatanen, R., Suominen, K. and Korpilahti, P. (2005) 'Similarities in the phenotype of the auditory neural substrate in children with Asperger syndrome and their parents.' *European Journal of Neuroscience 22*, 986–990.

Johnson, M. (2005) *Managing with Asperger Syndrome.* London: Jessica Kingsley Publishers.

Jolliffe, T., Lansdown, R. and Robinson, T. (1992) 'Autism: a personal account.' *Communication 26*, 12–19.

Jones, R., Quigney, C. and Huws, J. (2003) 'First-hand accounts of sensory perceptual experiences in autism: a qualitative analysis.' *Journal of Intellectual and Developmental Disability 28*, 112–121.

Jordan, R. (2003) 'School based intervention for children with specific learning difficulties.' In M. Prior (ed) *Learning and Behavior Problems in Asperger Syndrome.* New York: The Guilford Press.

Joseph, R., McGrath, L. and Tager-Flusberg, H. (2005) 'Executive dysfunction and its relation to language ability in verbal school-age children with autism.' *Developmental Neuropsychology 27*, 361–378.

Kadesjo, B. and Gillberg, C. (2000) 'Tourette's disorder: epidemiology and comorbidity in primary school children.' *Journal of the American Academy of Child and Adolescent Psychiatry 39*, 548–555.

Kadesjo, B., Gillberg, C. and Hagberg, B. (1999) 'Autism and Asperger syndrome in seven-year-old children: a total population study.' *Journal of Autism and Developmental Disorders 29*, 327–331.

Kaland, N., Moller-Nielsen, A., Callesen, K., Mortensen, E.L., Gottlieb, D. and Smith, L. (2002) 'A new "advanced" test of theory of mind: evidence from children and adolescents with Asperger syndrome.' *Journal of Child Psychology and Psychiatry 43*, 517–528.

Kanner, L. (1943) 'Autistic disturbances of affective contact.' *Nervous Child 2*, 217–250.

Kendall, P.C. (2000) *Child and Adolescent Therapy: Cognitive Behavioural Therapy Procedures.* New York: The Guilford Press.

Kerbel, D. and Grunwell, P. (1998) 'A study of idiom comprehension in children with semantic-pragmatic difficulties.' *International Journal of Language and Communication Disorders 33*, 23–44.

Kerbeshian, J. and Burd, L. (1986) 'Asperger's syndrome and Tourette syndrome: the case of the pinball wizard.' *British Journal of Psychiatry 148*, 731–736.

Kerbeshian, J. and Burd, L. (1996) 'Case study: comorbidity among Tourette's syndrome, autistic disorder and bipolar disorder.' *Journal of the American Academy of Child and Adolescent Psychiatry 35*, 681–685.

Kerbeshian, J., Burd, L. and Fisher, W. (1990) 'Asperger's Syndrome: to be or not to be?' *British Journal of Psychiatry 156*, 721–725.

Kerr, S. and Durkin, K. (2004) 'Understanding of thought bubbles as mental representations in children with autism: implications for Theory of Mind.' *Journal of Autism and Developmental Disorders 34*, 637–647.

Kim, J.A., Szatmari, P., Bryson, S.E., Streiner, D.L. and Wilson, F. (2000) 'The prevalence of anxiety and mood problems among children with autism and Asperger Syndrome.' *Autism 4*, 117–132.

Kleinhans, N., Akshoomoff, N. and Delis, D. (2005) 'Executive functions in autism and Asperger's disorder: flexibility, fluency and inhibition.' *Developmental Neuropsychology 27*, 379–401.

Kleinman, J., Marciano, P.L. and Ault, R.L. (2001) 'Advanced Theory of Mind in high-functioning adults with autism.' *Journal of Autism and Developmental Disorders 31*, 29–36.

Klin, A. (2000) 'Attributing social meaning to ambiguous visual stimuli in higher-functioning autism and Asperger syndrome: the Social Attribution Task.' *Journal of Child Psychology and Psychiatry 41*, 831–846.

Klin, A., Carter, A. and Sparrow, S.S. (1997) 'Psychological assessment of children with autism.' In D.J. Cohen and F.R. Volkmar (eds) *Handbook of Autism and Pervasive Developmental Disorders*, 2nd edition. New York: Wiley.

Klin, A., Jones, W., Schultz, R., Volkmar, F. and Cohen, D. (2002a) 'Defining and quantifying the social phenotype in autism.' *American Journal of Psychiatry 159*, 895–908.

Klin, A., Jones, W., Schultz, R., Volkmar, F. and Cohen, D. (2002b) 'Visual fixation patterns during viewing of naturalistic social situations as predictors of social competence in individuals with autism.' *Archives of General Psychiatry 59*, 809–816.

Klin, A., Sparrow, S., Marans, W., Carter, A. and Volkmar, F. (2000) 'Assessment issues in children and adolescents with Asperger syndrome.' In A. Klin, F. Volkmar and S. Sparrow (eds) *Asperger Syndrome*. New York: Guilford Press.

Klin, A. and Volkmar, F. (1997) 'Asperger's Syndrome.' In D.J. Cohen and F. Volkmar (eds) *Handbook of Autism and Pervasive Developmental Disorders*. New York: Guilford Press.

Klin, A., Volkmar, F., Sparrow, S., Cicchetti, D. and Rourke, B. (1995) 'Validity and neuropsychological characterization of Asperger Syndrome: convergence with Nonverbal Learning Disabilities Syndrome.' *Journal of Child Psychology and Psychiatry 36*, 1127–1140.

Knickmeyer, R., Baron-Cohen, S., Raggatt, P. and Taylor, K. (2005) 'Foetal testosterone, social relationships, and restricted interests in children.' *Journal of Child Psychology and Psychiatry 46*, 198–210.

Koning, C. and Magill-Evans, J. (2001) 'Social and language skills in adolescent boys with Asperger syndrome.' *Autism 5*, 23–36.

Konstantareas, M. (2005) 'Anxiety and depression in children and adolescents with Asperger syndrome.' In K. Stoddart (ed) *Children, Youth and Adults with Asperger Syndrome: Integrating Multiple Perspectives*. London: Jessica Kingsley Publishers.

Kopp, S. and Gillberg, C. (1997) 'Selective mutism: a population based study.' *Journal of Child Psychology and Psychiatry 32*, 43–46.

Kracke, I. (1994) 'Developmental prosopagnosia in Asperger syndrome: presentation and discussion of an individual case.' *Developmental Medicine and Child Neurology 36*, 873–876.

Kraemer, B., Delsignore, A., Gundelfinger, R., Schnyder, U. and Hepp, U. (2005) 'Comorbidity of Asperger syndrome and gender identity disorder.' *European Journal of Child and Adolescent Psychiatry 14*, 292–296.

Krug, D. and Arick, J. (2002) *Krug Asperger's Disorder Index*. Austin, TX: PRO-ED.

Kurita, H. (1999) 'Brief report: delusional disorder in a male adolescent with high-functioning PDDNOS.' *Journal of Autism and Developmental Disorders 29*, 419–423.

Kutscher, M. (2005) *Kids in the Syndrome Mix of ADHD, LD, Asperger's, Tourette's, Bipolar and More*. London: Jessica Kingsley Publishers.

Ladd, G. and Ladd, B.K. (1998) 'Parenting behaviours and parent–child relationships: correlates of peer victimization in kindergarten.' *Developmental Psychology 34*, 1450–1458.

Lainhart, J. and Folstein, S. (1994) 'Affective disorders in people with autism: a review of published cases.' *Journal of Autism and Developmental Disorders 24*, 587–601.

Landa, R. (2000) 'Social language use in Asperger syndrome and High-Functioning Autism.' In A. Klin, F. Volkmar and S. Sparrow (eds) *Asperger Syndrome*. New York: The Guilford Press.

Landa, R. and Goldberg, M. (2005) 'Language, social and executive functions in high-functioning autism: a continuum of performance.' *Journal of Autism and Developmental Disorders 35*, 557–573.

LaSalle, B. (2003) *Finding Ben: A Mother's Journey Through the Maze of Asperger's.* New York: Contemporary Books.

Laurent, A. and Rubin, E. (2004) 'Challenges in emotional regulation in Asperger Syndrome and High Functioning Autism.' *Topics in Language Disorders 24*, 286–297.

Lawson, W. (1998) *Life Behind Glass: A Personal Account of Autism Spectrum Disorder.* London: Jessica Kingsley Publishers.

Lawson, W. (2001) *Understanding and Working with the Spectrum of Autism: An Insider's View.* London: Jessica Kingsley Publishers.

Lawson, W. (2005) *Sex, Sexuality and the Autism Spectrum.* London: Jessica Kingsley Publishers.

Ledgin, N. (2002) *Asperger's and Self-esteem: Insight and Hope Through Famous Role Models.* Arlington, TX: Future Horizons.

Lee, A. and Hobson, R.P. (1998) 'On developing self-concepts: a controlled study of children and adolescents with autism.' *Journal of Child Psychology and Psychiatry 39*, 1131–1144.

Leekham, S., Libby, S., Wing, L., Gould, J. and Gillberg, C. (2000) 'Comparison of ICD-10 and Gillberg's criteria for Asperger syndrome.' *Autism 4*, 11–28.

Linblad, T. (2005) 'Communication and Asperger syndrome: the speech-language pathologist's role.' In K. Stoddart (ed) *Children, Youth and Adults with Asperger Syndrome: Integrating Multiple Perspectives.* London: Jessica Kingsley Publishers.

Lincoln, A., Courchesne, E., Kilman, B., Elmasian, R. and Allen, M. (1988) 'A study of intellectual abilities in high-functioning people with autism.' *Journal of Autism and Developmental Disorders 18*, 505–524.

Little, L. (2002) 'Middle-class mothers' perceptions of peer and sibling victimization among children with Asperger syndrome and non-verbal learning disorders.' *Issues in Comprehensive Pediatric Nursing 25*, 43–57.

Long, M. (2003) 'Roses and cacti.' In K. Rodman (ed) *Asperger's Syndrome and Adults: Is Anyone Listening?* London: Jessica Kingsley Publishers.

Lord, C., Risi, S., Lambrecht, L., Cook, E., Leventhal, B., DiLavore, P., Pickles, A. and Rutter, M. (2000) 'The Autism Diagnostic Observation Schedule – Generic: a standard measure of social and communication deficits associated with the spectrum of autism.' *Journal of Autism and Developmental Disorders 30*, 205–223.

Lord, C., Rutter, M. and Le Couteur, A. (1994) 'Autism Diagnostic Interview – Revised: a revised version of a diagnostic interview for caregivers of individuals with possible pervasive developmental disorders.' *Journal of Autism and Developmental Disorders 24*, 659–685.

Lorimer, P.A. (2002) 'The use of Social Stories as a preventative behavioural intervention in a home setting with a child with autism.' *Journal of Positive Behavior Interventions 4*, 53–60.

Lovecky, D. (2004) *Different Minds: Gifted Children with AD/HD, Asperger Syndrome, and Other Learning Deficits.* London: Jessica Kingsley Publishers.

Loveland, K.A. and Tunali, B. (1991) 'Social scripts for conversational interactions in Autism and Downs Syndrome.' *Journal of Autism and Developmental Disorders 21*, 177–186.

Lyons, V. and Fitzgerald, M. (2004) 'Humor in autism and Asperger syndrome.' *Journal of Autism and Developmental Disorders 34*, 521–531.

Lyons, V. and Fitzgerald, M. (2005) 'Early memory and autism: Letter to the editor.' *Journal of Autism and Developmental Disorders 35*, 683.

Mahoney, W.J., Szatmari, P., MacLean, J.E., Bryson, S.E., Bartolucci, G., Walter, S.D., Jones, M.B. and Zwaigenbaum, L. (1998) 'Reliability and accuracy of differentiating Pervasive Developmental Disorder subtypes.' *Journal of the American Academy of Child and Adolescent Psychiatry 37*, 278–285.

Manjiviona, J. (2003) 'Assessment of specific learning difficulties.' In M. Prior (ed) *Learning and Behavior Problems in Asperger Syndrome*. New York: The Guilford Press.

Manjiviona, J. and Prior, M. (1995) 'Comparison of Asperger syndrome and high-functioning autistic children on a test of motor impairment.' *Journal of Autism and Developmental Disorders 25*, 23–39.

Manjiviona, J. and Prior, M. (1999) 'Neuropsychological profiles of children with Asperger syndrome and autism.' *Autism 3*, 327–356.

Marriage, K., Miles, T., Stokes, D. and Davey, M. (1993) 'Clinical and research implications of the co-occurrence of Asperger's and Tourette's Syndrome.' *Australian and New Zealand Journal of Psychiatry 27*, 666–672.

Marriage, K.J., Gordon, V. and Brand, L. (1995) 'A social skills group for boys with Asperger's Syndrome.' *Australian and New Zealand Journal of Psychiatry 29*, 58–62.

Martin, I. and McDonald, S. (2004) 'An exploration of causes of non-literal language problems in individuals with Asperger syndrome.' *Journal of Autism and Developmental Disorders 34*, 311–328.

Matthews, A. (1990) *Making Friends: A Guide to Getting Along with People*. Singapore: Media Masters.

Mawson, D., Grounds, A. and Tantam, D. (1985) 'Violence and Asperger's Syndrome: a case study.' *British Journal of Psychiatry 147*, 566–569.

Mayes, L., Cohen, D. and Klin, A. (1993) 'Desire and fantasy: a psychoanalytic perspective on theory of mind and autism.' In S. Baron-Cohen, T. Tager-Flusberg and D. Cohen (eds) *Understanding Other Minds: Perspectives From Autism*. Oxford: Oxford Medical Publications.

Mayes, S. and Calhoun, S.L. (2001) 'Non-significance of early speech delay in children with autism and normal intelligence and implications for DSM-IV Asperger's Disorder.' *Autism 5*, 81–94.

McDougle, C., Kresch, L., Goodman, W. and Naylor, S. (1995) 'A case controlled study of repetitive thoughts and behavior in adults with autistic disorder and obsessive compulsive disorder.' *American Journal of Psychiatry 152*, 772–777.

McGee, G., Feldman, R. and Chernin, L. (1991) 'A comparison of emotional facial display by children with autism and typical preschoolers.' *Journal of Early Intervention 15*, 237–245.

McGregor, E., Whiten, A. and Blackburn, P. (1998) 'Teaching theory of mind by highlighting intentions and illustrating thoughts: a comparison of their effectiveness with three-year-olds and autistic subjects.' *British Journal of Developmental Psychology 16*, 281–300.

Mercier, C., Mottron, L. and Belleville, S. (2000) 'Psychosocial study on restricted interest in high-functioning persons with pervasive developmental disorders.' *Autism 4*, 406–425.

Mesibov, G.B. (1984) 'Social skills training with verbal autistic adolescents and adults: a program model.' *Journal of Autism and Developmental Disorders 14*, 395–404.

Micali, N., Chakrabarti, S. and Fombonne, E. (2004) 'The broad autism phenotype: findings from an epidemiological survey.' *Autism 8*, 21–37.

Miedzianik, D. (1986) *My Autobiography*. Nottingham: Child Development Research Unit, University of Nottingham.

Miller, J.N. and Ozonoff, S. (1997) 'Did Asperger's cases have Asperger Disorder? A research note.' *Journal of Child Psychology and Psychiatry 38*, 247–251.

Miller, J.N. and Ozonoff, S. (2000) 'The external validity of Asperger Disorder: lack of evidence from the domain of neuropsychology.' *Journal of Abnormal Psychology 109*, 227–238.

Minshew, N., Goldstein, G. and Siegel, D. (1997) 'Neuropsychologic functioning in autism: profile of a complex information processing disorder.' *Journal of the International Neuropsychological Society 3*, 303–316.

Miyahara, M., Tsujii, M., Hori, M., Nakanishi, K., Kageyama, H. and Sugiyama, T. (1997) 'Brief report: Motor incoordination in children with Asperger syndrome and learning disabilities.' *Journal of Autism and Developmental Disabilities 27*, 595–603.

Molloy, C., Dietrich, K. and Bhattacharya, A. (2003) 'Postural stability in children with Autism Spectrum Disorder.' *Journal of Autism and Developmental Disorders 33*, 643–652.

Molloy, H. and Vasil, L. (2004) *Asperger Syndrome, Adolescence and Identity. Looking Beyond the Label.* London: Jessica Kingsley Publishers.

Murray, D. (ed) (2006) *Coming Out Asperger: Diagnosis, Disclosure and Self-confidence.* London: Jessica Kingsley Publishers.

Murray, D., Lesser, M. and Lawson, W. (2005) 'Attention, monotropism and the diagnostic criteria for autism.' *Autism 9*, 139–156.

Murrie, D., Warren, J., Kristiansson, M. and Dietz, P. (2002) 'Asperger syndrome in forensic settings.' *International Journal of Forensic Mental Health 1*, 59–70.

Myer, R. (2001) *Asperger Syndrome Employment Workbook: An Employment Workbook for Adults with Asperger Syndrome.* London: Jessica Kingsley Publishers.

Myles, B.S., Bock, S.J. and Simpson, R.L. (2001) *Asperger Syndrome Diagnostic Scale Examiner's Manual.* Austin, TX: PRO-ED.

Nass, R. and Gutman, R. (1997) 'Boys with Asperger's disorder, exceptional verbal intelligence, tics and clumsiness.' *Developmental Medicine and Child Neurology 39*, 691–695.

National Autistic Society (2005) *Employing People with Asperger Syndrome: A Practical Guide.* London: The National Autistic Society.

Newsom, E. (1983) 'Pathological demand-avoidance syndrome.' *Communication 17*, 3–8.

Nieminen-von Wendt, T. (2004) 'On the origins and diagnosis of Asperger syndrome: a clinical, neuroimaging and genetic study.' Academic dissertation, Medical Faculty, University of Helsinki.

Nieminen-von Wendt, T., Metsahonkala, L., Kulomaki, T., Aalto, S., Autti, T., Vanhala, R., Eskola, O., Bergman, J., Hietala, J. and von Wendt, L. (2004) 'Increased presynaptic dopamine function in Asperger syndrome.' *Clinical Neuroscience and Neuropathology 15*, 757–760.

Njiokiktjien, C., Verschoor, A., de Sonneville, L., Huyser, C., Op het Veld, V. and Toorenaar, N. (2001) 'Disordered recognition of facial identity and emotions in three Asperger type autists.' *European Journal of Child and Adolescent Psychiatry 10*, 79–90.

Norris, C. and Dattilo, J. (1999) 'Evaluating effects of a Social Story intervention on a young girl with autism.' *Focus on Autism and Other Developmental Disabilities 14*, 180–186.

North, A., Russell, A. and Gudjonsson, G. (2005) 'An investigation of potential vulnerability during police interrogation of adults with autism spectrum disorder: a focus on interrogative suggestibility and compliance.' Paper presented at the 1st International Symposium on Autism Spectrum Disorder in a Forensic Context, September, Copenhagen, Denmark.

Nyden, A., Gillberg, C., Hjelmquist, E. and Heiman, M. (1999) 'Executive function/attention deficits in boys with Asperger syndrome, attention disorder and reading/writing disorder.' *Autism 3*, 213–228.

Nylander, L. and Gillberg, C. (2001) 'Screening for autism spectrum disorders in adult psychiatric out-patients.' *Acta Psychiatria Scandinavica 103*, 428–434.

Olweus, D. (1992) 'Victimization by peers: antecedents and long-term outcomes.' In K.H. Rubin and J.B. Asenddorf (eds) *Social Withdrawal, Inhibition, and Shyness in Childhood.* Hillsdale, NJ: Lawrence Erlbaum Associates.

Olweus, D. (1993) *Bullying at School: What We Know and What We Can Do.* Oxford: Blackwell.

O'Neill, M. and Jones, R. (1997) 'Sensory-perceptual abnormalities in autism: a case for more research?' *Journal of Autism and Developmental Disorders 27*, 283–293.

Ozonoff, S., Cook, I., Coon, H., Dawson, G., Joseph, R., Klin, A., McMahon, W., Minshew, N., Munson, J., Pennington, B., Rogers, S., Spence, M., Tager-Flusberg, H., Volkmar, F. and Wrathall, D. (2004) 'Performance on Cambridge Neuropsychological Test Automated Battery Subtests sensitive to frontal lobe function in people with autistic disorder: evidence from the collaborative programs of excellence in autism network.' *Journal of Autism and Developmental Disorders 34*, 139–150.

Ozonoff, S., Garcia, N., Clark, E. and Lainhart, J. (2005a) 'MMPI-2 personality profiles of high functioning adults with Autism Spectrum Disorders.' *Assessment 12*, 86–95.

Ozonoff, S. and Miller, J. (1995) 'Teaching Theory of Mind: a new approach to social skills training for individuals with autism.' *Journal of Autism and Developmental Disorders 25*, 415–433.

Ozonoff, S., South, M. and Miller, J. (2000) 'DSM-IV defined Asperger syndrome: cognitive, behavioural and early history differentiation from high-functioning autism.' *Autism 4*, 29–46.

Ozonoff, S., South, M. and Provencal, S. (2005b) 'Executive functions.' In F. Volkmar, R. Paul, A. Klin and D. Cohen (eds) *Handbook of Autism and Pervasive Developmental Disorders*, third edition. New Jersey: John Wiley and Sons.

Pakenham, K., Sofronoff, K. and Samios, C. (2004) 'Finding meaning in parenting a child with Asperger syndrome: correlates of sense making and benefit finding.' *Research in Developmental Disabilities 25*, 245–264.

Palmen, S., Hulshoff, H., Kemner, C., Schnack, H., Durston, S., Lahuis, B., Kahn, R. and Van Engeland, H. (2005) 'Increased grey matter volume in medication-naïve high-functioning children with autism spectrum disorder.' *Psychological Medicine 35*, 561–570.

Palmer, A. (2006) *Realizing the College Dream with Autism or Asperger Syndrome: A Parent's Guide to Student Success.* London: Jessica Kingsley Publishers.

Paradiz, V. (2002) *Elijah's Cup: A Family's Journey into the Community and Culture of High Functioning Autism and Asperger's Syndrome.* New York: The Free Press.

Paul, R., Augustyn, A., Klin., A. and Volkmar, F. (2005) 'Perception and production of prosody by speakers with Autism Spectrum Disorders.' *Journal of Autism and Developmental Disorders 35*, 205–220.

Paul, R., Spangle-Looney, S. and Dahm, P. (1991) 'Communication and socialization skills at ages two and three in "late-talking" young children.' *Journal of Speech and Hearing Research 34*, 858–865.

Paul, R. and Sutherland, D. (2003) 'Asperger Syndrome: the role of the speech-language pathologists in schools.' *Perspectives on Language, Learning and Education 10*, 9–15.

Pennington, B.F. and Ozonoff, S. (1996) 'Executive functions and developmental psychopathology.' *Journal of Child Psychology and Psychiatry Annual Research Review 37*, 51–87.

Pepler, D. and Craig, W. (1999) 'What should we do about bullying? research into practice.' *Peacebuilder 2*, 9–10.

Perlman, L. (2000) 'Adults with Asperger disorder misdiagnosed as schizophrenic.' *Professional Psychology: Research and Practice 31*, 221–225.

Perry, R. (1998) 'Misdiagnosed ADD/ADHD; re-diagnosed PDD.' *Journal of the American Academy of Child and Adolescent Psychiatry 37*, 113–114.

Perry, R. (2004) 'Early diagnosis of Asperger's disorder: lessons from a large clinical practice.' *Journal of the American Academy of Child and Adolescent Psychiatry 43*, 1445–1449.

Person, B. and Branden, S. (2005) 'An investigation of the prevalence of ASD in patients in the forensic psychiatric clinic in Vaxjo.' Paper presented at the 1st International Symposium on Autism Spectrum Disorder in a Forensic Context, September, Copenhagen, Denmark.

Pietz, J., Ebinger, F. and Rating, D. (2003) 'Prosopagnosia in a preschool child with Asperger syndrome.' *Developmental Medicine and Child Neurology 45*, 55–57.

Piven, J., Harper, J., Palmer, P. and Arndt, S. (1996) 'Course of behavioral change in autism: a retrospective study of high-IQ adolescents and adults.' *Journal of the American Academy of Child and Adolescent Psychiatry 35*, 523–529.

Piven, J. and Palmer, P. (1999) 'Psychological disorder and the broad autism phenotype: evidence from a family study of multiple-incidence autism families.' *American Journal of Psychiatry 156*, 557–563.

Pozzi, M. (2003) 'The use of observation in the psychoanalytic treatment of a 12-year-old boy with Asperger's syndrome.' *International Journal of Psychoanalysis 84*, 1333–1349.

Prior, M. and Hoffmann, W. (1990) 'Neuropsychological testing of autistic children through an exploration with frontal lobe tests.' *Journal of Autism and Developmental Disorders 20*, 581–590.

Pyles, L. (2002) *Hitchhiking Through Asperger Syndrome*. London: Jessica Kingsley Publishers.

Rajendran, G. and Mitchelle, P. (2000) 'Computer mediated interaction in Asperger's syndrome: the bubble dialogue program.' *Computers and Education 35*, 189–207.

Rapin, I. (1982) *Children with Brain Dysfunction*. New York: Raven Press.

Rastam, M., Gillberg, C., Gillberg, I.C. and Johansson, M. (1997) 'Alexithymia in anorexia nervosa: a controlled study using the 20-item Toronto Alexithymia Scale.' *Acta Psychiatrica Scandinavica 95*, 385–388.

Rastam, M., Gillberg, C. and Wentz, E. (2003) 'Outcome of teenage onset anorexia nervosa in a Swedish community based sample.' *European Journal of Child and Adolescent Psychiatry 12, Supplement 1*, 178–190.

Ray, F., Marks, C. and Bray-Garretson, H. (2004) 'Challenges to treating adolescents with Asperger's syndrome who are sexually abusive.' *Sexual Addiction and Compulsivity 11*, 265–285.

Realmuto, A. and August, G.J. (1991) 'Catatonia in autistic disorder: a sign of comorbidity or variable expression?' *Journal of Autism and Developmental Disorders 21*, 517–528.

Reaven, J. and Hepburn, S. (2003) 'Cognitive-behavioural treatment of obsessive-compulsive disorder in a child with Asperger syndrome.' *Autism 7*, 145–164.

Reitzel, J. and Szatmari, P. (2003) 'Cognitive and academic problems.' In M. Prior (ed) *Learning and Behavior Problems in Asperger Syndrome*. New York: The Guilford Press.

Rhode, M. and Klauber, T. (2004) *The Many Faces of Asperger's Syndrome*. London: Karnac Books.

Rieffe, C., Terwogt, M. and Stockman, L. (2000) 'Understanding atypical emotions among children with autism.' *Journal of Autism and Developmental Disorders 30*, 195–202.

Rigby, K. (1996) *Bullying in Schools: And What To Do About It*. London: Jessica Kingsley Publishers.

Rinehart, N., Bradshaw, J., Brereton, A. and Tonge, B. (2001) 'Movement preparation in High-Functioning Autism and Asperger Disorder.' *Journal of Autism and Developmental Disorders 31*, 79–88.

Ringman, J. and Jankovic, J. (2000) 'Occurrence of tics in Asperger's syndrome and autistic disorder.' *Journal of Child Neurology 15*, 394–400.

Rodman, K. (2003) *Asperger's Syndrome and Adults...Is Anyone Listening? Essays and Poems by Partners, Parents and Family Members of Adults with Asperger's Syndrome*. London: Jessica Kingsley Publishers.

Rogers, M.F. and Myles, B.S. (2001) 'Using Social Stories and Comic Strip Conversations to interpret social situations for an adolescent with Asperger's syndrome.' *Intervention in School and Clinic 38*, 310–313.

Rogers, S., Benneto, L., McEvoy, R. and Pennington, B. (1996) 'Imitation and pantomime in high-functioning adolescents with autism spectrum disorders.' *Child Development 67*, 2060–2073.

Rogers, S. and Ozonoff, S. (2005) 'Annotation: What do we know about sensory dysfunction in autism? A critical review of the empirical evidence.' *Journal of Child Psychology and Psychiatry 46*, 1255–1268.

Rourke, B. (1989) *Nonverbal Learning Disabilities: The Syndrome and the Model*. New York: The Guilford Press.

Rourke, B. and Tsatsanis, K. (2000) 'Nonverbal learning disabilities and Asperger syndrome.' In A. Klin, F. Volkmar and S. Sparrow (eds) *Asperger Syndrome*. New York: Guilford Press.

Rowe, C. (1999) 'Do Social Stories benefit children with autism in mainstream primary school?' *British Journal of Special Education 26*, 12–14.

Rubin, K. (2002) *The Friendship Factor*. New York: Viking.

Rumsey, J. and Hamburger, S. (1990) 'Neuropsychological divergence of high-level autism and severe dyslexia.' *Journal of Autism and Developmental Disorders 20*, 155–168.

Russell, A., Mataix Cols, D., Anson, M. and Murphy, D. (2005) 'Obsessions and compulsions in Asperger syndrome and high functioning autism.' *British Journal of Psychiatry 186*, 525–528.

Russell, E. and Sofronoff, K. (2004) 'Anxiety and social worries in children with Asperger syndrome.' *Australian and New Zealand Journal of Psychiatry 39*, 633–638.

Russell, J. (1997) *Autism as an Executive Disorder.* Oxford: Oxford University Press.

Russell Burger, N. (2004) *A Special Kind of Brain: Living With Nonverbal Learning Disability.* London: Jessica Kingsley Publishers.

Rutherford, M.D., Baron-Cohen, S. and Wheelwright, S. (2002) 'Reading the Mind in the Voice: a study with normal adults and adults with Asperger syndrome and high-functioning autism.' *Journal of Autism and Developmental Disorders 32*, 189–194.

Rutter, M., Le Couteur, A. and Lord, C. (2003) *Autism Diagnostic Interview – Revised.* Los Angeles, CA: Western Psychological Services.

Sainsbury, C. (2000) *Martian in the Playground: Understanding the Schoolchild with Asperger's Syndrome.* Bristol: Lucky Duck Publishing.

Sanders, R. (2002) *Overcoming Asperger's: Personal Experience and Insight.* Murfreesboro, TN: Armstrong Valley Publishing Company.

Santosi, F., Powell Smith, K. and Kincaid, D. (2004) 'A research synthesis of Social Story interventions for children with Autism Spectrum Disorders.' *Focus on Autism and Other Developmental Disabilities 19*, 194–204.

Scattone, D., Wilczynski, S.M., Edwards, R.P. and Rabian, B. (2002) 'Decreasing disruptive behaviours of children with autism using Social Stories.' *Journal of Autism and Developmental Disorders 32*, 535–543.

Schatz, A., Weimer, A. and Trauner, D. (2002) 'Brief report: Attention differences in Asperger syndrome.' *Journal of Autism and Developmental Disorders 32*, 333–336.

Schneider, E. (1999) *Discovering My Autism.* London: Jessica Kingsley Publishers.

Schroeder, A. (2003) *The Socially Speaking Game.* Wisbech: LDA.

Scott, F.J., Baron-Cohen, S., Bolton, P. and Brayne, C. (2002) 'The CAST (Childhood Asperger Syndrome Test): preliminary development of a UK screen for mainstream primary-school-age children.' *Autism 6*, 9–31.

Scragg, P. and Shah, A. (1994) 'Prevalence of Asperger's syndrome in a secure hospital.' *British Journal of Psychiatry 165*, 679–682.

Segar, M. (undated) 'The Battles of the Autistic Thicker.' Online at www.autismandcomputing.org.uk /marc1.en.html. Accessed 4 July 2006.

Sheindlin, Judge J. (2001) *You Can't Judge a Book by it's Cover: Cool Rules for School.* New York: HarperCollins.

Shore, S. (2001) *Beyond the Wall: Personal Experiences with Autism and Asperger Syndrome.* Kansas: Autism Asperger Publishing Company.

Shore, S. (ed) (2004) *Ask and Tell: Self-Advocacy and Disclosure for People on the Autism Spectrum.* Kansas: Autism Asperger Publishing Company.

Shriberg, L., Paul, R., McSweeney, J. and Klin, A. (2001) 'Speech and prosody characteristics of adolescents and adults with high-functioning autism and Asperger syndrome.' *Journal of Speech, Language and Hearing Research 44*, 1097–1115.

Shu, B., Lung, F., Tien, A. and Chen, B. (2001) 'Executive function deficits in non-retarded autistic children.' *Autism 5*, 165–174.

Silva, J., Ferrari, M. and Leong, G. (2002) 'The case of Jeffrey Dahmer: sexual serial homicide from a neuropsychiatric developmental perspective.' *Journal of Forensic Science 47*, 1347–1359.

Silver, M. and Oakes, P. (2001) 'Evaluation of a new computer intervention to teach people with autism or Asperger syndrome to recognize and predict emotions in others.' *Autism 5*, 299–316.

Siponmaa, L., Kristiansson, M., Jonson, C., Nyden, A. and Gillberg, C. (2001) 'Juvenile and young adult mentally disordered offenders: the role of child neuropsychiatric disorders.' *Journal of the American Academy of Psychiatry and the Law 29*, 420–426.

Slater-Walker, G. and Slater-Walker, C. (2002) *An Asperger Marriage*. London: Jessica Kingsley Publishers.

Slee, P. (1995) 'Peer victimization and its relationship to depression among Australian primary school students.' *Personal and Individual Differences 18*, 57–62.

Smith, C. (2001) 'Using Social Stories with children with autistic spectrum disorders: an evaluation.' *Good Autism Practice 2*, 16–23.

Smith, I. (2000) 'Motor functioning in Asperger syndrome.' In A. Klin, F. Volkmar and S. Sparrow (eds) *Asperger Syndrome*. New York: The Guilford Press.

Smith, I. and Bryson, S. (1998) 'Gesture imitation in autism: 1. Nonsymbolic postures and sequences.' *Cognitive Neuropsychology 15*, 747–770.

Smith, P., Pepler, D. and Rigby, K. (eds) (2004) *Bullying in Schools. How Successful Can Interventions Be?* Cambridge: Cambridge University Press.

Smith Myles, B., Hilgenfeld, T., Barnhill, G., Griswold, D., Hagiwara, T. and Simpson, R. (2002) 'Analysis of reading skills in individuals with Asperger syndrome.' *Focus on Autism and Other Developmental Disabilities 17*, 44–67.

Smith Myles, B., Tapscott Cook, K., Miller, N., Rinner, L. and Robbins, L. (2000) *Asperger Syndrome and Sensory Issues: Practical Solutions for Making Sense of the World*. Kansas: Autism Asperger Publishing Company.

Smyrnios, S. (2002) 'Adaptive behaviour, executive functions and theory of mind in children with Asperger's syndrome.' Thesis, Victoria University of Technology, Melbourne, Australia.

Sobanski, E., Marcus, A., Henninghausen, K., Hebebrand, J. and Schmidt, M. (1999) 'Further evidence for a low body weight in male children and adolescents with Asperger's disorder.' *European Journal of Child and Adolescent Psychiatry 8*, 312–314.

Soderstrom, H., Rastam, M. and Gillberg, C. (2002) 'Temperament and character in adults with Asperger syndrome.' *Autism 6*, 287–297.

Sofronoff, K., Attwood, T. and Hinton, S. (2005) 'A randomised controlled trial of a CBT intervention for anxiety in children with Asperger syndrome.' *Journal of Child Psychology and Psychiatry 46*, 1152–1160.

Soloman, M., Goodlin-Jones, B. and Anders, T. (2004) 'A social adjustment enhancement intervention for high-functioning autism, Asperger's syndrome and Pervasive Developmental Disorder NOS.' *Journal of Autism and Developmental Disorders 34*, 649–668.

South, M., Klin, A. and Ozonoff, S. (1999) The Yale Special Interest Interview. Unpublished measure.

South, M., Ozonoff, S. and McMahon, W. (2005) 'Repetitive behaviour profiles in Asperger syndrome and high-functioning autism.' *Journal of Autism and Developmental Disorders 35*, 145–158.

Sponheim, E. and Skjeldal, O. (1998) 'Autism and related disorders: epidemiological findings in a Norwegian study using ICD-10 diagnostic criteria.' *Journal of Autism and Developmental Disorders 28*, 217–227.

Ssucharewa, G.E. (1926) 'Die schizoiden Psychopathien im Kindesalter.' *Monatschrift fur Psychiatrie und Neurologie 60*, 235–261.

Ssucharewa, G.E. and Wolff, S. (1996) 'The first account of the syndrome Asperger described? Translation of a paper entitled "Die schizoiden Psychopathien im Kindesalter".' *European Journal of Child and Adolescent Psychiatry 5*, 119–132.

Stahlberg, O., Soderstrom, H., Rastam, M. and Gillberg, C. (2004) 'Bipolar disorder, schizophrenia and other psychotic disorders in adults with childhood onset AD/HD and/or autism spectrum disorders.' *Journal of Neural Transmission 111*, 891–902.

Stanford, A. (2003) *Asperger Syndrome and Long-term Relationships*. London: Jessica Kingsley Publishers.

Stuart-Hamilton, I. (2004) *An Asperger Dictionary of Everyday Expressions.* London: Jessica Kingsley Publishers.

Sturm, H., Fernell, E. and Gillberg, C. (2004) 'Autism spectrum disorders in children with normal intellectual levels: associated impairments and subgroups.' *Developmental Medicine and Child Neurology 46,* 444–447.

Sunday Mail, The (2005) Interview with Daniel Tammet. 5 June, p.69.

Sverd, J. (1991) 'Tourette syndrome and autistic disorder: a significant relationship.' *American Journal of Medical Genetics 39,* 173–179.

Swaggart, B.L., Gagnon, E., Bock, S.J., Earles, T.L., Quinn, C., Myles, B.S. and Simpson, R.L. (1995) 'Using Social Stories to teach social and behavioural skills to children with autism.' *Focus on Autistic Behavior 10,* 1–16.

Swettenham, J., Baron-Cohen, S., Gomez, J.C. and Walsh, S. (1996) 'What's inside a person's head? Conceiving of the mind as a camera helps children with autism develop an alternative theory of mind.' *Cognitive Neuropsychiatry 1,* 73–88.

Szatmari, P. (2000) 'Perspectives on the classification of Asperger syndrome.' In A. Klin, F. Volkmar and S. Sparrow (eds) *Asperger Syndrome.* New York: Guilford Press.

Szatmari, P. (2004) *A Mind Apart.* New York: Guilford Press.

Szatmari, P., Archer, L., Fisman, S., Streiner, D. and Wilson, F. (1995) 'Asperger's syndrome and autism: differences in behaviour, cognition, and adaptive functioning.' *Journal of the American Academy of Child and Adolescent Psychiatry 34,* 1662–1671.

Szatmari, P., Bartolucci, G. and Bremner, R. (1989a) 'Asperger's syndrome: comparison of early history and outcome.' *Developmental Medicine and Child Neurology 31,* 709–720.

Szatmari, P., Bremner, R. and Nagy, J. (1989b) 'Asperger's syndrome: a review of clinical features.' *Canadian Journal of Psychiatry 34,* 554–560.

Szatmari, P., Tuff, L., Finlayson, A. and Bartolucci, G. (1990) 'Asperger's syndrome and autism: neurocognitive aspects.' *Journal of the American Academy of Child and Adolescent Psychiatry 29,* 130–136.

Tanguay, P. (2002) *Nonverbal Learning Disabilities at School: Educating Students with NLD, Asperger Syndrome and Related Conditions.* London: Jessica Kingsley Publishers.

Tani, P., Joukamaa, M., Lindberg, N., Nieminen-von Wendt, T., Virkkala, J., Appelberg, B. and Porkka-Heiskanen, T. (2004) 'Asperger syndrome, alexithymia and sleep.' *Neuropsychobiology 49,* 64–70.

Tani, P., Lindberg, N., Appelberg, B., Nieminen-von Wendt, T., von Wendt, L. and Porkka-Heiskanen, T. (2006) 'Childhood inattention and hyperactivity symptoms self-reported by adults with Asperger syndrome.' *Psychopathology 39,* 49–54.

Tantam, D. (1988a) 'Asperger's syndrome.' *Journal of Child Psychology and Psychiatry 29,* 245–253.

Tantam, D. (1988b) 'Lifelong eccentricity and social isolation: Asperger's Syndrome or Schizoid Personality Disorder?' *British Journal of Psychiatry 153,* 783–791.

Tantam, D. (1991) 'Asperger's Syndrome in adulthood.' In U. Frith (ed) *Autism and Asperger's Syndrome.* Cambridge: Cambridge University Press.

Tantam, D. (2000a) 'Adolescence and adulthood of individuals with Asperger Syndrome.' In A. Klin, F. Volkmar and S. Sparrow (eds) *Asperger Syndrome.* New York: Guilford Press.

Tantam, D. (2000b) 'Psychological disorder in adolescents and adults with Asperger disorder.' *Autism 4,* 47–62.

Tantam, D., Evered, C. and Hersov, L. (1990) 'Asperger's Syndrome and ligamentous laxity.' *Journal of the American Academy for Child and Adolescent Psychiatry 29,* 892–896.

Taylor, B., Miller, E., Farrington, C., Petropoulos, M., Favot-Mayaud, I., Li, J. and Wraight, P. (1999) 'Autism and measles, mumps and rubella vaccine: no epidemiological evidence for a causal association.' *Lancet 353,* 2026–2029.

Teitelbaum, O., Benton, T., Shah, P., Prince, A., Kelly, J. and Teitelbaum, P. (2004) 'Eshkol-Wachman movement notation in diagnosis: the early detection of Asperger's syndrome.' *Proceedings of the National Academy of Science USA 101*, 11,909–11,914.

Thiemann, K.S. and Goldstein, H. (2001) 'Social Stories, written text cues and video feedback: effects on social communication of children with autism.' *Journal of Applied Behavior Analysis 34*, 425–446.

Tirosh, E. and Canby, J. (1993) 'Autism and hyperlexia: a distinct syndrome?' *American Journal on Mental Retardation 98*, 84–92.

Toal, F., Murphy, D. and Murphy, K. (2005) 'Autistic spectrum disorders: lessons from neuroimaging.' *British Journal of Psychiatry 187*, 395–397.

Tonge, B., Brereton, A., Gray, K. and Einfeld, S. (1999) 'Behavioural and emotional disturbance in high-functioning autism and Asperger Syndrome.' *Autism 3*, 117–130.

Towbin, K., Pradella, A., Gorrindo, T., Pine, D. and Leibenluft, E. (2005) 'Autism spectrum traits in children with mood and anxiety disorders.' *Journal of Child and Adolescent Psychpharmacology 15*, 452–464.

Turner, M. (1997) 'Toward an executive dysfunction account of repetitive behaviour in autism.' In J. Russell (ed) *Autism as an Executive Disorder*. Oxford: Oxford University Press.

Twachtman-Cullen, D. (1998) 'Language and communication in High-Functioning Autism and Asperger Syndrome.' In E. Schopler, G. Mesibov and L. Kunce (eds) *Asperger Syndrome or High-Functioning Autism*. New York: Plenum Press.

Volden, J. and Lord, C. (1991) 'Neologisms and idiosyncratic language in autistic speakers.' *Journal of Autism and Developmental Disorders 21*, 109–130.

Volkmar, F. and Klin, A. (2000) 'Diagnostic issues in Asperger syndrome.' In A. Klin, F. Volkmar and S. Sparrow (eds) *Asperger Syndrome*. New York: Guilford Press.

Volkmar, F., Klin, A. and Pauls, D. (1998) 'Nosological and genetic aspects of Asperger syndrome.' *Journal of Autism and Developmental Disorders 28*, 457–463.

Voors, W. (2000) *The Parent's Book About Bullying: Changing the Course of Your Child's Life*. Center City, MN: Hazelden.

Weimer, A., Schatz, A., Lincoln, A., Ballantyne, A. and Trauer, D. (2001) '"Motor" impairment in Asperger syndrome: evidence for a deficit in proprioception.' *Developmental and Behavioral Pediatrics 22*, 92–101.

Welchew, D., Ashwin, C., Berkouk, K., Salvador, R., Suckling, J., Baron-Cohen, S. and Bullmore, E. (2005) 'Functional disconnectivity of the medial temporal lobe in Asperger's syndrome.' *Biological Psychiatry 57*, 991–998.

Wellman, H.M., Baron-Cohen, S., Caswell, R., Gomez, J.C., Swettenham, J., Toye, E. and Lagattuta, K. (2002) 'Thought-bubbles help children with autism acquire an alternative theory of mind.' *Autism 6*, 343–363.

Wellman, H.M., Hollander, M. and Schult, C. (1996) 'Young children's understanding of thought bubbles and of thoughts.' *Child Development 67*, 768–788.

Welton, J. and Telford, J. (2004) *What Did You Say? What Do You Mean? An Illustrated Guide to Understanding Metaphors*. London: Jessica Kingsley Publishers.

Wentz, E., Lacey, J., Waller, G., Rastam, M., Turk, J. and Gillberg, C. (2005) 'Childhood onset neuropsychiatric disorders in adult eating disorder patients: a pilot study.' *European Journal of Child and Adolescent Psychiatry 14*, 431–437.

Wentz Nilsson, E., Gillberg, C., Gillberg, C.I. and Rastam, M. (1999) 'Ten year follow-up of adolescent onset anorexia nervosa: personality disorders.' *Journal of the American Academy of Child and Adolescent Psychiatry 38*, 1389–1395.

Werth, A., Perkins, M. and Boucher, J. (2001) 'Here's the weavery looming up.' *Autism 5*, 2, 111–125.

White, B.B. and White, M.S. (1987) 'Autism from the inside.' *Medical Hypotheses 24*, 223–229.

Wilkinson, L. (2005) 'Supporting the inclusion of a student with Asperger syndrome: a case study using Conjoint Behavioural Consultations and self-management.' *Educational Psychology in Practice 21*, 307–326.

Willey, L.H. (1999) *Pretending to be Normal: Living with Asperger's Syndrome.* London: Jessica Kingsley Publishers.

Willey, L.H. (2001) *Asperger Syndrome in the Family: Redefining Normal.* London: Jessica Kingsley Publishers.

Williams, D. (1998) *Nobody Nowhere: The Remarkable Autobiography of an Autistic Girl.* London: Jessica Kingsley Publishers.

Williams, J., Scott, F., Stott, C., Allison, C., Bolton, P., Baron-Cohen, S. and Brayne, C. (2005) 'The CAST (Childhood Asperger Syndrome Test): test accuracy.' *Autism 9*, 45–68.

Williams, T.A. (1989) 'A social skills group for autistic children.' *Journal of Autism and Developmental Disorders 19*, 143–155.

Wing, L. (1981) 'Asperger's Syndrome: a clinical account.' *Psychological Medicine 11*, 115–130.

Wing, L. (1992) 'Manifestations of social problems in high-functioning autistic people.' In E. Schopler and G.B. Mesibov (eds) *High-Functioning Individuals With Autism.* New York: Plenum Press.

Wing, L. and Attwood, A. (1987) 'Syndromes of autism and atypical development.' In D. Cohen and A. Donnellan (eds) *Handbook of Autism and Pervasive Developmental Disorders.* New York: John Wiley and Sons.

Wing, L., Leekham, S.R., Libby, S.J., Gould, J. and Larcombe, M. (2002) 'The Diagnostic Interview for Social and Communication Disorders: background, inter-rater reliability and clinical use.' *Journal of Child Psychology and Psychiatry 43*, 307–325.

Wing, L. and Shah, A. (2000) 'Catatonia in autistic spectrum disorders.' *British Journal of Psychiatry 176*, 357–362.

Wolff, S. (1995) *Loners: The Life Path of Unusual Children.* London: Routledge.

Wolff, S. (1998) 'Schizoid personality in childhood.' In E. Schopler, G. Mesibov and L. Kunce (eds) *Asperger Syndrome or High-Functioning Autism.* New York: Plenum Press.

Woodbury Smith, M., Robinson, J., Wheelwright, S. and Baron-Cohen, S. (2005) 'Screening adults for Asperger syndrome using the AQ: a preliminary study of its diagnostic validity in clinical practice.' *Journal of Autism and Developmental Disorders 35*, 331–335.

World Health Organization (1993) *International Classification of Diseases*, tenth edition. Geneva: World Health Organization.

Yoshida, Y. and Uchiyama, T. (2004) 'The clinical necessity for assessing Attention Deficit/ Hyperactivity Disorder (AD/HD) symptoms in children with high functioning Pervasive Developmental Disorders (PDD).' *European Journal of Child and Adolescent Psychiatry 13*, 307–314.

Yoshida, Y., Uchiyama, T., Tomari, S., Izuka, N., Hihara, N. and Muramatsu, Y. (2005) 'Letter for use when telling a child that he or she has an ASD.' Poster presentation at the National Autistic Conference, London.

Youell, B. (1999) 'Matthew: from numbers to numeracy: from knowledge to knowing in a ten-year-old boy with Asperger's syndrome.' In A. Alvarez and S. Reid (eds) *Autism and Personality: Findings from the Tavistock Autism Workshop.* London: Routledge.

Subject Index

Author Index